The Great Debates of the Constitutional Co

Other Books
by Saul K. Padover

ition of 1787, *Arranged According to Topics*

To
Secure
These
Blessings

by *Saul K. Padover*

Professor of Politics, Graduate Faculty
New School for Social Research

A Washington Square Press /
Ridge Press Book
New York

KRAUS REPRINT CO.
New York
1970

PICTURE SOURCES
(Numbers refer to pictures, not to pages.)

American Catholic Historical Society of Philadelphia: 27
American Numismatic Society: 64
American Scenic and Historic Preservation Society: 35
Brown Brothers: 73, 75
Charles Scribner's Sons: *George Washington,* W. C. Ford (1900): 20, 41
Chase Manhattan Bank Museum of Moneys of the World: 62-63
Courtesy of Harry Shaw Newman, The Old Print Shop Inc.: 60
Courtesy of the Atwater Kent Museum: 54-55, 57, 61, 65-66, 68-69, 86
Culver Service: 10
Free Library of Philadelphia: 67, 85
G. P. Putnam's Sons: *Little Journeys to the Homes of
     American Statesmen,* Elbert Hubbard (1898): 14
Kennedy Galleries, Inc., New York: 56
Library of Congress: 78
Metropolitan Museum of Art: 58
Miss Edith D. Johnston, Savannah, Georgia: 37
New-York Historical Society: 29-30, 40, 70-71, 79-80, 83
New York Public Library Manuscript Division: 59, 72, 74, 76, 84.
     Picture Collection: 7-8, 21, 26, 28, 31, 43, 47, 53, 82.
     Print Room: 3-6, 9, 11-13, 15-19, 22-25, 32-34, 36, 38-39,
     42, 44-46, 48-52, 81

Library of Congress Catalog Card Number: 77-129771

© *1962 by Saul K. Padover.*
Published by Washington Square Press and the Ridge Press, Inc.,

Reprinted with the permission of the Licensor
KRAUS REPRINT CO.
A U.S. Division of Kraus-Thomson Organization Limited
Printed in U.S.A.

To Peggy, of course

Contents

Chapter 2 Congress in General

Chapter 3 The House and Senate

Chapter 4 The Executive

Chapter 5 The Judiciary

Chapter 6 Amendment

Chapter 7 Ratification

Here, for the first time in topical form, are the remarkable debates that led to the formation of the Constitution of the United States.

Until now, the records and journals of the Founding Fathers' convention in Philadelphia during the spring and summer of 1787 have always been presented chronologically, exactly as the debates unfolded from day to day. This method, of course, is unswervingly faithful to history, but it is painfully deficient in clarity and continuity. For, as the proceedings of the convention reveal, the great task was not quickly or easily encompassed and the delegates rarely reached agreement or pursued a point to its conclusion upon first consideration. Topics often were taken up, discussed, dropped, postponed, referred to committees, and later resumed. For the student or reader interested in tracing the evolution of a constitutional paragraph from its inception to its final acceptance, the chronological record frequently is muddled and confusing.

This book undertakes to give consecutiveness and cohesion to the debates by rearranging them according to the sections of the Constitution to which they refer. Thus, fragments of discussion on the qualifications of the executive, the powers of the judiciary, or the functions of the Congress—discussion which may have taken place intermittently over a period of weeks—are grouped and blended into a continuous narrative. Nothing is lost by this procedure. In fact, it is clear that much has been gained. The ability to follow the closely reasoned argument, to see the gradual emergence of one idea from many —realizing that these were spontaneous utterances, delivered without prepared notes—gives one a new appreciation for the practicality, tough-mindedness, and sheer political sagacity of these remarkable men. Displayed here with new brilliance are the twists and turns of the prodigious mental and spiritual effort that reduced a variety of political philosophies and aspirations to the practical—and prescient

—document that has served as the underpinning of democratic government in America for more than one hundred and seventy years.

On any level—political, historical, literary—the debates make exciting reading. In spots they are drama of a high order. Nearly always they are illuminating and, in retrospect, significant. Gouverneur Morris was prophetic when he said that the proceedings of the convention would "affect the whole human race." The debates contain a lesson in moderation, realism, wisdom, and benevolence for all mankind. They are a treasury of freedom.

THE BACKGROUND

The historical background of the Constitutional Convention can best be understood in the light of the Articles of Confederation, which had gone into effect in July, 1778. It was under the government of the Articles that the thirteen Colonies had fought the Revolutionary War.

But when the war was over, in 1783, the weaknesses of the Articles became glaring. For the Confederation was, in effect, a league of independent states, rather than a sovereign national government. Article II stated specifically: "Each State retains its sovereignty, freedom and independence, and every power, jurisdiction and right, which is not by this Confederation expressly delegated to the United States, in Congress assembled."

Whatever national power the Confederation had was vested in a one-chamber Congress, which was a denial of Montesquieu's famous theory of the separation of powers. There was no national executive and no national judiciary.

The makeshift government of the Confederation suffered from at least half-a-dozen serious weaknesses:

1. The Congress did not represent the people as a whole, but only the thirteen individual states. Each state, regardless of its size, had only one vote, although it could send any number of delegates.

2. All important legislation required the consent of nine states. Since many delegations often were absent, one or two states were in a position to defeat proposals of pressing importance. In practice, this gave individual states a veto power.

3. The Congress had no authority to levy taxes, to borrow money, or to maintain armed forces. It could declare war, but had to rely upon the individual states to put the declaration into effect.

4. It had no power to execute its own laws, including treaties with foreign nations. The authority to enforce legislation was left to the state governments.

5. There was no provision for courts to settle disputes between states and among citizens.

6. The Congress had no power to regulate commerce among the states. This led to interstate trade barriers and the imposition of a variety of tariffs causing economic chaos.

As government under the Articles of Confederation found itself powerless to control the growing economic and financial confusion that prevailed after the Revolution, a number of leading citizens decided to remedy the situation. A convention was called by a Virginia delegation that included Edmund Randolph and James Madison, and met at Annapolis, Maryland, in September, 1786. Only five states attended, however, and the convention was unable to do anything effective. It decided to ask the states to send delegates to another convention, to meet at the State House, the old Independence Hall, in Philadelphia on the second Monday in May, 1787, for the purpose of examining the defects of the existing government and "digesting a plan for supplying such defects as may be discovered to exist."

THE DELEGATES

The Virginia legislature promptly accepted the recommendation and appointed a delegation of seven, one of whom was the country's most famous man, George Washington. The other six were: John Blair, James Madison, George Mason, James McClurg, Edmund Randolph, and George Wythe.

A few weeks later, the legislatures of New Jersey, Pennsylvania, North Carolina, Delaware, and Georgia appointed their delegates.

New Jersey named: David Brearly, Jonathan Dayton, William Churchill Houston, William Livingston, and William Paterson.

Pennsylvania appointed a delegation of eight, including her greatest citizen, the world-renowned Benjamin Franklin. The others were: George Clymer, Thomas Fitzsimmons,[1] Jared Ingersoll, Thomas Mifflin, Gouverneur Morris, Robert Morris, and James Wilson.

North Carolina's delegation consisted of five men: William Blount, William R. Davie, Alexander Martin, Richard Dobbs Spaight, and Hugh Williamson.

Delaware appointed an equal number: Richard Bassett, Gunning Bedford, Jacob Broom, John Dickinson, and George Read.

Georgia appointed four: Abraham Baldwin, William Few, William Houston, and William Pierce.

---

[1] Also spelled "Fitzsimins."

The remaining states—particularly those of New England and New *17*
York—hesitated to nominate delegations on the ground that only the
Congress could approve amendments to the Articles of Confederation.
Without such consent, any decisions of the convention would be of
dubious legality. After some delay, Congress accepted the suggestion
that the convention at Philadelphia could properly meet "for the sole
and express purpose of revising the Articles of Confederation and re-
porting to Congress and the several legislatures such alterations and
provisions therein as shall, when agreed to in Congress and confirmed
by the States, render the Federal Constitution adequate to the exigencies of Government and the preservation of the Union."

Thus empowered, and with the clear understanding that the
Philadelphia convention met only for the *"sole purpose of revising
the Articles of Confederation,"* the rest of the states, except Rhode
Island, appointed delegations.[1] New York named: Alexander Hamilton, John Lansing, and Robert Yates.

Connecticut appointed: Oliver Ellsworth, William Samuel Johnson,
and Roger Sherman.

The delegates from Massachusetts were: Elbridge Gerry, Nathaniel
Gorham, Rufus King, and Caleb Strong.

New Hampshire named two: Nicholas Gilman and John Langdon.

South Carolina appointed four: Pierce Butler, Charles Pinckney,
Charles Cotesworth Pinckney, and John Rutledge.

Maryland named five: Daniel Carroll, Daniel of St. Thomas Jenifer,
Luther Martin, James McHenry, and John Francis Mercer.

Altogether, fifty-five delegates were appointed to the Philadelphia
Convention, but not all of them served through the whole period of
sixteen weeks. Some left early and others arrived late. Virginia's
George Wythe resigned on June 16 because of "Mrs. W's state of
health." New York's whole delegation was absent during some of the
crucial debates. Alexander Hamilton left in discouragement on June
29 and did not come back until August. His colleagues, John Lansing and Robert Yates, protesting that the convention failed "to conform to our ideas," departed for good on July 5. Others kept coming
late. Maryland's Luther Martin arrived on June 9, Georgia's Abraham Baldwin on June 11, North Carolina's William Blount on June
20, Maryland's Daniel Carroll on July 9, and New Hampshire's two-
man delegation, Nicholas Gilman and John Langdon, on July 23,

[1] Rhode Island not only failed to send delegates to Philadelphia, but did not
ratify the Constitution until after the Federal Government had been in operation
for more than a year.

when the convention was already half over. A few, the foremost being James Madison, attended all the sessions. In the end, only thirty-nine of the delegates signed the completed Constitution.

THE RULES

The delegates were so slow in arriving at Philadelphia that the organization of the convention, scheduled to begin on May 14, had to be postponed for more than a week. The work of the convention did not begin until May 25, when twenty-nine delegates, representing nine states, had arrived and were present. On that day, George Washington was unanimously elected president of the convention and Major William Jackson its secretary. The rules that were to govern the convention were adopted three days later. These were strict and businesslike. One of the regulations required that: "Every member, rising to speak, shall address the president; and, whilst he shall be speaking, none shall pass between them, or hold discourse with another, or read a book, pamphlet, or paper, printed or manuscript. And of two members rising to speak at the same time, the president shall name him who shall be first heard."

A day later the rule of absolute secrecy was adopted. It provided "That nothing spoken in the House be printed, or otherwise published, or communicated, without leave." The rule of secrecy was vitally important, for the country was in a pitch of excitement over the Federal convention. The wildest rumors circulated. People were saying that the convention was planning to replace the thirteen states with three separate republics; that Rhode Island was to be expelled from the union; that a monarchy was being set up; that the Duke of York (son of George III) was being invited to become King. People apparently believed many of the rumors, judging by the mail of the delegates. Letters angrily accused the convention of pro-monarchist bias or anxiously sought information that would allay fears. To safeguard the debates and to guarantee the fullest freedom of speech from outside pressure and agitation, it was essential that secrecy prevail.

George Washington, who could freeze the boldest with a look, saw to it that the rules of secrecy were strictly observed. One answer the delegates gave the letter writers who worried over the establishment of a monarchy was: "While we cannot affirmatively tell you what we are doing, we can negatively tell you what we are not doing; we never once thought of a King" (*Pennsylvania Gazette*, August 22, 1787). Indeed, what went on in the convention was kept secret from the

American people for thirty-two years. It was not until 1819, during the administration of President James Monroe, that the first *Journal*, a bare record of the proceedings, was printed.

THE DELEGATES AS INDIVIDUALS

Who were the delegates? Without exception, they were substantial citizens, leaders in their respective states, and generally well-to-do. Among them were governors, judges, and generals. At least two delegates, Benjamin Franklin and George Washington, had world reputations. Some, Rufus King and Robert Morris, for example, were wealthy businessmen. A number, among them Pierce Butler and George Mason, were big planters. Three—James McClurg, James McHenry, and Hugh Williamson—were physicians. Sixty per cent were lawyers, including jurists of the highest distinction and erudition, notably John Dickinson, Edmund Randolph, and George Wythe.

Nearly half were college graduates, an astonishing proportion in view of the fact that formal higher education was then strictly confined to a minute fraction of the population. The overwhelming majority of the American people had no education at all. Only the offspring of the well-to-do, those whom Alexander Hamilton called "the rich and the well-born," received any education at that time, and even for them going to college was uncommon. Many of the delegates to the convention were either self-taught or privately tutored. Of those who went to college, some, notably the learned James Wilson and the distinguished John Dickinson, were graduated from Scottish or British institutions. The rest were educated in American colleges, primarily at Princeton (ten), William and Mary (four), Yale (three), Columbia and Harvard (two each).

We learn of the personalities of the delegates from contemporary records. Conscious of the historic occasion, a number of the delegates —Hamilton, King, McHenry, Madison, Paterson, Pierce, Charles Pinckney, and Yates—kept private notes. These were of varying value, ranging from the full and indispensable reports of James Madison to the character sketches written by Major William Pierce of Georgia. Pierce, a Savannah merchant who had served as an artillery officer during the Revolution, remained at the convention only a few weeks (not long enough to sign the Constitution), but his pen-portraits of his fellow-delegates have the flavor of a contemporary observer. Here are a few of them:

Benjamin Franklin: ". . . the greatest philosopher of the present age . . . He does not shine much in public council—he is no speaker . . . He is, however, a most extraordinary man, and tells a story in a style more engaging than anything I ever heard."

Rufus King: ". . . much distinguished for his eloquence . . . About five feet ten inches high, well-formed, and handsome face, with a strong expressive eye, and a sweet high-toned voice."

Elbridge Gerry: ". . . a hesitating and laborious speaker . . . goes extensively into all subjects . . . without respect to elegance or flower of diction."

Alexander Hamilton: ". . . convincing and engaging in his eloquence . . . Yet there is something feeble in his voice."

James Wilson: "All the political institutions of the world he knows in detail . . . No man is more clear, copious and comprehensive . . . yet he is no great orator."

John Dickinson: ". . . an indifferent Speaker. With an affected air of wisdom he labors to produce a trifle—his language is irregular and incorrect—his flourishes . . . are like expiring flames, they just shew themselves and go out."

Nathaniel Gorham: ". . . a Man of very good sense, but not much improved in his education. He is eloquent and easy in public debate, but has nothing fashionable or elegant in his style."

William Churchill Houston: "As to his legal or political knowledge he has very little to boast of. Nature seems to have done more for his corporeal than mental powers . . . In public debate [he] is confused and irregular."

William Livingston: ". . . he appears to me rather to indulge a sportiveness of wit, than a strength of thinking . . . He is no Orator, and seems little acquainted with the guiles of policy."

James McHenry: ". . . a Man of specious talents . . . Nothing remarkable in him, nor has he any of the graces of the Orator . . . However, a very respectable young Gentleman."

William Paterson: ". . . a Man of great modesty . . . Very happy in the choice of time and manner of engaging in a debate, and never speaks but when he understands his subject well."

George Read: ". . . his powers of Oratory are fatiguing and tiresome . . . his voice is feeble, and his articulation so bad that few can have patience to attend to him."

The debates in the convention produced several surprises. Some delegates with great reputations contributed little. A few obscure ones rose to heights of statesmanship and wisdom. Many changed their minds. The majority spoke little, or briefly, or sporadically, or unconvincingly, or off the point. The normally energetic and persuasive

Robert Morris, who had served the Revolution brilliantly as Supervisor of Finance, was unaccountably silent throughout the sessions. Alexander Hamilton made a few forensic splurges, but exerted no influence. James McClurg, a physician, had practically nothing to say. William Livingston, a satiric poet, seemed out of his depth. The learned and renowned John Dickinson was soon found to be a bore (although his exertions after the convention had important bearing on ratification of the Constitution by Delaware and Pennsylvania). Luther Martin was tiresome with his passion for the sacred rights of the small states. Gunning Bedford, a fat young lawyer from Delaware, blurted occasional foolishness that earned him sharp rebuke. The aged Benjamin Franklin, always listened to with respect, was still sensible and amusing, but garrulous.

George Washington's role as president of the convention was of incalculable importance. Aged fifty-five and the hero of America, the General was at the height of his fame. He was a big man in every way. Physically, to quote his own appraisal, he was "six feet high, and proportionably made—if anything rather slender than thick . . . with pretty long arms and thighs." His deportment, according to Jefferson, was "easy, erect and noble." Abigail Adams said he had more grace and dignity than the King of England.

General Washington asserted his personality without conscious effort. Cool, disciplined, self-controlled, he was a man who spoke sparingly. He had, in fact, little conversation, possessing, in the words of a contemporary, "neither copiousness of ideas nor fluency of words." As president of the convention he said practically nothing. He did not participate in the debates and made no effort to influence the delegates. But he presided impeccably, his mere presence being a guarantee of the seriousness of the occasion, a spur to loftiness, and a brake to passions. The convention was, indeed, remarkable for orderly behavior, despite the fact that feelings often were deep and the stakes high. George Washington, as one biographer has said, truly "supplied a ground anchor to the proceedings" of the convention.

The basic work of the convention was done by about a dozen men. They made the major proposals, worked out the compromises, argued the motions, and prepared the drafts. Contributing most, in terms of relevance and persuasiveness, were Ellsworth, Gerry, King, Madison, Mason, Gouverneur Morris, Paterson, Charles Pinckney, Randolph, Rutledge, Sherman, and Wilson. These may be considered the true architects of the Constitution.

Three of them—Gerry, Mason, and Wilson—may be described as liberals. The others were property-minded political conservatives with serious doubts about entrusting power to the people in general. All of them, however, were blessed with a gift for compromise. Of the liberals, Gerry and Mason refused to sign the Constitution because it was not democratic enough. Gerry was a Massachusetts businessman of enlightened views, and Mason an aristocratic democrat—a signer of the Declaration of Independence and the author of Virginia's great Bill of Rights—whom Jefferson admiringly described as "a man of the first order of wisdom."

Connecticut's Oliver Ellsworth was a jurist with moderate views on politics and theology. He was addicted to snuff and had a habit of talking to himself. It was the "tall, dignified, and commanding" Ellsworth who introduced the motion that led to the "Great Compromise." He was ably assisted by his like-minded colleague, Roger Sherman, a judge who had started life as a shoemaker and whose appearance was described as "grotesque and laughable." Sherman, however, was a solid man, and his opinions commanded respect. Similarly, Rufus King, who represented Massachusetts in the convention and later became U.S. Senator from New York, carried weight because of his moderation and tact. William Paterson of New Jersey and John Rutledge of South Carolina, both of them judges and governors of their respective states and future Justices of the United States Supreme Court, also made important contributions. So did Edmund Randolph, Virginia's brilliant and eloquent delegate, whose chief weakness was vacillation. After working long and hard on the Constitution, he finally refused to sign it. The following year, however, he changed his mind and supported it in the Virginia ratification convention.

The real surprises of the convention were three young men: James Madison, Gouverneur Morris, and Charles Pinckney. Madison was thirty-six, Morris thirty-five, and Pinckney twenty-nine. They worked hardest and longest and most consistently. Madison never missed a session; Morris spoke more frequently than any other delegate; Pinckney contributed a brilliant draft that served as a rich source for the final Constitution. Small, fragile Madison—"withered little applejohn," Washington Irving called him later—was a profound student of political history, a liberal in religion, and a conservative in politics.

Morris was a man of wealth, and despite the afflictions of a missing leg and a crippled arm, he was scintillating, worldly, articulate, and gifted. Major Pierce, clearly under his spell, said that he "throws around him such a glare that he charms, captivates, and leads away the senses of all who hear him." He was also cynical and profoundly anti-democratic, although outspoken against slavery. And it was he who polished the style and wrote the final draft of the Constitution.

Pinckney, too, was brilliant. Second youngest delegate (Major Jona-   *23*
than Dayton of New Jersey—aged twenty-six—was the youngest), he
was handsome and vain, and described as "something of a roué," something of a demagogue. His conservative opponents in South Carolina
later called him "Blackguard Charlie." But at the Convention, the
charming young South Carolinian was brimming with good ideas. In
later years—distinguished by service as senator, ambassador, and four-
term governor—he was to pretend that he himself had written the
Constitution! (General Charles Cotesworth Pinckney, also a delegate,
was his cousin.)

THE MIND OF THE DELEGATES

However else they may have differed, the delegates shared a common
cultural outlook. Their ethnic roots were British (including Northern
Irish), their religious background was Protestant, and the education
they received was based on the classics. All the formally educated men
had a knowledge of Latin and Greek, and some, like James Madison,
also knew Hebrew. Even those who had no formal education read,
and often referred to, the classics. The self-taught Franklin, for example, knew Cicero, Epictetus, Herodotus, Horace, Plato, Pliny,
Pythagoras, Sallust, Seneca, Tacitus, and Xenophon. Those who had a
college education were fond of citing personalities and examples of
antiquity. James Madison was intimately familiar with Plato,
Plutarch, and Polybius, among others. He and Alexander Hamilton scattered classical references throughout *The Federalist,* from
Cato to Zaleucus. Hamilton, indeed, was in the habit of using such
classical pseudonyms as "Camillus," "Pacificus," and "Publius."
For the delegates, the classics of antiquity were the underpinning of
an intellectual world that also drew heavily on certain authors of
the Seventeenth and Eighteenth Centuries. In the fields of legal ideas
and political theory, about half-a-dozen writers had the deepest influence. These were Sir Edward Coke (1552-1634), Henry Homes
(Lord Kames: 1696-1782), and Sir William Blackstone (1723-1780)
in the field of law; and Thomas Hobbes (1588-1679), John Locke
(1632-1704), and Baron de Montesquieu (1689-1755) in political
thought. Of all the books on political ideas and institutions known to
the delegates by far the most influential were Hobbes' *Leviathan*
(1651); Locke's *Letters on Toleration* (1689), *Treatises on Government* and *Essay Concerning Human Understanding* (1690), and Montesquieu's *Spirit of the Laws* (1748). Montesquieu, in particular, was
phenomenally popular in the Western world.

What these three political writers had in common—and what appealed to the Americans of the Eighteenth Century—was a rational approach to politics. They rejected political mysticism and the long-established idea that government was divinely ordained. While they disagreed in their conclusions, they agreed in the fundamental premise that men were of this world and that they were influenced by their ideas, passions, and interests. Hobbes, whose basic assumptions about humanity were accepted by many delegates to the Constitutional Convention, built his political analysis on a psychology that took for granted the existence of human hate, greed, and violence. Only a powerful government, a Leviathan, could keep the ugly human passions under control. Without it, Hobbes wrote, human life is "solitary, poor, nasty, brutish, and short."

Hobbes' advocacy of authoritarian government as the only type that was able to put a bridle on human passions was not acceptable to the majority of the delegates to the convention. Nevertheless, Hobbesian thought colored their attitudes and was never too far away from their debates. Hamilton did not shock the convention when he made his plea for aristocratic government on the ground that the human animal was too corrupt for self-government. Even so moderate a mind as James Madison's accepted a good deal of Hobbes, being, in general, distrustful of human nature but, unlike Hamilton, hopeful about some of its aspects. He felt—and much of his philosophy was incorporated into the Constitution—that political institutions should be so constructed as to avoid full reliance on human psychology and that the latter should be kept under constant control through such contrivances as "checks and balances." This underlying Hobbesian skepticism in regard to human nature was most clearly expressed in *The Federalist* (No. 51): "It may be a reflection on human nature that such devices [checks and balances] should be necessary to control the abuses of government. But what is government itself, but the greatest of all reflections on human nature? If men were angels, no government would be necessary. If angels were to govern men, neither external nor internal controls on government would be necessary."

But men were not angels.

THE INFLUENCE OF LOCKE

In the minds of the delegates to the convention, Hobbes' pessimistic philosophy was balanced by Locke's more optimistic approach. Locke supplied both a theory of politics and a social psychology. He argued that man came into the world with "natural" (inherent) rights and that he was a reasoning animal; as such, he voluntarily combined with others in organizing a commonwealth for the maintenance of order and the preservation of property. Having freely entered into such a "social contract," man assigns the governing power to a legislature. The latter always remains a servant, never a master. The legislature has no independent rights, except those obligations and duties allocated to it by the contract. This means that government is lawful only so long as it carries out the people's will. In general, these Lockean ideas were the common property of Eighteenth Century Americans.

Locke's political theory was reinforced by his social psychology. He rejected the prevalent belief that ideas (and passions) were innate and permanently fixed. He argued, instead, that men's ideas and, hence, their attitudes were simply the product of experience. Carried to its logical conclusions, this meant that people were not innately evil, as Hobbes (and Hamilton) argued, but were molded by their environment. The implications of this position were far-reaching. If men were the product of their environment and experience, it followed that the creation of a good political and social system would result in the production of good, not evil, people. Thus Locke countered Hobbes, and the spirits of both men were clearly present in the Constitutional Convention.

THE INFLUENCE OF MONTESQUIEU

Next to Hobbes and Locke, the intellect exerting greatest influence on the convention was that of Baron de Montesquieu, the French provincial lawyer and judge, and author of the monumental *Spirit of the Laws*. The *Spirit* is a systematic study of comparative government, symmetrically constructed with Cartesian logic and presumably based on universal laws. In the annals of mankind Montesquieu discerned three types of government: the republican, the monarchical, and the despotic. A believer in moderate monarchy, he considered despotism contrary to human nature. Why, then, did it exist throughout history? People submit to despotism, Montesquieu explained, because it is easy to do so. Governments that protect liberty are difficult to establish and take special effort to maintain: "To form a moderate government, it is necessary to combine powers, regulate them, temper them, activate them; to give, so to speak, a ballast to the one so as to enable the other to resist. This is a masterpiece of legislation which rarely happens by chance and is seldom left to prudence."

Montesquieu considered political freedom the highest good, and to attain it he proposed a system of laws that would restrain those who exercised power and at the same time would protect the citizen. To do this, he wrote, it was vital that political powers be distinctly separated. Legislative, executive, and judicial functions should be entrusted to three separate branches of government. For, he pointed out, where powers and functions were concentrated in the same hands, the result always was tyranny. A legislative body passing tyrannical laws, for example, would execute them oppressively and capriciously, since it would itself be judge, prosecutor, and executioner. There could be no appeal from such an accumulation of power. This was echoed by James Madison, a profound student of Montesquieu, who wrote in *The Federalist* (No. 47) that a concentration of legislative, executive, and judiciary powers in the same hands "may justly be pronounced the very definition of tyranny."

According to Montesquieu, each of the three separate branches of government should be dominant not only in its own sphere, but should have sufficient power to serve as a check on the other two, as well. The purpose of this counterpoise—or "ballast"—was to prevent any of the branches from overstepping its prescribed functions and encroaching upon the others. This is the principle of "checks and balances" that the students of Montesquieu incorporated into the Constitution at the Philadelphia convention.

THE BIG AND LITTLE STATES

Montesquieu's influence in the convention was apparent from the beginning. The delegates had come to Philadelphia with instructions merely to amend the Articles of Confederation. But within four days of the opening of the convention, on May 29, Edmund Randolph, speaking on behalf of the Virginia delegation, submitted his famous Virginia Plan, in the form of fifteen propositions, which actually provided for a new type of government. Among the crucial provisions of the Randolph resolutions were those that called for the establishment of a government with three separate branches—legislative, judicial, and executive—and two houses of Congress. Despite this radical departure from the existing Articles of Confederation, with its nondivision of powers and a single Congress, the Virginia—or Randolph—Plan immediately became the basis of the discussions.

As the debates unfolded, divisions of opinion came into the open. Although no position was absolutely clear cut, certain general tendencies among the delegates quickly became apparent. There were those, like Lansing and Yates, who felt that it was the business of the convention to do nothing more than amend certain weaknesses in the Articles of Confederation. There were others, notably Gouverneur Morris and James Madison, who believed that an altogether new, tripartite system of government should be established. But the sharpest division of opinion revolved around the question of the relationship between the big states and the little ones.

It soon became clear that the convention was sharply split. On the one side were the big and wealthy states—Massachusetts, Pennsylvania, Virginia, the two Carolinas, and Georgia. On the other side were four smaller states—Connecticut, Delaware, Maryland, and New Jersey. Of the remaining three, New York was divided, New Hampshire was absent a large part of the time, and Rhode Island was not represented.

Fundamentally, the problem reduced itself to the desire of the small states to preserve their status and individuality in any future national Congress that might be devised. They argued that unless their representation was equal to that of the big states, they would continually be outvoted and ever in danger of ultimate extinction (as Hamilton bluntly advocated). The big states took the position that it was unjust and inequitable to expect that Delaware, for instance, with less than 50,000 people, should have the same power and representation as, say, Virginia with a population of about 800,000.[1] The big states, therefore, demanded that they be represented in the Congress in proportion to their inhabitants (including the voteless Negro slaves in the South). Here was the most crucial of all issues, the one on which everything else hinged. Much of the drama of the convention's debates was focused on this point.

After Randolph, speaking for the Virginia delegation, had introduced his fifteen resolutions, the convention became a committee of the whole and debated them, one by one, for two weeks. On June 13, the resolutions, in amended form and providing for proportional representation in both houses of Congress, were reported out of committee. The small states protested. New Jersey's Paterson moved for an adjournment to allow time to prepare a substitute for the Randolph Plan. His motion was granted and, on June 15, Paterson submitted his own plan, consisting of nine propositions that called for an amendment of the Articles of Confederation, rather than a completely new government.

The Paterson Plan stirred up sharp and brilliant debate. Among the speakers were some of the best minds of the convention: Wilson, Hamilton, Madison, and, of course, Randolph himself. Their speeches

---

[1] The Census of 1800 reported Delaware's population as 64,273, Virginia's as 880,200.

are important lectures in political science (pages 85-109). After four days of debate, on June 19, the Paterson Plan (New Jersey Plan) was rejected and the convention resumed discussion of Randolph's propositions. The small states were adamant and some threatened withdrawal. On July 2, after a vote of five to five (one divided, one absent) on a motion to give each state equality in the Senate, the convention was deadlocked.

THE "GREAT COMPROMISE"

To break the nearly fatal impasse, a committee of eleven, one delegate from each state, was appointed to work out a compromise. Its report, brought in on July 5, recommended that in the upper house (Senate) each state should have an equal vote and that in the lower chamber (House of Representatives) the states should have one representative for every forty thousand of their population. Furthermore, all money bills should originate in the House.

The report aroused sharp opposition which, by deepening the dread of the consequences of continued disunion, finally resulted in the so-called "Great Compromise." The debates over the report were charged with strong emotions. Gouverneur Morris made a slashing assault on the small states. He considered their claims and pretensions inimical to America and to the human race in general. "State attachments," he said impatiently, "and state importance have been the bane of this country. We cannot annihilate, but we may perhaps take out the teeth of, the serpents." He warned that if they continued to stand in the way of union, the result could only be violence and foreign intervention: "This country must be united. If persuasion does not unite it, the sword will. The scenes of horror attending civil commotion cannot be described; and the conclusion of them will be worse than . . . their continuance. The stronger party will then make traitors of the weaker; and the gallows and halter will finish the work of the sword."

Morris' threatening language was resented by the spokesmen of the small states. Delaware's Gunning Bedford, who had himself threatened to ally with foreign powers in defense of the rights of the small states, cried out: "To hear such language without emotion would be to renounce the feelings of a man and the duty of a citizen." New Jersey's Paterson likewise objected to Morris' words: "he thought the sword and the gallows little calculated to produce conviction."

The effect of these emotional outbursts was to confirm the urgent need for an agreement. Ellsworth said: "Some compromise is necessary." Gerry agreed with him: "If no compromise should take place,

what will be the consequence? A secession." Mason concurred: "There
must be some accommodation . . . He (Mason) would bury his bones
in this city rather than expose his country to the consequences of a
dissolution of the convention without anything being done."

And so the compromises were worked out. It finally was agreed to
accept the committee report in favor of equality in the Senate, and
proportional representation in the House, with one delegate for every
forty-thousand inhabitants, including three-fifths of the Negro
slaves. The recommendation that money bills should originate in the
House also was accepted. On July 12, the convention adopted Gouverneur Morris' motion that taxation should be in proportion to representation. These were the basic compromises which broke the deadlock. Henceforth, the delegates proceeded to settle their lesser differences in a more amicable manner, determined to establish an effective
national government without sacrificing the independence or identity
of the individual states.

The "Great Compromise," giving the small states equality in the
Senate and thereby assuring their continued existence, removed the
main obstacle to union. Once they were no longer afraid of being extinguished, they were inclined to accede to other compromises. Debates over the Randolph resolutions—now expanded from fifteen to
twenty-three—continued for several more days. (The reader will
note that since the text observes continuity of topic, rather than
chronology, there is no specific break between debate on Randolph's
fifteen original resolutions and that on the expanded list of twenty-
three.) But these were, at bottom, details, although extremely important ones. The resolutions were debated with logic, common sense,
and reference to history, as well as to American colonial experience.
Since no basic principles were involved, compromises were achieved
with relative ease.

OTHER QUESTIONS DEBATED

Among the detailed questions considered in debate were the require-
ments, qualifications, characteristics, and contingencies of the executive, judiciary, and legislative branches. Each question was raised,
explored, defended, attacked, amended, and finally voted on. The decision was by simple majority, each state delegation being entitled to
one vote. Thus any motion needed seven votes to pass, if a full house
were present.

The convention changed its mind on a number of issues, even after
motions were passed. This was strikingly true of the executive's term

of office. Motions were made, and some of them were approved, to have the executive serve for six, nine, and fifteen years, and even for life—"during good behavior." In the course of many weeks this subject, clearly of considerable importance for the future, was debated, dropped, voted on, and reconsidered, until the delegates finally compromised on a term of four years, with no bar to re-eligibility. On this question, as on so many others, the debates are illuminating.

There also were serious discussions on the nature of the executive. Should there be one or many? Some delegates argued strongly in favor of a plural executive on the ground that it was desirable to have each of the three main sections of the country—the Northern, Middle, and Southern States—represented in that department. Fortunately, the proposals for a three-headed hydra were dropped in favor of a single President. Similarly, a suggestion was made that the executive should not be paid a salary but should serve as a matter of honor and patriotism. Franklin made an especially eloquent speech on this subject. Combine profit and honor, he argued, and you have a tyrant. But other counsel prevailed and it was decided that the executive, as well as all other officers of the Government, should be paid a regular salary while in office.

In regard to the other branches of government, the debates concerned themselves with such concrete questions as qualifications for office, mode of election, suffrage, length of term, enumerated powers, jurisdiction, oath of office, impeachment, and similar details. These were generally settled on the basis of common sense and the practical experience of the colonies.

THE FIRST DRAFT

By July 24, there had been sufficient agreement on important questions to warrant beginning a draft of a Constitution, and a Committee of Detail (Connecticut's Ellsworth, Massachusetts' Gorham, Virginia's Randolph, South Carolina's Rutledge, and Pennsylvania's Wilson) was appointed for that purpose. Two days later, on July 26, the convention adjourned to await the draft.

The delegates reassembled on August 6. For more than a month, until September 10, they debated the draft, item by item, section by section. This was, in a way, a systematic work of architecture. Perhaps the most difficult single point remaining to be settled was the method of electing the President. But a second brilliant piece of committee work—this time by the eleven-man Committee on Postponed

Matters, headed by Judge David Brearly oi New Jersey—came up with an acceptable solution on September 4.

On September 8, toward the end of the debates, another committee (New York's Hamilton, Connecticut's Johnson, Massachusetts' King, Virginia's Madison, and Pennsylvania's Gouverneur Morris) was named to "revise the style of and arrange the articles which had been agreed to by the house."

This "Committee of Style" completed the final drafting of the Constitution within a few days. Although various state constitutions and the Articles of Confederation contributed elements, the new Constitution was, in fact, an original document, based on the decisions of the convention. As polished by the Committee of Style, notably by Gouverneur Morris, it was comparatively short, about four thousand words, and comprised seven articles and twenty-one numbered sections. It contained a few repetitions, some loose arrangements, and an occasional imprecision of phrase. But in its entirety, it was a remarkable achievement, supple, simple, and terse. Lord Bryce, in *The American Commonwealth* (1888), justly ranked it "above every other written constitution for the intrinsic excellence of its scheme." British Prime Minister William E. Gladstone pronounced it "the most wonderful work ever struck off at a given time by the brain and purpose of man."

It had a magnificent, long-echoing preamble:

"We the People of the United States, in Order to form a more perfect Union, establish Justice, insure domestic Tranquility, provide for the common defence, promote the general Welfare, and secure the Blessings of Liberty to ourselves and our Posterity, do ordain and establish this Constitution for the United States of America."

THE HEART OF THE CONSTITUTION

Not the least remarkable thing about the Constitution was its system of compromises. It was, in fact, a kind of political symphony of compromises on all major points. Power was checked by countervailing power. Authority was balanced by counteracting authority. The whole tripartite structure was so delicately harmonized that each of the three was made independent of the other two, yet at the same time dependent on them in a number of subtle ways.

There was something in the Constitution for everybody, and nothing to please any extremist. The states were kept in balance by equality in the Senate and representation according to population in the

House. This also served in the years ahead to guarantee a continuation of the balance of power despite the admission of new states to the Union and growth of the population.

The executive was made both strong and limited. Those who advocated a powerful executive were assured by the independence of the presidential office and its control over the armed forces. Those who dreaded a potentially dictatorial or monarchist ruler were propitiated by the relative shortness of the President's term of office and by the congressional checks put on his authority (senatorial confirmation of appointments, control over the budget, impeachment).

The Federal judiciary was independent and yet dependent, too. The judges were to be immune from pressure and intimidation by their life tenure, but their appointment was made subject to senatorial confirmation and their good behavior assured by the congressional power of impeachment.

Large grants of power were given to the national Congress, but limits were put on it by means of specific enumeration of jurisdictions.

A great reservoir of rights was left to the individual states, but their range was restricted by the specific powers yielded to the Federal Government (for example, coinage, interstate commerce, foreign policy, national defense).

Representatives were to be elected directly by the people for short terms, but senators were to be chosen indirectly for terms long enough to assure security, so that the Senate could serve as a check on the "imprudence of democracy."

The President was to be selected indirectly by electors, but the people had the opportunity to choose and influence the electors in the individual states.

The people were denied the power to choose such vitally important officials as Federal judges, but they were guaranteed the indispensable right to live under republican governments in their states.

Underlying the whole spirit of the Constitution was the basic compromise between authoritarianism and democracy. The claims of each were partly satisfied and partly rejected. Neither those who strongly distrusted the people (Hamilton and Gouverneur Morris, for example), nor those who believed in a large measure of democracy (Mason and Wilson, for instance) won their points fully. Something was given to each—something of Hobbes and something of Locke. In essence, the Constitution was the creation of the moderates, as best personified by men like Ellsworth, King, and Madison. The latter in particular deserves the title of "Father of the Constitution."

In the perspective of history, one sees that a great deal of democracy

—such elements as free suffrage, periodic and frequent elections, guarantees of state and local self-government—was engrafted into the Constitution, which became the "supreme law" of the land. This was to be of decisive importance in the long run, for it enabled the American people to expand democratic practices and opportunities within the framework of the Constitution without doing violence to the whole fabric of society. For all its conservatism, the Constitution, as it was hammered out in Philadelphia by a group of strong-minded and cautious men, was what it still is—a democratic document.

This Constitution was printed, for the use of the delegates, on September 12, and for the next three days it was compared point by point with the recorded proceedings of the convention. On Saturday, September 15, the Constitution, thus completed, was ordered engrossed. It would be prepared for publication over the weekend.

THE SIGNING

On Monday, September 17, after sixteen weeks of debate, the convention met for the last time. The engrossed Constitution lay on the table in front of George Washington. Forty-two delegates were present, some of them disgruntled with the Constitution and viewing it as a worthless, makeshift, even dangerous, document. The majority felt the work was well done. There was a silence. Then the oldest and most renowned delegate—Benjamin Franklin—stood up, holding a paper. But his voice was too weak and he handed it to his colleague, James Wilson. Wilson read Franklin's touching plea for unity:

"I doubt . . . whether any other convention we can obtain may be able to make a better Constitution . . . It . . . astonishes me, sir, to find this system approaching so near to perfection as it does . . . Thus I consent, Sir, to this Constitution, because I expect no better, and because I am not sure that it is not the best . . . I hope, therefore, that for our own sakes . . . and for the sake of posterity, we shall act heartily and unanimously in recommending this Constitution . . . I cannot help expressing a wish that every member of the Convention . . . would with me, on this occasion, doubt a little of his own infallibility, and . . . put his name to this instrument."

But some refused to sign. They may have felt as did Luther Martin, who told his fellow delegate, Daniel of St. Thomas Jenifer: "I'll be hanged if ever the people of Maryland will agree to it." To which Jenifer replied: "I advise you to stay in Philadelphia lest you should be hanged."

Of the forty-two delegates present, thirty-nine "subscribed our

34 Names" to the document that contained the formula (devised by Gouverneur Morris "to gain the dissenting members")—"done in Convention by the Unanimous Consent of the States present." The first to sign was "G⁰ Washington, Presidᵗ and deputy from Virginia." Then the other delegates walked up to the table in the geographical order of their states—beginning with New Hampshire and going southward to Georgia—and affixed their signatures.

The Constitution was then made public. On Wednesday, September 19, *The Pennsylvania Packet, and Daily Advertiser* printed it on its front page.

THE STRUGGLE OVER THE CONSTITUTION

Two hurdles now had to be overcome before the Constitution could go into effect. One was the approval of the Congress of the Confederation. The other was ratification by nine of the thirteen states. The first was comparatively easy; the second caused a major crisis.

Three of the delegates to the convention—Gorham, King, and Madison—also were members of the Congress. They took the Constitution to New York, where Congress was then in session. After a short debate, the Congress, on September 28, agreed to submit the Constitution to the states for consideration. But it refrained from recommending adoption.

As the Constitution was submitted for ratification by state conventions, it stirred up a storm of controversy. Clearly, it proposed to replace the Articles of Confederation and, as such, it appeared to many people to be a kind of *coup d'état*. Throughout the country it was both violently attacked and warmly defended. Arguments against the Constitution, some rational and weighty and others emotional and trivial, were numerous, but in sum they amounted to a distrust of the men who made it and of the kind of government it contemplated. Those who defended the Constitution came to be known as Federalists and the opponents as anti-Federalists.

There were two main streams of opposition. One may be called popular, the other liberal. Popular hostility was based on the fear that by providing for a strong central government the Constitution would destroy the individual states, and that the proposed new government, being an instrument of the rich, would be a menace to the poor in such matters as taxation and other onerous burdens. Patrick Henry, in his violent attack on the Constitution in the Virginia ratification convention, described it as "extremely pernicious, impolitic and dangerous." Others argued that it would "take away all we have—all our property," that it contained "no proper restriction of power," that it was "founded on the principles of monarchy," and that it was "like a mad horse" that would run away with its rider. As one opponent said in the New York State ratification convention, anybody who trusted this newfangled Constitution was like a man getting on a horse without a bridle: he would "justly be deemed a mad man and deserve to have his neck broken."

The liberal opposition was more rational. This group granted that the Constitution contained a number of excellent features, but it protested against the absence of a bill of rights. The Constitution, the liberals said, contained safeguards for the protection of property, but not for individual liberty. This viewpoint was most clearly voiced by Thomas Jefferson, then American Minister in Paris, who, upon receiving a copy of the Constitution from his friend Madison, reacted to it as follows (December 20, 1787):

"I like much the general idea of framing a government which should go on of itself peaceably . . . I like the organization of the government into Legislative, Judiciary and Executive. I like the power given the Legislature to levy taxes; and for that reason solely approve of the greater house being chosen by the people directly . . . I am captivated by the compromise of the opposite claims of the great and little states . . . There are other good things. . . .

"I will now add what I do not like. First the omission of a bill of rights providing clearly and without the aid of sophisms for freedom of religion, freedom of the press, protection against standing armies, restriction against monopolies, the eternal and unremitting force of the habeas corpus laws, and trials by jury . . . Let me add that a bill of rights is what the people are entitled to against every government on earth, general or particular, and what no just government should refuse, or rest on inference."

The controversy over the Constitution produced at least one major piece of political literature. This was mostly the work of Hamilton and Madison.[1] About two weeks after the Constitution was signed, Hamilton threw himself into its defense by publishing, in the New York *Independent Journal*, on October 2, 1787, the first of a series of articles. The pieces continued, in the *Journal* and in other New York

---

[1] Of the eighty-five *Federalist* papers, Hamilton wrote fifty-one (Nos. 1, 6-9, 11-13, 15-17, 21-36, 59-61, 65-85); Madison fourteen (Nos. 10, 14, 37-48); John Jay five (Nos. 2-5, 64). Of the remaining fifteen, the authorship of twelve is uncertain: they were the work of either Hamilton or Madison; and three were written by both men in collaboration. See E. G. Bourne and P. L. Ford, in *American Historical Review*, April and July, 1897.

publications, until April, 1788. Later that year the collected articles were published in book form under the title, *The Federalist.*

Hamilton, although he was dubious about the democratic features in the Constitution, undertook to defend it on two main grounds. One was that, despite its shortcomings, it was the best obtainable under the circumstances; the other was that its rejection would lead to anarchy and perhaps dictatorship. As he pointed out pleadingly in the last *Federalist* paper (No. 85):

"I acknowledge that I cannot entertain an equal tranquillity with those who affect to treat the dangers of a longer continuance in our present situation as imaginary. A nation without a national government, is, in my view, an awful spectacle . . . I dread the more the consequences of new attempts [new Constitutional conventions], because I know that powerful individuals, in this and in other States, are enemies to a general national government in every possible shape."

Although written in the heat of a campaign, *The Federalist*'s tone and style are elevated to the point of making it a classic in political literature. It is a powerful analysis of political-social institutions, a comprehensive discussion of republican government, and a lucidly reasoned defense of the work of the Constitutional Convention. Every possible argument against the Constitution is raised, dissected, and explained with a wealth of cogent reasoning and historic example. Its tone and thought, in fact, are such that it has been frequently cited by the Supreme Court as an authoritative commentary on the Constitution and the intention of its framers.

A few of the states ratified the Constitution promptly and without dissent. The first of them was Delaware, which did so unanimously, on December 7, 1787. Unanimous ratifications also were voted in New Jersey (December 18) and Georgia (January 2, 1788).

In the bigger, more populous states—Pennsylvania, Massachusetts, Virginia, and New York—the struggle over ratification was fierce and the vote close. There the delegates split along class lines, with the wealthy and professional citizens generally supporting the Constitution and the economically less favored ones opposing it. In Pennsylvania, for example, of the forty-six delegates who voted for it (twenty-three opposed it), two were doctors, two clergymen, four merchants, eight lawyers, and twelve capitalists. Among those who opposed it, thirteen were representatives of the poorer farmers. Similarly, in Massachusetts, among the 187 who voted yea (against 168 nays), there were three justices of the state supreme court, twelve prominent lawyers, fifteen state senators, twenty-four clergymen, and a large number of army officers and government officials.

New Hampshire's ratification on June 21, 1788, meant that the *37* necessary nine states had approved and accepted the Constitution. (Virginia followed four days later, on June 25, and New York, thanks principally to the brilliant efforts of Alexander Hamilton, on July 26. North Carolina and Rhode Island did not ratify until the Constitution was already in effect.) And so, after more than a year of effort and struggle, the Constitution was launched on its historic career.

On September 13, the Continental Congress terminated itself by proclaiming the dates for establishing the new Government under the ratified Constitution. Three Wednesdays were selected for the successive stages in organizing the Government. The Congress resolved that the states should choose presidential electors on the first Wednesday in January, 1789; that these electors should vote for the President and Vice-President on the first Wednesday in February; and that both houses of the new national legislature should meet on the first Wednesday in March, which happened to fall on the fourth. New York City was selected as the temporary national capital.

There was little campaigning for the presidency. Practically everywhere the elections went off quietly. In five states presidential electors were chosen by the legislatures and in the rest by direct popular vote. Owing to bad roads, the count of the electoral vote was delayed for more than a month. It was not until April 6, 1789, that the first Congress met in New York City to count the votes. All sixty-nine had been cast for George Washington. Since in those days electors voted for two persons for President, the next highest vote—thirty-four—went to John Adams, who was thereupon declared Vice-President.

On April 30, George Washington, dressed in brown, wearing white stockings, and with a sword at his side, was inaugurated first President of the United States. In a tremulous voice he repeated the oath of office, as provided in the Constitution, and read to him by Chancellor Robert R. Livingston of New York: "I do solemnly swear that I will faithfully execute the office of President of the United States, and will to the best of my ability preserve, protect and defend the Constitution of the United States."

THE BILL OF RIGHTS

President Washington's inauguration was not the end of the struggle over the Constitution. In a number of states the defenders of the Constitution had promised to work for a bill of rights once the main document had been ratified. It was the price of ratification.

Precedents for a written bill of rights, specifically enumerating the liberties of the people, already existed. Apart from the historic bill of rights that William and Mary had granted the English people in 1689, a number of state constitutions contained such bills.

The promise to provide a national bill of rights that would, in the words of Washington's first inaugural address, promote the "characteristic rights of freemen," was promptly kept. On June 8, James Madison, representing Virginia in the House of Representatives, introduced there a list of amendments based on the seventy-eight proposals made in the various state ratification conventions. "We ought not," Madison said, "disregard their inclination, but on principle of amity, and moderation, conform to their wishes, and expressly declare the great rights of mankind secured under this Constitution."

A committee of the House of Representatives reported out seventeen of Madison's amendments and submitted them to the Senate for agreement. The printed copy of this list contained an explanatory preamble (August 24, 1789):

"The Convention of a Number of the States having, at the time of their adopting the Constitution, expressed a desire, in order to prevent misconstruction or abuse of its Powers, that further declaratory and restrictive Clauses should be added: And as extending the Ground of public Confidence in the Government, will best insure the beneficent ends of its Institutions."

The Senate reduced the seventeen amendments to twelve. These were agreed upon in a joint resolution of September 25, 1789. The President of the United States was then requested to "transmit to the Executives of the several States which have ratified the Constitution" copies of the proposed amendments. Under the Constitution, each amendment required ratification by three-fourths of the states.

The process of ratification took more than two years. By December 15, 1791, the date of ratification by Virginia, ten amendments—known as the Bill of Rights—had secured the necessary votes. Two amendments failed. One of these dealt with the question of membership in the House of Representatives; the second provided that a change in salaries of the members of Congress should take effect only after a succeeding election.

On December 15, 1791, the Bill of Rights was declared to be in force as an integral part of the Constitution.

NOTES ON THE TEXT

The official *Journal* of the Constitutional Convention is slim, meager, and confined mainly to motions and votes. Fortunately, some of the delegates, among them Yates, King, McHenry, Paterson, and Hamilton, kept notes which have helped us to amplify the record. But most of our knowledge of the proceedings comes from Madison's journal. Without him the essence of the debates would have been lost.

Although an active delegate who spoke often, Madison, nevertheless, took the trouble to jot down, in as much detail as possible, practically everything that was said on the floor of the convention. The strain of the effort nearly undermined his health, but it was a task voluntarily undertaken in the service of posterity. He tells us that:

"In pursuance of the task I had assumed, I chose a seat in front of the presiding member, with the other members on my right and left hands. In this favorable position for hearing all that passed, I noted, in terms legible and in abbreviations and marks intelligible to myself, what was read from the Chair or spoken by the members; and, losing not a moment unnecessarily between the adjournment and reassembling of the Convention, I was enabled to write out my daily notes during the session, or within a few finishing days after its close . . . In the labor and correctness of this I was not a little aided by practice, and by a familiarity with the style and the train of observation and reasoning which characterized the principal speakers. It happened, also, that I was not absent a single day, not more than a casual fraction of an hour in any day, so that I could not have lost a single speech, unless a very short one."

(At the same time, the reader must realize that Madison did not leave us a stenographic transcript. All discussion, therefore, does not inevitably lead to a constitutional paragraph, and votes on issues are not invariably preceded by relevant debate. Many constitutional guarantees most important to us today were accepted without debate or dissent. It should also be recalled that articles, motions, and resolutions read and accepted on the convention floor may later have been reworked and reworded in committee.)

The fullest publication of the records, notes, journals, and other materials relating to the convention is Professor Max Farrand's admirable work, *The Records of the Federal Convention,* in four volumes (1911, 1937). The present text, however, is not based on Farrand, but on an earlier work, Jonathan Elliot's *Debates . . . of the Congress of the Confederation* and *Debates in the Several State Conventions,* four volumes (1827) and five volumes (1861).

The choice of Elliot's text was dictated by the desire for simplicity. In Farrand's volumes, materials and notes are reproduced as given in the original, retaining the spellings, abbreviations, punctuation, and shorthand as they were recorded at the time. Thus, Gorham is sometimes spelled "Gorum," Paterson has one "t" too many, and Ellsworth one "l" too few. *Would* appears as "wd," *should* as "shd." *Doctor* is "Dcr," *the* is "ye," *and* is "&." Since the notes were written in haste, verbs, definite articles, and negatives frequently are left out. All this, while it may be important for the specialist, makes difficult reading.

The Elliot text is simplified without loss of contemporary flavor. The words are spelled out and generally "modernized." It is easy to read. The essential debates are hereby reproduced in full. The few omissions are generally recordings of votes and other technicalities, or obvious repetitions.

Saul K. Padover

MAY 25, 1787	*Constitutional Convention opens with twenty-nine delegates from nine states present.*
	George Washington unanimously elected convention president.
MAY 28-29	*Rules governing convention adopted.*
MAY 29	*Edmund Randolph introduces fifteen resolutions (the Virginia Plan).*
MAY 30	*Convention becomes a committee of the whole and Randolph resolutions are debated for two weeks.*
JUNE 13	*Randolph resolutions, in amended form, reported out of committee.*
JUNE 14	*William Paterson requests and is granted adjournment.*
JUNE 15	*Paterson submits for debate nine proposals to reform Articles of Confederation.*
JUNE 19	*Paterson plan rejected.*
JUNE 20	*Debate on Randolph resolutions resumed.*
JULY 2	*Debate deadlocked. Committee of eleven appointed to seek compromise.*
JULY 5	*Committee reports basic elements of "Great Compromise." Debate continues to July 24.*
JULY —	*Randolph's original fifteen resolutions increased to twenty-three.*
JULY 24	*Randolph, Oliver Ellsworth, Nathaniel Gorham, John Rutledge, and James Wilson appointed a Committee of Detail to draft a Constitution.*
JULY 26	*Convention adjourns to await draft.*
AUGUST 6	*Convention reassembles to debate Committee's completed draft.*
SEPTEMBER 8	*Alexander Hamilton, William Johnson, Rufus King, James Madison, and Gouverneur Morris appointed a Committee of Style to revise and arrange articles agreed to so far.*
SEPTEMBER 10	*Debates end.*
SEPTEMBER 12	*Constitution printed for use of delegates and*

compared point by point with record of the   *43*
proceedings.

SEPTEMBER 15   Constitution ordered engrossed (copied in a
large, fair hand).

SEPTEMBER 17   Thirty-nine of forty-two delegates present sign
the Constitution.

SEPTEMBER 19   Constitution made public. Printed in **Pennsylvania Packet, and Daily Advertiser.**

SEPTEMBER 28   Congress of Confederation, without approving
Constitution, agrees to submit it to the states
for consideration.

OCTOBER 2, 1787-   Federalist papers of Hamilton, Madison, and
APRIL, 1788   John Jay published to explain and defend
Constitution.

DECEMBER 7, 1787   Delaware ratifies the Constitution, 30 to 0.

DECEMBER 12   Pennsylvania ratifies, 46 to 23.

DECEMBER 18   New Jersey ratifies unanimously.

JANUARY 2, 1788   Georgia ratifies unanimously.

JANUARY 9   Connecticut ratifies, 128 to 40.

FEBRUARY 6   Massachusetts ratifies, 187 to 168.

APRIL 18   Maryland ratifies, 63 to 11.

MAY 23   South Carolina ratifies, 149 to 73.

JUNE 21   New Hampshire ratifies, 57 to 46. Necessary
acceptance by nine states achieved.

JUNE 25   Virginia ratifies, 89 to 79.

JULY 26   New York ratifies, 30 to 27.

SEPTEMBER 13   Continental Congress terminates itself.

APRIL 6, 1789   Electors meeting in New York vote George
Washington as first President of the United
States, John Adams as Vice President.

APRIL 30   Washington inaugurated.

JUNE 8   Madison introduces a Bill of Rights in the
House of Representatives.

SEPTEMBER 25   Joint House-Senate committee agrees to twelve
amendments.

NOVEMBER 21   North Carolina ratifies the Constitution,
184 to 77.

MAY 29, 1790   Rhode Island ratifies, 34 to 32.

DECEMBER 15, 1791   Virginia's ratification of Bill of Rights assures
necessary number of states to make first ten
amendments a part of Constitution. (Two
others failed of passage in the states.)

Plans and Proposals

CHAPTER ONE

Organization   47

THE OPENING

Monday, May 14, 1787, was the day fixed for the meeting of the deputies in convention for revising the federal system of government. On that day a small number only had assembled. Seven states were not convened till May 25, when the following members appeared:

Massachusetts: Rufus King.

New York: Robert Yates and Alexander Hamilton.

New Jersey: David Brearly, William Churchill Houston, and William Paterson.

Pennsylvania: Robert Morris, Thomas Fitzsimmons, James Wilson, and Gouverneur Morris.

Delaware: George Read, Richard Basset, and Jacob Broom.

Virginia: George Washington, Edmund Randolph, John Blair, James Madison, George Mason, George Wythe, and James McClurg.

North Carolina: Alexander Martin, William Richardson Davie, Richard Dobbs Spaight, and Hugh Williamson.

South Carolina: John Rutledge, (General) Charles Cotesworth Pinckney, Charles Pinckney, and Pierce Butler.

Georgia: William Few.

Mr. Robert Morris informed the members assembled that by the instruction and in behalf of the deputation of Pennsylvania, he proposed George Washington, Esq., late Commander-in-Chief, for president of the convention. Mr. John Rutledge seconded the motion, expressing his confidence that the choice would be unanimous and observing that the presence of General Washington forbade any observations on the occasion which might otherwise be proper.

Gen. Washington was accordingly unanimously elected by ballot and conducted to the chair by Mr. R. Morris and Mr. Rutledge, from which, in a very emphatic manner, he thanked the convention for the honor they had conferred on him, reminded them of the novelty of the scene of business in which he was to act, lamented his want of better qualifications, and claimed the indulgence of the house towards the involuntary errors which his inexperience might occasion.

Mr. Wilson moved that a secretary be appointed, and nominated Mr. Temple Franklin.

Mr. Hamilton nominated Major Jackson. On the ballot, Major Jackson had five votes and Mr. Franklin two votes.

The appointment of a committee, on the motion of Mr. C. Pinckney, consisting of Messrs. Wythe, Hamilton, and C. Pinckney to prepare standing rules and orders was the only remaining step taken on this day.

THE RULES / *May 28*

From Massachusetts, Nathaniel Gorham and Caleb Strong; from Connecticut, Oliver Ellsworth; from Delaware, Gunning Bedford; from Maryland, James Henry; from Pennsylvania, Benjamin Franklin, George Clymer, Thomas Mifflin, and Jared Ingersoll—took their seats.

Mr. Wythe from the committee for preparing rules made a report which employed the deliberations of this day.

Mr. King objected to one of the rules in the report authorizing any member to call for the yeas and nays and have them entered on the minutes. He urged that as the acts of the convention were not to bind the constituents, it was unnecessary to exhibit this evidence of the votes, and improper, as changes of opinion would be frequent in the course of the business and would fill the minutes with contradictions.

Mr. Mason seconded the objection, adding that such a record of the opinions of members would be an obstacle to a change of them on conviction, and in case of its being hereafter promulged, must furnish handles to the adversaries of the result of the meeting.

The proposed rule was rejected. The standing rules agreed to were as follows:

A house to do business shall consist of the deputies of not less than seven states, and all questions shall be decided by the greater number of these which shall be fully represented. But a lesser number than seven may adjourn from day to day.

Immediately after the president shall have taken the chair and the members their seats, the minutes of the preceding day shall be read by the secretary.

Every member rising to speak shall address the president, and whilst he shall be speaking, none shall pass between them, or hold discourse with another, or read a book, pamphlet, or paper, printed or manuscript. And of two members rising to speak at the same time, the president shall name him who shall be first heard.

A member shall not speak oftener than twice without special leave upon the same question, and not the second time before every other who had been silent shall have been heard if he choose to speak upon the subject.

A motion made and seconded shall be repeated, and if written, as it shall be when any member shall so require, read aloud by the secretary before it shall be debated, and may be withdrawn at any time before the vote upon it shall have been declared.

Orders of the day shall be read next after the minutes and either discussed or postponed before any other business shall be introduced.

When a debate shall arise upon a question, no motion other than to amend the question, to commit it, or to postpone the debate shall be received.

A question which is complicated shall at the request of any member be divided and put separately upon the propositions of which it is compounded.

The determination of a question, although fully debated, shall be postponed if the deputies of any state desire it until the next day.

A writing which contains any matter brought on to be considered shall be read once throughout for information, then by paragraphs to be debated, and again with the amendments if any made on the second reading, and afterwards the question shall be put upon the whole, amended, or approved in its original form as the case shall be.

Committees shall be appointed by ballot, and the members who have the greatest number of ballots, although not a majority of the votes present, shall be the committee. When two or more members have an equal number of votes, the member standing first on the list in the order of taking down the ballots shall be preferred.

A member may be called to order by any other member as well as by the president and may be allowed to explain his conduct or expressions supposed to be reprehensible. And all questions of order shall be decided by the president without appeal or debate.

Upon a question to adjourn for the day, which may be made at any time, if it be seconded, the question shall be put without a debate.

When the house shall adjourn, every member shall stand in his place until the president pass him.

/ May 29

John Dickinson and Elbridge Gerry, the former from Delaware, the latter from Massachusetts, took their seats. The following rules were added on the report of Mr. Wythe from the committee;

That no member be absent from the house, so as to interrupt the representation of the state, without leave.

That committees do not sit whilst the house shall be or ought to be sitting.

That no copy be taken of any entry on the journal during the sitting of the house without leave of the house.

That members only be permitted to inspect the journal.

That nothing spoken in the house be printed, or otherwise published, or communicated without leave.

That a motion to reconsider a matter which has been determined by a majority may be made with leave unanimously given on the same day on which the vote passed, but otherwise, not without one day's previous notice; in which last case if the house agree to the reconsideration, some future day shall be assigned for that purpose.

The Randolph Plan

Editor's note: On May 29, speaking for the Virginia delegation, Edmund Randolph submitted his plan of government consisting of fifteen propositions. On the following day, the convention went into a committee of the whole to discuss the Randolph Plan in detail. The debates continued until June 13.

RANDOLPH OPENS THE DEBATES / *May 29*

Mr. Randolph then opened the main business. He expressed his regret that it should fall to him rather than those who were of longer standing in life and political experience to open the great subject of their mission. But as the convention had originated from Virginia, and his colleagues supposed that some proposition was expected from them, they had imposed this task on him.

He then commented on the difficulty of the crisis and the necessity of preventing the fulfillment of the prophecies of the American downfall.

He observed that in revising the federal system we ought to inquire, first, into the properties which such a government ought to possess; secondly, the defects of the Confederation; thirdly, the danger of our situation, and, fourthly, the remedy.

1. The character of such a government ought to secure, first, against foreign invasion; secondly, against dissensions between members of the Union or seditions in particular states; thirdly, to procure to the several states various blessings of which an isolated situation was incapable; fourthly, it should be able to defend itself against encroachment, and fifthly, to be paramount to the state constitutions.

2. In speaking of the defects of the Confederation, he professed a high respect for its authors and considered them as having done all

that patriots could do in the then infancy of the science of constitutions and of confederacies when the inefficiency of requisitions was unknown—no commercial discord had arisen among any states—no rebellion had appeared, as in Massachusetts—foreign debts had not become urgent—the havoc of paper money had not been foreseen—treaties had not been violated—and perhaps nothing better could be obtained from the jealousy of the states with regard to their sovereignty.

He then proceeded to enumerate the defects:

First, that the Confederation produced no security against foreign invasion, Congress not being permitted to prevent a war, nor to support it by their own authority. Of this he cited many examples, most of which tended to show that they could not cause infractions of treaties, or of the law of nations to be punished; that particular states might by their conduct provoke war without control, and that neither militia nor drafts being fit for defense on such occasions, enlistments only could be successful, and these could not be executed without money.

Secondly, that the Federal Government could not check the quarrel between states, nor a rebellion in any not having constitutional power, nor means to interpose according to the exigency.

Thirdly, that there were many advantages which the United States might acquire which were not attainable under the Confederation, such as a productive impost, counteraction of the commercial regulations of other nations, pushing of commerce ad libitum, and so forth.

Fourthly, that the Federal Government could not defend itself against encroachments from the states.

Fifthly, that it was not even paramount to the state constitutions, ratified as it was in many of the states.

3. He next reviewed the danger of our situation and appealed to the sense of the best friends of the United States, to the prospect of anarchy from the laxity of government everywhere, and to other considerations.

4. He then proceeded to the remedy; the basis of which, he said, must be the republican principle.

HIS FIFTEEN RESOLUTIONS / *May 29*

Mr. Randolph proposed the following resolutions, which he explained one by one:

1. Resolved, that the Articles of Confederation ought to be so corrected and enlarged as to accomplish the objects proposed by their in-

stitution, namely common defense, security of liberty, and general welfare.

2. Resolved, therefore, that the rights of suffrage in the national legislature ought to be proportioned to the quotas of contribution or to the number of free inhabitants as the one or the other rule may seem best in different cases.

3. Resolved, that the national legislature ought to consist of two branches.

4. Resolved, that the members of the first branch of the national legislature ought to be elected by the people of the several states every _____ for the term of _____; to be of the age of _____ years at least; to receive liberal stipends by which they may be compensated for the devotion of their time to the public service; to be ineligible to any office established by a particular state or under the authority of the United States, except those peculiarly belonging to the functions of the first branch, during the term of service and for the space of _____ after its expiration; to be incapable of re-election for the space of _____ after the expiration of their terms of service, and to be subject to recall.

5. Resolved, that the members of the second branch of the national legislature ought to be elected by those of the first, out of a proper number of persons nominated by the individual legislatures; to be of the age of _____ years at least; to hold their offices for a term sufficient to insure their independency; to receive liberal stipends by which they may be compensated for the devotion of their time to the public service, and to be ineligible to any office established by a particular state or under the authority of the United States, except those peculiarly belonging to the functions of the second branch, during the term of service and for the space of _____ after the expiration thereof.

6. Resolved, that each branch ought to possess the right of originating acts; that the national legislature ought to be empowered to enjoy the legislative rights vested in Congress by the Confederation, and moreover to legislate in all cases to which the separate states are incompetent or in which the harmony of the United States may be interrupted by the exercise of individual legislation; to negative all laws passed by the several states contravening in the opinion of the national legislature the Articles of Union or any treaty subsisting under the authority of the Union, and to call forth the force of the Union against any member of the Union failing to fulfill its duty under the articles thereof.

7. Resolved, that a national executive be instituted to be chosen by the national legislature for the term of _____; to receive punctually

at stated times a fixed compension [compensation] for the services
rendered in which no increase or diminution shall be made so as to
affect the magistracy existing at the time of increase or diminution;
and to be ineligible a second time, and that besides a general authority
to execute the national laws, it ought to enjoy the executive rights
vested in Congress by the Confederation.

8. Resolved, that the executive and a convenient number of the
national judiciary ought to compose a council of revision with authority to examine every act of the national legislature before it shall be
final, and that the dissent of the said council shall amount to a rejection, unless the act of the national legislature be again passed, or that
of a particular legislature be again negatived by _____ of the members of each branch.

9. Resolved, that a national judiciary be established to consist of
one or more supreme tribunals and of inferior tribunals, to be chosen
by the national legislature, to hold their offices during good behavior,
and to receive punctually, at stated times, fixed compension for their
services in which no increase or diminution shall be made so as to affect the persons actually in office at the time of such increase or
diminution. That the jurisdiction of the inferior tribunals shall be to
hear and determine in the first instance, and of the supreme tribunal
to hear and determine in the *dernier* resort, all piracies and felonies
on the high seas, captures from an enemy, cases in which foreigners or
citizens of other states applying to such jurisdictions may be interested,
or which respect the collection of the national revenue, impeachments
of any national officers, and questions which may involve the national
peace and harmony.

10. Resolved, that provision ought to be made for the admission of
states lawfully arising within the limits of the United States, whether
from a voluntary junction of government and territory, or otherwise,
with the consent of a number of voices in the national legislature less
than the whole.

11. Resolved, that a republican government and the territory of
each state, except in the instance of a voluntary junction of government and territory, ought to be guaranteed by the United States to
each state.

12. Resolved, that provision ought to be made for the continuance
of Congress and their authorities and privileges until a given day after
the reform of the Articles of Union shall be adopted and for the com-
pletion of all their engagements.

13. Resolved, that provision ought to be made for the amendment
of the Articles of Union whensoever it shall seem necessary, and that

the assent of the national legislature ought not to be required thereto.

14. Resolved, that the legislative, executive, and judiciary powers within the several states ought to be bound by oath to support the Articles of Union.

15. Resolved, that the amendments which shall be offered to the Confederation by the convention ought, at a proper time or times after the approbation of Congress, be submitted to an assembly or assemblies of representatives, recommended by the several legislatures, to be expressly chosen by the people, to consider, and decided thereon.

These resolutions were referred to a committee of the whole house.

GENERAL AGREEMENT TO FORM
A NATIONAL GOVERNMENT / *May 30*

The propositions of Mr. Randolph, which had been referred to the committee (of the whole house) being taken up, he moved on the suggestion of Mr. Gouverneur Morris that the first of his propositions, to wit: "Resolved, that the Articles of Confederation ought to be so corrected and enlarged as to accomplish the objects proposed by their institution, namely, common defense, security of liberty, and general welfare," should mutually be postponed in order to consider the three following:

1. That a union of the states merely federal will not accomplish the objects proposed by the Articles of Confederation—namely, common defense, security of liberty, and general welfare.

2. That no treaty or treaties among the whole or part of the states as individual sovereignties would be sufficient.

3. That a national government ought to be established, consisting of a supreme legislative, executive, and judiciary.

The motion for postponing was seconded by Mr. Gouverneur Morris and unanimously agreed to.

Some verbal criticisms were raised against the first proposition, and it was agreed on motion of Mr. Butler, seconded by Mr. Randolph, to pass on to the third, which underwent a discussion, less, however, on its general merits than on the force and extent of the particular terms national and supreme.

Mr. Charles Pinckney wished to know of Mr. Randolph whether he meant to abolish the state governments altogether. Mr. Randolph replied that he meant by these general propositions merely to introduce the particular ones which explained the outlines of the system he had in view.

Mr. Butler said he had not made up his mind on the subject and was open to the light which discussion might throw on it. After some general observations, he concluded with saying that he had opposed the grant of powers to Congress heretofore because the whole power was vested in one body. The proposed distribution of the powers with different bodies changed the case and would induce him to go great lengths.

Gen. Pinckney expressed a doubt whether the Act of Congress recommending the convention, or the commissions of the deputies to it, would authorize a discussion of a system founded on different principles from the Federal Constitution.

Mr. Gerry seemed to entertain the same doubt.

Mr. Gouverneur Morris explained the distinction between a federal and a national supreme government, the former being a mere compact resting on the good faith of the parties, the latter having a complete and compulsive operation. He contended that in all communities there must be one supreme power, and one only.

Mr. Mason observed not only that the present Confederation was deficient in not providing for coercion and punishment against delinquent states, but argued very cogently that punishment could not in the nature of things be executed on the states collectively and, therefore, that such a government was necessary as could directly operate on individuals and would punish those only whose guilt required it.

Mr. Sherman admitted that the Confederation had not given sufficient power to Congress and that additional powers were necessary, particularly that of raising money, which he said would involve many other powers. He admitted also that the general and particular jurisdictions ought in no case to be concurrent. He seemed, however, not to be disposed to make too great inroads on the existing system, intimating as one reason, that it would be wrong to lose every amendment by inserting such as would not be agreed to by the states.

The question, as moved by Mr. Butler on the third proposition— it was resolved by the committee of the whole "that a national government ought to be established, consisting of a supreme legislative, executive, and judiciary"—passed, 6 to 1.

THE QUESTION OF
PROPORTIONAL REPRESENTATION / *May 30*

The following resolution, being the second of those proposed by Mr. Randolph, was taken up:

"That the rights of suffrage in the national legislature ought to be proportioned to the quotas of contribution or to the number of free inhabitants, as the one or the other rule may seem best in different cases."

Mr. Madison, observing that the words "or to the number of free inhabitants" might occasion debates which would divert the committee from the general question whether the principle of representation should be changed, moved that they might be struck out.

Mr. King observed that the quotas of contribution which would alone remain as the measure of representation would not answer, because waiving every other view of the matter, the revenue might hereafter be so collected by the General Government that the sums respectively drawn from the states would not appear and would besides be continually varying.

Mr. Madison admitted the propriety of the observation and that some better rule ought to be found.

Mr. Hamilton moved to alter the resolution so as to read "that the rights of suffrage in the national legislature ought to be proportioned to the number of free inhabitants." Mr. Spaight seconded the motion.

It was then moved that the resolution be postponed, which was agreed to.

Mr. Randolph and Mr. Madison then moved the following resolution: "That the rights of suffrage in the national legislature ought to be proportioned."

It was moved and seconded to amend it by adding "and not according to the present system," which was agreed to.

It was then moved and seconded to alter the resolution so as to read "That the rights of suffrage in the national legislature ought not to be according to the present system."

It was then moved and seconded to postpone the resolution moved by Mr. Randolph and Mr. Madison, which being agreed to, Mr. Madison moved, in order to get over the difficulties, the following resolution: "That the equality of suffrage established by the Articles of Confederation ought not to prevail in the national legislature, and that an equitable ratio of representation ought to be substituted." This was seconded by Mr. Gouverneur Morris and being generally relished, would have been agreed to when Mr. Read moved that the whole clause relating to the point of representation be postponed, reminding the committee that the deputies from Delaware were restrained by their commission from assenting to any change of the rule of suffrage, and in case such a change should be fixed on, it might become their duty to retire from the convention.

Mr. Gouverneur Morris observed that the valuable assistance of those members could not be lost without real concern and that so early a proof of discord in the convention as the secession of a state would add much to the regret; that the change proposed was, however, so fundamental an article in a national government that it could not be dispensed with.

Mr. Madison observed that whatever reason might have existed for the equality of suffrage when the union was a federal one among sovereign states, it must cease when a national government should be put into the place. In the former case, the acts of Congress depended so much for their efficacy on the co-operation of the states that these had a weight, both within and without Congress, nearly in proportion to their extent and importance. In the latter case, as the acts of the General Government would take effect without the intervention of the state legislatures, a vote from a small state would have the same efficacy and importance as a vote from a large one, and there was the same reason for different numbers of representatives from different states as from counties of different extents within particular states. He suggested as an expedient for at once taking the sense of the members on this point and saving the Delaware deputies from embarrassment, that the question should be taken in committee and the clause on report to the house be postponed without a question there. This, however, did not appear to satisfy Mr. Read.

By several it was observed that no just construction of the act of Delaware could require or justify a secession of her deputies, even if the resolution were to be carried through the house as well as the committee. It was finally agreed, however, that the clause should be postponed; it being understood that in the event the proposed change of representation would certainly be agreed to, no objection or difficulty being started from any other quarter than from Delaware.

The motion of Mr. Read to postpone being agreed to, the committee then rose, the chairman reported progress, and the house, having resolved to resume the subject in committee tomorrow, adjourned to ten o'clock.

Question postponed.

• Article I, Section 1: All legislative Powers herein granted shall be vested in a Congress of the United States, which shall consist of a Senate and House of Representatives. THE CONSTITUTION OF THE UNITED STATES

Mr. Randolph's third resolution "that the national legislature ought to consist of two branches" was agreed to without debate or dissent, except that of Pennsylvania—given probably from complaisance to Dr. Franklin, who was understood to be partial to a single house of legislation.

Two-branch legislature approved, 7 to 1.

SHOULD THE PEOPLE ELECT THE HOUSE? / *May 31*

The fourth resolution, first clause, "that the members of the first branch of the national legislature ought to be elected by the people of the several states," being taken up, Mr. Sherman opposed the election by the people, insisting that it ought to be by the state legislatures. The people, he said, immediately should have as little to do as may be about the government. They want information and are constantly liable to be misled.

Mr. Gerry: The evils we experience flow from the excess of democracy. The people do not want virtue, but are the dupes of pretended patriots. In Massachusetts, it had been fully confirmed by experience that they are daily misled into the most baneful measures and opinions by the false reports circulated by designing men which no one on the spot can refute. One principal evil arises from the want of due provision for those employed in the administration of government. It would seem to be a maxim of democracy to starve the public servants. He mentioned the popular clamor in Massachusetts for the reduction of salaries and the attack made on that of the governor, though secured by the spirit of the constitution itself. He had, he said, been too republican heretofore: he was still, however, republican, but had been taught by experience the danger of the leveling spirit.

Mr. Mason argued strongly for an election of the larger branch by the people. It was to be the grand depository of the democratic principle of the government. It was, so to speak, to be our House of Commons. It ought to know and sympathize with every part of the community and ought, therefore, to be taken, not only from different parts of the whole republic, but also from different districts of the larger members of it, which had in several instances, particularly in Virginia, different interests and views arising from difference of produce, of habits, and so forth. He admitted that we had been too democratic, but was afraid we should incautiously run into the opposite extreme. We ought to attend to the rights of every class of the people. He had

often wondered at the indifference of the superior classes of society
to this dictate of humanity and policy; considering that, however
affluent their circumstances or elevated their situations might be, the
course of a few years not only might, but certainly would, distribute
their posterity throughout the lowest classes of society. Every selfish
motive, therefore, every family attachment, ought to recommend such
a system of policy as would provide no less carefully for the rights and
happiness of the lowest than of the highest order of citizens.

Mr. Wilson contended strenuously for drawing the most numerous
branch of the legislature immediately from the people. He was for
raising the federal pyramid to a considerable altitude, and for that
reason wished to give it as broad a basis as possible. No government
could long subsist without the confidence of the people. In a republican government, this confidence was peculiarly essential. He
also thought it wrong to increase the weight of the state legislatures
by making them the electors of the national legislature. All interference between the general and local governments should be obviated
as much as possible. On examination, it would be found that the opposition of states to federal measures had proceeded much more from
the officers of the states than from the people at large.

Mr. Madison considered the popular election of one branch of the
national legislature as essential to every plan of free government. He
observed that in some of the states, one branch of the legislature was
composed of men already removed from the people by an intervening
body of electors; that if the first branch of the general legislature
should be elected by the state legislatures, the second branch elected
by the first, the executive by the second together with the first, and
other appointments again made for subordinate purposes by the executive, the people would be lost sight of altogether and the necessary
sympathy between them and their rulers and officers too little felt. He
was an advocate for the policy of refining the popular appointments
by successive filtrations, but thought it might be pushed too far. He
wished the expedient to be resorted to only in the appointment of the
second branch of the legislature and in the executive and judiciary
branches of the government. He thought, too, that the great fabric to
be raised would be more stable and durable if it should rest on the
solid foundation of the people themselves than if it should stand
merely on the pillars of the legislatures.

Mr. Gerry did not like the election by the people. The maxims
taken from the British constitution were often fallacious when applied
to our situation, which was extremely different. Experience, he said,
had shown that the state legislatures drawn immediately from the peo-

ple did not always possess their confidence. He had no objection, however, to an election by the people if it were so qualified that men of honor and character might not be unwilling to be joined in the appointments. He seemed to think the people might nominate a certain number out of which the state legislatures should be bound to choose.

Mr. Butler thought an election by the people an impracticable mode.

Election of the House of Representatives by the people approved, 6 to 2.

SHOULD THE STATE LEGISLATURES ELECT THE SENATE? / *May 31*

The committee proceeded to the fifth resolution, "that the second (or senatorial) branch of the national legislature ought to be chosen by the first branch out of persons nominated by the state legislatures."

Mr. Spaight contended that the second branch ought to be chosen by the state legislatures and moved an amendment to that effect.

Mr. Butler apprehended that the taking so many powers out of the hands of the states as was proposed tended to destroy all that balance and security of interests among the states which it was necessary to preserve, and called on Mr. Randolph, the mover of the propositions to explain the extent of his ideas, and particularly the number of members he meant to assign to this second branch.

Mr. Randolph observed that he had at the time of offering his propositions stated his ideas as far as the nature of general propositions required, that details made no part of the plan and could not perhaps with propriety have been introduced. If he was to give an opinion as to the number of the second branch, he should say that it ought to be much smaller than that of the first, so small as to be exempt from the passionate proceedings to which numerous assemblies are liable. He observed that the general object was to provide a cure for the evils under which the United States labored; that in tracing these evils to their origin, every man had found it in the turbulence and follies of democracy; that some check, therefore, was to be sought for against this tendency of our governments, and that a good Senate seemed most likely to answer the purpose.

Mr. King reminded the committee that the choice of the second branch (as proposed by Mr. Spaight) by the state legislatures would be impracticable unless it was to be very numerous or the idea of proportion among the states was to be disregarded. According to this idea,

there must be eighty or a hundred members to entitle Delaware to
the choice of one of them.

61

Mr. Spaight withdrew his motion.

Mr. Wilson opposed both a nomination by the state legislatures and
an election by the first branch of the national legislature, because the
second branch of the latter ought to be independent of both. He
thought both branches of the national legislature ought to be chosen
by the people, but was not prepared with a specific proposition. He
suggested the mode of choosing the Senate of New York—to wit, of
uniting several election districts for one branch in choosing members
for the other branch—as a good model.

Mr. Madison observed that such a mode would destroy the influence
of the smaller states associated with larger ones in the same district,
as the latter would choose from within themselves, although better
men might be found in the former. The election of senators in Virginia, where large and small counties were often formed into one district for the purpose, had illustrated this consequence. Local partiality would often prefer a resident within the county or state to a
candidate of superior merit residing out of it. Less merit also in a
resident would be more known throughout his own state.

Mr. Sherman favored an election of one member by each of the state
legislatures.

Mr. Pinckney moved to strike out the "nomination by the state legislatures."

Motion defeated.

*On the whole question for electing by the first branch out of
nominations by the state legislatures, the motion was defeated, 7 to 3.*

So the clause was disagreed to and a chasm left in this part of the
plan.

QUESTION RESUMED / *June 7*

The clause providing for the appointment of the second branch of
the national legislature having lain blank since the last vote on the
mode of electing it—to wit, by the first branch—Mr. Dickinson now
moved "that the members of the second branch ought to be chosen
by the individual legislatures."

Mr. Sherman seconded the motion, observing that the particular
states would thus become interested in supporting the national Government and that a due harmony between the two governments would
be maintained. He admitted that the two ought to have separate and

distinct jurisdictions, but that they ought to have a mutual interest in supporting each other.

Mr. Pinckney: If the small states should be allowed one senator only, the number will be too great; there will be eighty at least.

Mr. Dickinson had two reasons for his motion—first, because the sense of the states would be better collected through their governments than immediately from the people at large; secondly, because he wished the Senate to consist of the most distinguished characters, distinguished for their rank in life and their weight of property, and bearing as strong a likeness to the British House of Lords as possible, and he thought such characters more likely to be selected by the state legislatures than in any other mode. The greatness of the number was no objection with him. He hoped there would be eighty, and twice eighty, of them. If their number should be small, the popular branch could not be balanced by them. The legislature of a numerous people ought to be a numerous body.

Mr. Williamson preferred a small number of senators, but wished that each state should have at least one. He suggested twenty-five as a convenient number. The different modes of representation in the different branches will serve as a mutual check.

Mr. Butler was anxious to know the ratio of representation before he gave any opinion.

Mr. Wilson: If we are to establish a national government, that government ought to flow from the people at large. If one branch of it should be chosen by the legislatures and the other by the people, the two branches will rest on different foundations, and dissensions will naturally arise between them. He wished the Senate to be elected by the people as well as the other branch; the people might be divided into proper districts for the purpose, and he moved to postpone the motion of Mr. Dickinson in order to take up one of that import.

Mr. Gouverneur Morris seconded him.

Mr. Read proposed "that the Senate should be appointed by the executive magistrate out of a proper number of persons to be nominated by the individual legislatures." He said he thought it his duty to speak his mind frankly. Gentlemen, he hoped, would not be alarmed at the idea. Nothing short of this approach toward a proper model of government would answer the purpose, and he thought it best to come directly to the point at once. His proposition was not seconded, nor supported.

Mr. Madison: If the motion (of Mr. Dickinson) should be agreed to, we must either depart from the doctrine of proportional representation or admit into the Senate a very large number of members. The

first is inadmissible, being evidently unjust. The second is inexpedient.
The use of the Senate is to consist in its proceeding with more coolness,
with more system, and with more wisdom than the popular branch.
Enlarge their number and you communicate to them the vices which
they are meant to correct. He differed from Mr. Dickinson who
thought that the additional number would give additional weight to
the body. On the contrary, it appeared to him that their weight would
be in an inverse ratio to their numbers. The example of the Roman
tribunes was applicable. They lost their influence and power in proportion as their number was augmented. The reason seemed to be
obvious. They were appointed to take care of the popular interests
and pretensions at Rome, because the people by reason of their numbers could not act in concert and were liable to fall into factions
among themselves and to become a prey to their aristocratic adversaries. The more they partook of the infirmities of their constituents,
the more liable they became to be divided among themselves either
from their own indiscretions or the artifices of the opposite faction,
and, of course, the less capable of fulfilling their trust. When the
weight of a set of men depends merely on their personal characters,
the greater the number, the greater the weight. When it depends on
the degree of political authority lodged in them, the smaller the number, the greater the weight. These considerations might perhaps be
combined in the intended Senate, but the latter was the material one.

Mr. Gerry: Four modes of appointing the Senate have been mentioned. First, by the first branch of the national legislature. This would
create a dependence contrary to the end proposed. Secondly, by the
national executive. This is a stride toward monarchy that few will
think of. Thirdly, by the people. The people have two great interests,
the landed interest and the commercial, including the stockholders.
To draw both branches from the people will leave no security to the
latter interest, the people being chiefly composed of the landed interest
and erroneously supposing that the other interests are adverse to it.
Fourthly, by the individual legislatures. The elections being carried
through this refinement will be most likely to provide some check in
favor of the commercial interest against the landed, without which,
oppression will take place, and no free government can last long where
that is the case. He was, therefore, in favor of this last.

Mr. Dickinson: The preservation of the states in a certain degree of
agency is indispensable. It will produce that collision between the different authorities which should be wished for in order to check each
other. To attempt to abolish the states altogether would degrade the
councils of our country, would be impracticable, would be ruinous.

He compared the proposed national system to the solar system in which the states were the planets and ought to be left to move freely in their proper orbits. The gentleman from Pennsylvania (Mr. Wilson) wished, he said, to extinguish these planets. If the state governments were excluded from all agency in the national one, and all power drawn from the people at large, the consequence would be that the national Government would move in the same direction as the state governments now do and would run into all the same mischiefs. The reform would only unite the thirteen small streams into one great current pursuing the same course without any opposition whatever. He adhered to the opinion that the Senate ought to be composed of a large number and that their influence from family weight and other causes would be increased thereby. He did not admit that the tribunes lost their weight in proportion as their number was augmented and gave an historical sketch of this institution. If the reasoning of Mr. Madison was good, it would prove that the number of the Senate ought to be reduced below ten, the highest number of the tribunitial corps.

Mr. Wilson: The subject, it must be owned, is surrounded with doubts and difficulties. But we must surmount them. The British Government cannot be our model. We have no materials for a similar one. Our manners, our laws, the abolition of entails and of primogeniture, the whole genius of the people, are opposed to it. He did not see the danger of the states being devoured by the national Government. On the contrary, he wished to keep them from devouring the national Government. He was not, however, for extinguishing these planets as was supposed by Mr. Dickinson; neither did he, on the other hand, believe that they would warm or enlighten the sun. Within their proper orbits, they must still be suffered to act for subordinate purposes for which their existence is made essential by the great extent of our country. He could not comprehend in what manner the landed interest would be rendered less predominant in the Senate by an election through the medium of the legislatures than by the people themselves. If the legislatures, as was now complained, sacrificed the commercial to the landed interest, what reason was there to expect such a choice from them as would defeat their own views? He was for an election by the people in large districts, which would be most likely to obtain men of intelligence and uprightness, subdividing the districts only for the accommodation of voters.

Mr. Madison could as little comprehend in what manner family weight, as desired by Mr. Dickinson, would be more certainly conveyed into the Senate through elections by the state legislatures than

in some other modes. The true question was in what mode the best 65
choice would be made. If an election by the people, or through any
other channel than the state legislatures, promised as uncorrupt and
impartial a preference of merit, there could surely be no necessity for
an appointment by those legislatures. Nor was it apparent that a more
useful check would be derived through that channel than from the
people through some other. The great evils complained of were that
the state legislatures ran into schemes of paper money and so forth
whenever solicited by the people and sometimes without even the
sanction of the people. Their influence, then, instead of checking a
like propensity in the national legislature, may be expected to promote
it. Nothing can be more contradictory than to say that the national
legislature without a proper check will follow the example of the state
legislatures and in the same breath that the state legislatures are the
only proper check.

Mr. Sherman opposed elections by the people, in districts, as not
likely to produce such fit men as elections by the state legislatures.

Mr. Gerry insisted that the commercial and moneyed interest would
be more secure in the hands of the state legislatures than of the people
at large. The former have more sense of character and will be
restrained by that from injustice. The people are for paper money
when the legislatures are against it. In Massachusetts, the county conventions had declared a wish for a depreciating paper that would sink
itself. Besides, in some states there are two branches in the legislature,
one of which is somewhat aristocratic. There would, therefore, be so
far a better chance of refinement in the choice. There seemed,
he thought, to be three powerful objections against elections by districts. First, it is impracticable; the people cannot be brought to one
place for the purpose, and whether brought to the same place or not,
numberless frauds would be unavoidable. Secondly, small states forming part of the same district with a large one or a large part of a large
one would have no chance of gaining an appointment for its citizens
of merit. Thirdly, a new source of discord would be opened between
different parts of the same district.

Mr. Pinckney thought the second branch ought to be permanent
and independent and that the members of it would be rendered more
so by receiving their appointments from the state legislatures. This
mode would avoid the rivalships and discontents incident to the election by districts. He was for dividing the states into three classes according to their respective sizes and for allowing to the first class three
members; to the second, two, and to the third, one.

The question for postponing Mr. Dickinson's motion referring the appointment of the Senate to the state legislatures in order to consider Mr. Wilson's for referring it to the people was defeated, 10 to 1.

Mr. Mason: Whatever power may be necessary for the national Government, a certain portion must necessarily be left with the states. It is impossible for one power to pervade the extreme parts of the United States so as to carry equal justice to them. The state legislatures also ought to have some means of defending themselves against encroachments of the national Government. In every other department, we have studiously endeavored to provide for its self-defense. Shall we leave the states alone unprovided with the means for this purpose? And what better means can we provide than the giving them some share in, or rather to make them a constituent part of, the national establishment? There is danger on both sides no doubt, but we have only seen the evils arising on the side of the state governments. Those on the other side remain to be displayed. The example of Congress does not apply. Congress had no power to carry their acts into execution, as the national Government will have.

Mr. Dickinson's motion for an appointment of the Senate by the state legislatures passed unanimously.

THE POWERS OF THE
NATIONAL LEGISLATURE DISCUSSED / *May 31*

On the proposition for giving legislative power in all cases to which the state legislatures were individually incompetent, Mr. Pinckney and Mr. Rutledge objected to the vagueness of the term "incompetent" and said they could not well decide how to vote until they should see an exact enumeration of the powers comprehended by this definition.

Mr. Butler repeated his fears that we were running into an extreme in taking away the powers of the states and called on Mr. Randolph for the extent of his meaning.

Mr. Randolph disclaimed any intention to give indefinite powers to the national legislature, declaring that he was entirely opposed to such an inroad on the state jurisdictions and that he did not think any considerations whatever could ever change his determination. His opinion was fixed on this point.

Mr. Madison said that he had brought with him into the convention a strong bias in favor of an enumeration and definition of the powers necessary to be exercised by the national legislature, but had also brought doubts concerning its practicability. His wishes remained unaltered, but his doubts had become stronger. What his opinion might ultimately be, he could not yet tell. But he should shrink from nothing which should be found essential to such a form of government as would provide for the safety, liberty, and happiness of the community. This being the end of all our deliberations, all the necessary means for attaining it must, however reluctantly, be submitted to.

The question for giving power in cases to which the states are not competent approved.

The other clauses, giving powers necessary to preserve harmony among the states, to negative all state laws contravening in the opinion of the national legislature the Articles of Union, down to the last clause (the words "or any treaties subsisting under the authority of the Union," being added after the words "contravening and so forth, the articles of the Union," on motion of Dr. Franklin), were agreed to without debate or dissent.

The last clause of the sixth resolution, authorizing an exertion of the force of the whole against a delinquent state, came next into consideration.

Mr. Madison observed that the more he reflected on the use of force, the more he doubted the practicability, the justice, and the efficacy of it when applied to people collectively and not individually. A union of the states containing such an ingredient seemed to provide for its own destruction. The use of force against a state would look more like a declaration of war than an infliction of punishment and would probably be considered by the party attacked as a dissolution of all previous compacts by which it might be bound. He hoped that such a system would be framed as might render this resource unnecessary and moved that the clause be postponed.

This motion was agreed to. The committee then rose and the house adjourned.

• Article IV, Section 4: The United States shall guarantee to every State in this Union a Republican Form of Government, and shall protect each of them against Invasion; and on Application of the Legislature, or of the Executive (when the Legislature cannot be convened) against domestic Violence.

THE CONSTITUTION OF THE UNITED STATES

In committee of the whole. Mr. Pinckney, according to previous notice and rule obtained, moved "that the first branch of the national legislature be elected by the state legislatures, and not by the people," contending that the people were less fit judges in such a case and that the legislatures would be less likely to promote the adoption of the new Government if they were to be excluded from all share in it.

Mr. Gerry: Much depends on the mode of election. In England, the people will probably lose their liberty from the smallness of the proportion having a right of suffrage. Our danger arises from the opposite extreme. Hence, in Massachusetts the worst men get into the legislature. Several members of that body had lately been convicted of infamous crimes. Men of indigence, ignorance, and baseness spare no pains, however dirty, to carry their point against men who are superior to the artifices practiced. He was not disposed to run into extremes. He was as much principled as ever against aristocracy and monarchy. It was necessary, on the one hand, that the people should appoint one branch of the government in order to inspire them with the necessary confidence, but he wished the election, on the other, to be so modified as to secure more effectually a just preference of merit. His idea was that the people should nominate certain persons in certain districts out of whom the state legislatures should make the appointment.

Mr. Wilson: He wished for vigor in the government, but he wished that vigorous authority to flow immediately from the legitimate source of all authority. The government ought to possess not only, first, the force, but second, the mind or sense of the people at large. The legislature ought to be the most exact transcript of the whole society. Representation is made necessary only because it is impossible for the people to act collectively. The opposition was to be expected, he said, from the governments, not from the citizens of the states. The latter had parted, as was observed by Mr. King, with all the necessary powers, and it was immaterial to them by whom they were exercised, if well exercised. The state officers were to be the losers of power. The people, he supposed, would be rather more attached to the national Government than to the state governments, as being more important in itself and more flattering to their pride. There is no danger of improper elections if made by large districts. Bad elections proceed from the smallness of the districts, which give an opportunity to bad men to intrigue themselves into office.

Mr. Sherman: If it were in view to abolish the state governments, the elections ought to be by the people. If the state governments are to be continued, it is necessary in order to preserve harmony between the national and state governments that the elections to the former should be made by the latter. The right of participating in the national Government would be sufficiently secured to the people by their election of the state legislatures. The objects of the Union, he thought, were few—first, defense against foreign danger; secondly, against internal disputes and a resort to force; thirdly, treaties with foreign nations; fourthly, regulating foreign commerce and drawing revenue from it. These and perhaps a few lesser objects alone rendered a confederation of the states necessary. All other matters, civil and criminal, would be much better in the hands of the states. The people are more happy in small than in large states. States may, indeed, be too small, as Rhode Island, and thereby be too subject to faction. Some others were, perhaps, too large, the powers of government not being able to pervade them. He was for giving the General Government power to legislate and execute within a defined province.

Mr. Mason: Under the existing Confederacy, Congress represents the states and not the people of the states; their acts operate on the states not on the individuals. The case will be changed in the new plan of government. The people will be represented; they ought, therefore, to choose the representatives. The requisites in actual representation are that the representatives should sympathize with their constituents, should think as they think and feel as they feel, and that for these purposes they should be residents among them. Much, he said, had been alleged against democratic elections. He admitted that much might be said, but it was to be considered that no government was free from imperfections and evils and that improper elections in many instances were inseparable from republican governments. But compare these with the advantage of this form in favor of the rights of the people—in favor of human nature. He was persuaded there was a better chance for proper elections by the people, if divided into large districts, than by the state legislatures. Paper money had been issued by the latter when the former were against it. Was it to be supposed that the state legislatures, then, would not send to the national legislature patrons of such projects if the choice depended on them?

Mr. Madison considered an election of one branch, at least, of the legislature by the people immediately as a clear principle of free government and that this mode under proper regulations had the additional advantage of securing better representatives as well as of avoiding too great an agency of the state governments in the general one. He differed from the member from Connecticut (Mr. Sherman) in thinking the objects mentioned to be all the principal ones that required a national government. Those were certainly important and necessary objects, but he combined with them the necessity of providing more effectually for the security of private rights and the steady dispensation of justice. Interferences with these were evils which had, more perhaps than anything else, produced this convention. Was it to be supposed that republican liberty could long exist under the abuses of it practiced in some of the states? The gentleman (Mr. Sherman) had admitted that in a very small state faction and oppression would prevail. It was to be inferred, then, that wherever these prevailed, the state was too small. Had they not prevailed in the largest as well as the smallest, though less than in the smallest? And were we not thence admonished to enlarge the sphere as far as the nature of the government would admit? This was the only defense against the inconveniences of democracy consistent with the democratic form of government. All civilized societies would be divided into different sects, factions, and interests as they happened to consist of rich and poor, debtors and creditors, the landed, the manufacturing, the commercial interests, the inhabitants of this district or that district, the followers of this political leader or that political leader, the disciples of this religious sect or that religious sect. In all cases where a majority are united by a common interest or passion, the rights of the minority are in danger. What motives are to restrain them? A prudent regard to the maxim that honesty is the best policy is found by experience to be as little regarded by bodies of men as by individuals. Respect for character is always diminished in proportion to the number among whom the blame or praise is to be divided. Conscience—the only remaining tie —is known to be inadequate in individuals; in large numbers little is to be expected from it. Besides, religion itself may become a motive to persecution and oppression. These observations are verified by the histories of every country, ancient and modern. In Greece and Rome, the rich and poor, the creditors and debtors, as well as the patricians and plebeians, alternately oppressed each other with equal unmercifulness. What a source of oppression was the relation between the parent cities of Rome, Athens, and Carthage and their respective provinces! The former possessing the power, and the latter being sufficiently distinguished to be separate objects of it. Why was America so justly apprehensive of parliamentary injustice? Because Great Britain had a separate interest, real or supposed, and if her authority had been admitted, could have pursued that interest at our expense. We have seen the mere distinction of color made in the most enlightened period of time a ground of the most oppressive dominion ever exercised by man over man. What has been the source of those unjust laws complained of among ourselves? Debtors have defrauded their creditors. The landed interest has borne hard on the mercantile interest. The holders of one species of property have thrown a disproportion of taxes on the holders of another species. The lesson we are to draw from the whole is that where a majority are united by a common sentiment and have an opportunity, the rights of the minor party become insecure. In a republican government, the majority, if united, have always an opportunity. The only remedy is to enlarge the sphere, and thereby divide the community into so great a number of interests and parties that in the first place, a majority will not be likely at the same moment to have a common interest separate from that of the whole or of the minority, and in the second place, that in case they should have such an interest, they may not be so apt to unite in the pursuit of it. It was incumbent on us, then, to try this remedy, and with that view to frame a republican system on such a scale and in such a form as will control all the evils which have been experienced.

Mr. Dickinson considered it essential that one branch of the legislature should be drawn immediately from the people and expedient that the other should be chosen by the legislatures of the states. This combination of the state governments with the national Government was as politic as it was unavoidable. In the formation of the Senate, we ought to carry it through such a refining process as will assimilate it as nearly as may be to the House of Lords in England. He repeated his warm eulogiums on the British constitution. He was for a strong national government, but for leaving the states a considerable agency in the system. The objection against making the former dependent on the latter might be obviated by giving to the Senate an authority permanent and irrevocable for three, five, or seven years. Being thus independent, they will check and decide with uncommon freedom.

Mr. Read: Too much attachment is betrayed to the state governments. We must look beyond their continuance. A national government must soon of necessity swallow them all up. They will soon be reduced to the mere office of electing the national Senate. He was against patching up the old federal system; he hoped the idea would be dismissed. It would be like putting new cloth on an old garment. The Confederation was founded on temporary principles. It cannot last; it cannot be amended. If we do not establish a good government on new principles, we must either go to ruin or have the work to do over again. The people at large are wrongly suspected of being averse to a general government. The aversion lies among interested men who possess their confidence.

72   Mr. Pierce was for an election by the people as to the first branch and by the states as to the second branch, by which means the citizens of the states would be represented both individually and collectively.

Gen. Pinckney wished to have a good national government and at the same time to leave a considerable share of power in the states. An election of either branch by the people, scattered as they are in many states, particularly in South Carolina, was totally impracticable. He differed from gentlemen who thought that a choice by the people would be a better guard against bad measures than by the legislatures. A majority of the people in South Carolina were notoriously for paper money as a legal tender; the legislature had refused to make it a legal tender. The reason was that the latter had some sense of character and were restrained by that consideration. The state legislatures also, he said, would be more jealous and more ready to thwart the national Government if excluded from a participation in it. The idea of abolishing these legislatures would never go down.

Mr. Wilson would not have spoken again, but for what had fallen from Mr. Read; namely, that the idea of preserving the state governments ought to be abandoned. He saw no incompatibility between the national and state governments, provided the latter were restrained to certain local purposes, nor any probability of their being devoured by the former. In all confederated systems, ancient and modern, the reverse had happened, the generality being destroyed gradually by the usurpations of the parts composing it.

Election by state legislatures of representatives to the House defeated, 8 to 3.

PROPORTIONAL REPRESENTATION RESUMED / *June 9*

Mr. Paterson moved that the committee resume the clause relating to the rule of suffrage in the national legislature.

Mr. Brearly seconds him. He was sorry, he said, that any question on this point was brought into view. It had been much agitated in Congress at the time of forming the Confederation and was then rightly settled by allowing to each sovereign state an equal vote. Otherwise, the smaller states must have been destroyed instead of being saved. The substitution of a ratio, he admitted, carried fairness on the face of it, but on a deeper examination was unfair and unjust. Judging the disparity of the states by the quota of Congress, Virginia would have sixteen votes and Georgia but one. A like proportion to the others will make the whole number ninety. There will be three large states and ten small ones. The large states, by which he meant Massachusetts, Pennsylvania, and Virginia, will carry everything before them. It had been admitted, and was known to him from facts within New Jersey, that where large and small counties were united into a district for electing representatives for the district, the large counties always carried their point, and consequently the large states would do so. Virginia with her sixteen votes will be a solid column indeed, a formidable phalanx. While Georgia with her solitary vote and the other little states will be obliged to throw themselves constantly into the scale of some large one in order to have any weight at all. He had come to the convention with a view of being as useful as he could in giving energy and stability to the Federal Government. When the proposition for destroying the equality of votes came forward, he was astonished, he was alarmed. Is it fair then, it will be asked, that Georgia should have an equal vote with Virginia? He would not say it was. What remedy then? One only: that a map of the United States be spread out, that all the existing boundaries be erased, and that a new partition of the whole be made into thirteen equal parts.

Mr. Paterson considered the proposition for a proportional representation as striking at the existence of the lesser states. He would premise, however, to an investigation of this question some remarks on the nature, structure, and powers of the convention. The convention, he said, was formed in pursuance of an Act of Congress; that this act was recited in several of the commissions, particularly that of Massachusetts, which he required to be read; that the amendment of the Confederacy was the object of all the laws and commissions on the subject; that the Articles of the Confederation were, therefore, the proper basis of all the proceedings of the convention; that we ought to keep within its limits or we should be charged by our constituents with usurpation; that the people of America were sharp-sighted and not to be deceived. But the commissions under which we acted were not only the measure of our power, they denoted also the sentiments of the states on the subject of our deliberation. The idea of a national government, as contradistinguished from a federal one, never entered into the mind of any of them, and to the public mind we must accommodate ourselves. We have no power to go beyond the federal scheme, and if we had, the people are not ripe for any other. We must follow the people; the people will not follow us. The proposition could not be maintained, whether considered in reference to us as a nation or as a confederacy. A confederacy supposes sovereignty in the members composing it, and sovereignty supposes equality. If we are to be considered as a nation, all state distinctions must be abolished, the whole must be thrown into hotchpot, and when an equal division is made, then there may be fairly an equality of representation. He held up Virginia, Massachusetts, and Pennsylvania as the three large states, and the other ten as small ones, repeating the calculations of Mr. Brearly as to the disparity of votes which would take place and affirming that the small states would never agree to it. He said there was no more reason that a great individual state contributing much should have more votes than a small one contributing a little than that a rich individual citizen should have more votes than an indigent one. If the ratable property of A was to that of B as forty to one, ought A for that reason to have forty times as many votes as B? Such a principle would never be admitted, and if it were admitted, would put B entirely at the mercy of A. As A has more to be protected than B, so he ought to contribute more for the common protection. The same may be said of a large state which has more to be protected than a small one. Give the large states an influence in proportion to their magnitude and what will be the consequences? Their ambition will be proportionally increased, and the small states will have everything to fear. It was once proposed by Galloway[1] and some others that America should be represented in the British Parliament and then be bound by its laws. America could not have been entitled to more than one third of the representatives which would fall to the share of Great Britain: Would American rights and interests have been safe under an authority thus constituted? It has been said that if a national government is to be formed so as to operate on the people, and not on the states, the representatives ought to be drawn from the people. But why so? May not a legislature filled by the state legislatures operate on the people who choose the state legislatures? Or may not a practicable coercion be found? He admitted that there was none such in the existing system. He was attached strongly to the plan of the existing Confederacy in which the people choose their legislative representatives, and the legislatures their Federal representatives. No other amendments were wanting than to mark the orbits of the states with due precision and provide for the use of coercion, which was the great point. He alluded to the hint thrown out by Mr. Wilson of the necessity to which the large states might be reduced, of confederating among themselves by a refusal of the others to concur. Let them unite if they please, but let them remember that they have no authority to compel the others to unite. New Jersey will never confederate on the plan before the committee. She would be swallowed up. He had rather submit to a monarch, to a despot, than to such a fate. He would not

---

[1] Joseph Galloway, Philadelphia lawyer and member of the Continental Congress, was a loyalist who opposed independence for the Colonies.

only oppose the plan here, but on his return home do everything in his power to defeat it there.

Mr. Wilson hoped if the Confederacy should be dissolved that a majority—nay, a minority of the states—would unite for their safety. He entered elaborately into the defense of a proportional representation, stating for his first position that as all authority was derived from the people, equal numbers of people ought to have an equal number of representatives, and different numbers of people, different numbers of representatives. This principle had been improperly violated in the Confederation owing to the urgent circumstances of the time. As to the case of A and B stated by Mr. Paterson, he observed that in districts as large as the states, the number of people was the best measure of their comparative wealth. Whether, therefore, wealth or numbers was to form the ratio, it would be the same. Mr. Paterson admitted persons, not property, to be the measure of suffrage. Are not the citizens of Pennsylvania equal to those of New Jersey? Does it require one hundred and fifty of the former to balance fifty of the latter? Representatives of different districts ought clearly to hold the same proportion to each other as their respective constituents hold to each other. If the small states will not confederate on this plan, Pennsylvania and, he presumed, some other states, would not confederate on any other. We have been told that each state being sovereign, all are equal. So each man is naturally a sovereign over himself, and all men are, therefore, naturally equal. Can he retain this equality when he becomes a member of civil government? He cannot. As little can a sovereign state when it becomes a member of a federal government. If New Jersey will not part with her sovereignty, it is vain to talk of government. A new partition of the states is desirable, but evidently and totally impracticable.

Mr. Williamson illustrated the cases by a comparison of the different states to counties of different sizes within the same state, observing that proportional representation was admitted to be just in the latter case and could not, therefore, be fairly contested in the former.

The question being about to be put, Mr. Paterson hoped that as so much depended on it, it might be thought best to postpone the decision till tomorrow, which was done.

The committee rose and the house adjourned.

/ *June 11*

In committee of the whole. The clause concerning the rule of suffrage in the national legislature postponed on Saturday was resumed.

Mr. Sherman proposed that the proportion of suffrage in the first branch should be according to the respective numbers of free inhabitants, and that in the second branch, or Senate, each state should have one vote and no more. He said as the states would remain possessed of certain individual rights, each state ought to be able to protect itself; otherwise, a few large states will rule the rest. The House of Lords in England, he observed, had certain particular rights under the constitution, and hence they have an equal vote with the House of Commons that they may be able to defend their rights.

Mr. Rutledge proposed that the proportion of suffrage in the first branch should be according to the quotas of contribution. The justice of this rule, he said, could not be contested. Mr. Butler urged the same idea, adding that money was power and that the states ought to have weight in the government in proportion to their wealth.

Mr. King and Mr. Wilson in order to bring the question to a point moved "that the right of suffrage in the first branch of the national legislature ought not to be according to the rule established in the Articles of Confederation, but according to some equitable ratio of representation." The clause so far as it related to suffrage in the first branch was postponed in order to consider this motion. (*In the printed journal of the convention, Mr. Rutledge is named as the seconder of the motion.*)

Mr. Dickinson contended for the actual contributions of the states as the rule of their representation and suffrage in the first branch. By thus connecting the interests of the states with their duty, the latter would be sure to be performed.

Mr. King remarked that it was uncertain what mode might be used in levying a national revenue, but that it was probable imposts would be one source of it. If the actual contributions were to be the rule, the non-importing states, as Connecticut and New Jersey, would be in a bad situation indeed. It might so happen that they would have no representation. This situation of particular states had been always one powerful argument in favor of the five-per-cent impost.

The question being about to be put, Dr. Franklin said he had thrown his ideas of the matter on a paper which Mr. Wilson read to the committee in the words following:

"Mr. Chairman: It has given me great pleasure to observe that till this point—the proportion of representation—came before us, our debates were carried on with great coolness and temper. If anything of a contrary kind has on this occasion appeared, I hope it will not be repeated, for we are sent here to consult, not to contend with each other, and declarations of a fixed opinion and of determined resolution never to change it, neither enlighten, nor convince us. Positiveness and warmth on one side naturally beget their like on the other and tend to create and augment discord and division in a great concern wherein harmony and union are extremely necessary to give weight to our councils and render them effectual in promoting and securing the common good.

"I must own that I was originally of opinion it would be better if every member of Congress or our national council were to consider himself rather as a representative of the whole than as an agent for the interests of a particular state, in which case the proportion of members for each state would be of less consequence, and it would not be very material whether they voted by states or individually. But as I find this is not to be expected, I now think the number of representatives should bear some proportion to the number of the represented, and that the decisions should be by the majority of members, not by the majority of the states. This is objected to from an apprehension that the greater states would then swallow up the smaller. I do not at present clearly see what advantage the greater states could propose to themselves by swallowing up the smaller and, therefore, do not apprehend they would attempt it. I recollect that in the beginning of this century when the union was proposed of the two kingdoms, England and Scotland, the Scotch patriots were full of fears that unless they had an equal number of representatives in Parliament, they should be ruined by the superiority of the English. They finally agreed, however, that the different proportions of importance in the union of the two nations should be attended to, whereby they were to have only forty members in the House of Commons and only sixteen in the House of Lords—a very great inferiority of numbers. And yet to this day I do not recollect that anything has been done in the Parliament of Great Britain to the prejudice of Scotland, and whoever looks over the lists of public officers, civil and military, of that nation will find, I believe, that the North Britons enjoy at least their full proportion of emolument.

"But, sir, in the present mode of voting by states, it is equally in the power of the lesser states to swallow up the greater, and this is mathematically demonstrable. Suppose, for example, that seven smaller states had each three members in the House, and the six larger to have, one with another, six members; and that upon a question, two members of each smaller state should be in the affirmative and one in the negative, they would make affirmatives, fourteen; negatives, seven, and that all the larger states should be unanimously in the negative, they would make negatives, thirty-six; in all, affirmatives, fourteen, negatives, forty-three.

"It is then apparent that the fourteen carry the question against the forty-three, and the minority overpowers the majority, contrary to the common practice of assemblies in all countries and ages.

"The greater states, sir, are naturally as unwilling to have their property left in the disposition of the smaller, as the smaller are to have theirs in the disposition of the greater. An honorable gentleman has, to avoid this difficulty, hinted a proposition of equalizing the states. It appears to me an equitable one and I should, for my own part, not be against such a measure if it might be found practicable. Formerly, indeed, when almost every province had a different constitution—some with greater, others with fewer, privileges—it was of importance to the borderers when their boundaries were contested, whether by running the division lines they were placed on one side or the other. At present, when such differences are done away, it is less material. The interest of a state is made up of the interests of its individual members. If they are not injured, the state is not injured. Small states are more easily well and happily governed than large ones. If, therefore, in such an equal division, it should be found necessary to diminish Pennsylvania, I should not be averse to the giving a part of it to New Jersey and another to Delaware. But as there would probably be considerable difficulties in adjusting such a division; and however equally made at first, it would be continually varying by the augmentation of inhabitants in some states and their fixed proportion in others and, thence, frequently occasion new divisions, I beg leave to propose for the consideration of the committee another mode which appears to me to be as equitable, more easily carried into practice, and more permanent in its nature.

"Let the weakest state say what proportion of money or force it is able and willing to furnish for the general purposes of the Union;

"Let all the others oblige themselves to furnish each an equal proportion;

"The whole of these joint supplies to be absolutely in the disposition of Congress;

"The Congress, in this case, to be composed of an equal number of delegates from each state;

"And their decisions to be by the majority of individual members voting.

"If these joint and equal supplies should on particular occasions not be sufficient, let Congress make requisitions on the richer and more powerful states for further aids to be voluntarily afforded, leaving to each state the right of considering the necessity and utility of the aid desired and of giving more or less as it should be found proper.

"This mode is not new. It was formerly practiced with success by the British Government with respect to Ireland and the colonies. We sometimes gave even more than they expected or thought just to accept; and in the last war, carried on while we were united, they gave us back in five years a million sterling. We should probably have continued such voluntary contributions whenever the occasion appeared to require them for the common good of the empire. It was not till they chose to force us and to deprive us of the merit and pleasure of voluntary contributions that we refused and resisted. These contributions, however, were to be disposed of at the pleasure of a government in which we had no representative. I am, therefore, persuaded that they will not be refused to one in which the representation shall be equal.

"My learned colleague (Mr. Wilson) has already mentioned that the present method of voting by states was submitted to originally by Congress under a conviction of its impropriety, inequality, and injustice. This appears in the words of their resolution. It is of the sixth of September, 1774. The words are:

" 'Resolved, that in determining questions in this Congress, each colony or province shall have one vote, the Congress not being possessed of, or at present able to procure, materials for ascertaining the importance of each colony.' "

Proportional representation of states in House approved, 7 to 3.

RATIO OF REPRESENTATION DISCUSSED / *June 11*

It was then moved by Mr. Rutledge, seconded by Mr. Butler, to add to the words "equitable ratio of representation" at the end of the motion just agreed to, the words "according to the quotas of contribution." On motion of Mr. Wilson, seconded by Mr. Pinckney, this was postponed in order to add after the words "equitable ratio of representation," the words following—"in proportion to the whole number of white and other free citizens and inhabitants of every age, sex, and condition, including those bound to servitude for a term of years, and three-fifths of all other persons not comprehended in the foregoing description, except Indians not paying taxes, in each state"—this being the rule in the Act of Congress agreed to by eleven states for apportioning quotas of revenue on the states and requiring a census only every five, seven, or ten years.

Mr. Gerry thought property not the rule of representation. Why, then, should the blacks who were property in the South be in the rule of representation more than the cattle and horses of the North?

Representation in House in proportion to the total number of free men plus three-fifths of the slaves approved, 9 to 2.

EQUALITY IN THE SENATE DEBATED / *June 11*

Mr. Sherman moved that a question be taken whether each state shall have one vote in the second branch. Everything, he said, depended on this. The smaller states would never agree to the plan on any other principle than an equality of suffrage in this branch.

Mr. Ellsworth seconded the motion.

The question for allowing each state one vote in the second branch was defeated, 6 to 5.

Mr. Wilson and Mr. Hamilton moved that the right of suffrage in the second branch ought to be according to the same rule as in the first branch.

On this question for making the ratio of representation the same in the second as in the first branch, it passed, 6 to 5.

• **Article VI: . . . The Senators and Representatives before mentioned, and the Members of the several State Legislatures, and all executive and judicial Officers, both of the United States and of the several States, shall be bound by Oath or Affirmation, to support this Constitution; but no religious Test shall ever be required as a Qualification to any Office or public Trust under the United States.**

THE CONSTITUTION OF THE UNITED STATES

OATH OF OFFICE DISCUSSED / *June 11*

The fourteenth resolution, requiring oaths from the members of the state governments to observe the national Constitution and laws, being considered, Mr. Sherman opposed it as unnecessarily intruding into the state jurisdictions.

Mr. Randolph considered it necessary to prevent that competition between the national Constitution and laws and those of the particular states, which had already been felt. The officers of the states are already under oath to the states. To preserve a due impartiality, they ought to be equally bound to the national Government. The national authority needs every support we can give it. The executive and judiciary of the states, notwithstanding their nominal independence on the state legislatures, are in fact so dependent on them that unless they be brought under some tie to the national system, they will always lean too much to the state system whenever a contest arises between the two.

Mr. Gerry did not like the clause. He thought there was as much reason for requiring an oath of fidelity to the states from national officers as vice versa.

Mr. Luther Martin moved to strike out the words requiring such an oath from the state officers, namely, "within the several states," observing that if the new oath should be contrary to that already taken by them, it would be improper; if coincident, the oaths already taken will be sufficient.

Oath of support for the Constitution from state officers passed, 6 to 5.

/ July 23

The eighteenth resolution [Randolph's original fifteen have now been increased to twenty-three], requiring the legislative, executive, and judiciary of the states to be bound by oath to support the Articles of Union, was taken into consideration.

Mr. Williamson suggests that a reciprocal oath should be required from the national officers to support the governments of the states.

Mr. Gerry moved to insert as an amendment that the oath of the officers of the national Government also should extend to the support of the national Government, which was agreed to unanimously.

Mr. Wilson said he was never fond of oaths, considering them as a left-handed security only. A good government did not need them, and a bad one could not or ought not to be supported. He was afraid they might too much trammel the members of the existing government in case future alterations should be necessary and prove an obstacle to the seventeenth resolution just agreed to.

Mr. Gorham did not know that oaths would be of much use, but could see no inconsistency between them and the seventeenth resolution, or any regular amendment of the Constitution. The oath could only require fidelity to the existing Constitution. A constitutional alteration of the Constitution could never be regarded as a breach of the Constitution or of any oath to support it.

Mr. Gerry thought, with Mr. Gorham, there could be no shadow of inconsistency in the case. Nor could he see any other harm that could result from the resolution. On the other side, he thought, one good effect would be produced by it. Hitherto the officers of the two governments had considered them as distinct from, and not as parts of, the general system and had in all cases of interference given a preference to the state governments. The proposed oath will cure that error.

The eighteenth resolution was agreed to unanimously.

The Paterson Plan

Editor's note: On June 13, Randolph's Plan in amended form was reported out of committee. The small states protested. On June 14, William Paterson of New Jersey asked for an adjournment to prepare a substitute. His request granted, he submitted his own plan on the following day. It consisted of nine proposals for the reform of the Articles of Confederation. The Paterson Plan was debated until June 19, when it was rejected.

PATERSON'S NINE RESOLUTIONS / *June 14*

Mr. Paterson observed to the convention that it was the wish of several deputations, particularly that of New Jersey, that further time might be allowed them to contemplate the plan reported from the committee of the whole and to digest one purely federal, and contradistinguished from the reported plan. He said they hoped to have such a one ready by tomorrow to be laid before the convention, and the convention adjourned that leisure might be given for the purpose.

/ *June 15*

In convention. Mr. Paterson laid before the convention the plan which, he said, several of the deputations wished to be substituted in place of that proposed by Mr. Randolph. After some little discussion of the most proper mode of giving it a fair deliberation, it was agreed that it should be referred to a committee of the whole, and that in order to place the two plans in due comparison, the other should be recommitted. At the earnest request of Mr. Lansing and some other gentleman, it was also agreed that the convention should not go into committee of the whole on the subject till tomorrow; by which delay the friends of the plan proposed by Mr. Paterson would be better prepared to explain and support it, and all would have an opportunity of taking copies.

The propositions from New Jersey moved by Mr. Paterson were in the words following:

1. Resolved, that the Articles of Confederation ought to be so revised, corrected, and enlarged as to render the Federal Constitution adequate to the exigencies of government and the preservation of the Union.

2. Resolved, that in addition to the powers vested in the United States in Congress by the present existing Articles of Confederation, they be authorized to pass acts for raising a revenue by levying a duty or duties on all goods or merchandises of foreign growth or manufacture imported into any part of the United States by stamps on paper, vellum, or parchment, and by a postage on all letters or packages passing through the general post office—to be applied to such federal purposes as they shall deem proper and expedient; to make rules and regulations for the collection thereof, and the same from time to time to alter and amend in such manner as they shall think proper; to pass acts for the regulation of trade and commerce, as well with foreign nations as with each other, provided that all punishments, fines, forfeitures, and penalties to be incurred for contravening such acts, rules, and regulations shall be adjudged by the common-law judiciaries of the state in which any offense contrary to the true intent and meaning of such acts, rules, and regulations, shall have been committed or perpetrated, with liberty of commencing in the first instance all suits and prosecutions for that purpose in the superior common-law judiciary in such state; subject, nevertheless, for the correction of all errors both in law and fact in rendering judgment to an appeal to the judiciary of the United States.

3. Resolved, that whatever requisitions shall be necessary, instead of the rule for making requisitions mentioned in the Articles of Confederation, the United States in Congress be authorized to make such requisitions in proportion to the whole number of white and other free inhabitants of every age, sex, and condition, including those bound to servitude for a term of years and three-fifths of all other persons not comprehended in the foregoing description, except Indians not paying taxes; that if such requisitions be not complied with in the time specified therein, to direct the collection thereof in the noncomplying states and for the purpose to devise and pass acts directing and authorizing the same, provided that none of the powers hereby vested in the United States in Congress shall be exercised without the consent of at least _____ states, and in that proportion if the number of confederated states should hereafter be increased or diminished.

4. Resolved, that the United States in Congress be authorized to

elect a Federal executive to consist of _____ persons; to continue in office for the term of _____ years; to receive punctually at stated times a fixed compensation for their services, in which no increase nor diminution shall be made so as to affect the persons composing the executive at the time of such increase or diminution; to be paid out of the Federal treasury; to be incapable of holding any other office or appointment during their time of service, and for _____ years thereafter; to be ineligible a second time, and removable by Congress on application by a majority of the executives of the several states: that the executive, besides their general authority to execute the Federal acts, ought to appoint all Federal officers not otherwise provided for and to direct all military operations, provided that none of the persons composing the Federal executive shall on any occasion take command of any troops so as personally to conduct any military enterprise as general or in any other capacity.

5. Resolved, that a Federal judiciary be established to consist of a supreme tribunal, the judges of which to be appointed by the executive and to hold their offices during good behavior; to receive punctually at stated times a fixed compensation for their services, in which no increase or diminution shall be made so as to affect the persons actually in office at the time of such increase or diminution. That the judiciary so established shall have authority to hear and determine, in the first instance on all impeachments of Federal officers, and by way of appeal in the *dernier* resort in all cases touching the rights of ambassadors, in all cases of captures from an enemy, in all cases of piracies and felonies on the high seas, in all cases in which foreigners may be interested, in the construction of any treaty or treaties, or which may arise on any of the acts for the regulation of trade, or the collection of the Federal revenue: that none of the judiciary shall during the time they remain in office be capable of receiving or holding any other office or appointment during their term of service or for _____ thereafter.

6. Resolved, that all acts of the United States in Congress made by virtue and in pursuance of the powers hereby, and by the Articles of Confederation vested in them, and all treaties made and ratified under the authority of the United States, shall be the supreme law of the respective states, so far forth as those acts or treaties shall relate to the said states or their citizens; and that the judiciary of the several states shall be bound thereby in their decisions, anything in the respective laws of the individual states to the contrary notwithstanding; and that if any state or any body of men in any state shall oppose or prevent the carrying into execution such acts or treaties, the Federal exec-

utive shall be authorized to call forth the power of the confederated
states, or so much thereof as may be necessary, to enforce and compel
an obedience to such acts or an observance of such treaties.

7. Resolved, that provision be made for the admission of new states
into the Union.

8. Resolved, that the rule for naturalization ought to be the same
in every state.

9. Resolved, that a citizen of one state committing an offense in another state of the Union shall be deemed guilty of the same offense as
if it had been committed by a citizen of the state in which the offense
was committed.

OPPOSITION TO PATERSON
AND RANDOLPH PLANS / *June 16*

In committee of the whole. On the resolutions proposed by Mr. Paterson and Mr. Randolph, Mr. Lansing called for the reading of the
first resolution of each plan, which he considered as involving principles directly in contrast. That of Mr. Paterson, says he, stains the sovereignty of the respective states, that of Mr. Randolph destroys it.
The latter requires a negative on all the laws of the particular states,
the former only certain general power for the general good. The plan
of Mr. Randolph, in short, absorbs all power, except what may be
exercised in the little local matters of the states which are not objects
worthy of the supreme cognizance. He grounded his preference to Mr.
Paterson's plan chiefly on two objections to that of Mr. Randolph,
first, want of power in the convention to discuss and propose it;
secondly, the improbability of its being adopted.

1. He was decidedly of opinion that the power of the convention
was restrained to amendments of a federal nature and having for
their basis the Confederacy in being. The Acts of Congress, the tenor
of the acts of the states, the commissions produced by the several deputations, all proved this. And this limitation of the power to an amendment of the Confederacy marked the opinion of the states that it was
unnecessary and improper to go farther. He was sure that this was the
case with his state. New York would never have concurred in sending
deputies to the convention if she had supposed the deliberations were
to turn on a consolidation of the states and a national government.

2. Was it probable that the states would adopt and ratify a scheme
which they had never authorized us to propose and which so far exceeded what they regarded as sufficient? We see by their several acts,
particularly in relation to the plan of revenue proposed by Congress

in 1783, not authorized by the Articles of Confederation, what were the ideas they then entertained. Can so great a change be supposed to have already taken place? To rely on any change which is hereafter to take place in the sentiments of the people would be trusting to too great an uncertainty. We know only what their present sentiments are, and it is in vain to propose what will not accord with these. The states will never feel a sufficient confidence in a general government to give it a negative on their laws. The scheme is itself totally novel. There is no parallel to it to be found. The authority of Congress is familiar to the people and an augmentation of the powers of Congress will be readily approved by them.

PATERSON DEFENDS HIS PLAN / *June 16*

Mr. Paterson said as he had on a former occasion given his sentiments on the plan proposed by Mr. Randolph, he would now give his reasons in favor of that proposed by himself. He preferred it because it accorded, first, with the powers of the convention; secondly, with the sentiments of the people. If the Confederacy was radically wrong, let us return to our states and obtain larger powers, not assume them ourselves. I came here not to speak my own sentiments, but the sentiments of those who sent me. Our object is not such a government as may be best in itself, but such a one as our constituents have authorized us to prepare, and as they will approve. If we argue the matter on the supposition that no confederacy at present exists, it cannot be denied that all the states stand on the footing of equal sovereignty. All, therefore, must concur before any can be bound. If a proportional representation be right, why do we not vote so here? If we argue on the fact that a federal compact actually exists and consult the articles of it, we still find an equal sovereignty to be the basis of it. (He read the Fifth Article of the Confederation, giving each state one vote, and the Thirteenth, declaring that alterations required unanimous consent.[1]) This is the nature of all treaties.

What is unanimously done, must be unanimously undone. It was observed (by Mr. Wilson) that the larger states gave up the point, not because it was right, but because the circumstances of the moment

---

[1] Article Five: "In determining questions in the United States, in Congress assembled, each state shall have one vote."
Article Thirteen: ". . . nor shall any alteration . . . be made . . . , unless such alteration be agreed to in a Congress of the United States, and be afterwards confirmed by the legislatures of every state."

urged the concession. Be it so. Are they for that reason at liberty to take it back? Can the donor resume his gift without the consent of the donee? This doctrine may be convenient, but it is a doctrine that will sacrifice the lesser states. The larger states acceded readily to the Confederacy. It was the small ones that came in reluctantly and slowly. New Jersey and Maryland were the two last, the former objecting to the want of power in Congress over trade, both of them to the want of power to appropriate the vacant territory to the benefit of the whole. If the sovereignty of the states is to be maintained, the representatives must be drawn immediately from the states, not from the people, and we have no power to vary the idea of equal sovereignty. The only expedient that will cure the difficulty is that of throwing the states into hotchpot. To say that this is impracticable will not make it so. Let it be tried, and we shall see whether the citizens of Massachusetts, Pennsylvania, and Virginia accede to it. It will be objected that coercion will be impracticable. But will it be more so in one plan than the other? Its efficacy will depend on the quantum of power collected, not on its being drawn from the states or from the individuals, and according to his plan, it may be exerted on individuals as well as according to that of Mr. Randolph. A distinct executive and judiciary also were equally provided by his plan. It is urged that two branches in the legislature are necessary. Why? For the purpose of a check. But the reason for the precaution is not applicable to this case. Within a particular state, where party heats prevail, such a check may be necessary. In such a body as Congress it is less necessary, and, besides, the delegations of the different states are checks on each other. Do the people at large complain of Congress? No. What they wish is that Congress may have more power. If the power now proposed be not enough, the people hereafter will make additions to it. With proper powers Congress will act with more energy and wisdom than the proposed national legislature, being fewer in number, and more secreted, and refined by the mode of election. The plan of Mr. Randolph will also be enormously expensive. Allowing Georgia and Delaware two representatives each in the popular branch, the aggregate number of that branch will be one hundred and eighty. Add to it half as many for the other branch and you have two hundred and seventy members coming once, at least, a year from the most distant as well as the most central parts of the republic. In the present deranged state of our finances can so expensive a system be seriously thought of? By enlarging the powers of Congress, the greatest part of this expense will be saved, and all purposes will be answered. At least a trial ought to be made.

Mr. Wilson entered into a contrast of the principal points of the two plans, so far, he said, as there had been time to examine the one last proposed. These points were: 1. In the Virginia plan there are two, and in some degree three, branches in the legislature; in the plan from New Jersey there is to be a single legislature only. 2. Representation of the people at large is the basis of one; the state legislatures the pillars of the other. 3. Proportional representation prevails in one, equality of suffrage in the other. 4. A single executive magistrate is at the head of the one; a plurality is held out in the other. 5. In the one, a majority of the people of the United States must prevail; in the other, a minority may prevail. 6. The national legislature is to make laws in all cases to which the separate states are incompetent; in place of this, Congress are to have additional power in a few cases only. 7. A negative on the laws of the states; in place of this, coercion to be substituted. 8. The executive to be removable on impeachment and conviction in one plan; in the other, to be removable at the instance of a majority of the executives of the states. 9. Revision of the laws provided for in one; no such check in the other. 10. Inferior national tribunals in one; none such in the other. 11. In the one, jurisdiction of national tribunals to extend; an appellate jurisdiction only allowed in the other. 12. Here, the jurisdiction is to extend to all cases affecting the national peace and harmony; there, a few cases only are marked out. 13. Finally, the ratification is in this to be by the people themselves; in that, by the legislative authorities according to the Thirteenth Article of the Confederation.

With regard to the power of the convention, he conceived himself authorized to conclude nothing, but to be at liberty to propose anything. In this particular, he felt himself perfectly indifferent to the two plans.

With regard to the sentiments of the people, he conceived it difficult to know precisely what they are. Those of the particular circle in which one moved were commonly mistaken for the general voice. He could not persuade himself that the state governments and sovereignties were so much the idols of the people, nor a national government so obnoxious to them as some supposed. Why should a national government be unpopular? Has it less dignity? Will each citizen enjoy under it less liberty or protection? Will a citizen of Delaware be degraded by becoming a citizen of the United States? Where do the people look at present for relief from the evils of which they complain? Is it from an internal reform of their governments? No, sir. It is from the national councils that relief is expected. For these reasons, he did not fear that the people would not follow us into a national government, and it will be a further recommendation of Mr. Randolph's plan that it is to be submitted to them, and not to the legislatures, for ratification.

Proceeding now to the first point on which he had contrasted the two plans, he observed that anxious as he was for some augmentation of the Federal powers, it would be with extreme reluctance, indeed, that he could ever consent to give powers to Congress. He had two reasons, either of which was sufficient—first, Congress, as a legislative body, does not stand on the people; secondly, it is a single body.

1. He would not repeat the remarks he had formerly made on the principles of representation. He would only say that an inequality in it has ever been a poison contaminating every branch of government. In Great Britain, where this poison has had a full operation, the security of private rights is owing entirely to the purity of her tribunals of justice, the judges of which are neither appointed nor paid by a venal parliament. The political liberty of that nation, owing to the inequality of representation, is at the mercy of its rulers. He means not to insinuate that there is any parallel between the situation of that country and ours at present. But it is a lesson we ought not to disregard that the smallest bodies in Great Britain are notoriously the most corrupt. Every other source of influence must also be stronger in small than in large bodies of men. When Lord Chesterfield had told us that one of the Dutch provinces had been seduced into the views of France, he need not have added that it was not Holland, but one of the smallest of them. There are facts among ourselves which are known to all. Passing over others, we will only remark that the impost so anxiously wished for by the public was defeated not by any of the larger states in the Union.

2. Congress is a single legislature. Despotism comes on mankind in different shapes—sometimes in an executive, sometimes in a military one. Is there no danger of a legislative despotism? Theory and practice both proclaim it. If the legislative authority be not restrained, there can be neither liberty nor stability, and it can only be restrained by dividing it within itself into distinct and independent branches. In a single house there is no check, but the inadequate one of the virtue and good sense of those who compose it.

On another great point, the contrast was equally favorable to the plan reported by the committee of the whole. It vested the executive powers in a single magistrate. The plan of New Jersey vested them in a plurality. In order to control the legislative authority, you must divide it. In order to control the executive, you must unite it. One man will be more responsible than three. Three will contend among themselves till one becomes the master of his colleagues. In the triumvirates of Rome, first Caesar, then Augustus are witnesses of this truth. The kings of Sparta and the consuls of Rome prove also the factious consequences of dividing the executive magistracy. Having already taken up so much time, he would not, he said, proceed to any of the other points. Those on which he had dwelt are sufficient of themselves, and on the decision of them the fate of the others will depend.

COMMENTS / *June 16*

Gen. Pinckney: The whole comes to this as he conceived. Give New Jersey an equal vote and she will dismiss her scruples and concur in the national system. He thought the convention authorized to go any length in recommending which they found necessary to remedy the evils which produced this convention.

Mr. Ellsworth proposed, as a more distinctive form of collecting the mind of the committee on the subject, that the legislative power of the United States should remain in Congress. This was not seconded; though it seemed better calculated for the purpose than the first proposition of Mr. Paterson, in place of which Mr. Ellsworth wished to substitute it.

RANDOLPH DEFENDS HIS PLAN / *June 16*

Mr. Randolph was not scrupulous on the point of power. When the salvation of the republic was at stake, it would be treason to our trust not to propose what we found necessary. He painted in strong colors the imbecility of the existing Confederacy and the danger of delaying a substantial reform. In answer to the objection drawn from the sense of our constituents, as denoted by their acts relating to the convention and the objects of their deliberation, he observed that as each state acted separately in the case, it would have been indecent for it to have charged the existing Constitution with all the vices which it might have perceived in it. The first state that set on foot this experiment would not have been justified in going so far, ignorant as it was of the opinion of others and sensible as it must have been of the uncertainty of a successful issue to the experiment. There are reasons certainly of a peculiar nature where the ordinary cautions must be dispensed with, and this is certainly one of them. He would not, as far as depended on him, leave anything that seemed necessary undone. The present moment is favorable and is probably the last that will offer.

The true question is whether we shall adhere to the federal plan or introduce the national plan. The insufficiency of the former has been fully displayed by the trial already made. There are but two modes by which the end of a general government can be attained: the first, by coercion, as proposed by Mr. Paterson's plan; the second, by real legislation, as proposed by the other plan. Coercion he pronounced to be impracticable, expensive, cruel to individuals. It tended also to habituate the instruments of it to shed the blood and riot in the spoils of their fellow-citizens, and consequently train them up for the service of ambition. We must resort, therefore, to a national legislation over individuals for which Congress are unfit. To vest such power in them would be blending the legislative with the executive, contrary to the received maxim on this subject. If the union of these powers, heretofore, in Congress has been safe, it has been owing to the general impotency of that body. Congress are, moreover, not elected by the people, but by the legislatures who retain even a power of recall. They have, therefore, no will of their own; they are a mere diplomatic body and are always obsequious to the views of the states, who are always encroaching on the authority of the United States. A provision for harmony among the states, as in trade, naturalization, and so forth, for crushing rebellion whenever it may rear its crest and for certain other general benefits, must be made.

The powers for these purposes can never be given to a body inadequate as Congress are in point of representation, elected in the mode in which they are, and possessing no more confidence than they do. For notwithstanding what has been said to the contrary, his own experience satisfied him that a rooted distrust of Congress pretty generally prevailed. A national government alone, properly constituted, will answer the purpose, and he begged it to be considered that the present is the last moment for establishing one. After this select experiment, the people will yield to despair.

The committee rose and the house adjourned.

PATERSON'S PLAN POSTPONED / *June 18*

In committee of the whole, on the propositions of Mr. Paterson and Mr. Randolph. On motion of Mr. Dickinson to postpone the first resolution in Mr. Paterson's plan in order to take up the following: "That the Articles of Confederation ought to be revised so as to render the Government of the United States adequate to the exigencies, the preservation, and the prosperity of the Union," the postponement was agreed to by ten states, Pennsylvania divided.

Mr. Hamilton had been hitherto silent on the business before the convention, partly from respect to others whose superior abilities, age, and experience rendered him unwilling to bring forward ideas dissimilar to theirs, and partly from his delicate situation with respect to his own state, to whose sentiments, as expressed by his colleagues. he could by no means accede. The crisis, however, which now marked our affairs was too serious to permit any scruples whatever to prevail over the duty imposed on every man to contribute his efforts for the public safety and happiness. He was obliged, therefore, to declare himself unfriendly to both plans. He was particularly opposed to that from New Jersey, being fully convinced that no amendment of the Confederation leaving the states in possession of their sovereignty could possibly answer the purpose. On the other hand, he confessed he was much discouraged by the amazing extent of country in expecting the desired blessings from any general sovereignty that could be substituted. As to the powers of the convention, he thought the doubts started on that subject had arisen from distinctions and reasonings too subtle. A federal government he conceived to mean an association of independent communities into one. Different confederacies have different powers and exercise them in different ways. In some instances, the powers are exercised over collective bodies; in others over individuals, as in the German Diet, and among ourselves in cases of piracy. Great latitude, therefore, must be given to the signification of the term. The plan last proposed departs itself from the federal idea as understood by some, since it is to operate eventually on individuals. He agreed, moreover, with the honorable gentleman from Virginia (Mr. Randolph) that we owed it to our country to do on this emergency whatever we should deem essential to its happiness. The states sent us here to provide for the exigencies of the Union. To rely on and propose any plan not adequate to these exigencies, merely because it was not clearly within our powers, would be to sacrifice the means to the end. It may be said that the states cannot ratify a plan not within the purview of the Article of the Confederation providing for alterations and amendments. But may not the states, themselves, in which no constitutional authority equal to this purpose exists in the legislatures, have had in view a reference to the people at large? In the Senate of New York, a proviso was moved that no act of the convention should be binding until it should be referred to the people and ratified, and the motion was lost by a single voice only, the reason assigned against it being that it might possibly be found an inconvenient shackle.

The great question is what provision shall we make for the happiness of our country? He would first make a comparative examination of the two plans, prove that there were essential defects in both, and point out such changes as might render a national one efficacious. The great and essential principles necessary for the support of government are: 1. An active and constant interest in supporting it. This principle does not exist in the states in favor of the Federal Government. They have evidently in a high degree the *esprit de corps*. They constantly pursue internal interests adverse to those of the whole. They have their particular debts, their particular plans of finance, and so forth. All these, when opposed to, invariably prevail over the requisitions and plans of Congress. 2. The love of power. Men love power. The same remarks are applicable to this principle. The states have constantly shown a disposition rather to regain the powers delegated by them than to part with more or to give effect to what they had parted with. The ambition of their demagogues is known to hate the control of the General Government. It may be remarked too that the citizens have not that anxiety to prevent a dissolution of the General Government as of the particular governments. A dissolution of the latter would be fatal, of the former would still leave the purposes of government attainable to a considerable degree. Consider what such a state as Virginia will be in a few years—a few compared with the life of nations. How strongly will it feel its importance and self-sufficiency! 3. An habitual attachment of the people. The whole force of this tie is on the side of the state government. Its sovereignty is immediately before the eyes of the people; its protection is immediately enjoyed by them. From its hand distributive justice and all those acts which familiarize and endear a government to a people are dispensed to them. 4. Force, by which may be understood a coercion of laws or coercion of arms. Congress have not the former, except in few cases. In particular states, this coercion is nearly sufficient; though he held it in most cases not entirely so. A certain portion of military force is absolutely necessary in large communities. Massachusetts is now feeling this necessity and making provision for it. But how can this force be exerted on the states collectively? It is impossible. It amounts to a war between the parties. Foreign powers also will not be idle spectators. They will interpose; the confusion will increase, and a dissolution of the Union will ensue. 5. Influence—he did not mean corruption, but a dispensation of those regular honors and emoluments which produce an attachment to the government. Almost all the weight of these is on the side of the states and must continue so, as long as the states continue to exist. All the passions, then, we see, of avarice, ambition, interest, which govern most individuals and all public bodies, fall into the current of the states and do not flow into the stream of the General Government. The former, therefore, will generally be an overmatch for the General Government and render any confederacy in its very nature precarious. Theory is in this case fully confirmed by experience. The Amphictyonic Council had, it would seem, ample powers for general purposes. It had, in particular, the power of fining and using force against delinquent members. What was the consequence? Their decrees were mere signals of war. The Phocian war is a striking example of it. Philip, at length, taking advantage of their disunion and insinuating himself into their councils, made himself master of their fortunes. The German confederacy affords another lesson. The authority of Charlemagne seemed to be as great as could be necessary. The great feudal chiefs, however, exercising their local sovereignties, soon felt the spirit and found the means of encroachments which reduced the imperial authority to a nominal sovereignty. The Diet has succeeded; which though aided by a prince, at its head, of great authority independently of his imperial attributes, is a striking illustration of the weakness of confederated governments. Other examples instruct us in the same truth. The Swiss Cantons have scarcely any union at all and have been more than once at war with one another. How then are all these evils to be avoided? Only by such a complete sovereignty in the General Government as will turn all the strong principles and passions above mentioned on its side. Does the scheme of New Jersey produce this effect? Does it afford any substantial remedy whatever? On the contrary, it labors under great defects, and the defect of some of its provisions will destroy the efficacy of others. It gives a direct revenue to Congress, but this will not be sufficient. The balance can only be supplied by requisitions, which experience proves cannot be relied on. If states are to deliberate on the mode, they will also deliberate on the object of the supplies and will grant or not grant as they approve or disapprove of it. The delinquency of one will invite and countenance it in others. Quotas, too, must in the nature of things be so unequal as to produce the same evil. To what standard will you resort? Land is a fallacious one. Compare Holland with Russia; France or England with other countries of Europe; Pennsylvania with North Carolina—will the relative pecuniary abilities in those instances correspond with the relative value of land? Take numbers of inhabitants for the rule and make like comparison of different countries and you will find it to be equally unjust. The different degrees of industry and improvement in different countries render

the first object a precarious measure of wealth. Much depends, too,
on situation. Connecticut, New Jersey, and North Carolina, not being
commercial states and contributing to the wealth of the commercial
ones, can never bear quotas assessed by the ordinary rules of proportion. They will, and must, fail in their duty. Their example will be
followed, and the Union itself be dissolved. Whence, then, is the national revenue to be drawn? From commerce, even from exports,
which, notwithstanding the common opinion, are fit objects of moderate taxation; from excise, and so forth. These, though not equal, are
less unequal than quotas. Another destructive ingredient in the plan
is that equality of suffrage which is so much desired by the small states.
It is not in human nature that Virginia and the large states should
consent to it, or if they did, that they should long abide by it. It shocks
too much all ideas of justice and every human feeling. Bad principles
in a government, though slow, are sure in their operation and will
gradually destroy it. A doubt has been raised whether Congress at present have a right to keep ships or troops in time of peace. He leans to
the negative. Mr. Paterson's plan provides no remedy. If the powers
proposed were adequate, the organization of Congress is such that
they could never be properly and effectually exercised. The members
of Congress, being chosen by the states and subject to recall, represent
all the local prejudices. Should the powers be found effectual, they
will from time to time be heaped on them till a tyrannic sway shall be
established. The general power, whatever be its form, if it preserves
itself, must swallow up the state powers. Otherwise, it will be
swallowed up by them. It is against all the principles of a good government to vest the requisite powers in such a body as Congress. Two
sovereignties cannot coexist within the same limits. Giving powers to
Congress must eventuate in a bad government or in no government.
The plan of New Jersey, therefore, will not do. What then is to be
done? Here he was embarrassed. The extent of the country to be
governed discouraged him. The expense of a general government
was also formidable, unless there were such a diminution of expense
on the side of the state governments as the case would admit. If they
were extinguished, he was persuaded that the great economy might be
obtained by substituting a general government. He did not mean,
however, to shock the public opinion by proposing such a measure.
On the other hand, he saw no other necessity for declining it. They
are not necessary for any of the great purposes of commerce, revenue,
or agriculture. Subordinate authorities, he was aware, would be necessary. There must be district tribunals, corporations for local purposes. But *cui bono* the vast and expensive apparatus now ap-

pertaining to the states? The only difficulty of a serious nature which occurred to him was that of drawing representatives from the extremes to the center of the community. What inducements can be offered that will suffice? The moderate wages for the first branch could only be a bait to little demagogues. Three dollars or thereabouts, he supposed, would be the utmost. The Senate, he feared, from a similar cause would be filled by certain undertakers who wish for particular offices under the government.

This view of the subject almost led him to despair that a republican government could be established over so great an extent. He was sensible at the same time that it would be unwise to propose one of any other form. In his private opinion, he had no scruple in declaring, supported as he was by the opinion of so many of the wise and good, that the British Government was the best in the world, and that he doubted much whether anything short of it would do in America. He hoped gentlemen of different opinions would bear with him in this and begged them to recollect the change of opinion on this subject which had taken place and was still going on. It was once thought that the power of Congress was amply sufficient to secure the end of their institution. The error was now seen by everyone. The members most tenacious of republicanism, he observed, were as loud as any in declaiming against the vices of democracy. This progress of the public mind led him to anticipate the time when others as well as himself would join in the praise bestowed by Mr. Neckar on the British constitution—namely, that it is the only government in the world "which unites public strength with individual security." In every community where industry is encouraged there will be a division of it into the few and the many. Hence, separate interests will arise. There will be debtors and creditors, and so forth. Give all power to the many, they will oppress the few. Give all power to the few, they will oppress the many. Both, therefore, ought to have the power that each may defend itself against the other. To the want of this check, we owe our paper money, installment laws, and so forth. To the proper adjustment of it, the British owe the excellence of their constitution. Their House of Lords is a most noble institution. Having nothing to hope for by a change, and a sufficient interest by means of their property in being faithful to the national interest, they form a permanent barrier against every pernicious innovation, whether attempted on the part of the crown or of the commons. No temporary senate will have firmness enough to answer the purpose. The Senate of Maryland, which seems to be so much appealed to, has not yet been sufficiently tried. Had the people been unanimous and eager in the late appeal to them on the subject of a paper emission, they would have yielded to the torrent. Their acquiescing in such an appeal is a proof of it. Gentlemen differ in their opinions concerning the necessary checks from the different estimates they form of the human passions. They suppose seven years a sufficient period to give the Senate an adequate firmness from not duly considering the amazing violence and turbulence of the democratic spirit. When a great object of government is pursued which seizes the popular passions, they spread like wildfire and become irresistible. He appealed to the gentlemen from New England states whether experience had not there verified the remark. As to the executive, it seemed to be admitted that no good one could be established on republican principles. Was not this giving up the merits of the question; for can there be a good government without a good executive? The English model was the only good one on this subject. The hereditary interest of the king was so interwoven with that of the nation, and his personal emolument so great, that he was placed above the danger of being corrupted from abroad, and at the same time was both sufficiently independent and sufficiently controlled to answer the purpose of the institution at home. One of the weak sides of republics was their being liable to foreign influence and corruption. Men of little character acquiring great power become easily the tools of intermeddling neighbors. Sweden was a striking instance. The French and English had each their parties during the late revolution, which was effected by the predominant influence of the former. What is the inference from all these observations? That we ought to go as far in order to attain stability and permanency as republican principles will admit. Let one branch of the legislature hold their places for life, or at least during good behavior. Let the executive also be for life. He appealed to the feelings of the members present whether a term of seven years would induce the sacrifices of private affairs which an acceptance of public trust would require so as to insure the services of the best citizens. On this plan, we should have in the Senate a permanent will, a weighty interest, which would answer essential purposes. But is this a republican government, it will be asked. Yes, if all the magistrates are appointed and vacancies are filled by the people or a process of election originating with the people. He was sensible that an executive, constituted as he proposed, would have in fact but little of the power and independence that might be necessary. On the other plan of appointing him for seven years, he thought the executive ought to have but little power. He would be ambitious with the means of making creatures, and as the object of his ambition would be to prolong his power, it is probable that in case of war he would avail himself of the emergency to evade or refuse a degradation from his place. An executive for life has not this motive for forgetting his fidelity and will, therefore, be a safer depository of power. It will be objected, probably, that such an executive will be an elective monarch and will give birth to the tumults which characterize that form of government. He would reply that monarch is an indefinite term. It marks not either the degree or duration of power. If this executive magistrate would be a monarch for life, the other proposed by the report from the committee of the whole would be a monarch for seven years. The circumstance of being elective was also applicable to both. It had been observed by judicious writers that elective monarchies would be the best if they could be guarded against the tumults excited by the ambition and intrigues of competitors. He was not sure that tumults were an inseparable evil. He thought this character of elective monarchies had been taken rather from particular cases than from general principles. The election of Roman emperors was made by the army. In Poland, the election is made by great rival princes with independent power and ample means of raising commotions. In the German empire, the appointment is made by the electors and princes, who have equal motives and means for exciting cabals and parties. Might not such a mode of election be devised among ourselves as will defend the community against these effects in any dangerous degree? Having made these observations, he would read to the committee a sketch of a plan which he should prefer to either of those under consideration. He was aware that it went beyond the ideas of most members. But will such a plan be adopted out-of-doors? In return he would ask, will the people adopt the other plan? At present, they will adopt neither. But he sees the Union dissolving or already dissolved—he sees evils operating in the states which must soon cure the people of their fondness for democracies—he sees that a great progress has been already made, and is still going on, in the public mind. He thinks, therefore, that the people will in time be unshackled from their prejudices, and whenever that happens, they will themselves not be satisfied at stopping where the plan of Mr. Randolph would place them, but be ready to go as far at least as he proposes. He did not mean to offer the paper he had sketched as a proposition to that committee. It was meant only to give a more correct view of his ideas and to suggest the amendments which he should probably propose to the plan of Mr. Randolph in the proper stages of its future discussion. He reads his sketch in the words following, to wit:

1. The supreme legislative power of the United States of America to be vested in two different bodies of men: the one to be called the

Assembly, the other the Senate; who, together shall form the Legislature of the United States, with power to pass all laws whatsoever, subject to the negative hereafter mentioned.

2. The Assembly to consist of persons elected by the people, to serve for three years.

3. The Senate to consist of persons elected to serve during good behavior; the election to be made by electors chosen for that purpose by the people. In order for this, the states to be divided into election districts. On the death, removal, or resignation of any senator, his place to be filled out of the district from which he came.

4. The supreme executive authority of the United States to be vested in a governor, to be elected to serve during good behavior; the election to be made by electors chosen by the people in the election districts aforesaid. The authorities and functions of the executive to be as follows: to have a negative on all laws about to be passed and the execution of all laws passed; to have the direction of war when authorized or begun; to have with the advice and approbation of the Senate the power of making all treaties; to have the sole appointment of the heads or chief officers of the departments of finance, war, and foreign affairs; to have the nomination of all other officers (ambassadors to foreign nations included), subject to the approbation or rejection of the Senate; to have the power of pardoning all offenses except treason, which he shall not pardon without the approbation of the Senate.

5. On the death, resignation, or removal of the governor, his authorities to be exercised by the president of the Senate till a successor be appointed.

6. The Senate to have the sole power of declaring war; the power of advising and approving all treaties; the power of approving or rejecting all appointments of officers, except the heads or chiefs of the departments of finance, war, and foreign affairs.

7. The supreme judicial authority to be vested in judges, to hold their offices during good behavior, with adequate and permanent salaries. This court to have original jurisdiction in all causes of capture and an appellative jurisdiction in all causes in which the revenues of the General Government or the citizens of foreign nations are concerned.

8. The Legislature of the United States to have power to institute courts in each state for the determination of all matters of general concern.

9. The governor, senators, and all officers of the United States to be liable to impeachment for mal and corrupt conduct; and upon con-

viction, to be removed from office and disqualified for holding any place of trust or profit; all impeachments to be tried by a court to consist of the chief⸺, or judge of the superior court of law of each state, provided such judge shall hold his place during good behavior and have a permanent salary.

10. All laws of the particular states contrary to the Constitution or laws of the United States to be utterly void, and the better to prevent such laws being passed, the governor or president of each state shall be appointed by the General Government and shall have a negative upon the laws about to be passed in the state of which he is the governor or president.

11. No state to have any forces, land or naval; and the militia of all the states to be under the sole and exclusive direction of the United States, the officers of which to be appointed and commissioned by them.

On these several articles he entered into explanatory observations corresponding with the principles of his introductory reasoning.

The committee rose and the house adjourned.

MADISON DISCUSSES PATERSON'S PLAN / *June 19*

In committee of the whole, on the propositions of Mr. Paterson. *The substitute offered yesterday by Mr. Dickinson was rejected by a vote of 6 to 4, and Mr. Paterson's plan was again at large before the committee.*

Mr. Madison: Much stress has been laid by some gentlemen on the want of power in the convention to propose any other than a federal plan. To what had been answered by others, he would only add that neither of the characteristics attached to a federal plan would support this objection. One characteristic was that in a federal government the power was exercised not on the people *individually,* but on the people collectively, on the states. Yet in some instances, as in piracies, captures, and so forth, the existing Confederacy, and in many instances the amendments to it proposed by Mr. Paterson, must operate immediately on individuals. The other characteristic was that a federal government derived its appointments not immediately from the people, but from the states which they respectively composed. Here, too, were facts on the other side. In two of the states, Connecticut and Rhode Island, the delegates to Congress were chosen, not by the legislatures, but by the people at large, and the plan of Mr. Paterson intended no change in this particular.

It had been alleged (by Mr. Paterson) that the Confederation, having been formed by unanimous consent, could be dissolved by unanimous consent only. Does this doctrine result from the nature of compacts? Does it arise from any particular stipulation in the Articles of Confederation? If we consider the Federal Union as analogous to the fundamental compact by which individuals compose one society and which must, in its theoretic origin at least, have been the unanimous act of the component members, it cannot be said that no dissolution of the compact can be effected without unanimous consent. A breach of the fundamental principles of the compact by a part of the society would certainly absolve the other part from their obligations to it. If the breach of any article by any of the parties does not set the others at liberty, it is because the contrary is implied in the compact itself, and particularly by that law of it which gives an indefinite authority to the majority to bind the whole in all cases. This latter circumstance shows that we are not to consider the Federal Union as analogous to the social compact of individuals: For if it were so, a majority would have a right to bind the rest and even to form a new constitution for the whole, which the gentleman from New Jersey would be among the last to admit. If we consider the Federal Union as analogous, not to the social compacts among individual men, but to the conventions among individual states, what is the doctrine resulting from these conventions? Clearly, according to the expositors of the law of nations, that a breach of any one article by any one party leaves all the other parties at liberty to consider the whole convention as dissolved, unless they choose rather to compel the delinquent party to repair the breach. In some treaties, indeed, it is expressly stipulated that a violation of particular articles shall not have this consequence and even that particular articles shall remain in force during war, which is in general understood to dissolve all subsisting treaties. But are there any exceptions of this sort to the Articles of Confederation? So far from it that there is not even an express stipulation that force shall be used to compel an offending member of the Union to discharge its duty. He observed that the violations of the Federal Articles had been numerous and notorious. Among the most notorious was an act of New Jersey, herself, by which she expressly refused to comply with a constitutional requisition of Congress and yielded no further to the expostulations of their deputies than barely to rescind her vote of refusal without passing any positive act of compliance. He did not wish to draw any rigid inferences from these observations. He thought it proper, however, that the true nature of the existing Confederacy should be investigated, and he was not anxious to strengthen the foundations on which it now stands.

Proceeding to the consideration of Mr. Paterson's plan, he stated the object of a proper plan to be twofold—first, to preserve the Union; secondly, to provide a government that will remedy the evils felt by the states, both in their united and individual capacities. Examine Mr. Paterson's plan and say whether it promises satisfaction in these respects.

1. Will it prevent the violations of the law of nations and of treaties, which if not prevented, must involve us in the calamities of foreign wars? The tendency of the states to these violations has been manifested in sundry instances. The files of Congress contain complaints already from almost every nation with which treaties have been formed. Hitherto indulgence has been shown to us. This cannot be the permanent disposition of foreign nations. A rupture with other powers is among the greatest of national calamities; it ought, therefore, to be effectually provided that no part of a nation shall have it in its power to bring them on the whole. The existing Confederacy does not sufficiently provide against this evil. The proposed amendment to it does not supply the omission. It leaves the will of the states as uncontrolled as ever.

2. Will it prevent encroachments on the Federal authority? A tendency to such encroachments has been sufficiently exemplified among ourselves as well as in every other confederated republic, ancient and modern. By the Federal Articles, transactions with the Indians appertain to Congress; yet in several instances the states have entered into treaties and wars with them. In like manner, no two or more states can form among themselves any treaties, and so forth, without the consent of Congress; yet Virginia and Maryland in one instance—Pennsylvania and New Jersey in another—have entered into compacts without previous application or subsequent apology. No state, again, can of right raise troops in time of peace without the like consent. Of all cases of the league, this seems to require the most scrupulous observance. Has not Massachusetts, notwithstanding (the most powerful member of the Union), already raised a body of troops? Is she not now augmenting them without having even deigned to apprise Congress of her intentions? In fine, have we not seen the public land dealt out to Connecticut to bribe her acquiescence in the decree constitutionally awarded against her claim on the territory of Pennsylvania? For no other possible motive can account for the policy of Congress in that measure. If we recur to the examples of other confederacies, we shall find in all of them the same tendency of the parts to encroach on the authority of the whole. He then reviewed the Amphictyonic and

Achaean confederacies among the ancients, and the Helvetic, Germanic, and Belgic among the moderns; tracing their analogy to the United States in the constitution and extent of their federal authorities, in the tendency of the particular members to usurp on these authorities, and to bring confusion and ruin on the whole. He observed that the plan of Mr. Paterson, besides omitting a control over the states as a general defense of the Federal prerogatives, was particularly defective in two of its provisions. In the first place, its ratification was not to be by the people at large, but by the legislatures. It could not, therefore, render the Acts of Congress in pursuance of their powers even legally paramount to the acts of the states. And in the second place, it gave to the Federal tribunal an appellate jurisdiction only even in the criminal cases enumerated. The necessity of any such provision supposed a danger of undue acquittal in the state tribunals: of what avail would an appellate tribunal be after an acquittal? Besides, in most if not all of the states, the executives have by their respective constitutions the right of pardoning: How could this be taken from them by a legislative ratification only?

3. Will it prevent trespasses of the states on each other? Of these enough has been already seen. He instanced acts of Virginia and Maryland which gave a preference to their own citizens in cases where the citizens of other states are entitled to equality of privileges by the Articles of Confederation. He considered the emissions of paper money and other kindred measures as also aggressions. The states, relatively to one another, being each of them either debtor or creditor, the creditor states must suffer unjustly from every emission by the debtor states. We have seen retaliating acts on the subject, which threatened danger, not to the harmony only, but the tranquillity of the Union. The plan of Mr. Paterson, not giving even a negative on the acts of the states, left them as much at liberty as ever to execute their unrighteous projects against each other.

4. Will it secure the internal tranquillity of the states themselves? The insurrections in Massachusetts admonished all the states of the danger to which they were exposed. Yet the plan of Mr. Paterson contained no provisions for supplying the defect of the Confederation on this point. According to the republican theory, indeed, right and power, being both vested in the majority, are held to be synonymous. According to fact and experience, a minority may in an appeal to force be an overmatch for the majority—in the first place, if the minority happen to include all such as possess the skill and habits of military life with such as possess the great pecuniary resources, one third may conquer the remaining two thirds; in the second place, one third of

those who participate in the choice of rulers may be rendered a majority by the accession of those whose poverty disqualifies them from a suffrage and who for obvious reasons must be more ready to join the standard of sedition than that of established government, and in the third place, where slavery exists, the republican theory becomes still more fallacious.

5. Will it secure a good internal legislation and administration to the particular states? In developing the evils which vitiate the political system of the United States, it is proper to take into view those which prevail within the states individually, as well as those which affect them collectively, since the former indirectly affect the whole, and there is great reason to believe that the pressure of them had a full share in the motives which produced the present convention. Under this head he enumerated and animadverted on: first, the multiplicity of the laws passed by the several states; secondly, the mutability of their laws; thirdly, the injustice of them, and fourthly, the impotence of them, observing that Mr. Paterson's plan contained no remedy for this dreadful class of evils and could not, therefore, be received as an adequate provision for the exigencies of the community.

6. Will it secure the Union against the influence of foreign powers over its members? He pretended not to say that any such influence had yet been tried, but it was naturally to be expected that occasions would produce it. As lessons which claimed particular attention, he cited the intrigues practiced among the Amphictyonic confederates, first by the kings of Persia and, afterwards, fatally by Philip of Macedon; among the Achaeans, first by Macedon and, afterwards, no less fatally by Rome; among the Swiss, by Austria, France, and the lesser neighboring powers; among the members of the Germanic body, by France, England, Spain, and Russia, and in the Belgic republic, by all the great neighboring powers. The plan of Mr. Paterson, not giving to the general councils any negative on the will of the particular states, left the door open for the like pernicious machinations among ourselves.

7. He begged the smaller states, which were most attached to Mr. Paterson's plan, to consider the situation in which it would leave them. In the first place, they would continue to bear the whole expense of maintaining their delegates in Congress. It ought not to be said that if they were willing to bear this burden, no others had a right to complain. As far as it led the smaller states to forbear keeping up a representation by which the public business was delayed, it was evidently a matter of common concern. An examination of the minutes of Congress would satisfy everyone that the public business had been frequently

delayed by this cause, and that the states most frequently unrepre-
sented in Congress were not the larger states. He reminded the convention of another consequence of leaving on a small state the burden
of maintaining a representation in Congress. During a considerable
period of the war, one of the representatives of Delaware, in whom
alone before the signing of the Confederation the entire vote of that
state and after that event one half of its vote frequently resided, was a
citizen and resident of Pennsylvania and held an office in his own state
incompatible with an appointment from it to Congress. During another period, the same state was represented by three delegates, two
of whom were citizens of Pennsylvania and the third a citizen of New
Jersey. These expedients must have been intended to avoid the burden of supporting delegates from their own state. But whatever might
have been the cause, was not, in effect, the vote of one state doubled
and the influence of another increased by it? In the second place, the
coercion on which the efficacy of the plan depends can never be exerted
but on themselves. The larger states will be impregnable, the smaller
only can feel the vengeance of it. He illustrated the position by the
history of the Amphictyonic confederates and the ban of the German
empire. It was the cobweb which could entangle the weak, but would
be the sport of the strong.

8. He begged them to consider the situation in which they would
remain in case their pertinacious adherence to an inadmissible plan
should prevent the adoption of any plan. The contemplation of such
an event was painful, but it would be prudent to submit to the task
of examining it at a distance, that the means of escaping it might be
the more readily embraced. Let the Union of the States be dissolved
and one of two consequences must happen. Either the states must remain individually independent and sovereign, or two or more confederacies must be formed among them. In the first event, would the
small states be more secure against the ambition and power of their
larger neighbors than they would be under a general government
pervading with equal energy every part of the empire and having an
equal interest in protecting every part against every other part? In the
second, can the smaller expect that their larger neighbors would confederate with them on the principle of the present Confederacy, which
gives to each member an equal suffrage, or that they would exact less
severe concessions from the smaller states than are proposed in the
scheme of Mr. Randolph?

The great difficulty lies in the affair of representation, and if this
could be adjusted, all others would be surmountable. It was admitted
by both the gentlemen from New Jersey (Mr. Brearly and Mr. Pater-

son) that it would not be just to allow Virginia, which was sixteen times as large as Delaware, an equal vote only. Their language was that it would not be safe for Delaware to allow Virginia sixteen times as many votes. The expedient proposed by them was that all the states should be thrown into one mass and a new partition be made into thirteen equal parts. Would such a scheme be practicable? The dissimilarities existing in the rules of property, as well as in the manners, habits, and prejudices of different states, amounted to a prohibition of the attempt. It had been found impossible for the power of one of the most absolute princes of Europe (the King of France), directed by the wisdom of one of the most enlightened and patriotic ministers (Mr. Neckar) that any age has produced, to equalize in some points only the different usages and regulations of the different provinces. But admitting a general amalgamation and repartition of the states to be practicable, and the danger apprehended by the smaller states from a proportional representation to be real, would not a particular and voluntary coalition of these with their neighbors be less inconvenient to the whole community and equally effectual for their own safety? If New Jersey or Delaware conceived that an advantage would accrue to them from an equalization of the states, in which case they would necessarily form a junction with their neighbors, why might not this end be attained by leaving them at liberty by the Constitution to form such a junction whenever they pleased? And why should they wish to obtrude a like arrangement on all the states when it was, to say the least, extremely difficult, would be obnoxious to many of the states, and when neither the inconvenience nor the benefit of the expedient to themselves would be lessened by confining it to themselves? The prospect of many new states to the westward was another consideration of importance. If they should come into the Union at all, they would come when they contained but few inhabitants. If they should be entitled to vote according to their proportion of inhabitants, all would be right and safe. Let them have an equal vote, and a more objectionable minority than ever might give law to the whole.

Motion to postpone Paterson's plan passed, 9 to 2.

PATERSON'S PLAN REJECTED
AND RANDOLPH'S RESUMED / *June 19*

On the question moved by Mr. King whether the committee should rise and Mr. Randolph's proposition be reported without alteration,

which was in fact a question whether Mr. Randolph's should be ad-
hered to as preferable to those of Mr. Paterson, passed 7 to 3.

Mr. Randolph's plan as reported from the committee (June 13) being before the house, and the first resolution, "that a national government ought to be established, consisting, and so forth," being taken up, Mr. Wilson observed that by a national government he did not mean one that would swallow up the state governments, as seemed to be wished by some gentlemen. He was tenacious of the idea of preserving the latter. He thought, contrary to the opinion of Mr. Hamilton, that they might not only subsist, but subsist on friendly terms with the former. They were absolutely necessary for certain purposes which the former could not reach. All large governments must be subdivided into lesser jurisdictions. As examples he mentioned Persia, Rome, and particularly the divisions and subdivisions of England by Alfred.

Mr. Hamilton coincided with the proposition as it stood in the report. He had not been understood yesterday. By an abolition of the states, he meant that no boundary could be drawn between the national and state legislatures; that the former must, therefore, have indefinite authority. If it were limited at all, the rivalship of the states would gradually subvert it. Even as corporations, the extent of some of them, as Virginia, Massachusetts, and so forth, would be formidable. As states, he thought they ought to be abolished. But he admitted the necessity of leaving in them subordinate jurisdictions. The examples of Persia and the Roman Empire, cited by Mr. Wilson, were, he thought, in favor of his doctrine, the great powers delegated to the satraps and proconsuls having frequently produced revolts and schemes of independence.

Mr. King wished, as everything depended on this proposition, that no objection might be improperly indulged against the phraseology of it. He conceived that the import of the terms "states," "sovereignty," "national," "federal" had been often used and applied in the discussions inaccurately and delusively. The states were not "sovereigns" in the sense contended for by some. They did not possess the peculiar features of sovereignty—they could not make war, nor peace, nor alliances, nor treaties. Considering them as political beings, they were dumb, for they could not speak to any foreign sovereign whatever. They were deaf, for they could not hear any propositions from such sovereign. They had not even the organs or faculties of defense or offense, for they could not of themselves raise troops or equip vessels for war. On the other side, if the Union of the States comprises the idea of a confederation, it comprises that also of consolidation. A union of the states is a union of the men composing them from whence a national character results to the whole. Congress can act alone without the states; they can act (and their acts will be binding) against the instructions of the states. If they declare war, war is *de jure* declared; captures made in pursuance of it are lawful; no acts of the states can vary the situation or prevent the judicial consequences. If the states, therefore, retained some portion of their sovereignty, they had certainly divested themselves of essential portions of it. If they formed a confederacy in some respects, they formed a nation in others. The convention could clearly deliberate on and propose any alterations that Congress could have done under the Federal Articles. And could not Congress propose by virtue of the last article a change in any article whatever—and as well that relating to the equality of suffrage as any other? He made these remarks to obviate some scruples which had been expressed. He doubted much the practicability of annihilating the states, but thought that much of their power ought to be taken from them.

Mr. Martin said he considered that the separation from Great Britain placed the thirteen states in a state of nature toward each other; that they would have remained in that state till this time, but for the Confederation; that they entered into the Confederation on the footing of equality; that they met now to amend it on the same footing, and that he could never accede to a plan that would introduce an inequality and lay ten states at the mercy of Virginia, Massachusetts, and Pennsylvania.

Mr. Wilson could not admit the doctrine that when the colonies became independent of Great Britain, they became independent also of each other. He read the Declaration of Independence, observing thereon, that the United Colonies were declared to be free and independent states, and inferring that they were independent, not individually but unitedly, and that they were confederated, as they were independent states.

Mr. Hamilton assented to the doctrine of Mr. Wilson. He denied the doctrine that the states were thrown into a state of nature. He was not yet prepared to admit the doctrine that the Confederacy could be dissolved by partial infractions of it. He admitted that the states met now on an equal footing, but could see no inference from that against concerting a change of the system in this particular. He took this occasion of observing for the purpose of appeasing the fear of the small states that two circumstances would render them secure under a national government in which they might lose the equality of rank which they now held: one was the local situation of the three largest states —Virginia, Massachusetts, and Pennsylvania. They were separated from each other by distance of place and equally so by all the peculiarities which distinguish the interests of one state from those of another. No combination, therefore, could be dreaded. In the second place, as there was a gradation in the states from Virginia, the largest, down to Delaware, the smallest, it would always happen that ambitious combinations among a few states might and would be counteracted by defensive combinations of greater extent among the rest. No combination has been seen among the large counties, merely as such, against lesser counties. The more close the union of the states and the more complete the authority of the whole, the less opportunity will be allowed to the stronger states to injure the weaker.

Resumption of the Randolph Plan

Editor's note: On June 20, after the Paterson Plan was rejected, debate over the Randolph Plan was resumed. It continued for the next twelve days, but the small states were discontented. They insisted on an equal vote in the Senate. On this issue, the convention remained deadlocked.

TERM "UNITED STATES" GOVERNMENT
SUBSTITUTED FOR "NATIONAL" / June 20

Mr. Ellsworth, seconded by Mr. Gorham, moves to alter it [one of Randolph's propositions of May 30, see page 54] so as to run "that the Government of the United States ought to consist of a supreme legislative, executive, and judiciary." This alteration, he said, would drop the word "national" and retain the proper title, "the United States." He could not admit the doctrine that a breach of any of the Federal Articles could dissolve the whole. It would be highly dangerous not to consider the Confederation as still subsisting. He wished, also, the plan of the convention to go forth as an amendment of the Articles of the Confederation, since under this idea the authority of the legislatures could ratify it. If they are unwilling, the people will be so too. If the plan goes forth to the people for ratification, several succeeding conventions within the states would be unavoidable. He did not like these conventions. They were better fitted to pull down than to build up constitutions.

Mr. Randolph did not object to the change of expression, but apprised the gentleman who wished for it that he did not admit it for the reasons assigned, particularly that of getting rid of a reference to the people for ratification.

The motion of Mr. Ellsworth was acquiesced in.

QUESTION OF A TWO-BRANCH LEGISLATURE / *June 20*

The third resolution, "That the national legislature ought to consist of two branches," being taken up, the "national" (was) struck out, as (a matter) of course.

Mr. Lansing observed that the true question here was whether the convention would adhere to or depart from the foundation of the present Confederacy, and moved, instead of the third resolution, "that the powers of legislation be vested in the United States in Congress." He had already assigned two reasons against such an innovation as was proposed—first, the want of competent powers in the convention; secondly, the state of the public mind. It had been observed (by Mr. Madison) in discussing the first point that in two states the delegates to Congress were chosen by the people. Notwithstanding the first appearance of this remark, it had in fact no weight as the delegates, however chosen, did not represent the people merely as so many individuals, but as forming a sovereign state. Mr. Randolph put it, he said, on its true footing—namely, that the public safety superseded the scruple arising from the review of our powers. But in order to feel the force of this consideration, the same impression must be had of the public danger. He had not himself the same impression and could not, therefore, dismiss his scruple.

Mr. Wilson contended that as the convention were only to recommend, they might recommend what they pleased. He differed much from him. Any act whatever of so respectable a body must have a great effect, and if it does not succeed will be a source of great dissensions. He admitted that there was no certain criterion of the public mind on the subject. He, therefore, recurred to the evidence of it given by the opposition in the states to the scheme of an impost. It could not be expected that those possessing sovereignty could ever voluntarily part with it. It was not to be expected from any one state, much less from thirteen. He proceeded to make some observations on the plan itself and the arguments urged in support of it. The point of representation could receive no elucidation from the case of England. The corruption of the boroughs did not proceed from their comparative smallness, but from the actual fewness of the inhabitants, some of them not having more than one or two. A great inequality existed in the counties of England. Yet the like complaint of peculiar corruption in the small ones had not

been made. It had been said that Congress represent the state of prejudices—will not any other body, whether chosen by the legislatures or
people of the states, also represent their prejudices? It had been asserted
by his colleague (Mr. Hamilton) that there was no coincidence of interests among the large states that ought to excite fears of oppression
in the smaller. If it were true that such a uniformity of interests existed
among the states, there was equal safety for all of them whether the
representation remained as heretofore or were proportioned as now
proposed. It is proposed that the general legislature shall have a negative on the laws of the states. Is it conceivable that there will be leisure for such a task? There will on the most moderate calculation be
as many acts sent up from the states as there are days in the year. Will
the members of the general legislature be competent judges? Will a
gentleman from Georgia be a judge of the expediency of a law which
is to operate in New Hampshire? Such a negative would be more injurious than that of Great Britain heretofore was. It is said that the
national Government must have the influence arising from the grant
of offices and honors. In order to render such a government effectual,
he believed such an influence to be necessary. But if the states will not
agree to it, it is in vain, worse than in vain, to make the proposition.
If this influence is to be attained, the states must be entirely abolished.
Will anyone say this would ever be agreed to? He doubted whether
any General Government equally beneficial to all can be attained.
That now under consideration, he is sure, must be utterly unattainable. He had another objection. The system was too novel and complex. No man could foresee what its operation will be either with
respect to the General Government or the state governments. One or
other, it has been surmised, must absorb the whole.

Mr. Mason did not expect this point would have been reagitated.
The essential differences between the two plans had been clearly
stated. The principal objections against that of Mr. Randolph were
the want of power and the want of practicability. There can be no
weight in the first, as the fiat is not to be here, but in the people. He
thought with his colleague (Mr. Randolph) that there were, besides,
certain crises in which all the ordinary cautions yielded to public necessity. He gave as an example the eventual treaty with Great Britain,
in forming which the commissioners of the United States had boldly
disregarded the improvident shackles of Congress, had given to their
country an honorable and happy peace, and instead of being censured
for the transgression of their powers, had raised to themselves a monu-
ment more durable than brass. The impracticability of gaining the
public concurrence, he thought, was still more groundless. Mr. Lan-

sing had cited the attempts of Congress to gain an enlargement of their powers and had inferred from the miscarriage of these attempts the hopelessness of the plan which he (Mr. Lansing) opposed. He thought a very different inference ought to have been drawn, namely, that the plan which Mr. Lansing espoused and which proposed to augment the powers of Congress never could be expected to succeed. He meant not to throw any reflections on Congress as a body, much less on any particular members of it. He meant, however, to speak his sentiments without reserve on this subject; it was a privilege of age, and perhaps the only compensation which nature had given for the privation of so many other enjoyments, and he should not scruple to exercise it freely. Is it to be thought that the people of America, so watchful over their interests, so jealous of their liberties, will give up their all, will surrender both the sword and the purse, to the same body—and that, too, not chosen immediately by themselves? They never will. They never ought. Will they trust such a body with the regulation of their trade, with the regulation of their taxes, with all the other great powers which are in contemplation? Will they give unbounded confidence to a secret journal—to the intrigues, to the factions which in the nature of things appertain to such an assembly? If any man doubts the existence of these characters of Congress, let him consult their journals for the years '78, '79, and '80. It will be said that if the people are averse to parting with power, why is it hoped that they will part with it to a national legislature? The proper answer is that in this case they do not part with power; they only transfer it from one set of immediate representatives to another set. Much has been said of the unsettled state of the mind of the people. He believed the mind of the people of America, as elsewhere, was unsettled as to some points, but settled as to others. In two points he was sure it was well settled—first, in an attachment to republican government; secondly, in an attachment to more than one branch in the legislature. Their constitutions accord so generally in both these circumstances that they seem almost to have been preconcerted. This must either have been a miracle or have resulted from the genius of the people. The only exceptions to the establishment of two branches in the legislature are the state of Pennsylvania, and Congress, and the latter the only single one not chosen by the people themselves. What has been the consequence? The people have been constantly averse to giving that body further powers. It was acknowledged by Mr. Paterson that this plan could not be enforced without military coercion. Does he consider the force of this concession? The most jarring elements of nature, fire and water themselves, are not more incompatible than

such a mixture of civil liberty and military execution. Will the militia
march from one state into another in order to collect the arrears of
taxes from the delinquent members of the republic? Will they maintain an army for this purpose? Will not the citizens of the invaded
state assist one another till they rise as one man and shake off the
Union altogether? Rebellion is the only case in which the military
forces of the state can be properly exerted against its citizens. In one
point of view, he was struck with horror at the prospect of recurring to
this expedient. To punish the non-payment of taxes with death was a
severity not yet adopted by despotism itself; yet this unexampled
cruelty would be mercy compared to a military collection of revenue in
which the bayonet could make no discrimination between the innocent and the guilty. He took this occasion to repeat that, notwithstanding his solicitude to establish a national government, he never
would agree to abolish the state governments or render them absolutely insignificant. They were as necessary as the General Government, and he would be equally careful to preserve them. He was aware
of the difficulty of drawing the line between them, but hoped it was
not insurmountable. The convention, though comprising so many
distinguished characters, could not be expected to make a faultless
government, and he would prefer trusting to posterity the amendment of its defects, rather than to push the experiment too far.

Mr. Luther Martin agreed with Mr. Mason as to the importance of
the state governments: He would support them at the expense of the
General Government, which was instituted for the purpose of that support. He saw no necessity for two branches and if it existed, Congress
might be organized into two. He considered Congress as representing the people, being chosen by the legislatures, who were chosen by
the people. At any rate, Congress represented the legislatures, and it
was the legislatures, not the people, who refused to enlarge their powers. Nor could the rule of voting have been the ground of objection,
otherwise ten of the states must always have been ready to place
further confidence in Congress. The causes of repugnance must therefore be looked for elsewhere. At the separation from the British empire, the people of America preferred the establishment of themselves
into thirteen separate sovereignties instead of incorporating themselves into one. To these they look up for the security of their lives,
liberties, and properties; to these they must look up. The Federal
Government they formed to defend the whole against foreign nations
in time of war and to defend the lesser states against the ambition of
the larger. They are afraid of granting power unnecessarily, lest they
should defeat the original end of the Union; lest the powers should

prove dangerous to the sovereignties of the particular states which the Union was meant to support, and expose the lesser to being swallowed up by the larger. He conceived, also, that the people of the states, having already vested their powers in their respective legislatures, could not resume them without a dissolution of their governments. He was against conventions in the states—was not against assisting states against rebellious subjects—thought the federal plan of Mr. Paterson did not require coercion more than the national one, as the latter must depend for the deficiency of its revenues on requisitions and quotas—and that a national judiciary extended into the states would be ineffectual and would be viewed with a jealousy inconsistent with its usefulness.

Mr. Sherman seconded and supported Mr. Lansing's motion. He admitted two branches to be necessary in the state legislatures, but saw no necessity in a confederacy of states. The examples were all of a single council. Congress carried us through the war, and perhaps as well as any government could have done. The complaints at present are not that the views of Congress are unwise or unfaithful, but that their powers are insufficient for the execution of their views. The national debt and the want of power somewhere to draw forth the national resources are the great matters that press. All the states were sensible of the defect of power in Congress. He thought much might be said in apology for the failure of the state legislatures to comply with the Confederation. They were afraid of leaning too hard on the people by accumulating taxes; no constitutional rule had been or could be observed in the quotas; the accounts also were unsettled, and every state supposed itself in advance rather than in arrears. For want of a general system, taxes to a due amount had not been drawn from trade, which was the most convenient resource. As almost all the states had agreed to the recommendation of Congress on the subject of an impost, it appeared clearly that they were willing to trust Congress with power to draw a revenue from trade. There is no weight, therefore, in the argument drawn from a distrust of Congress; for money matters being the most important of all, if the people will trust them with power as to them, they will trust them with any other necessary powers. Congress, indeed, by the Confederation have in fact the right of saying how much the people shall pay and to what purpose it shall be applied, and this right was granted to them in the expectation that it would in all cases have its effect. If another branch were to be added to Congress, to be chosen by the people, it would serve to embarrass. The people would not much interest themselves in the elections; a few designing men in the large districts would carry their points, and the people would have no more confidence in their new representatives than in Congress. He saw no reason why the state legislatures should be unfriendly, as had been suggested, to Congress. If they appoint Congress and approve of their measures, they would be rather favorable and partial to them. The disparity of the states in point of size, he perceived, was the main difficulty. But the large states had not yet suffered from the equality of votes enjoyed by the smaller ones. In all great and general points, the interests of all the states were the same. The state of Virginia, notwithstanding the equality of votes, ratified the Confederation without even proposing any alteration. Massachusetts also ratified without any material difficulty. In none of the ratifications is the want of two branches noticed or complained of. To consolidate the states, as some had proposed, would dissolve our treaties with foreign nations which had been formed with us as confederated states. He did not, however, suppose that the creation of two branches in the legislature would have such an effect. If the difficulty on the subject of representation cannot be otherwise got over, he would agree to have two branches and a proportional representation in one of them, provided each state had an equal voice in the other. This was necessary to secure the rights of the lesser states, otherwise three or four of the large states would rule the others as they please. Each state, like each individual, had its peculiar habits, usages, and manners, which constituted its happiness. It would not, therefore, give to others a power over this happiness, any more than an individual would do when he could avoid it.

Mr. Wilson urged the necessity of two branches, observed that if a proper model was not to be found in other confederacies, it was not to be wondered at. The number of them was small, and the duration of some, at least, short. The Amphictyonic and Achaean were formed in the infancy of political science and appear by their history and fate to have contained radical defects. The Swiss and Belgic confederacies were held together, not by any vital principle of energy, but by the incumbent pressure of formidable neighboring nations. The German owed its continuance to the influence of the House of Austria. He appealed to our own experience for the defects of our Confederacy. He had been six years of the twelve since the commencement of the revolution a member of Congress and had felt all its weaknesses. He appealed to the recollection of others, whether on many important occasions the public interest had not been obstructed by the small members of the Union. The success of the Revolution was owing to other causes than the constitution of Congress. In many instances, it went on even against the difficulties arising from Congress themselves.

He admitted that the large states did accede, as had been stated, to the Confederation in its present form, but it was the effect of necessity, not of choice. There are other instances of their yielding from the same motive to the unreasonable measures of the small states. The situation of things is now a little altered. He insisted that a jealousy would exist between the state legislatures and the general legislature, observing that the members of the former would have views and feelings very distinct in this respect from their constituents. A private citizen of a state is indifferent whether power be exercised by the general or state legislatures, provided it be exercised most for his happiness. His representative has an interest in its being exercised by the body to which he belongs. He will therefore view the national legislature with the eye of a jealous rival. He observed that the address of Congress to the people at large had always been better received and produced greater effect than those made to the legislatures.

On motion of the deputies from Delaware, the question on the third resolution in the report from the committee of the whole was postponed till tomorrow, and the house adjourned.

AGREEMENT ON A TWO-BRANCH LEGISLATURE / *June 21*

Dr. Johnson: On a comparison of the two plans which had been proposed from Virginia and New Jersey, it appeared that the peculiarity which characterized the latter was its being calculated to preserve the individuality of the states. The plan from Virginia did not profess to destroy this individuality altogether, but was charged with such a tendency. One gentleman alone (Mr. Hamilton) in his animadversions on the plan of New Jersey boldly and decisively contended for an abolition of the state governments. Mr. Wilson and the gentleman from Virginia, who also were adversaries of the plan of New Jersey, held a different language. They wished to leave the states in possession of a considerable, though a subordinate, jurisdiction. They had not yet, however, shown how this could consist with, or be secured against, the general sovereignty and jurisdiction which they proposed to give to the national Government. If this could be shown in such a manner as to satisfy the patrons of the New Jersey propositions that the individuality of the states would not be endangered, many of their objections would, no doubt, be removed. If this could not be shown, their objections would have their full force. He wished it, therefore, to be well considered, whether in case the states, as was proposed, should retain some portion of sovereignty at least, this portion could be preserved without allowing them to participate effectually in the General Gov-

ernment—without giving them each a distinct and equal vote for the 117
purpose of defending themselves in the general councils.

Mr. Wilson's respect for Dr. Johnson, added to the importance of
the subject, led him to attempt, unprepared as he was, to solve the
difficulty which had been started. It was asked how the General
Government and individuality of the particular states could be reconciled to each other—and how the latter could be secured against the
former? Might it not, on the other side, be asked how the former was
to be secured against the latter? It was generally admitted that a jealousy and rivalship would be felt between the general and particular
governments. As the plan now stood, though indeed contrary to his
opinion, one branch of the General Government (the Senate or second
branch) was to be appointed by the state legislatures. The state legislatures, therefore, by this participation in the General Government
would have an opportunity of defending their rights. Ought not a
reciprocal opportunity to be given to the General Government of defending itself by having an appointment of some one constituent
branch of the state governments? If a security be necessary on one side,
it would seem reasonable to demand it on the other. But taking the
matter in a more general view, he saw no danger to the states from the
General Government. In case a combination should be made by the
large ones, it would produce a general alarm among the rest and the
project would be frustrated. But there was no temptation to such a
project. The states having in general a similar interest, in case of any
propositions in the national legislature to encroach on the state legislatures, he conceived a general alarm would take place in the national legislature itself; that it would communicate itself to the state
legislatures, and would finally spread among the people at large.
The General Government will be as ready to preserve the rights of
the states as the latter are to preserve the rights of individuals—all the
members of the former having a common interest, as representatives of
all the people of the latter, to leave the state governments in possession
of what the people wish them to retain. He could not discover, therefore, any danger whatever on the side from which it was apprehended.
On the contrary, he conceived that in spite of every precaution, the
General Government would be in perpetual danger of encroachments
from the state governments.

Mr. Madison was of the opinion in the first place that there was less
danger of encroachment from the General Government than from
the state governments, and in the second place that the mischiefs
from encroachments would be less fatal if made by the former than
if made by the latter.

1. All the examples of other confederacies prove the greater tendency in such systems to anarchy than to tyranny, to a disobedience of the members than usurpations of the Federal head. Our own experience had fully illustrated this tendency. But it will be said that the proposed change in the principles and form of the Union will vary the tendency; that the General Government will have real and greater powers and will be derived, in one branch at least, from the people, not from the governments of the states. To give full force to this objection, let it be supposed for a moment that indefinite power should be given to the general legislature, and the states reduced to corporations dependent on the general legislature—why should it follow that the General Government would take from the states any branch of their power, as far as its operation was beneficial and its continuance desirable to the people? In some of the states, particularly in Connecticut, all the townships are incorporated and have a certain limited jurisdiction: Have the representatives of the people of the townships in the legislature of the state ever endeavored to despoil the townships of any part of their local authority? As far as this local authority is convenient to the people, they are attached to it, and their representatives, chosen by and amenable to them, naturally respect their attachment to this as much as their attachment to any other right or interest. The relation of a general government to state governments is parallel.

2. Guards were more necessary against encroachments of the state governments on the General Government than of the latter on the former. The great objection made against an abolition of the state governments was that the General Government could not extend its care to all the minute objects which fall under the cognizance of the local jurisdictions. The objection as stated lay not against the probable abuse of the general power, but against the imperfect use that could be made of it throughout so great an extent of country and over so great a variety of objects. As far as its operation would be practicable, it could not in this view be improper; as far as it would be impracticable, the convenience of the General Government itself would concur with that of the people in the maintenance of subordinate governments. Were it practicable for the General Government to extend its care to every requisite object without the co-operation of the state governments, the people would not be less free as members of one great republic than as members of thirteen small ones. A citizen of Delaware was not more free than a citizen of Virginia, nor would either be more free than a citizen of America. Supposing, therefore, a tendency in the General Government to absorb the state governments, no fatal consequence could result. Taking the reverse as the

supposition, that a tendency should be left in the state governments toward an independence on the General Government, and the gloomy consequences need not be pointed out. The imagination of them must have suggested to the states the experiment we are now making to prevent the calamity and must have formed the chief motive with those present to undertake the arduous task.

Motion "that the legislature ought to consist of two branches" passed, 7 to 3.

ELECTION OF THE HOUSE
BY THE PEOPLE RESUMED / *June 21*

The fourth resolution of the report being taken into consideration, Gen. Pinckney moved "that the first branch, instead of being elected by the people, should be elected in such manner as the legislature of each state should direct." He urged, first, that this liberty would give more satisfaction, as the legislatures could then accommodate the mode to the convenience and opinions of the people; secondly, that it would avoid the undue influence of large counties, which would prevail if the elections were to be made in districts, as must be the mode intended by the report of the committee; thirdly, that otherwise disputed elections must be referred to the general legislature, which would be attended with intolerable expense and trouble to the distant parts of the Republic.

Mr. L. Martin seconded the motion.

Mr. Hamilton considered the motion as intended manifestly to transfer the election from the people to the state legislatures, which would essentially vitiate the plan. It would increase that state influence which could not be too watchfully guarded against. All, too, must admit the possibility, in case the General Government should maintain itself, that the state governments might gradually dwindle into nothing. The system, therefore, should not be engrafted on what might possibly fail.

Mr. Mason urged the necessity of retaining the election by the people. Whatever inconvenience may attend the democratic principle, it must actuate one part of the government. It is the only security for the rights of the people.

Mr. Sherman would like an election by the legislatures best, but is content with the plan as it stands.

Mr. Rutledge could not admit the solidity of the distinction between a mediate and immediate election by the people. It was the same thing to act by oneself and to act by another. An election by the legislature would be more refined than an election immediately by the people and would be more likely to correspond with the sense of the whole community. If this convention had been chosen by the people in districts, it is not to be supposed that such proper characters would have been preferred. The delegates to Congress, he thought, had also been fitter men than would have been appointed by the people at large.

Mr. Wilson considered the election of the first branch by the people not only as the cornerstone, but as the foundation of the fabric, and that the difference between a mediate and immediate election was immense. The difference was particularly worthy of notice in this respect—that the legislatures are actuated not merely by the sentiment of the people, but have an official sentiment opposed to that of the General Government and perhaps to that of the people themselves.

Mr. King enlarged on the same distinction. He supposed the legislatures would constantly choose men subservient to their own views as contrasted to the general interest, and that they might even devise modes of election that would be subversive of the end in view. He remarked several instances in which the views of a state might be at variance with those of the General Government, and mentioned particularly a competition between the national and state debts for the most certain and productive funds.

Gen. Pinckney was for making the state governments a part of the general system. If they were to be abolished or lose their agency, South Carolina and the other states would have but a small share of the benefits of government.

Gen. Pinckney's motion, election by state legislatures, defeated, 6 to 4.

Gen. Pinckney then moved "that the first branch be elected by the people in such mode as the legislatures should direct," but waived it on its being hinted that such a provision might be more properly tried in the detail of the plan.

Election of the first branch "by the people" passed, 9 to 1.

ELECTION OF THE SENATE BY LEGISLATURES APPROVED / *June 25*

Mr. Gorham inclined to a compromise as to the rule of proportion. He thought there was some weight in the objections of the small states. If Virginia should have sixteen votes and Delaware with several other states together sixteen, those from Virginia would be more likely to unite than the others and would therefore have an undue influence. This remark was applicable not only to states, but to counties or other districts of the same state. Accordingly, the Constitution of Massachusetts had provided that the representatives of the larger districts should not be in an exact ratio to their numbers, and experience, he thought, had shown the provision to be expedient.

Mr. Read: The states have heretofore been in a sort of partnership. They ought to adjust their old affairs before they open a new account. He brought into view the appropriation of the common interest in the western lands to the use of particular states. Let justice be done on this head: Let the fund be applied fairly and equally to the discharge of the general debt, and the smaller states who had been injured would listen then, perhaps, to those ideas of just representation which had been held out.

Mr. Gorham could not see how the convention could interpose in the case. Errors, he allowed, had been committed on the subject. But Congress were now using their endeavors to rectify them. The best remedy would be such a government as would have vigor enough to do justice throughout. This was certainly the best chance that could be afforded to the smaller states.

Mr. Wilson: The question is shall the members of the second branch be chosen by the legislatures of the states? When he considered the amazing extent of country, the immense population which is to fill it, the influence of the government we are to form will have, not only on the present generation of our people and their multiplied posterity, but on the whole globe, he was lost in the magnitude of the object. The project of Henry IV and his statesmen was but the picture in miniature of the great portrait to be exhibited. He was opposed to an election by the state legislatures. In explaining his reasons, it was necessary to observe the twofold relation in which the people would stand —first, as citizens of the General Government, and secondly, as citizens of their particular state. The General Government was meant for them in the first capacity, the state governments in the second. Both governments were derived from the people; both meant for the people; both, therefore, ought to be regulated on the same principles. The same train of ideas which belonged to the relation of the citizens to their state governments was applicable to their relation to the General Government, and in forming the latter we ought to proceed by abstracting as much as possible from the idea of the state governments. With respect to the province and object of the General Government, they should be considered as having no existence. The election of the second branch by the legislatures will introduce and cherish local interests and local prejudices. The General Government is not an assemblage of states, but of individuals, for certain political purposes. It is not meant for the states, but for the individuals composing them; the individuals, therefore, not the states, ought to be represented in it. A proportion in this representation can be preserved in the second as well as in the first branch, and the election can be made by electors chosen by the people for that purpose. He moved an amendment to that effect, which was not seconded.

Mr. Ellsworth saw no reason for departing from the mode contained in the report. Whoever chooses the member, he will be a citizen of the state he is to represent and will feel the same spirit and act the same part, whether he be appointed by the people or the legislature. Every state has its particular views and prejudices, which will find their way into the general council, through whatever channel they may flow. Wisdom was one of the characteristics which it was in contemplation to give the second branch: Would not more of it issue from the legislatures than from an immediate election by the people? He urged the necessity of maintaining the existence and agency of the states. Without their co-operation it would be impossible to support a republican government over so great an extent of country. An army could scarcely render it practicable. The largest states are the worst governed. Virginia is obliged to acknowledge her incapacity to extend her government to Kentucky. Massachusetts cannot keep the peace one hundred miles from her capital and is now forming an army for its support. How long Pennsylvania may be free from a like situation cannot be foreseen. If the principles and materials of our government are not adequate to the extent of these single states, how can it be imagined that they can support a single government throughout the United States? The only chance of supporting a general government lies in grafting it on those of the individual states.

Dr. Johnson urged the necessity of preserving the state governments, which would be at the mercy of the General Government on Mr. Wilson's plan.

Mr. Madison thought it would obviate difficulty if the present resolution were postponed and the eighth taken up, which is to fix the right of suffrage in the second branch.

Mr. Williamson professed himself a friend to such a system as would secure the existence of the state governments. The happiness of the people depended on it. He was at a loss to give his vote as to the Senate until he knew the number of its members. In order to ascertain this, he moved to insert after "second branch of the national legislature" the words "who shall bear such proportion to the number of the first branch as one to_____." He was not seconded.

Mr. Mason: It has been agreed on all hands that an efficient government is necessary; that to render it such, it ought to have the faculty of self-defense; that to render its different branches effectual, each of them ought to have the same power of self-defense. He did not wonder that such an agreement should have prevailed on these points. He only wondered that there should be any disagreement about the necessity of allowing the state governments the same self-defense. If they are to be preserved, as he conceived to be essential, they certainly ought to have this power, and the only mode left of giving it to them was by allowing them to appoint the second branch of the national legislature.

Mr. Butler, observing that we were put to difficulties at every step by the uncertainty whether an equality or a ratio of representation would prevail finally in the second branch, moved to postpone the fifth resolution and to proceed to the eighth resolution on that point. Mr. Madison seconded him.

Election to the Senate by state legislatures approved, 9 to 2.

The mode of constituting the second branch being under consideration, the word "national" was struck out and "United States" inserted.

PINCKNEY ANALYZES THE POLITICAL SITUATION / *June 25*

The fourth resolution being taken up, Mr. Pinckney spoke as follows:

The efficacy of the system will depend on this article. In order to form a right judgment in the case, it will be proper to examine the situation of this country more accurately than it has yet been done.

The people of the United States are perhaps the most singular of any we are acquainted with. Among them there are fewer distinctions of fortune and less of rank than among the inhabitants of any other nation. Every freeman has a right to the same protection and security, and a very moderate share of property entitles him to the possession of all the honors and privileges the public can bestow. Hence arises a greater equality than is to be found among the people of any other country, and an equality which is more likely to continue. I say this equality is likely to continue because in a new country, possessing immense tracts of uncultivated lands, where every temptation is offered to emigration and where industry must be rewarded with competency, there will be few poor and few dependent. Every member of the society, almost, will enjoy an equal power of arriving at the supreme offices, and consequently of directing the strength and sentiments of the whole community. None will be excluded by birth and few by fortune from voting for proper persons to fill the offices of government. The whole community will enjoy in the fullest sense that kind of political liberty which consists in the power the members of the state reserve to themselves of arriving at the public offices or, at least, of having votes in the nomination of those who fill them.

If this state of things is true, and the prospect of its continuance probable, it is perhaps not politic to endeavor too close an imitation of a government calculated for a people whose situation is, and whose views ought to be, extremely different.

Much has been said of the constitution of Great Britain. I will confess that I believe it to be the best constitution in existence, but at the same time I am confident it is one that will not or cannot be introduced into this country for many centuries. If it were proper to go here into an historical dissertation on the British constitution, it might easily be shown that the peculiar excellence, the distinguishing feature, of that government cannot possibly be introduced into our system; that its balance between the crown and the people cannot be made a part of our Constitution; that we neither have, nor can have the members to compose it, nor the rights, privileges, and properties of so distinct a class of citizens to guard; that the materials for forming this balance or check do not exist, nor is there a necessity for having so permanent a part of our legislative until the executive power is so constituted as to have something fixed and dangerous in its principle. By this I mean a sole, hereditary, though limited, executive.

That we cannot have a proper body for forming a legislative balance between the inordinate power of the executive and the people is evident from a review of the accidents and circumstances which gave rise to the peerage of Great Britain. I believe it is well ascertained that the parts which compose the British constitution arose immediately from the forests of Germany, but the antiquity of the establishment of nobility is by no means clearly defined. Some authors are of opinion that the dignity denoted by the titles of *dux* and *comes* was derived from the old Roman to the German empire; while others are of opinion that they existed among the Germans long before the Romans were acquainted with them. The institution, however, of nobility is immemorial among the nations who may properly be termed the ancestors of Great Britain. At the time they were summoned in England to become a part of the national council, the circumstances which contributed to make them a constituent part of that constitution must be well known to all gentlemen who have had industry and curiosity enough to investigate the subject. The nobles, with their possessions and dependents, composed a body permanent in their nature and formidable in point of power. They had a distinct interest both from the king and the people—an interest which could only be represented by themselves and the guardianship of which could not be safely entrusted to others. At the time they were originally called to form a part of the national council, necessity perhaps, as much as other causes, induced the monarch to look up to them. It was necessary to demand the aid of his subjects in personal and pecuniary services. The power and possessions of the nobility would not permit taxation from any assembly of which they were not a part; and the blending of the deputies of the commons with them, and thus forming what they called their *parler-ment,* was perhaps as much the effect of chance as of anything else. The commons were at that time completely subordinate to the nobles, whose consequence and influence seem to have been the only reasons for their superiority; a superiority so degrading to the commons that in the first summons we find the peers are called upon to consult, the commons to consent. From this time the peers have composed a part of the British legislature, and notwithstanding their power and influence have diminished, and those of the commons have increased, yet still they have always formed an excellent balance against either the encroachments of the crown or the people.

I have said that such a body cannot exist in this country for ages, and that until the situation of our people is exceedingly changed, no necessity will exist for so permanent a part of the legislature. To illustrate this, I have remarked that the people of the United States are more equal in their circumstances than the people of any other country; that they have very few rich men among them—by rich men I mean those whose riches may have a dangerous influence, or such as are esteemed rich in Europe—perhaps there are not one hundred such on the continent; that it is not probable this number will be greatly increased; that the genius of the people, their mediocrity of situation, and the prospects which are afforded their industry in a country which must be a new one for centuries are unfavorable to the rapid distinction of ranks. The destruction of the right of primogeniture and the equal division of the property of intestates will also have an effect to preserve this mediocrity; for laws invariably affect the manners of people. On the other hand, that vast extent of unpeopled territory which opens to the frugal and industrious a sure road to competency and independence will effectually prevent for a considerable time the increase of the poor or discontented and be the means of preserving that equality of condition which so eminently distinguishes us.

If equality is, as I contend, the leading feature of the United States, where then are the riches and wealth whose representation and protection is the peculiar province of this permanent body? Are they in the hands of the few who may be called rich—in the possession of less than a hundred citizens? Certainly not. They are in the great body of the people, among whom there are no men of wealth and very few of real poverty. Is it probable that a change will be created and that a new order of men will arise? If under the British Government for a century no such change was produced, I think it may be fairly concluded it will not take place while even the semblance of republicanism remains. How is this change to be effected? Where are the sources from whence it is to flow? From the landed interest? No. That is too unproductive and too much divided in most of the states. From the moneyed interest? If such exist at present, little is to be apprehended from that source. Is it to spring from commerce? I believe it would be the first instance in which a nobility sprang from merchants. Besides, sir, I apprehend that on this point the policy of the United States has been much mistaken. We have unwisely considered ourselves as the inhabitants of an old, instead of a new, country. We have adopted the maxims of a state full of people and manufactures and established in credit. We have deserted our true interest, and instead of applying closely to those improvements in domestic policy which would have insured the future importance of our commerce, we have rashly and prematurely engaged in schemes as extensive as they are imprudent. This, however, is an error which daily corrects itself and I have no doubt that a few more severe trials will convince us that very different commercial principles ought to govern the conduct of these states.

The people of this country are not only very different from the inhabitants of any state we are acquainted with in the modern world, but I assert that their situation is distinct from either the people of Greece or Rome or of any states we are acquainted with among the ancients. Can the orders introduced by the institution of Solon—can they be found in the United States? Can the military habits and manners of Sparta be resembled to ours in habits and manners? Are the distinctions of patrician and plebeian known among us? Can the Helvetic or Belgic confederacies, or can the unwieldy, unmeaning body called the Germanic empire—can they be said to possess either the same or a situation like ours? I apprehend not. They are perfectly different in their distinctions of rank, their constitutions, their manners, and their policy.

Our true situation appears to me to be this—a new, extensive country, containing within itself the materials for forming a government capable of extending to its citizens all the blessings of civil and religious liberty—capable of making them happy at home. This is the great end of republican establishments. We mistake the object of our

government if we hope or wish that it is to make us respectable abroad.
Conquests or superiority among other powers is not, or ought not
ever to be, the object of republican systems. If they are sufficiently active and energetic to rescue us from contempt and preserve our domestic happiness and security, it is all we can expect from them—it is
more than almost any other government insures to its citizens.

I believe this observation will be found generally true—that no
two people are so exactly alike in their situation or circumstances as
to admit the exercise of the same government with equal benefit; that
a system must be suited to the habits and genius of the people it is to
govern and must grow out of them.

The people of the United States may be divided into three classes—
professional men, who must from their particular pursuits always have
a considerable weight in the government while it remains popular;
commercial men, who may or may not have weight, as a wise or in-
judicious commercial policy is pursued. If that commercial policy is
pursued which I conceive to be the true one, the merchants of this
country will not, or ought not, for a considerable time to have much
weight in the political scale. The third is the landed interest, the owners and cultivators of the soil, who are, and ought ever to be the governing spring in the system. These three classes, however, distinct in
their pursuits, are individually equal in the political scale and may be
easily proved to have but one interest. The dependence of each on the
other is mutual. The merchant depends on the planter. Both must,
in private as well as public affairs, be connected with the professional
men, who in their turn must in some measure depend on them. Hence
it is clear from this manifest connection and the equality which I before stated exists and must, for the reasons then assigned, continue,
that after all there is one, but one great and equal body of citizens composing the inhabitants of this country, among whom there are no distinctions of rank and very few or none of fortune.

For a people thus circumstanced are we, then, to form a government, and the question is what sort of government is best suited
to them?

Will it be the British Government? No. Why? Because Great Britain
contains three orders of people distinct in their situation, their possessions, and their principles. These orders combined form the great
body of the nation, and as in national expenses the wealth of
the whole community must contribute, so ought each component part
to be duly and properly represented. No other combination of power
could form this due representation but the one that exists. Neither the
peers or the people could represent the royalty, nor could the royalty

and the people form a proper representation for the peers. Each, there, fore, must of necessity be represented by itself, of the sign of itself, and this accidental mixture had certainly formed a government admirably well balanced.

But the United States contain but one order that can be assimilated to the British nation—this is the order of Commons. They will not, surely then, attempt to form a government consisting of three branches, two of which shall have nothing to represent. They will not have an executive and senate (hereditary) because the King and lords of England are so. The same reasons do not exist, and, therefore, the same provisions are not necessary.

We must, as has been observed, suit our government to the people it is to direct. These are, I believe, as active, intelligent, and susceptible of good government as any people in the world. The confusion which has produced the present relaxed state is not owing to them. It is owing to the weakness and defects of a government incapable of combining the various interests it is intended to unite, and destitute of energy. All that we have to do, then, is to distribute the powers of government in such a manner and for such limited periods, as, while it gives a proper degree of permanency to the magistrate, will reserve to the people the right of election they will not or ought not frequently to part with. I am of opinion that this may easily be done, and that with some amendments, the propositions before the committee will fully answer this end.

No position appears to me more true than this: that the General Government cannot effectually exist without reserving to the states the possession of their local rights. They are the instruments upon which the Union must frequently depend for the support and execution of their powers, however immediately operating upon the people and not upon the states.

RIGHTS OF STATES DEFENDED / *June 27*

In convention. Mr. Rutledge moved to postpone the sixth resolution, defining the powers of Congress, in order to take up the seventh and eighth, which involved the most fundamental points, the rules of suffrage in the two branches, which was agreed to unanimously.

A question being proposed on the seventh resolution, declaring that the suffrage in the first branch should be according to an equitable ratio, Mr. L. Martin contended at great length and with great eagerness that the General Government was meant merely to preserve the state governments, not to govern individuals; that its powers ought to

The Delegates

The Constitution was the creation of
strong-minded, yet moderate men whose idealism
persists because they had
a genius for the democratic compromise

GEORGE WASHINGTON: *His very presence was a spur to loftiness.*　　1

OLIVER ELLSWORTH AND WIFE
CONNECTICUT

*He gave strong support to the
Constitution and later became a U.S. Senator and
Chief Justice of the U.S. Supreme Court.*

ABRAHAM BALDWIN   3
GEORGIA

He played a conservative role, was a man
of culture, learning, and eloquence.

RICHARD BASSETT
DELAWARE   4

e became U.S. Senator, Governor, and
Federal Circuit Court judge.

6

GUNNING BEDFORD, JR.

DELAWARE

Although rebuked for his impetuo[us]
manner, Bedford signed the Constitut[ion]
later became a Federal judge.

JOHN BLAIR   5

VIRGINIA

Washington appointed this jurist
to the U.S. Supreme Court.

BENJAMIN FRANKLIN

PENNSYLVANIA

Eighty-two years old at the time o[f]
the convention, the world-famous and
Franklin still had a nimble mind

8

DAVID BREARLY
NEW JERSEY

*An esteemed judge, he
helped to ratify
Constitution in his state.*

9

WILLIAM BLOUNT
NORTH CAROLINA

*He later moved to Tennessee, founded
the city of Knoxville.*

10

JACOB BROOM
DELAWARE

A politician in his home state,
he was quiet, but
"cheerful" in convention.

11

PIERCE BUTLER
SOUTH CAROLINA

A wealthy planter of Irish
origin, he later was
elected to the U.S. Senate.

ALEXANDER HAMIL'
NEW YORK

He made a brilliant
defense of
the Constitution in
The Federalist.

DANIEL CARROLL   12
MARYLAND

Washington appointed him a Commissioner
of the District of Columbia.

GEORGE CLYMER   13
PENNSYLVANIA

Subsequently elected to Congress, he was a
liberal and defended the Constitution.

15

RUFUS KING

MASSACHUSETTS

*One of the most active in the debates, he
strove for harmony between extremes.*

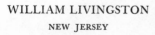

WILLIAM RICHARDSON DAVIE
NORTH CAROLINA

*A vigorous supporter of
the Constitution,
he was subsequently Governor
of North Carolina.*

16

WILLIAM LIVINGSTON
NEW JERSEY

*Livingston was later elected
Governor of his state.*

17

JONATHAN DAYTON
NEW JERSEY

Major Dayton was, at twenty-seven,
the youngest delegate. 18

JOHN DICKINSON
DELAWARE

His influence was largely
responsible for ratification by
Pennsylvania and Delaware. 19

JAMES MADISON
VIRGINIA

He never missed a session, made major
contributions to the debates.

22   NICHOLAS GILMAN

NEW HAMPSHIRE

A lawyer, he served for nearly
eighteen years in Congress.

23   WILLIAM FEW

GEORGIA

Few moved to New York and served
in the state legislature.

GEORGE MASON

VIRGINIA

Mason felt the
Constitution was not
democratic enough,
did not sign.

21

24   JOHN RUTLEDGE

SOUTH CAROLINA

A conservative, he was appointed a justice
of the U.S. Supreme Court.

25   **JARED INGERSOLL**

PENNSYLVANIA

A competent, well-educated attorney,
he was also an able speaker.

27

THOMAS FITZSIMMONS
PENNSYLVANIA

A signer, he was also elected to the nation's first Congress.

26

ELBRIDGE GERRY
MASSACHUSETTS

beral Gerry was a non-signer, but a major contributor to the debates.

28

NATHANIEL GORHAM
MASSACHUSETTS

He was chairman of the convention's committee of the whole.

DANIEL OF ST. THOMAS JENIFER
MARYLAND

*A confirmed bachelor, he was
active in state politics.*

29

WILLIAM SAMUEL JOHNSON
CONNECTICUT

*He was first to propose the Senate as
a separate legislative branch.*

30

GOUVERNEUR MORRIS
PENNSYLVANIA

*Morris wrote the final draft of
the Constitution.*

31

JOHN LANGDON

NEW HAMPSHIRE

*He was one of New Hampshire's
first U.S. Senators.*

JOHN LANSING

NEW YORK

*He was inflexibly opposed to any
new plan of government.*

34

WILLIAM PATERSON
NEW JERSEY

*His proposal for equal state representation
in the Senate was accepted.*

36 DR. JAMES McCLURG

VIRGINIA

*He became a delegate when
Patrick Henry declined.*

37 WILLIAM HOUSTON

GEORGIA

*Lawyer, state legislator, he was
one of the non-signers.*

CHARLES PINCKNEY

SOUTH CAROLINA

*A serious student of politics,
his ideas influenced the
final shape of the Constitution.*

35

38 JAMES McHENRY

MARYLAND

*Washington selected him to be
Secretary of War.*

JOHN FRANCIS MERCER
MARYLAND

*He did not sign Constitution,
opposed ratification.*

39

ALEXANDER MARTIN
NORTH CAROLINA

*A non-signer, he subsequently held a
U.S. Senate seat for one term.*

40

41

EDMUND RANDOLPH

VIRGINIA

*Although he refused to sign Constitution,
he supported its ratification.*

THOMAS MIFFLIN
PENNSYLVANIA

*He spoke only once in convention,
became Governor of his state.*

42

43

ROBERT MORRIS
PENNSYLVANIA

*Although he was unaccountably
silent at the convention,
he favored the Constitution.*

44

GEORGE READ
DELAWARE

*Small and fragile, he spoke feebly
for strong government.*

RICHARD DOBBS SPAIGHT
NORTH CAROLINA

*One of the youngest, most active
delegates, later a Governor.*

45

CHARLES COTESWORTH PINCKN[E]

SOUTH CAROLINA

Cousin of Charles Pinckney, he
was an ardent Federalist.

47

CALEB STRONG

MASSACHUSETTS

He did not sign Constitution,
but aided ratification.

46

48

ROGER SHERMAN
CONNECTICUT

*Odd in appearance and awkward in
manner, he was widely
respected for his sturdy sense.*

DR. HUGH WILLIAMSON
NORTH CAROLINA

A well-educated physician, he was the
most active of his delegation.

LUTHER MARTIN
MARYLAND

49

The Attorney General of his state,
he was a non-signer.

GEORGE WYTHE

VIRGINIA

*...te's most famous jurist, he
was law teacher of
...rson and John Marshall.*

52

JAMES WILSON

PENNSYLVANIA

This liberal, Scottish-born jurist was one
of the dozen most important delegates.

be kept within narrow limits; that if too little power was given to it, *129*
more might be added, but that if too much, it could never be resumed;
that individuals, as such, have little to do but with their own states;
that the General Government has no more to apprehend from
the states composing the Union while it pursues proper measures than
a government over individuals has to apprehend from its subjects;
that to resort to the citizens at large for their sanction to a new government will be throwing them back into a state of nature; that the dissolution of the state governments is involved in the nature of the process; that the people have no right to do this without the consent of
those to whom they have delegated their power for state purposes:
through their tongues only they can speak, through their ears only
they can hear; that the states have shown a good disposition to comply
with the Acts of Congress, weak, contemptibly weak, as that body has
been, and have failed through inability alone to comply; that the
heaviness of the private debts and the waste of property during the war
were the chief causes of this inability; that he did not conceive the instances mentioned by Mr. Madison of compacts between Virginia and
Maryland, between Pennsylvania and New Jersey, or of troops raised
by Massachusetts for defense against the rebels to be violations of the
Articles of Confederation; that an equal vote in each state was essential to the federal idea and was founded in justice and freedom, not
merely in policy; that though the states may give up this right of sovereignty, yet they had not and ought not; that the states, like individuals, were in a state of nature equally sovereign and free. In order to
prove that individuals in a state of nature are equally free and independent, he read passages from Locke, Vattel, Lord Somers, Priestly.
To prove that the case is the same with states till they surrender their
equal sovereignty, he read other passages in Locke and Vattel and also
Rutherford: that the states, being equal, cannot treat or confederate
so as to give up an equality of votes without giving up their liberty;
that the propositions on the table were a system of slavery for ten
states; that as Virginia, Massachusetts, and Pennsylvania have forty-
two ninetieths of the votes, they can do as they please without a mi-
raculous union of the other ten; that they will have nothing to do but
to gain over one of the ten to make them complete masters of the rest;
that they can then appoint an executive and judiciary and legislature
for them, as they please; that there was, and would continue, a natural
predilection and partiality in men for their own states; that the states,
particularly the smaller, would never allow a negative to be exercised
over their laws; that no state in ratifying the Confederation had objected to the equality of votes; that the complaints at present ran not

against this equality, but the want of power; that sixteen members from Virginia would be more likely to act in concert than a like number formed of members from different states; that instead of a junction of the small states as a remedy, he thought a division of the large states would be more eligible. This was the substance of a speech which was continued more than three hours. He was too much exhausted, he said, to finish his remarks and reminded the house that he should tomorrow resume them.

ARGUMENT CONTINUED / *June 28*

Mr. L. Martin resumed his discourse, contending that the General Government ought to be formed for the states, not for individuals; that if the states were to have votes in proportion to their numbers of people, it would be the same thing whether their representatives were chosen by the legislatures or the people: the smaller states would be equally enslaved; that if the large states have the same interest with the smaller, as was urged, there could be no danger in giving them an equal vote: they would not injure themselves, and they could not injure the large ones on that supposition without injuring themselves, and if the interests were not the same, the inequality of suffrage would be dangerous to the smaller states; that it will be in vain to propose any plan offensive to the rulers of the states, whose influence over the people will certainly prevent their adopting it; that the large states were weak at present in proportion to their extent and could only be made formidable to the small ones by the weight of their votes; that in case a dissolution of the Union should take place, the small states would have nothing to fear from their power; that if in such a case the three great states should league themselves together, the other ten could do so too, and that he had rather see partial confederacies take place than the plan on the table. This was the substance of the residue of his discourse, which was delivered with much diffuseness and considerable vehemence.

Mr. Lansing and Mr. Dayton moved to strike out "not" so that the seventh article might read "that the right of suffrage in the first branch ought to be according to the rule established by the Confederation."

Mr. Dayton expressed great anxiety that the question might not be put till tomorrow, Governor Livingston being kept away by indisposition and the representation of New Jersey thereby suspended.

Mr. Williamson thought that if any political truth could be grounded on mathematical demonstration, it was that if the states were equally sovereign now and parted with equal proportions of sovereignty, that they would remain equally sovereign. He could not comprehend how the smaller states would be injured in the case and wished some gentleman would vouchsafe a solution of it. He observed that the small states if they had a plurality of votes would have an interest in throwing the burdens off their own shoulders on those of the large ones. He begged that the expected addition of new states from the westward might be taken into view. They would be small states; they would be poor states; they would be unable to pay in proportion to their numbers, their distance from market, rendering the produce of their labor less valuable; they would, consequently, be tempted to combine for the purpose of laying burdens on commerce and consumption, which would fall with greater weight on the old states.

Mr. Madison said he was much disposed to concur in any expedient not inconsistent with fundamental principles that could remove the difficulty concerning the rule of representation. But he could neither be convinced that the rule contended for was just, nor that it was necessary for the safety of the small states against the large states. That it was not just had been conceded by Mr. Brearly and Mr. Paterson themselves. The expedient proposed by them was a new partition of the territory of the United States. The fallacy of the reasoning drawn from the equality of sovereign states in the formation of compacts lay in confounding mere treaties in which were specified certain duties to which the parties were to be bound, and certain rules by which their subjects were to be reciprocally governed in their intercourse with a compact by which an authority was created, paramount to the parties, and making laws for the government of them. If France, England, and Spain were to enter into a treaty for the regulation of commerce, and so forth, with the Prince of Monacho and four or five other of the smallest sovereigns of Europe, they would not hesitate to treat as equals and to make the regulations perfectly reciprocal. Would the case be the same if a council were to be formed of deputies from each, with authority and discretion to raise money, levy troops, determine the value of coin, and so forth? Would thirty or forty millions of people submit their fortunes into the hands of a few thousand? If they did, it would only prove that they expected more from the terror of their superior force than they feared from the selfishness of their feeble associates. Why are counties of the same states represented in proportion to their numbers? Is it because the representatives are chosen by the people themselves? So will be the representatives in the national legislature. Is it because the larger have more at stake than the smaller? The case will be the same with the larger and smaller states. Is it because the laws are to operate immediately on their per-

131

sons and properties? The same is the case in some degree as the Articles of Confederation stand; the same will be the case in a far greater degree under the plan proposed to be substituted. In the cases of captures, of piracies, and of offenses in a federal army, the property and persons of individuals depend on the laws of Congress. By the plan proposed, a complete power of taxation—the highest prerogative of supremacy—is proposed to be vested in the national Government. Many other powers are added which assimilate it to the government of individual states. The negative proposed on the state laws will make it an essential branch of the state legislatures and, of course, will require that it should be exercised by a body established on like principles with the branches of those legislatures. That it is not necessary to secure the small states against the large ones he conceived to be equally obvious. Was a combination of the large ones dreaded? This must arise either from some interest common to Virginia, Massachusetts, and Pennsylvania, and distinguishing them from the other states, or from the mere circumstance of similarity of size. Did any such common interest exist? In point of situation, they could not have been more effectually separated from each other by the most jealous citizen of the most jealous states. In point of manners, religion, and the other circumstances which sometimes beget affection between different communities, they were not more assimilated than the other states. In point of the staple productions, they were as dissimilar as any three other states in the Union. The staple of Massachusetts was fish, of Pennsylvania flour, of Virginia tobacco. Was a combination to be apprehended from the mere circumstance of equality of size? Experience suggested no such danger. The Journals of Congress did not present any peculiar association of these states in the votes recorded. It had never been seen that different counties in the same state, conformable in extent, but disagreeing in other circumstances, betrayed a propensity to such combinations. Experience rather taught a contrary lesson. Among individuals of superior eminence and weight in society, rivalships were much more frequent than coalitions. Among independent nations, pre-eminent over their neighbors, the same remark was verified. Carthage and Rome tore one another to pieces instead of uniting their forces to devour the weaker nations of the earth. The houses of Austria and France were hostile as long as they remained the greatest powers of Europe. England and France have succeeded to the pre-eminence and to the enmity. To this principle, we owe perhaps our liberty. A coalition between those powers would have been fatal to us. Among the principal members of ancient and modern confederacies, we find the same effect from the same cause. The contentions, not the coalitions, of Sparta, Athens, and Thebes proved fatal to the smaller members of the Amphictyonic confederacy. The contentions, not the combinations, of Russia and Austria have distracted and oppressed the German Empire. Were the large states formidable singly to their smaller neighbors? On this supposition, the latter ought to wish for such a general government as will operate with equal energy on the former as on themselves. The more lax the band, the more liberty the larger will have to avail themselves of their superior force. Here again experience was an instructive monitor. What is the situation of the weak compared with the strong in those stages of civilization in which the violence of individuals is least controlled by an efficient government? The heroic period of ancient Greece, the feudal licentiousness of the Middle Ages of Europe, the existing condition of the American savages answer this question. What is the situation of the minor sovereigns in the great society of independent nations in which the more powerful are under no control but the nominal authority of the law of nations? Is not the danger to the former exactly in proportion to their weakness? But there are cases still more in point. What was the condition of the weaker members of the Amphictyonic confederacy? Plutarch (see Life of Themistocles) will inform us that it happened but too often that the strongest cities corrupted and awed the weaker and that judgment went in favor of the more powerful party. What is the condition of the lesser states in the German confederacy? We all know that they are exceedingly trampled upon, and that they owe their safety, as far as they enjoy it, partly to their enlisting themselves under the rival banners of the pre-eminent members, partly to alliances with neighboring princes, which the constitution of the empire does not prohibit. What is the state of things in the lax system of the Dutch confederacy? Holland contains about half the people, supplies about half the money, and by her influence silently and indirectly governs the whole republic. In a word, the two extremes before us are a perfect separation and a perfect incorporation of the thirteen states. In the first case, they would be independent nations, subject to no law but the law of nations. In the last, they would be mere counties of one entire republic, subject to one common law. In the first case, the smaller states would have everything to fear from the larger. In the last, they would have nothing to fear. The true policy of the small states, therefore, lies in promoting those principles and that form of government which will most approximate the states to the condition of counties. Another consideration may be added. If the General Government be feeble, the larger states, distrusting its continuance, and foreseeing that their importance and security may depend on their own size and strength, will never submit to a partition. Give to the General Government sufficient energy and permanency, and you remove the objection. Gradual partitions of the large, and junctions of the small, states will be facilitated, and time may effect that equalization which is wished for by the small states now, but can never be accomplished at once.

Mr. Wilson: The leading argument of those who contend for equality of votes among the states is that the states, as such, being equal, and being represented, not as districts of individuals, but in their political and corporate capacities, are entitled to an equality of suffrage. According to this mode of reasoning, the representation of the boroughs in England, which has been allowed on all hands to be the rotten part of the constitution, is perfectly right and proper. They are, like the states, represented in their corporate capacity; like the states, therefore, they are entitled to equal voices—Old Sarum to as many as London. And instead of the injury supposed hitherto to be done to London, the true ground of complaint lies with Old Sarum, for London, instead of two, which is her proper share, sends four representatives to Parliament.

Mr. Sherman: The question is not what rights naturally belong to man, but how they may be most equally and effectually guarded in society. And if some give up more than others in order to obtain this end, there can be no room for complaint. To do otherwise, to require an equal concession from all, if it would create danger to the rights of some, would be sacrificing the end to the means. The rich man who enters into society along with the poor man gives up more than the poor man; yet with an equal vote, he is equally safe. Were he to have more votes than the poor man in proportion to his superior stake, the rights of the poor man would immediately cease to be secure. This consideration prevailed when the Articles of Confederation were formed.

The determination of the question for striking out the word "not," was put off till tomorrow at the request of the deputies from New York.

Dr. Franklin: Mr. President, the small progress we have made after four or five weeks' close attendance and continual reasonings with each other—our different sentiments on almost every question, several of the last producing as many noes as ayes—is, methinks, a melancholy proof of the imperfection of the human understanding. We indeed seem to feel our own want of political wisdom, since we have been running about in search of it. We have gone back to ancient history for models of government and examined the different forms of those republics which, having been formed with the seeds of their own dissolution, now no longer exist. And we have viewed modern states all around Europe, but find none of their constitutions suitable to our circumstances.

In this situation of this assembly, groping, as it were, in the dark, to find political truth, and scarce able to distinguish it when presented to us, how has it happened, sir, that we have not hitherto once thought of humbly applying to the Father of Lights to illuminate our understanding? In the beginning of the contest with Great Britain, when we were sensible of danger, we had daily prayer in this room for the divine protection. Our prayers, sir, were heard, and they were graciously answered. All of us who were engaged in the struggle must have observed frequent instances of a superintending Providence in our favor. To that kind Providence we owe this happy opportunity of consulting in peace on the means of establishing our future national felicity. And have we now forgotten that powerful Friend? Or do we imagine that we no longer need His assistance? I have lived, sir, a long time, and the longer I live, the more convincing proofs I see of this truth—that God governs in the affairs of men. And if a sparrow cannot fall to the ground without His notice, is it probable that an empire can rise without His aid? We have been assured, sir, in the sacred writings that "except the Lord build the house, they labor in vain that build it." I firmly believe this, and I also believe that without His concurring aid we shall succeed in this political building no better than the builders of Babel. We shall be divided by our little partial local interests; our projects will be confounded, and we ourselves shall become a reproach and byword down to future ages. And what is worse, mankind may hereafter from this unfortunate instance despair of establishing governments by human wisdom and leave it to chance, war, and conquest.

I, therefore, beg leave to move that, henceforth, prayers imploring the assistance of Heaven and its blessings on our deliberations be held in this assembly every morning before we proceed to business, and that one or more of the clergy of this city be requested to officiate in the service.

Mr. Sherman seconded the motion.

Mr. Hamilton and several others expressed their apprehensions that, however proper such a resolution might have been at the beginning of the convention, it might at this late day, in the first place, bring on it some disagreeable animadversions, and in the second, lead the public to believe that the embarrassments and dissensions within the convention had suggested this measure. It was answered by Dr.

Franklin, Mr. Sherman, and others that the past omission of a duty could not justify a further omission; that the rejection of such a proposition would expose the convention to more unpleasant animadversions than the adoption of it, and that the alarm out of doors that might be excited for the state of things within would at least be as likely to do good as ill.

Mr. Williamson observed that the true cause of the omission could not be mistaken. The convention had no funds.

Mr. Randolph proposed in order to give a favorable aspect to the measure that a sermon be preached at the request of the convention on the Fourth of July, the anniversary of Independence, and thenceforward prayers, and so forth, to be read in the convention every morning. Dr. Franklin seconded this motion. After several unsuccessful attempts for silently postponing this matter by adjourning, the adjournment was at length carried without any vote on the motion.

ARGUMENT BECOMES "ENDLESS CONTROVERSY" / *June 29*

In convention. Dr. Johnson: The controversy must be endless whilst gentlemen differ in the grounds of their arguments: those on one side considering the states as districts of people composing one political society; those on the other considering them as so many political societies. The fact is that the states do exist as political societies, and a government is to be formed for them in their political capacity, as well as for the individuals composing them. Does it not seem to follow that if the states, as such, are to exist, they must be armed with some power of self-defense? This is the idea of Col. Mason, who appears to have looked to the bottom of this matter. Besides the aristocratic and other interests, which ought to have the means of defending themselves, the states have their interests as such and are equally entitled to like means. On the whole, he thought that as, in some respects, the states are to be considered in their political capacity and, in others, as districts of individual citizens, the two ideas embraced on different sides, instead of being opposed to each other, ought to be combined— that in one branch the people ought to be represented; in the other, the states.

Mr. Gorham: The states as now confederated have no doubt a right to refuse to be consolidated or to be formed into any new system. But he wished the small states, which seemed most ready to object, to consider which are to give up most, they or the larger ones. He conceived that a rupture of the Union would be an event unhappy for all, but surely the large states would be least unable to take care of themselves and to make connections with one another. The weak, therefore, were most interested in establishing some general system for maintaining order. If among individuals composed partly of weak and partly of strong, the former most need the protection of law and government; the case is exactly the same with weak and powerful states. What would be the situation of Delaware (for these things, he found, must be spoken out, and it might as well be done at first as last); what would be the situation of Delaware in case of a separation of the states? Would she not be at the mercy of Pennsylvania? Would not her true interest lie in being consolidated with her, and ought she not now to wish for such a union with Pennsylvania, under one government, as will put it out of the power of Pennsylvania to oppress her? Nothing can be more ideal than the danger apprehended by the states from their being formed into one nation. Massachusetts was originally three colonies, namely, old Massachusetts, Plymouth, and the Province of Maine. These apprehensions existed then. An incorporation took place, all parties were safe and satisfied, and every distinction is now forgotten. The case was similar with Connecticut and New Haven. The dread of union was reciprocal; the consequence of it equally salutary and satisfactory. In like manner, New Jersey has been made one society out of two parts. Should a separation of the states take place, the fate of New Jersey would be worst of all. She has no foreign commerce and can have but little. Pennsylvania and New York will continue to levy taxes on her consumption. If she consults her interest, she would beg of all things to be annihilated. The apprehensions of the small states ought to be appeased by another reflection. Massachusetts will be divided. The Province of Maine is already considered as approaching the term of its annexation to it, and Pennsylvania will probably not increase, considering the present state of her population and other events that may happen. On the whole, he considered a union of the states as necessary to their happiness and a firm general government as necessary to their union. He should consider it his duty, if his colleagues viewed the matter in the same light he did, to stay here as long as any other state would remain with them in order to agree on some plan that could, with propriety, be recommended to the people.

Mr. Ellsworth did not despair. He still trusted that some good plan of government would be devised and adopted.

Mr. Read: He should have no objection to the system if it were truly national, but it has too much of a federal mixture in it. The little states, he thought, had not much to fear. He suspected that the large states felt their want of energy and wished for a general government to supply the defect. Massachusetts was evidently laboring under her weakness, and he believed Delaware would not be in much danger if in her neighborhood. Delaware had enjoyed tranquillity and, he flattered himself, would continue to do so. He was not, however, so selfish as not to wish for a good general government. In order to obtain one the whole states must be incorporated. If the states remain, the representatives of the large ones will stick together and carry everything before them. The executive also will be chosen under the influence of this partiality and will betray it in his administration. These jealousies are inseparable from the scheme of leaving the states in existence. They must be done away with. The ungranted lands, also, which have been assumed by particular states, must be given up. He repeated his approbation of the plan of Mr. Hamilton and wished it to be substituted for that on the table.

Mr. Madison agreed with Dr. Johnson that the mixed nature of the government ought to be kept in view, but thought too much stress was laid on the rank of the states as political societies. There was a gradation, he observed, from the smallest corporation with the most limited powers to the largest empire with the most perfect sovereignty. He pointed out the limitations on the sovereignty of the states as now confederated. Their laws in relation to the paramount law of the Confederacy were analogous to that of bylaws to the supreme law within a state. Under the proposed government, the powers of the states will be much further reduced. According to the views of every member, the General Government will have powers far beyond those exercised by the British Parliament when the states were part of the British Empire. It will, in particular, have the power, without the consent of the state legislatures, to levy money directly from the people themselves and, therefore, not to divest such unequal portions of the people as composed the several states of an equal voice, would subject the system to the reproaches and evils which have resulted from the vicious representation in Great Britain.

He entreated the gentlemen representing the small states to renounce a principle which was confessedly unjust, which could never be admitted, and which, if admitted, must infuse mortality into a constitution which we wished to last forever. He prayed them to ponder well the consequences of suffering the Confederacy to go to pieces. It had been said that the want of energy in the large states would be a security to the small. It was forgotten that this want of energy proceeded from the supposed security of the states against all external danger. Let each state depend on itself for its security, and let apprehensions arise of danger from distant powers or from neighboring states, and the languishing condition of all the states, large as well as small, would soon be transformed into vigorous and high-toned governments. His great fear was that their governments would then have too much energy; that this might not only be formidable in the large to the small states, but fatal to the internal liberty of all. The same causes which have rendered the old world the theater of incessant wars and have banished liberty from the face of it would soon produce the same effects here. The weakness and jealousy of the small states would quickly introduce some regular military force against sudden danger from their powerful neighbors. The example would be followed by others and would soon become universal. In time of actual war, great discretionary powers are constantly given to the executive magistrate. Constant apprehension of war has the same tendency to render the head too large for the body. A standing military force with an overgrown executive will not long be safe companions to liberty. The means of defense against foreign danger have been always the instruments of tyranny at home. Among the Romans, it was a standing maxim to excite a war whenever a revolt was apprehended. Throughout all Europe, the armies kept up under the pretext of defending have enslaved the people. It is perhaps questionable whether the best-concerted system of absolute power in Europe could maintain itself in a situation where no alarms of external danger could tame the people to the domestic yoke. The insular situation of Great Britain was the principal cause of her being an exception to the general fate of Europe. It has rendered less defense necessary and admitted a kind of defense which could not be used for the purpose of oppression. These consequences, he conceived, ought to be apprehended whether the states should run into a total separation from each other or should enter into partial confederacies. Either event would be truly deplorable, and those who might be necessary to either could never be forgiven by their country, nor by themselves.

Mr. Hamilton[1] observed that individuals forming political societies modify their rights differently with regard to suffrage. Examples of it are found in all the states. In all of them some individuals are deprived of the right altogether, not having the requisite qualification of property. In some of the states, the right of suffrage is allowed in some cases and refused in others. To vote for a member in one branch, a certain quantum of property, to vote for a member in another branch of the legislature, a higher quantum of property, is required. In like manner, states may modify their right of suffrage differently, the larger exercis-

_139_

[1] From this date, Hamilton was absent until September.

ing a larger, the smaller a smaller, share of it. But as states are a collection of individual men, which ought we to respect most: the rights of the people composing them or of the artificial beings resulting from the composition? Nothing could be more preposterous or absurd than to sacrifice the former to the latter. It has been said that if the smaller states renounce their equality, they renounce, at the same time, their liberty. The truth is, it is a contest for power, not for liberty. Will the men composing the small states be less free than those composing the larger? The state of Delaware, having forty-thousand souls, will lose power if she has one-tenth only of the votes allowed to Pennsylvania, having four hundred thousand, but will the people of Delaware be less free if each citizen has an equal vote with each citizen of Pennsylvania? He admitted that common residence within the same state would produce a certain degree of attachment, and that this principle might have a certain influence on public affairs. He thought, however, that this might by some precautions be in a great measure excluded, and that no material inconvenience could result from it, as there could not be any ground for combination among the states whose influence was most dreaded. The only considerable distinction of interests lay between the carrying and non-carrying states —which divides, instead of uniting, the largest states. No considerable inconvenience had been found from the division of the state of New York into different districts of different sizes.

Some of the consequences of a dissolution of the Union and the establishment of partial confederacies had been pointed out. He would add another of a most serious nature. Alliances will immediately be formed with different rival and hostile nations of Europe, who will foment disturbances among ourselves and make us parties to all their own quarrels. Foreign nations having American dominion are, and must be, jealous of us. Their representatives betray the utmost anxiety for our fate and for the result of this meeting, which must have an essential influence on it. It had been said that respectability in the eyes of foreign nations was not the object at which we aimed, that the proper object of republican government was domestic tranquillity and happiness. This was an ideal distinction. No government could give us tranquillity and happiness at home which did not possess sufficient stability and strength to make us respectable abroad. This was the critical moment for forming such a government. We should run every risk in trusting to future amendments. As yet we retain the habits of union. We are weak and sensible of our weakness. Henceforward, the motives will become feebler and the difficulties greater. It is a miracle that we are now here, exercising

our tranquil and free deliberations on the subject. It would be mad- *141*
ness to trust to future miracles. A thousand causes must obstruct a re-
production of them.

Mr. Pierce considered the equality of votes under the Confederation
as the great source of the public difficulties. The members of Congress
were advocates for local advantages. State distinctions must be sacrificed as far as the general good required, but without destroying the
states. Though from a small state, he felt himself a citizen of the
United States.

Mr. Gerry urged that we never were independent states, were not
such now, and never could be, even on the principles of the Confederation. The states and the advocates for them were intoxicated with the
idea of their sovereignty. He was a member of Congress at the time
the Federal Articles were formed. The injustice of allowing each state
an equal vote was long insisted on. He voted for it, but it was against
his judgment and under the pressure of public danger and the obstinacy of the lesser states. The present Confederation he considered as
dissolving. The fate of the Union will be decided by the convention.
If they do not agree on something, few delegates will probably be appointed to Congress. If they do, Congress will probably be kept up till
the new system should be adopted. He lamented that instead of coming here like a band of brothers belonging to the same family,
we seemed to have brought with us the spirit of political negotiators.

Mr. L. Martin remarked that the language of the states being sovereign and independent was once familiar and understood; though it
seemed now so strange and obscure. He read those passages in the
Articles of Confederation which describe them in that language.

*The motion that the rule of suffrage in the first branch ought not
to be according to that established by the Articles of the Confederation
passed, 6 to 4.*

Dr. Johnson and Mr. Ellsworth moved to postpone the residue of
the clause and take up the eighth resolution.

EQUALITY OF STATES IN THE SENATE MOVED / *June 29*

Mr. Ellsworth moved "that the rule of suffrage in the second branch
be the same with that established by the Articles of Confederation."
He was not sorry on the whole, he said, that the vote just passed had
determined against this rule in the first branch. He hoped it would become a ground of compromise with regard to the second branch. We
were partly national, partly federal. The proportional representation

in the first branch was conformable to the national principle and would secure the large states against the small. An equality of voices was conformable to the federal principle and was necessary to secure the small states against the large. He trusted that on this middle ground a compromise would take place. He did not see that it could on any other, and if no compromise should take place, our meeting would not only be in vain, but worse than in vain. To the eastward, he was sure Massachusetts was the only state that would listen to a proposition for excluding the states as equal political societies from an equal voice in both branches. The others would risk every consequence rather than part with so dear a right. An attempt to deprive them of it was at once cutting the body of America in two, and as he supposed would be the case, somewhere about this part of it. The large states, he conceived, would, notwithstanding the equality of votes, have an influence that would maintain their superiority. Holland, as had been admitted (by Mr. Madison), had, notwithstanding a like equality in the Dutch confederacy, a prevailing influence in the public measures. The power of self-defense was essential to the small states. Nature had given it to the smallest insect of the creation. He could never admit that there was no danger of combinations among the large states. They will, like individuals, find out and avail themselves of the advantage to be gained by it. It was true the danger would be greater if they were contiguous and had a more immediate and common interest. A defensive combination of the small states was rendered more difficult by their greater number. He would mention another consideration of great weight. The existing Confederation was founded on the equality of the states in the article of suffrage—was it meant to pay no regard to this antecedent plighted faith? Let a strong executive, a judiciary, and legislative power be created, but let not too much be attempted by which all may be lost. He was not in general a half-way man, yet he preferred doing half the good we could, rather than do nothing at all. The other half may be added when the necessity shall be more fully experienced.

Mr. Baldwin could have wished that the powers of the general legislature had been defined before the mode of constituting it had been agitated. He should vote against the motion of Mr. Ellsworth, though he did not like the resolution as it stood in the report of the committee of the whole. He thought the second branch ought to be the representation of property, and that in forming it, therefore, some reference ought to be had to the relative wealth of their constituents and to the principles on which the Senate of Massachusetts was constituted. He concurred with those who thought it would be impossible

for the general legislature to extend its cares to the local matters of   *143*
the states.

EQUALITY OF STATES ARGUED / *June 30*

Mr. Wilson did not expect such a motion after the establishment of
the contrary principle in the first branch, and considering the reasons
which would oppose it even if an equal vote had been allowed in the
first branch. The gentleman from Connecticut (Mr. Ellsworth) had
pronounced that if the motion should not be acceded to, of all the
states north of Pennsylvania one only would agree to any general government. He entertained more favorable hopes of Connecticut and of
the other northern states. He hoped the alarms exceeded their cause,
and that they would not abandon a country to which they were bound
by so many strong and endearing ties. But should the deplored event
happen, it would neither stagger his sentiments nor his duty. If the
minority of the people of America refuse to coalesce with the majority
on just and proper principles, if a separation must take place, it could
never happen on better grounds. The votes of yesterday against the
just principle of representation were as twenty-two to ninety of the
people of America. Taking the opinions to be the same on this point,
and he was sure if there was any room for change it could not be on
the side of the majority, the question will be, shall less than one-quar-
ter of the United States withdraw themselves from the Union, or shall
more than three-quarters renounce the inherent, indisputable, and un-
alienable rights of men in favor of the artificial systems of states. If
issue must be joined, it was on this point he would choose to join. The
gentleman from Connecticut, in supposing that the preponderancy
secured to the majority in the first branch had removed the objections
to an equality of votes in the second branch for the security of the minority, narrowed the case extremely. Such an equality will enable the
minority to control in all cases whatsoever, the sentiments and interests of the minority. Seven states will control six: seven states according to the estimates that had been used, composed twenty-four
nintieths of the whole people. It would be in the power then of less
than one-third to overrule two-thirds whenever a question should happen to divide the states in that manner. Can we forget for whom we
are forming a government? Is it for *men,* or for the imaginary beings
called *states?* Will our honest constituents be satisfied with metaphys-
ical distinctions? Will they, ought they to be satisfied with being told
that the one-third compose the greater number of states. The rule of

suffrage ought on every principle to be the same in the second as in the first branch. If the government be not laid on this foundation, it can be neither solid nor lasting; any other principle will be local, confined, and temporary. This will expand with the expansion and grow with the growth of the United States. Much has been said of an imaginary combination of three states. Sometimes a danger of monarchy, sometimes of aristocracy has been charged on it. No explanation, however, of the danger has been vouchsafed. It would be easy to prove both from reason and history that rivalships would be more probable than coalitions and that there are no coinciding interests that could produce the latter. No answer has yet been given to the observations of Mr. Madison on this subject. Should the executive magistrate be taken from one of the large states, would not the other two be thereby thrown into the scale with the other states? Whence then the danger of monarchy? Are the people of the three large states more aristocratic than those of the small ones? Whence then the danger of aristocracy from their influence? It is all a mere illusion of names. We talk of states till we forget what they are composed of. Is a real fair majority the natural hotbed of aristocracy? It is a part of the definition of this species of government, or rather of tyranny, that the smaller number governs the greater. It is true that a majority of states in the second branch can not carry a law against a majority of the people in the first. But this removes half only of the objection. Bad governments are of two sorts: 1. That which does too little; 2. That which does too much; that which fails through weakness, and that which destroys through oppression. Under which of these evils do the United States at present groan? Under the weakness and inefficiency of its government. To remedy this weakness we have been sent to this convention. If the motion should be agreed to, we shall leave the United States fettered precisely as heretofore, with the additional mortification of seeing the good purposes of fair representation of the people in the first branch defeated in the second. Twenty-four will still control sixty-six. He lamented that such a disagreement should prevail on the point of representation as he did not foresee that it would happen on the other point most contested, the boundary between the general and the local authorities. He thought the states necessary and valuable parts of a good system.

MOVE FOR EQUALITY DEFENDED / *June 30*

Mr. Ellsworth: The capital objection of Mr. Wilson, "that the minority will rule the majority," is not true. The power is given to the few to save them from being destroyed by the many. If an equality of votes **145** had been given to them in both branches, the objection might have had weight. Is it a novel thing that the few should have a check on the many? Is it not the case in the British constitution, the wisdom of which so many gentlemen have united in applauding? Have not the House of Lords, who form so small a proportion of the nation, a negative on the laws as a necessary defense of their peculiar rights against the encroachments of the Commons? No instance of a confederacy has existed in which an equality of voices has not been exercised by the members of it. We are running from one extreme to another. We are razing the foundations of the building when we need only repair the roof. No salutary measure has been lost for want of a majority of the states to favor it. If security be all that the great states wish for, the first branch secures them. The danger of combinations among them is not imaginary. Although no particular abuses could be foreseen by him, the possibility of them would be sufficient to alarm him. But he could easily conceive cases in which they might result from such combinations. Suppose that in pursuance of some commercial treaty or arrangement, three or four free ports, and no more, were to be established, would not combinations be formed in favor of Boston, Philadelphia, and some port of the Chesapeake? A like concert might be formed in the appointment of the great offices. He appealed again to the obligations of the Federal pact, which was still in force and which had been entered into with so much solemnity, persuading himself that some regard would still be paid to the plighted faith under which each state, small as well as great, held an equal right of suffrage in the general councils. His remarks were not the result of partial or local views. The state he represented (Connecticut) held a middle rank.

MOVE FOR EQUALITY ATTACKED / *June 30*

Mr. Madison did justice to the able and close reasoning of Mr. Ellsworth but must observe that it did not always accord with itself. On another occasion, the large states were described by him as the aristocratic states, ready to oppress the small. Now the small are the House of Lords, requiring a negative to defend them against the more numerous Commons. Mr. Ellsworth had also erred in saying that no instance had existed in which confederated states had not retained to themselves a perfect equality of suffrage. Passing over the German system, in which the King of Prussia has nine voices, he reminded Mr. Ellsworth of the Lycian confederacy in which the component members had votes proportioned to their importance and which Montesquieu recommends as the fittest model for that form of government. Had the fact been as stated by Mr. Ellsworth, it would have been of little avail to him, or rather would have strengthened the arguments against him; the history and fate of the several confederacies, modern as well as ancient, demonstrating some radical vice in their structure. In reply to the appeal of Mr. Ellsworth to the faith plighted in the existing Federal compact, he remarked that the party claiming from others an adherence to a common engagement ought at least to be guiltless itself of a violation. Of all the states, however, Connecticut was perhaps least able to urge this plea. Besides the various omissions to perform the stipulated acts from which no state was free, the legislature of that state had by a pretty recent vote positively refused to pass a law for complying with the requisitions of Congress and had transmitted a copy of the vote to Congress. It was urged, he said, continually, that an equality of votes in the second branch was not only necessary to secure the small, but would be perfectly safe to the large ones, whose majority in the first branch was an effectual bulwark. But notwithstanding this apparent defense, the majority of states might still injure the majority of the people. In the first place, they could obstruct the wishes and interests of the majority. Secondly, they could extort measures repugnant to the wishes and interest of the majority. Thirdly, they could impose measures adverse thereto, as the second branch will probably exercise some great powers in which the first will not participate. He admitted that every peculiar interest, whether in any class of citizens or any description of states, ought to be secured as far as possible. Wherever there is danger of attack, there ought to be given a constitutional power of defense. But he contended that the states were divided into different interests, not by their difference of size, but by other circumstances; the most material of which resulted partly from climate, but principally from the effects of their having or not having slaves. These two causes concurred in forming the great division of interests in the United States. It did not lie between the large and small states. It lay between the northern and southern, and if any defensive power were necessary, it ought to be mutually given to these two interests. He was so strongly impressed with this important truth that he had been casting about in his mind for some expedient that would answer the purpose. The one which had occurred was that instead of proportioning the votes of the states in both branches to their respective numbers of inhabitants, computing the slaves in the ratio of five to three, they should be represented in one branch according to the number of free inhabitants only, and in the other, according to the whole number, counting the slaves as free. By this arrangement the southern scale would have the advantage in one house, and the northern in the other. He had been restrained from proposing this expedient by two considerations: one was his unwillingness to urge any diversity of interests on an occasion where it is but too apt to arise of it- self; the other was the inequality of powers that must be vested in the two branches and which would destroy the equilibrium of interests.

Mr. Ellsworth assured the house that, whatever might be thought of the representatives of Connecticut, the state was entirely federal in her disposition. He appealed to her great exertions during the war in supplying both men and money. The muster-rolls would show she had more troops in the field than Virginia. If she had been delinquent, it had been from inability and not more so than other states.

DEBATE DEADLOCKED / *June 30*

Mr. Sherman: Mr. Madison animadverted on the delinquency of the states when his object required him to prove that the constitution of Congress was faulty. Congress is not to blame for the faults of the states. Their measures have been right and the only thing wanting has been a further power in Congress to render them effectual.

Mr. Davie was much embarrassed and wished for explanations. The report of the committee allowing the legislatures to choose the Senate, and establishing a proportional representation in it seemed to be im- practicable. There will, according to this rule, be ninety members in the outset and the number will increase as new states are added. It was impossible that so numerous a body could possess the activity and other qualities required in it. Were he to vote on the comparative merits of the report as it stood, and the amendment, he should be constrained to prefer the latter. The appointment of the Senate by electors chosen by the people for that purpose was, he conceived, liable to an insupera- ble difficulty. The larger counties or districts, thrown into a general district, would certainly prevail over the smaller counties or districts, and merit in the latter would be excluded altogether. The report, therefore, seemed to be right in referring the appointment to the legis- latures, whose agency in the general system did not appear to him ob- jectionable, as it did to some others. The fact was that the local prej- udices and interests, which could not be denied to exist, would find their way into the national councils, whether the representatives should be chosen by the legislatures or by the people themselves. On the other hand, if a proportional representation was attended with in- superable difficulties, making the Senate the representative of the states looked like bringing us back to Congress again and shutting out all the advantages expected from it. Under this view of the subject, he could not vote for any plan for the Senate yet proposed. He thought that in general there were extremes on both sides. We were partly federal, partly national, in our union, and he did not see why the government might not in some respects operate on the states, in others on the people.

Mr. Wilson admitted the question concerning the number of senators to be embarrassing. If the smallest states be allowed one, and the others in proportion, the Senate will certainly be too numerous. He looked forward to the time when the smallest states will contain a hundred-thousand souls at least. Let there be then one senator in each for every hundred-thousand souls, and let the states not having that number of inhabitants be allowed one. He was willing himself to submit to this temporary concession to the small states and threw out the idea as a ground of compromise.

Dr. Franklin: The diversity of opinions turns on two points. If a proportional representation takes place, the small states contend that their liberties will be in danger. If an equality of votes is to be put in its place, the large states say their money will be in danger. When a broad table is to be made and the edges of planks do not fit, the artist takes a little from both and makes a good joint. In like manner here both sides must part with some of their demands in order that they may join in some accommodating proposition. He had prepared one, which he would read, that it might lie on the table for consideration. The proposition was in the words following:

"That the legislatures of the several states shall choose and send an equal number of delegates, namely _____, who are to compose the second branch of the general legislature.

"That in all cases or questions wherein the sovereignty of individual states may be affected, or whereby their authority over their own citizens may be diminished, or the authority of the General Government within the several states augmented, each state shall have equal suffrage.

"That in the appointment of all civil officers of the General Government, in the election of whom the second branch may by the Constitution have part, each state shall have equal suffrage.

"That in fixing the salaries of such officers, and in all allowances for public services, and generally in all appropriations and dispositions of money to be drawn out of the general treasury, and in all laws for supplying that treasury, the delegates of the several states shall have suffrage in proportion to the sums which their respective states do actually contribute to the treasury."

Where a ship had many owners, this was the rule of deciding on her expedition. He had been one of the ministers from this country to France during the joint war and would have been very glad if allowed a vote in distributing the money to carry it on.

Mr. King observed that the simple question was whether each state should have an equal vote in the second branch; that it must be apparent to those gentlemen who liked neither the motion for this equality nor the report as it stood that the report was as susceptible of melioration as the motion; that a reform would be nugatory and nominal only if we should make another Congress of the proposed Senate; that if the adherence to an equality of votes was fixed and unalterable, there could not be less obstinacy on the other side; and that we were in fact cut asunder already, and it was in vain to shut our eyes against it; that he was, however, filled with astonishment that if we were convinced that every man in America was secured in all his rights, we should be ready to sacrifice this substantial good to the phantom of state sovereignty; that his feelings were more harrowed and his fears more agitated for his country than he could express; that he conceived this to be the last opportunity of providing for its liberty and happiness; that he could not, therefore, but repeat his amazement that when a just government founded on a fair representation of the people of America was within our reach, we should renounce the blessing from an attachment to the ideal freedom and importance of states; that should this wonderful illusion continue to prevail his mind was prepared for every event rather than sit down under a government founded on a vicious principle of representation and which must be as short-lived as it would be unjust. He might prevail on himself to accede to some such expedient as had been hinted by Mr. Wilson, but he never could listen to an equality of votes, as proposed in the motion.

Mr. Dayton: When assertion is given for proof and terror substituted for argument, he presumed they would have no effect, however eloquently spoken. It should have been shown that the evils we have experienced have proceeded from the equality now objected to and that the seeds of dissolution for the state governments are not sown in the General Government. He considered the system on the table as a novelty, an amphibious monster, and was persuaded that it never would be received by the people.

Mr. Martin would never confederate if it could not be done on just principles.

Mr. Madison would acquiesce in the concession hinted by Mr. Wilson on condition that a due independence should be given to the Senate. The plan in its present shape makes the Senate absolutely dependent on the states. The Senate, therefore, is only another edition of Congress. He knew the faults of that body and had used a bold language against it. Still he would preserve the state rights as carefully as the trial by jury.

Mr. Bedford contended that there was no middle way between a perfect consolidation and a mere confederacy of the states. The first is out of the question, and in the latter they must continue, if not perfectly, yet equally, sovereign. If political societies possess ambition, avarice, and all the other passions which render them formidable to each other, ought we not to view them in this light here? Will not the same motives operate in America as elsewhere? If any gentleman doubts it, let him look at the votes. Have they not been dictated by interest, by ambition? Are not the large states evidently seeking to aggrandize themselves at the expense of the small? They think, no doubt, that they have right on their side, but interest has blinded their eyes. Look at Georgia. Though a small state at present, she is actuated by the prospect of soon being a great one. South Carolina is actuated both by present interest and future prospects. She hopes, too, to see the other states cut down to her own dimensions. North Carolina has the same motives of present and future interest. Virginia follows. Maryland is not on that side of the question. Pennsylvania has a direct and future interest. Massachusetts has a decided and palpable interest in the part she takes. Can it be expected that the small states will act from pure disinterestedness? Look at Great Britain. Is the representation there less unequal? But we shall be told again that that is the rotten part of the constitution. Have not the boroughs, however, held fast their constitutional rights? And are we to act with greater purity than the rest of mankind? An exact proportion in the representation is not preserved in any one of the states. Will it be said that an inequality of power will not result from an inequality of votes? Give the opportunity, and ambition will not fail to abuse it. The whole history of mankind proves it. The three large states have a common interest to bind them together in commerce. But whether a combination, as we supposed, or a competition, as others supposed, shall take place among them, in either case the small states must be ruined. We must, like Solon, make such a government as the people will approve. Will the smaller states ever agree to the proposed degradation of them? It is not true that the people will not agree to enlarge the powers of the present Congress. The language of the people has been that Congress ought to have the power of collecting an impost and of coercing the states where it may be necessary. On the first point they have been explicit and, in a manner, unanimous in their declarations. And must they not agree to this and similar measures if they ever mean to discharge their engagements? The little states are willing to observe their engagements, but will meet the large ones on no ground but that of the Confederation. We have been told with a dictatorial air that this is the last moment for a fair trial in favor of a good government. It will be the last, indeed, if the propositions reported from the committee go forth to the people. He was under no apprehensions. The large states dare not dissolve the Confederation. If they do, the small ones will find some foreign ally of more honor and good faith who will take them by the hand and do them justice. He did not mean by this to intimidate or alarm. It was a natural consequence, which ought to be avoided by enlarging the federal powers, not annihilating the federal system. This is what the people expect. All agree in the necessity of a more efficient government, and why not make such a one as they desire?

Mr. Ellsworth: Under a national government, he should participate in the national security, as remarked by Mr. King, but that was all. What he wanted was domestic happiness. The national Government could not descend to the local objects on which this depended. It could only embrace objects of a general nature. He turned his eyes, therefore, for the preservation of his rights to the state governments. From these alone he could derive the greatest happiness he expects in this life. His happiness depends on their existence, as much as a newborn infant on its mother for nourishment. If this reasoning was not satisfactory, he had nothing to add that could be so.

Mr. King was for preserving the states in a subordinate degree and as far as they could be necessary for the purposes stated by Mr. Ellsworth. He did not think a full answer had been given to those who apprehended a dangerous encroachment on their jurisdictions. Expedients might be devised, as he conceived, that would give them all the security the nature of things would admit of. In the establishment of societies, the Constitution was to the legislature what the laws were to individuals. As the fundamental rights of individuals are secured by express provisions in the state constitutions, why may not a like security be provided for the rights of states in the national Constitution? The articles of union between England and Scotland furnish an example of such a provision in favor of sundry rights of Scotland. When that union was in agitation, the same language of apprehension which has been heard from the smaller states was in the mouths of the Scotch patriots. The articles, however, have not been violated, and the Scotch have found an increase of prosperity and happiness. He was aware that this will be called a mere paper security. He thought it a sufficient answer to say that if fundamental articles of compact are no sufficient defense against physical power, neither will there be any safety against it if there be no compact. He could not sit down without taking some notice of the language of the honorable gentleman from Delaware (Mr. Bedford). It was not he that had uttered a dictatorial language. This intemperance had marked the honorable gentleman himself. It was not he who with a vehemence unprecedented in that house had declared himself ready to turn his hopes from our common country and court the protection of some foreign hand. This, too, was the language of the honorable member himself. He was grieved that such an expression had entered his heart. He was more grieved that such an expression had dropped from his lips. The gentleman could only excuse it to himself on the score of passion. For himself, whatever might be his distress, he would never court relief from a foreign power.

The "Great Compromise"

Editor's note: To break the deadlock over the question of equality of representation in the Senate, the convention on July 2 elected a committee of eleven—one from each state. Three days later, on July 5, the committee submitted its report which formed the basis of the "Great Compromise." This provided that each state should have an equal vote in the Senate, that each should have one representative in the House of Representatives for every 40,000 persons in the population, and that money bills should originate in the latter.

After debates that lasted until July 24, when a committee of five was appointed to draft a constitution, these proposals were finally adopted.

ALL-STATE COMMITTEE TO BREAK DEADLOCK / *July 2*

On the question for allowing each state one vote in the second branch as moved by Mr. Ellsworth, it was lost by an equal division of votes, 5 to 5.

Mr. Pinckney thought an equality of votes in the second branch inadmissible. At the same time, candor obliged him to admit that the large states would feel a partiality for their own citizens and give them a preference in appointments, that they might also find some common

points in their commercial interests and promote treaties favorable *153*
to them. There is a real distinction between the northern and southern interests. North Carolina, South Carolina, and Georgia, in their
rice and indigo, had a peculiar interest which might be sacrificed.
How, then, shall the larger states be prevented from administering
the General Government as they please without being themselves
unduly subjected to the will of the smaller? By allowing them some,
but not a full proportion. He was extremely anxious that something
should be done, considering this as the last appeal to a regular experiment. Congress have failed in almost every effort for an amendment
of the federal system. Nothing has prevented a dissolution of it but
the appointment of this convention and he could not express his
alarms for the consequence of such an event. He read his motion to
form the states into classes with an apportionment of senators among
them.

Gen. Pinckney was willing the motion might be considered. He did
not entirely approve it. He liked better the motion of Dr. Franklin.
Some compromise seemed to be necessary, the states being exactly divided on the question for an equality of votes in the second branch.
He proposed that a committee consisting of a member from each state
should be appointed to devise and report some compromise.

Mr. L. Martin had no objection to a commitment, but no modifications whatever could reconcile the smaller states to the least diminution of their equal sovereignty.

Mr. Sherman: We are now at a full stop, and nobody, he supposed,
meant that we should break up without doing something. A committee
he thought most likely to hit on some expedient.

Mr. Gouverneur Morris thought a committee advisable as the convention had been equally divided. He had a stronger reason also. The
mode of appointing the second branch tended, he was sure, to defeat
the object of it. What is this object? To check the precipitation,
changeableness, and excesses of the first branch. Every man of observation had seen in the democratic branches of the state legislatures precipitation—in Congress, changeableness—in every department, excesses against personal liberty, private property, and personal safety.
What qualities are necessary to constitute a check in this case? Abilities and virtue are equally necessary in both branches. Something
more then is now wanted. In the first place, the checking branch must
have a personal interest in checking the other branch. One interest
must be opposed to another interest. Vices, as they exist, must be
turned against each other. In the second place, it must have great personal property; it must have the aristocratic spirit; it must love to lord

it through pride. Pride is, indeed, the great principle that actuates both the poor and the rich. It is this principle which in the former resists, in the latter abuses, authority. In the third place, it should be independent. In religion, the creature is apt to forget its Creator. That it is otherwise in political affairs, the late debates here are an unhappy proof. The aristocratic body should be as independent and as firm as the democratic. If the members of it are to revert to a dependence on the democratic choice, the democratic scale will preponderate. All the guards contrived by America have not restrained the senatorial branches of the legislatures from a servile complaisance to the democratic. If the second branch is to be dependent, we are better without it. To make it independent, it should be for life. It will then do wrong, it will be said. He believed so; he hoped so. The rich will strive to establish their dominion and enslave the rest. They always did. They always will. The proper security against them is to form them into a separate interest. The two forces will then control each other. Let the rich mix with the poor and in a commercial country they will establish an oligarchy. Take away commerce and the democracy will triumph. Thus it has been all the world over. So it will be among us. Reason tells us we are but men, and we are not to expect any particular interference of Heaven in our favor. By thus combining and setting apart the aristocratic interest, the popular interest will be combined against it. There will be a mutual check and mutual security. In the fourth place, an independence for life involves the necessary permanency. If we change our measures nobody will trust us, and how avoid a change of measures, but by avoiding a change of men? Ask any man if he confides in Congress—if he confides in the state of Pennsylvania—if he will lend his money or enter into contract? He will tell you no. He sees no stability. He can repose no confidence. If Great Britain were to explain her refusal to treat with us, the same reasoning would be employed. He disliked the exclusion of the second branch from holding offices. It is dangerous. It is like the imprudent exclusion of the military officers during the war from civil appointments. It deprives the executive of the principal source of influence. If danger be apprehended from the executive, what a left-handed way is this of obviating it! If the son, the brother, or the friend can be appointed, the danger may be even increased, as the disqualified father, and so forth, can then boast of a disinterestedness which he does not possess. Besides, shall the best, the most able, the most virtuous citizens, not be permitted to hold offices? Who then are to hold them? He was also against paying the senators. They will pay themselves if they can. If they cannot, they will be rich and can do without it. Of such the second branch ought to consist and none but such can compose it if they are not to be paid. He contended that the executive should appoint the Senate and fill up vacancies. This gets rid of the difficulty in the present question. You may begin with any ratio you please; it will come to the same thing. The members being independent, and for life, may be taken as well from one place as from another. It should be considered, too, how the scheme could be carried through the states. He hoped there was strength of mind enough in this house to look truth in the face. He did not hesitate, therefore, to say that loaves and fishes must bribe the demagogues. They must be made to expect higher offices under the general than the state governments. A Senate for life will be a noble bait. Without such captivating prospects, the popular leaders will oppose and defeat the plan. He perceived that the first branch was to be chosen by the people of the states, the second by those chosen by the people. Is not here a government by the states—a government by compact between Virginia in the first and second branch, Massachusetts in the first and second branch, and so forth? This is going back to mere treaty. It is no government at all. It is altogether dependent on the states and will act over again the part which Congress has acted. A firm government alone can protect our liberties. He fears the influence of the rich. They will have the same effect here as elsewhere if we do not by such a government keep them within their proper spheres. We should remember that the people never act from reason alone. The rich will take the advantage of their passions and make these the instruments for oppressing them. The result of the contest will be a violent aristocracy or a more violent despotism. The schemes of the rich will be favored by the extent of the country. The people in such distant parts cannot communicate and act in concert. They will be the dupes of those who have more knowledge and intercourse. The only security against encroachments will be a select and sagacious body of men instituted to watch against them on all sides. He meant only to hint these observations without grounding any motion on them.

Mr. Randolph favored the commitment, though he did not expect much benefit from the expedient. He animadverted on the warm and rash language of Mr. Bedford on Saturday; reminded the small states that if the large states should combine, some danger of which he did not deny, there would be a check in the revisionary power of the executive, and intimated that in order to render this still more effectual, he would agree that in the choice of an executive each state should have an equal vote. He was persuaded that two such opposite bodies as Mr. Morris had planned could never long co-exist. Dissensions would arise, as has been seen even between the senate and house of delegates in Maryland, appeals would be made to the people, and in a little time commotions would be the result. He was far from thinking the large states could subsist of themselves any more than the small; an avulsion would involve the whole in ruin, and he was determined to pursue such a scheme of government as would secure us against such a calamity.

Mr. Strong was for the commitment and hoped the mode of constituting both branches would be referred. If they should be established on different principles, contentions would prevail, and there would never be a concurrence in necessary measures.

Dr. Williamson: If we do not concede on both sides, our business must soon be at an end. He approved of the commitment, supposing that as the committee would be a smaller body, a compromise would be pursued with more coolness.

Mr. Wilson objected to the committee, because it would decide according to that very rule of voting which was opposed on one side. Experience in Congress had also proved the inutility of committees consisting of members from each state.

Mr. Lansing would not oppose the commitment, though expecting little advantage from it.

Mr. Madison opposed the commitment. He had rarely seen any other effect than delay from *such* committees in Congress. Any scheme of compromise that could be proposed in the committee might as easily be proposed in the house, and the report of the committee, where it contained merely the *opinion* of the committee, would neither shorten the discussion, nor influence the decision of the house.

Mr. Gerry was for the commitment. Something must be done or we shall disappoint not only America, but the whole world. He suggested a consideration of the state we should be thrown into by the failure of the Union. We should be without an umpire to decide controversies and must be at the mercy of events. What, too, is to become of our treaties—what of our foreign debts—what of our domestic? We must make concessions on both sides. Without these, the constitutions of the several states would never have been formed.

Motion passed, 9 to 2.

The committee elected by ballot were Mr. Gerry, Mr. Ellsworth, Mr. Yates, Mr. Paterson, Dr. Franklin, Mr. Bedford, Mr. Martin, Mr. Mason, Mr. Davie, Mr. Rutledge, Mr. Baldwin.

That time might be given to the committee and to such as choose to attend to the celebrations on the anniversary of Independence, the convention adjourned till Thursday.

Mr. Gerry delivered in from the committee appointed on Monday last the following report:

"The committee to whom was referred the eighth resolution of the report from the committee of the whole house, and so much of the seventh as has not been decided on, submit the following report:

"That the subsequent propositions be recommended to the convention on condition that both shall be generally adopted.

"1. That in the first branch of the legislature, each of the states now in the Union shall be allowed one member for every forty-thousand inhabitants of the description reported in the seventh resolution of the committee of the whole house; that each state not containing that number shall be allowed one member; that all bills for raising or appropriating money and for fixing the salaries of the officers of the Government of the United States shall originate in the first branch of the legislature and shall not be altered or amended by the second branch, and that no money shall be drawn from the public treasury but in pursuance of appropriations to be originated in the first branch.

"2. That in the second branch, each state shall have an equal vote."

Mr. Gorham observed that as the report consisted of propositions mutually conditional, he wished to hear some explanations touching the grounds on which the conditions were estimated.

Mr. Gerry: The committee were of different opinions, as well as the deputations from which the committee were taken, and agreed to the report merely in order that some ground of accommodation might be proposed. Those opposed to the equality of votes have only assented conditionally, and if the other side do not generally agree, will not be under any obligation to support the report.

Mr. Wilson thought the committee had exceeded their powers.

Mr. Martin was for taking the question of the whole report.

Mr. Wilson was for a division of the question; otherwise it would be a leap in the dark.

Mr. Madison could not regard the privilege of originating money bills as any concession on the side of the small states. Experience proved that it had no effect. If seven states in the upper branch wished a bill to be originated, they might surely find some member from some of the same states in the lower branch who would originate it. The restriction as to amendments was of as little consequence. Amendments could be handed privately by the Senate to members of the other house. Bills could be negatived that they might be sent up in the desired shape. If the Senate should yield to the obstinacy of the first branch, the use of that body as a check would be lost. If the first branch should yield to that of the Senate, the privilege would be nugatory. Experience had also shown, both in Great Britain and the states having a similar regulation, that it was a source of frequent and obstinate altercations. These considerations had produced a rejection of a like motion on a former occasion when judged by its own merits. It could not, therefore, be deemed any concession on the present, and left in force all the objections which had prevailed against allowing each state an equal voice. He conceived that the convention was reduced to the alternative of either departing from justice in order to conciliate the smaller states and the minority of the people of the United States, or of displeasing these by justly ratifying the larger states and the majority of the people. He could not himself hesitate as to the option he ought to make. The convention, with justice and a majority of the people on their side, had nothing to fear. With injustice and the minority on their side they had everything to fear. It was in vain to purchase concord in the convention on terms which would perpetuate discord among their constituents. The convention ought to pursue a plan which would bear the test of examination, which would be espoused and supported by the enlightened and impartial part of America, and which they could themselves vindicate and urge. It should be considered that although at first many may judge of the system recommended by their opinion of the convention, yet finally all will judge of the convention by the system. The merits of the system alone can finally and effectually obtain the public suffrage. He was not apprehensive that the people of the small states would obstinately refuse to accede to a government founded on just principles and promising them substantial protection. He could not suspect that Delaware would brave the consequences of seeking her fortunes apart from the other states rather than submit to such a government; much less could he suspect that she would pursue the rash policy of courting foreign support, which the warmth of one of her representatives (Gunning Bedford) had suggested; or if she should, that any foreign nation would be so rash as to harken to the overture. As little could he suspect that the people of New Jersey, notwithstanding the decided tone of the gentlemen from that state, would choose rather to stand on their own legs and bid defiance to events than to acquiesce under an establishment founded on principles, the justice of which they could not dispute, and absolutely necessary to redeem them from the exactions levied on them by the commerce of the neighboring states. A review of other states would prove that there was as little reason to apprehend an inflexible opposition elsewhere. Harmony in the convention was, no doubt, much to be desired. Satisfaction to all the states, in the first instance, still more so. But if the principal states, comprehending a majority of the people of the United States, should concur in a just and judicious plan, he had the firmest hopes that all the other states would by degrees accede to it.

Mr. Butler said he could not let down his idea of the people of America so far as to believe they would from mere respect to the convention adopt a plan evidently unjust. He did not consider the privilege concerning money bills as of any consequence. He urged that the second branch ought to represent the states according to their property.

Mr. Gouverneur Morris thought the form as well as the matter of the report objectionable. It seemed, in the first place, to render amendment impracticable. In the next place, it seemed to involve a pledge to agree to the second part if the first should be agreed to. He conceived the whole aspect of it to be wrong. He came here as a representative of America; he flattered himself he came here in some degree as a representative of the whole human race, for the whole human race will be affected by the proceedings of this convention. He wished gentlemen to extend their views beyond the present moment of time, beyond the narrow limits of place from which they derive their political origin. If he were to believe some things which he had heard, he should suppose that we were assembled to truck and bargain for our particular states. He cannot descend to think that any gentlemen are really actuated by these views. We must look forward to the effects of what we do. These alone ought to guide us. Much has been said of the sentiments of the people. They were unknown. They could not be known. All that we can infer is that if the plan we recommend be reasonable and right, all who have reasonable minds and sound intentions will embrace it, notwithstanding what had been said by some gentlemen. Let us suppose that the larger states shall agree and that the smaller refuse, and let us trace the consequences. The opponents of the system in the smaller states will not, no doubt, make a party and a noise for a time, but the ties of interest, of kindred, and of common habits which connect them with other states, will be too strong to be easily broken. In New Jersey, particularly, he was sure a great many would follow the sentiments of Pennsylvania and New York. This country must be united. If persuasion does not unite it, the sword will. He begged this consideration might have its due weight. The scenes of horror attending civil commotion cannot be described, and the conclusion of them will be worse than the term of their continuance. The stronger party will then make traitors of the weaker and the gallows and halter will finish the work of the sword. How far foreign powers would be ready to take part in the confusions, he would not say. Threats that they will be invited have, it seems, been thrown out. He drew the melancholy picture of foreign intrusions as exhibited in the history of Germany and urged it as a standing lesson to other nations. He trusted that the gentlemen who may have hazarded such expressions did not entertain them till they reached their own lips. But returning to the report, he could not think it in any respect calculated for the public good. As the second branch is now constituted, there will be constant disputes and appeals to the states, which will undermine the General Government and control and annihilate the first branch. Suppose that the delegates from Massachusetts and Rhode Island in the upper house disagree, and that the former are outvoted. What results? They will immediately declare that their state will not abide by the decision and make such representations as will produce that effect. The same may happen as to Virginia and other states. Of what avail, then, will be what is on paper? State attachments and state importance have been the bane of this country. We cannot annihilate, but we may perhaps take out the teeth of the serpents. He wished our ideas to be enlarged to the true interest of man instead of being circumscribed within the narrow compass of a particular spot. And after all, how little can be the motive yielded by selfishness for such a policy! Who can say whether he himself, much less whether his children, will the next year be an inhabitant of this or that state?

Mr. Bedford: He found that what he had said as to the small states being taken by the hand had been misunderstood, and he rose to explain. He did not mean that the small states would court the aid and interposition of foreign powers. He meant that they would not consider the Federal compact as dissolved until it should be so by the acts of the large states. In this case, the consequence of the breach of faith on their part and the readiness of the small states to fulfill their engagements, would be that foreign nations having demands on this country would find it to their interest to take the small states by the hand in order to do themselves justice. This was what he meant. But no man can foresee to what extremities the small states may be driven by oppression. He observed, also, in apology, that some allowance ought to be made for the habits of his profession in which warmth was natural and sometimes necessary. But is there not an apology in what was said (by Gouverneur Morris), that the sword is to unite; by Mr. Gorham, that Delaware must be annexed to Pennsylvania, and New

Jersey divided between Pennsylvania and New York? To hear such language without emotion would be to renounce the feelings of a man and the duty of a citizen. As to the propositions of the committee, the lesser states have thought it necessary to have a security somewhere. This has been thought necessary for the executive magistrate of the proposed government, who has a sort of negative on the laws, and is it not of more importance that the states should be protected than that the executive branch of the government should be protected? In order to obtain this, the smaller states have conceded as to the constitution of the first branch and as to money bills. If they be not gratified by correspondent concessions as to the second branch, is it to be supposed they will ever accede to the plan? And what will be the consequence if nothing should be done? The condition of the United States requires that something should be immediately done. It will be better that a defective plan should be adopted than that none should be recommended. He saw no reason why defects might not be supplied by meetings ten, fifteen, or twenty years hence.

Mr. Ellsworth said he had not attended the proceedings of the committee, but was ready to accede to the compromise they had reported. Some compromise was necessary and he saw none more convenient or reasonable.

Mr. Williamson hoped that the expressions of individuals would not be taken for the sense of their colleagues, much less of their states, which was not and could not be known. He hoped, also, that the meaning of those expressions would not be misconstrued or exaggerated. He did not conceive that Gouverneur Morris meant that the sword ought to be drawn against the smaller states. He only pointed out the probable consequences of anarchy in the United States. A similar exposition ought to be given of the express of Mr. Gorham. He was ready to hear the report discussed, but thought the propositions contained in it the most objectionable of any he had yet heard.

Mr. Paterson said that he had, when the report was agreed to in the committee, reserved to himself the right of freely discussing it. He acknowledged that the warmth complained of was improper, but he thought the sword and the gallows little calculated to produce conviction. He complained of the manner in which Mr. Madison and Mr. G. Morris had treated the small states.

Mr. Gerry: Though he had assented to the report in the committee, he had very material objections to it. We were, however, in a peculiar situation. We were neither the same nation, nor different nations. We ought not, therefore, to pursue the one or the other of these ideas too closely. If no compromise should take place, what will be the consequence? A secession, he foresaw, would take place; for some gentlemen seemed decided on it. Two different plans will be proposed and the result no man could foresee. If we do not come to some agreement among ourselves, some foreign sword will probably do the work for us.

Mr. Madison: The report was meant not as specific propositions to be adopted, but merely as a general ground of accommodation. There must be some accommodation on this point, or we shall make little further progress in the work. Accommodation was the object of the house in the appointment of the committee and of the committee in the report they had made. And however liable the report might be to objections, he thought it preferable to an appeal to the world by the different sides as had been talked of by some gentlemen. It could not be more inconvenient to any gentleman to remain absent from his private affairs than it was for him, but he would bury his bones in this city rather than expose his country to the consequences of a dissolution of the convention without anything being done.

The first proposition in the report for fixing the representation in the first branch—"one member for every forty-thousand inhabitants" —being taken up, Mr. Gouverneur Morris objected to that scale of apportionment. He thought property ought to be taken into the estimate as well as the number of inhabitants. Life and liberty were generally said to be of more value than property. An accurate view of the matter would nevertheless prove that property was the main object of society. The savage state was more favorable to liberty than the civilized, and sufficiently so to life. It was preferred by all men who had not acquired a taste for property; it was only renounced for the sake of property, which could only be secured by the restraints of regular government. These ideas might appear new to some, but they were nevertheless just. If property, then, was the main object of government, certainly it ought to be one measure of the influence due to those who were to be affected by the government. He looked forward also to that range of new states which would soon be formed in the West. He thought the rule of representation ought to be so fixed as to secure to the Atlantic states a prevalence in the national councils. The new states will know less of the public interest than these; will have an interest in many respects different; in particular, will be little scrupulous of involving the community in wars, the burdens and operations of which would fall chiefly on the maritime states. Provision ought, therefore, to be made to prevent the maritime states from being hereafter outvoted by them. He thought this might easily be done by irrevocably fixing the number of representatives which the Atlantic states should respectively have and the number which each new state will have. This would not be unjust, as the western settlers would previously know the conditions on which they were to possess their lands. It would be politic, as it would recommend the plan to the present as well as future interest of the states which must decide the fate of it.

Mr. Rutledge: The gentlemen last up had spoken some of his sentiments precisely. Property was certainly the principle object of society. If numbers should be made the rule of representation, the Atlantic states would be subjected to the western. He moved that the first proposition in the report be postponed in order to take up the following:

"That the suffrages of the several states be regulated and proportioned according to the sums to be paid toward the general revenue by the inhabitants of each state, respectively; that an apportionment of suffrages according to the ratio aforesaid shall be made and regulated at the end of_____years from the first meeting of the legislature of the United States, and at the end of every_____years; but that for the present, and until the period above mentioned, the suffrages shall be for New Hampshire_____, for Massachusetts_____, etc."

Mr. Mason said the case ot new states was not unnoticed in the committee, but it was thought, and he was himself decidedly of opinion, that if they made a part of the Union, they ought to be subject to no unfavorable discriminations. Obvious considerations required it.

Mr. Randolph concurred with Mr. Mason.

Mr. Rutledge's motion defeated, 9 to 1. Adjourned.

RATIO OF REPRESENTATION DEBATED AGAIN / *July 6*

In convention. Mr. Gouverneur Morris moved to commit so much of the report as relates to "one member for every forty-thousand inhabitants." His view was that they might absolutely fix the number for each state in the first instance, leaving the legislature at liberty to provide for changes in the relative importance of the states and for the case of new states.

Mr. Wilson seconded the motion, but with a view of leaving the committee under no implied shackles.

Mr. Gorham apprehended great inconvenience from fixing directly the number of representatives to be allowed to each state. He thought the number of inhabitants the true guide, though perhaps some departure might be expedient from the full proportion. The states also would vary in their relative extent by separations of parts of the largest states. A part of Virginia is now on the point of a separation. In the province of Maine, a convention is at this time deliberating on a sepa-

163

ration from Massachusetts. In such events the number of representatives ought certainly to be reduced. He hoped to see all the states made small by proper divisions instead of their becoming formidable, as was apprehended, to the small states. He conceived that, let the government be modified as it might, there would be a constant tendency in the state governments to encroach upon it; it was of importance, therefore, that the extent of the states should be reduced as much and as fast as possible. The stronger the government shall be made in the first instance, the more easily will these divisions be effected; as it will be of less consequence, in the opinion of the states, whether they be of great or small extent.

Mr. Gerry did not think with his colleague that the larger states ought to be cut up. This policy has been inculcated by the middling and small states ungenerously and contrary to the spirit of the Confederation. Ambitious men will be apt to solicit needless divisions, till the states be reduced to the size of counties. If this policy should still actuate the small states, the large ones could not confederate safely with them, but would be obliged to consult their safety by confederating only with one another. He favored the commitment and thought that representation ought to be in the combined ratio of numbers of inhabitants and of wealth, and not of either singly.

Mr. King wished the clause to be committed chiefly in order to detach it from the report with which it had no connection. He thought, also, that the ratio of representation proposed could not be safely fixed, since in a century and a half our computed increase of population would carry the number of representatives to an enormous excess; that the number of inhabitants was not the proper index of ability and wealth; that property was the primary object of society, and that in fixing a ratio, this ought not to be excluded from the estimate. With regard to new states, he observed that there was something peculiar in the business which had not been noticed. The United States were now admitted to be proprietors of the country northwest of the Ohio. Congress by one of their ordinances have impoliticly laid it out into ten states, and have made it a fundamental article of compact with those who may become settlers, that as soon as the number in any one state shall equal that of the smallest of the thirteen original states, it may claim admission into the Union. Delaware does not contain, it is computed, more than thirty-five thousand souls and for obvious reasons will not increase much for a considerable time. It is possible, then, that if this plan be persisted in by Congress, ten new votes may be added without a greater addition of inhabitants than are represented by the single vote of Pennsylvania. The plan, as it respects one of the new states, is already irrevocable—the sale of the lands having commenced, and the purchasers and settlers will immediately become entitled to all the privileges of the compact.

Mr. Butler agreed to the commitment if the committee were to be left at liberty. He was persuaded that the more the subject was examined, the less it would appear that the number of inhabitants would be a proper rule of proportion. If there were no other objection, the changeableness of the standard would be sufficient. He concurred with those who thought some balance was necessary between the old and the new states. He contended strenuously that property was the only just measure of representation. This was the great object of government, the great cause of war, the great means of carrying it on.

Mr. Pinckney saw no good reason for committing. The value of land had been found on full investigation to be an impracticable rule. The contributions of revenue, including imports and exports, must be too changeable in their amount, too difficult to be adjusted, and too injurious to the noncommercial states. The number of inhabitants appeared to him the only just and practicable rule. He thought the blacks ought to stand on an equality with the whites, but would agree to the ratio settled by Congress. He contended that Congress had no right under the Articles of Confederation to authorize the admission of new states; no such case having been provided for.

Mr. Davie was for committing the clause in order to get at the merits of the question arising on the report. He seemed to think that wealth or property ought to be represented in the second branch and numbers in the first branch.

Motion for one member for every 40,000 inhabitants recommitted, 7 to 3.

THE QUESTION OF NEGRO REPRESENTATION / July 11

The next clause as to three-fifths of the Negroes being considered, Mr. King, being much opposed to fixing numbers as the rule of representation, was particularly so on account of the blacks. He thought the admission of them along with whites at all would excite great discontents among the states having no slaves. He had never said as to any particular point that he would in no event acquiesce in and support it, but he would say that if in any case such a declaration was to be made by him, it would be in this. He remarked that in the temporary allotment of representatives made by the committee, the southern states had received more than the number of their white and three-fifths of their black inhabitants entitled them to.

Mr. Sherman: South Carolina had not more beyond her proportion than New York and New Hampshire, nor either of them more than was necessary in order to avoid fractions, or reducing them below their proportion. Georgia had more, but the rapid growth of that state seemed to justify it. In general, the allotment might not be just, but considering all circumstances, he was satisfied with it.

Mr. Gorham supported the propriety of establishing numbers as the rule. He said that in Massachusetts estimates had been taken in the different towns and that persons had been curious enough to compare these estimates with the respective numbers of people, and it had been found, even including Boston, that the most exact proportion prevailed between numbers and property. He was aware that there might be some weight in what had fallen from his colleague as to the umbrage which might be taken by the people of the eastern states. But he recollected that when the proposition of Congress for changing the eighth article of the Confederation was before the Legislature of Massachusetts, the only difficulty then was to satisfy them that the Negroes ought not to have been counted equally with the whites, instead of being counted in the ratio of three-fifths only.

Mr. Wilson did not well see on what principle the admission of blacks in the proportion of three-fifths could be explained. Are they admitted as citizens? Then why are they not admitted on an equality with white citizens? Are they admitted as property? Then why is not other property admitted into the computation? These were difficulties, however, which he thought must be overruled by the necessity of compromise. He had some apprehensions, also, from the tendency of the blending of the blacks with the whites to give disgust to the people of Pennsylvania, as had been intimated by his colleague (Mr. Gouverneur Morris). But he differed from him in thinking numbers of inhabitants so incorrect a measure of wealth. He had seen the western settlements of Pennsylvania, and on a comparison of them with the city of Philadelphia, could discover little other difference than that property was more unequally divided here than there. Taking the same number in the aggregate in the two situations, he believed there would be little difference in their wealth and ability to contribute to the public wants.

Mr. Gouverneur Morris was compelled to declare himself reduced to the dilemma of doing injustice to the southern states or to human nature, and he must, therefore, do it to the former; for he could never agree to give such encouragement to the slave trade as would be given by allowing them a representation for their Negroes, and he did not *167* believe those states would ever confederate on terms that would deprive them of that trade.

Question for agreeing to include three-fifths of the blacks defeated, 6 to 4.

NEGRO REPRESENTATION RESUMED / *August 8*

Mr. King wished to know what influence the vote just passed was meant to have on the succeeding part of the report concerning the admission of slaves into the rule of representation. He could not reconcile his mind to the article if it was to prevent objections to the latter part. The admission of slaves was a most grating circumstance to his mind and he believed would be so to a great part of the people of America. He had not made a strenuous opposition to it heretofore, because he had hoped that this concession would have produced a readiness, which had not been manifested, to strengthen the General Government and to mark a full confidence in it. The report under consideration had by the tenor of it put an end to all those hopes. In two great points, the hands of the legislature were absolutely tied. The importation of slaves could not be prohibited. Exports could not be taxed. Is this reasonable? What are the great objects of the general system? First, defense against foreign invasion; secondly, against internal sedition. Shall all the states, then, be bound to defend each, and shall each be at liberty to introduce a weakness which will render defense more difficult? Shall one part of the United States be bound to defend another part, and that other part be at liberty, not only to increase its own danger, but to withhold the compensation for the burden? If slaves are to be imported, shall not the exports produced by their labor supply a revenue the better to enable the General Government to defend their masters? There was so much inequality and unreasonableness in all this that the people of the northern states could never be reconciled to it. No candid man could undertake to justify it to them. He had hoped that some accommodation would have taken place on this subject; that, at least, a time would have been limited for the importation of slaves. He never could agree to let them be imported without limitation, and then be represented in the national legislature. Indeed, he could so little persuade himself of the rectitude of such a practice that he was not sure he could assent to it under any circumstances. At all events, either slaves should not be represented or exports should be taxable.

Mr. Sherman regarded the slave trade as iniquitous; but the point of representation having been settled after much difficulty and deliberation, he did not think himself bound to make opposition, especially as the present article as amended did not preclude any arrangement whatever on that point in another place of the report.

Mr. Madison objected to one for every forty-thousand inhabitants as a perpetual rule. The future increase of population, if the Union should be permanent, will render the number of representatives excessive.

Mr. Gorham: It is not to be supposed that the government will last so long as to produce this effect. Can it be supposed that this vast country, including the western territory, will one hundred and fifty years hence remain one nation?

Mr. Ellsworth: If the government should continue so long, alterations may be made in the Constitution in the manner proposed in a subsequent article.

Mr. Sherman and Mr. Madison moved to insert the words "not exceeding" before the words "one for every forty-thousand," which was agreed to unanimously.

Mr. Gouverneur Morris moved to insert "free" before the word "inhabitants." Much, he said, would depend on this point. He never would concur in upholding domestic slavery. It was a nefarious institution. It was the curse of Heaven on the states where it prevailed. Compare the free regions of the middle states, where a rich and noble cultivation marks the prosperity and happiness of the people, with the misery and poverty which overspread the barren wastes of Virginia, Maryland, and the other states having slaves. Travel through the whole continent and you behold the prospect continually varying with the appearance and disappearance of slavery. The moment you leave the eastern states and enter New York, the effects of the institution become visible. Passing through the Jerseys and entering Pennsylvania, every criterion of superior improvement witnesses the change. Proceed southwardly, and every step you take through the great regions of slaves presents a desert increasing with the increasing proportion of these wretched beings. Upon what principle is it that the slaves shall be computed in the representation? Are they men? Then make them citizens and let them vote. Are they property? Why then is no other property included? The houses in this city (Philadelphia) are worth more than all the wretched slaves who cover the rice swamps of South Carolina. The admission of slaves into the representation when fairly explained comes to this: that the inhabitant of Georgia and South Carolina who goes to the coast of Africa and in defiance of the most sacred laws of humanity tears away his fellow-creatures from their dearest connections and damns them to the most cruel bondage shall 169 have more votes in a government instituted for the protection of the rights of mankind than the citizen of Pennsylvania or New Jersey who views with a laudable horror so nefarious a practice. He would add that domestic slavery is the most prominent feature in the aristocratic countenance of the proposed Constitution. The vassalage of the poor has ever been the favorite offspring of aristocracy. And what is the proposed compensation to the northern states for a sacrifice of every principle of right, of every impulse of humanity? They are to bind themselves to march their militia for the defense of the southern states, for their defense against those very slaves of whom they complain. They must supply vessels and seamen in case of foreign attack. The legislature will have indefinite power to tax them by excises and duties on imports, both of which will fall heavier on them than on the southern inhabitants; for the bohea tea (a superior Chinese black tea) used by a northern freeman will pay more tax than the whole consumption of the miserable slave, which consists of nothing more than his physical subsistence and the rag that covers his nakedness. On the other side, the southern states are not to be restrained from importing fresh supplies of wretched Africans at once to increase the danger of attack and the difficulty of defense; nay, they are to be encouraged to it by an assurance of having their votes in the national Government increased in proportion, and are at the same time to have their exports and their slaves exempt from all contributions for the public service. Let it not be said that direct taxation is to be proportioned to representation. It is idle to suppose that the General Government can stretch its hand directly into the pockets of the people scattered over so vast a country. They can only do it through the medium of exports, imports, and excises. For what, then, are all the sacrifices to be made? He would sooner submit himself to a tax for paying for all the Negroes in the United States than saddle posterity with such a Constitution.

Mr. Dayton seconded the motion. He did it, he said, that his sentiments on the subject might appear, whatever might be the fate of the amendment.

Mr. Sherman did not regard the admission of the Negroes into the ratio of representation as liable to such insuperable objections. It was the freemen of the southern states who were in fact to be represented according to the taxes paid by them, and the Negroes are only included in the estimate of the taxes. This was his idea of the matter.

Mr. Pinckney considered the fisheries and the western frontier as more burdensome to the United States than the slaves. He thought this could be demonstrated if the occasion were a proper one.

Mr. Wilson thought the motion premature. An agreement to the clause would be no bar to the object of it.

The motion to insert "free" before "inhabitants" defeated, 10 to 1.

On the suggestion of Mr. Dickinson, the words "provided that each state shall have one representative, at least," were added.

ONE VOTE PER STATE
IN THE SENATE APPROVED / *July 7*

In convention. The question, shall the clause "allowing each state one vote in the second branch, stand as part of the report," being taken up, Mr. Gerry said this is the critical question. He had rather agree to it than have no accommodation. A government short of a proper national plan, if generally acceptable, would be preferable to a proper one which, if it could be carried at all, would operate on discontented states. He thought it would be best to suspend this question till the committee appointed yesterday should make report.

Mr. Sherman supposed that it was the wish of everyone that some general government should be established. An equal vote in the second branch would, he thought, be most likely to give it the necessary vigor. The small states have more vigor in their governments than the large ones; the more influence, therefore, the large ones have, the weaker will be the government. In the large states it will be most difficult to collect the real and fair sense of the people; fallacy and undue influence will be practiced with the most success, and improper men will most easily get into office. If they vote by states in the second branch and each state has an equal vote, there must be always a majority of states as well as a majority of the people on the side of public measures, and the government will have decision and efficacy. If this be not the case in the second branch, there may be a majority of states against public measures, and the difficulty of compelling them to abide by the public determination will render the government feebler than it has ever yet been.

Mr. Wilson was not deficient in a conciliating temper, but firmness was sometimes a duty of higher obligation. Conciliation was also misapplied in this instance. It was pursued here rather among the representatives than among the constituents, and it would be of little consequence if not established among the latter, and there could be little hope of its being established among them if the foundation should not be laid in justice and right.

The question, shall the words stand as part of the report, passed, 171
6 to 3.

EQUALITY OF STATES IN SENATE POSTPONED / *July 7*

Mr. Gerry thought it would be proper to proceed to enumerate and define the powers to be vested in the General Government before a question on the report should be taken as to the rule of representation in the second branch.

Mr. Madison observed that it would be impossible to say what powers could be safely and properly vested in the government before it was known in what manner the states were to be represented in it. He was apprehensive that if a just representation were not the basis of the government, it would happen, as it did when the Articles of Confederation were depending, that every effectual prerogative would be withdrawn or withheld and the new government would be rendered as impotent and as short-lived as the old.

Mr. Paterson would not decide whether the privilege concerning money bills were a valuable consideration or not; but he considered the mode and rule of representation in the first branch as fully so, and that after the establishment of that point, the small states would never be able to defend themselves without an equality of votes in the second branch. There was no other ground of accommodation. His resolution was fixed. He would meet the large states on that ground, and no other. For himself, he should vote against the report because it yielded too much.

Mr. Gouverneur Morris: He had no resolution unalterably fixed except to do what should finally appear to him right. He was against the report because it maintained the improper constitution of the second branch. It made it another Congress, a mere whisp of straw. It had been said (by Mr. Gerry) that the new government would be partly national, partly federal; that it ought in the first quality to protect individuals; in the second, the states. But in what quality was it to protect the aggregate interest of the whole? Among the many provisions which had been urged, he had seen none for supporting the dignity and splendor of the American empire. It had been one of our greatest misfortunes that the great objects of the nation had been sacrificed constantly to local views in like manner as the general interest of states had been sacrificed to those of the counties. What is to be the check in the Senate? None, unless it be to keep the majority of the people from injuring particular states. But particular states ought to be injured for the sake of a majority of the people in case their conduct should deserve it. Suppose they should insist on claims evidently unjust and pursue them in a manner detrimental to the whole body; suppose they should give themselves up to foreign influence, ought they to be protected in such cases? They were originally nothing more than colonial corporations. On the Declaration of Independence a government was to be formed. The small states, aware of the necessity of preventing anarchy and taking advantage of the moment, extorted from the large ones an equality of votes. Standing now on that ground, they demand under the new system greater rights as men than their fellow-citizens of the large states. The proper answer to them is that the same necessity of which they formerly took advantage does not now exist, and that the large states are at liberty now to consider what is right rather than what may be expedient. We must have an efficient government, and if there be an efficiency in the local governments, the former is impossible. Germany alone proves it. Notwithstanding their common diet, notwithstanding the great prerogatives of the emperor as head of the empire and his vast resources as sovereign of his particular dominions, no union is maintained; foreign influence disturbs every internal operation and there is no energy whatever in the General Government. Whence does this proceed? From the energy of the local authorities, from its being considered of more consequence to support the Prince of Hesse than the happiness of the people of Germany. Do gentlemen wish this to be the case here? Good God, sir, is it possible they can so delude themselves? What if all the charters and constitutions of the states were thrown into the fire and all their demagogues into the ocean—what would it be to the happiness of America? And will not this be the case here if we pursue the train in which the business lies? We shall establish an Aulic Council without an emperor to execute its decrees. The same circumstances which unite the people here unite them in Germany. They have there a common language, a common law, common usages and manners, and a common interest in being united; yet their local jurisdictions destroy every tie. The case was the same in the Grecian states. The United Netherlands are at this time torn in factions. With these examples before our eyes shall we form establishments which must necessarily produce the same effects? It is of no consequence from what districts the second branch shall be drawn if it be so constituted as to yield an asylum against these evils. As it is now constituted, he must be against its being drawn from the states in equal portions, but shall be ready to join in devising such an amendment of the plan as will be most likely to secure our liberty and happiness.

Mr. Sherman and Mr. Ellsworth moved to postpone the question   *173*
on the report from the committee (composed) of a member from each
state in order to wait for the report from the committee of five last appointed.
Question of equal Senate representation postponed, 6 to 5.

THE "ENDLESS CONTROVERSY" RESUMED / *July 13*

It being moved to postpone the clause in the report of the committee of
eleven as to the originating of money bills in the first branch in order
to take up the following, "that in the second branch each state shall
have an equal voice," Mr. Gerry moved to add as an amendment to
the last clause agreed to by the house "that from the first meeting of
the legislature of the United States till a census shall be taken, all
moneys to be raised for supplying the public treasury by direct taxation shall be assessed on the inhabitants of the several states according
to the number of their representatives, respectively, in the first
branch." He said this would be as just before as after the census, according to the general principle that taxation and representation
ought to go together.

Mr. Williamson feared that New Hampshire will have reason to
complain. Three members were allotted to her as a liberal allowance
for this reason among others, that she might not suppose any advantage to have been taken of her absence. As she was still absent and
had no opportunity of deciding whether she would choose to retain
the number on the condition of her being taxed in proportion to it,
he thought the number ought to be reduced from three to two before
the question was taken on Mr. Gerry's motion.

Mr. Read could not approve of the proposition. He had observed,
he said, in the committee a backwardness in some of the members
from the large states to take their full proportion of representatives.
He did not then see the motive. He now suspects it was to avoid their
due share of taxation. He had no objection to a just and accurate adjustment of representation and taxation to each other.

Mr. Gouverneur Morris and Mr. Madison answered that the charge
itself involved an acquittal; since, notwithstanding the augmentation
of the number of members allotted to Massachusetts and Virginia, the
motion for proportioning the burdens thereto was made by a member
from the former state and was approved by Mr. Madison, from the latter, who was on the committee. Mr. Gouverneur Morris said that he
thought Pennsylvania had her due share in eight members, and he
could not in candor ask for more. Mr. Madison said that having always

conceived that the difference of interest in the United States lay not between the large and small, but the northern and southern states, and finding that the number of members allotted to the northern states was greatly superior, he should have preferred an addition of two members to the southern states—to wit, one to North and one to South Carolina, rather than of one member to Virginia. He liked the present motion because it tended to moderate the views both of the opponents and advocates for rating very high the Negroes.

Mr. Ellsworth hoped the proposition would be withdrawn. It entered too much into detail. The general principle was already sufficiently settled. As fractions cannot be regarded in apportioning the number of representatives, the rule will be unjust until an actual census shall be made. After that, taxation may be precisely proportioned, according to the principle established, to the number of inhabitants.

Mr. Wilson hoped the motion would not be withdrawn. If it should, it will be made from another quarter. The rule will be as reasonable and just before, as after, a census. As to fractional numbers, the census will not destroy, but ascertain them. And they will have the same effect after, as before, the census; for as he understands the rule, it is to be adjusted not to the number of inhabitants, but of representatives.

Mr. Sherman opposed the motion. He thought the legislature ought to be left at liberty; in which case they would probably conform to the principles observed by Congress.

Mr. Mason did not know that Virginia would be a loser by the proposed regulation, but had some scruples as to the justice of it. He doubted much whether the conjectural rule which was to precede the census would be as just as it would be rendered by an actual census.

Mr. Ellsworth and Mr. Sherman moved to postpone the motion of Mr. Gerry.

/ July 14

The reconsideration being tacitly agreed to, Mr. Pinckney moved that instead of an equality of votes, the states should be represented in the second branch as follows: New Hampshire by two members; Massachusetts, four; Rhode Island, one; Connecticut, three; New York, three; New Jersey, two; Pennsylvania, four: Delaware, one; Maryland, three; Virginia, five; North Carolina, three; South Carolina, three; Georgia, two; making in the whole thirty-six.

Mr. Wilson seconds the motion.

Mr. Dayton: The smaller states can never give up their equality. For himself, he would in no event yield that security for their rights.

Mr. Sherman urged the equality of votes, not so much as a security for the small states, as for the state governments, which could not be preserved unless they were represented and had a negative in the General Government. He had no objection to the members in the second branch voting per capita, as had been suggested by Mr. Gerry.

Mr. Madison concurred in this motion of Mr. Pinckney as a reasonable compromise.

Mr. Gerry said he should like the motion, but could see no hope of success. An accommodation must take place and it was apparent from what had been seen that it could not do so on the ground of the motion. He was utterly against a partial confederacy leaving other states to accede or not accede, as had been intimated.

Mr. King said it was always with regret that he differed from his colleagues, but it was his duty to differ from Mr. Gerry on this occasion. He considered the proposed government as substantially and formally a general and national government over the people of America. There never will be a case in which it will act as a federal government on the states and not on the individual citizens. And is it not a clear principle that in a free government, those who are to be the objects of a government ought to influence the operations of it? What reason can be assigned why the same rule of representation should not prevail in the second as in the first branch? He could conceive none. On the contrary, every view of the subject that presented itself seemed to require it. Two objections had been raised against it, drawn, first, from the terms of the existing compact; secondly, from a supposed danger to the smaller states. As to the first objection, he thought it inapplicable. According to the existing Confederation, the rule by which the public burden is to be apportioned is fixed and must be pursued. In the proposed government, it cannot be fixed because indirect taxation is to be substituted. The legislature, therefore, will have full discretion to impose taxes in such modes and proportions as they may judge expedient. As to the second objection, he thought it of as little weight. The General Government can never wish to intrude on the state governments. There could be no temptation. None had been pointed out. In order to prevent the interference of measures which seemed most likely to happen, he would have no objection to throwing all the state debts into the Federal debt, making one aggregate debt of about $70,000,000, and leaving it to be discharged by the General Government. According to the idea of securing the state governments, there ought to be three distinct legislative branches. The second was admitted to be necessary and was actually meant to check the first branch —to give more wisdom, system, and stability to the government, and ought clearly, as it was to operate on the people, to be proportioned to them. For the third purpose of securing the states, there ought then to be a third branch, representing the states as such, and guarding by equal votes their rights and dignities. He would not pretend to be as thoroughly acquainted with his immediate constituents as his colleagues, but it was his firm belief that Massachusetts would never be prevailed on to yield to an equality of votes. In New York (he was sorry to be obliged to say anything relative to that state in the absence of its representatives, but the occasion required it), he had seen that the most powerful argument used by the considerate opponents to the grant of the impost to Congress was pointed against the vicious constitution of Congress with regard to representation and suffrage. He was sure that no government would last that was not founded on just principles. He preferred the doing of nothing to an allowance of an equal vote to all the states. It would be better, he thought, to submit to a little more confusion and convulsion than to submit to such an evil. It was difficult to say what the views of different gentlemen might be. Perhaps there might be some who thought no government coextensive with the United States could be established with a hope of its answering the purpose. Perhaps there might be other fixed opinions incompatible with the object we are pursuing. If there were, he thought it but candid that gentlemen should speak out that we might understand one another.

Mr. Strong: The convention had been much divided in opinion. In order to avoid the consequences of it, an accommodation had been proposed. A committee had been appointed, and though some of the members of it were averse to an equality of votes, a report had been made in favor of it. It is agreed on all hands that Congress are nearly at an end. If no accommodation takes place, the Union itself must soon be dissolved. It has been suggested that if we cannot come to any general agreement, the principal states may form and recommend a scheme of government. But will the small states in that case ever accede to it? Is it probable that the large states themselves will, under such circumstances, embrace and ratify it? He thought the small states had made a considerable concession in the article of money bills and that they might naturally expect some concessions on the other side. From this view of the matter, he was compelled to give his vote for the report taken altogether.

Mr. Madison expressed his apprehensions that if the proper foundation of government was destroyed by substituting an equality in place of a proportional representation, no proper superstructure would be raised. If the small states really wish for a government armed with

the powers necessary to secure their liberties and to enforce obedience
on the larger members as well as themselves, he could not help thinking them extremely mistaken in the means. He reminded them of the
consequences of laying the existing Confederation on improper principles. All the principal parties to its compilation joined immediately
in mutilating and fettering the government in such a manner that it
has disappointed every hope placed on it. He appealed to the doctrine
and arguments used by themselves on a former occasion. It had been
very properly observed (by Mr. Paterson) that representation was an
expedient by which the meeting of the people themselves was rendered unnecessary and that the representatives ought, therefore, to
bear a proportion to the votes which their constituents, if convened,
would respectively have. Was not this remark as applicable to one
branch of the representation as to the other? But it had been said
that the government would in its operation be partly federal, partly
national; that although in the latter respect the representatives of the
people ought to be in proportion to the people, yet in the former it
ought to be according to the number of states. If there was any solidity
in this distinction, he was ready to abide by it; if there was none, it
ought to be abandoned. In all cases where the General Government is
to act on the people, let the people be represented and the votes be
proportional. In all cases where the government is to act on the states
as such, in like manner as Congress now acts on them, let the states be
represented and the votes be equal. This was the true ground of compromise if there was any ground at all. But he denied that there was
any ground. He called for a single instance in which the General Government was not to operate on the people individually. The practicability of making laws with coercive sanctions for the states as political
bodies had been exploded on all hands. He observed that the people of
the large states would, in some way or other, secure to themselves a
weight proportioned to the importance accruing from their superior
numbers. If they could not effect it by a proportional representation
in the government, they would probably accede to no government
which did not in a great measure depend for its efficacy on their voluntary co-operation; in which case they would indirectly secure their object. The existing Confederacy proved that where the acts of the General Government were to be executed by the particular governments,
the latter had a weight in proportion to their importance. No one
would say that either in Congress or out of Congress Delaware had
equal weight with Pennsylvania. If the latter was to supply ten times
as much money as the former and no compulsion could be used, it
was of ten times more importance that she should voluntarily furnish

the supply. In the Dutch confederacy the votes of the provinces were equal, but Holland, which supplies about half the money, governed the whole republic. He enumerated the objections against an equality of votes in the second branch, notwithstanding the proportional representation in the first: 1. The minority could negative the will of the majority of the people. 2. They could extort measures by making them a condition of their assent to other necessary measures. 3. They could obtrude measures on the majority by virtue of the peculiar powers which would be vested in the Senate. 4. The evil instead of being cured by time would increase with every new state that should be admitted, as they must all be admitted on the principle of equality. 5. The perpetuity it would give to the preponderance of the northern against the southern scale was a serious consideration. It seemed now to be pretty well understood that the real difference of interest lay, not between the large and small, but between the northern and southern states. The institution of slavery and its consequences formed the line of discrimination. There were five states on the southern, eight on the northern side of this line. Should a proportional representation take place, it was true the northern would still outnumber the other, but not in the same degree, at this time, and everyday would tend towards an equilibrium.

Mr. Wilson would add a few words only. If equality in the second branch was an error that time would correct, he should be less anxious to exclude it, being sensible that perfection was unattainable in any plan, but being a fundamental and a perpetual error it ought by all means to be avoided. A vice in the representation, like an error in the first concoction, must be followed by disease, convulsions, and finally death itself. The justice of the general principle of proportional representation has not, in argument at least, been yet contradicted. But it is said that a departure from it, so far as to give the states an equal vote in one branch of the legislature, is essential to their preservation. He had considered this position maturely, but could not see its application. That the states ought to be preserved, he admitted. But does it follow that an equality of votes is necessary for the purpose? Is there any reason to suppose that if their preservation should depend more on the large than on the small states, the security of the states against the General Government would be diminished? Are the large states, less attached to their existence, more likely to commit suicide than the small? An equal vote, then, is not necessary as far as he can conceive and is liable, among other objections, to this insuperable one: The great fault of the existing Confederacy is the inactivity. It has never been a complaint against Congress that they governed overmuch. The complaint has been that they have governed too little. To remedy this defect we were sent here. Shall we effect the cure by establishing an equality of votes as is proposed? No, this very equality carries us directly to Congress—to the system which it is our duty to rectify. The small states cannot indeed act by virtue of this equality, but they may control the government as they have done in Congress. This very measure is here prosecuted by a minority of the people of America. Is, then, the object of the convention likely to be accomplished in this way? Will not our constituents say, "We sent you to form an efficient government, and you have given us one more complex, indeed, but having all the weakness of the former government"? He was anxious for uniting all the states under one government. He knew there were some respectable men who preferred three confederacies united by offensive and defensive alliances. Many things may be plausibly said, some things may be justly said, in favor of such a project. He could not, however, concur in it himself, but he thought nothing so pernicious as bad first principles.

Mr. Ellsworth asked two questions. One of Mr. Wilson, whether he had ever seen a good measure fail in Congress for want of a majority of states in its favor. He had himself never known such an instance. The other of Mr. Madison, whether a negative lodged with the majority of the states, even the smallest, could be more dangerous than the qualified negative proposed to be lodged in a single executive magistrate who must be taken from some one state.

Mr. Sherman signified that his expectation was that the general legislature would in some cases act on the federal principle of requiring quotas. But he thought it ought to be empowered to carry their own plans into execution if the states should fail to supply their respective quotas.

Attempt at proportional representation in the Senate defeated, 6 to 4.

• Article VI: This Constitution, and the Laws of the United States which shall be made in Pursuance thereof; and all Treaties made, or which shall be made, under the Authority of the United States, shall be the supreme Law of the Land; and the Judges in every State shall be bound thereby, any Thing in the Constitution or Laws of any State to the Contrary notwithstanding.
• Article I, Section 10: No State shall enter into any Treaty, Alliance, or Confederation; grant Letters of Marque and Reprisal; coin Money; emit Bills of Credit; make any Thing but gold and silver Coin a Tender in Payment of Debts; pass any Bill of Attainder, ex post facto Law, or Law impairing the Obligation of Contracts, or grant any Title of Nobility.

No State shall, without the Consent of the Congress, lay any Imposts or Duties on Imports or Exports, except what may be absolutely necessary for executing its inspection Laws; and the net Produce of all Duties and Imposts, laid by any State on Imports or Exports, shall be for the Use of the Treasury of the United States; and all such Laws shall be subject to the Revision and Control of the Congress.

No State shall, without the Consent of Congress, lay any Duty of Tonnage, keep Troops, or Ships of War in time of Peace, enter into any Agreement or Compact with another State, or with a foreign Power, or engage in War, unless actually invaded, or in such imminent Danger as will not admit of delay.

· Tenth Amendment, Bill of Rights, 1791: The powers not delegated to the United States by the Constitution, nor prohibited by it to the States, are reserved to the States respectively, or to the people.

THE CONSTITUTION OF THE UNITED STATES

STATE POWERS VERSUS NATIONAL POWERS / July 17

In convention. Mr. Gouverneur Morris moved to reconsider the whole resolution agreed to yesterday concerning the constitution of the two branches of the legislature. His object was to bring the house to a consideration in the abstract of the powers necessary to be vested in the General Government. It had been said: Let us know how the government is to be modeled and then we can determine what powers can be properly given to it. He thought the most eligible course was, first, to determine on the necessary powers and then so to modify the government as that it might be justly and properly enabled to administer them. He feared if we proceeded to a consideration of the powers whilst the vote of yesterday, including an equality of the states in the second branch, remained in force, a reference to it, either mental or expressed, would mix itself with the merits of every question concerning the powers. This motion was not seconded.

The sixth resolution in the report of the committee of the whole, relating to the powers, which had been postponed in order to consider the seventh and eighth, relating to the constitution of the national legislature, was now resumed.

Mr. Sherman observed that it would be difficult to draw the line between the powers of the general legislature and those to be left with the states; that he did not like the definition contained in the resolution; and proposed in its place to the words "individual legislation," inclusive, to insert "to make laws binding on the people of the United States in all cases which may concern the common interests of the

Union, but not to interfere with the government of the individual *181* states in any matters of internal police which respect the government of such states only and wherein the general welfare of the United States is not concerned."

Mr. Wilson seconded the amendment as better expressing the general principle.

Mr. Gouverneur Morris opposed it. The internal police, as it would be called and understood by the states, ought to be infringed in many cases, as in the case of paper money and other tricks by which citizens of other states may be affected.

Mr. Sherman, in explanation of his idea, read an enumeration of powers, including the power of levying taxes on trade, but not the power of direct taxation.

Mr. Gouverneur Morris remarked the omission and inferred that for the deficiencies of taxes on consumption, it must have been the meaning of Mr. Sherman that the General Government should recur to quotas and requisitions, which are subversive of the idea of government.

Mr. Sherman acknowledged that his enumeration did not include direct taxation. Some provision, he supposed, must be made for supplying the deficiency of other taxation, but he had not formed any.

On the question on Mr. Sherman's motion, it passed in the negative.

Attempt to clarify state–national legislative jurisdiction defeated, 8 to 2.

THE "SUPREME LAW" ACCEPTED / *July 17*

Mr. L. Martin moved the following resolution: "That the legislative acts of the United States, made by virtue and in pursuance of the Articles of Union, and all treaties made and ratified under the authority of the United States shall be the supreme law of the respective states as far as those acts or treaties shall relate to the said states or their citizens and inhabitants, and that the judiciaries of the several states shall be bound thereby in their decisions, anything in the respective laws of the individual states to the contrary notwithstanding."

Which was agreed to.

• Article IV, Section 1: Full Faith and Credit shall be given in each State to the public Acts, Records, and judicial Proceedings of every other State. And the

Congress may by general Laws prescribe the Manner in which such Acts, Records and Proceedings shall be proved, and the Effect thereof.

• Article IV, Section 2: The Citizens of each State shall be entitled to all Privileges and Immunities of Citizens in the several States.

• Article IV, Section 3: New States may be admitted by the Congress into this Union; but no new State shall be formed or erected within the Jurisdiction of any other State; nor any State be formed by the Junction of two or more States, or Parts of States, without the Consent of the Legislatures of the States concerned as well as of the Congress.

The Congress shall have Power to dispose of and make all needful Rules and Regulations respecting the Territory or other Property belonging to the United States; and nothing in this Constitution shall be so construed as to Prejudice any Claims of the United States, or of any particular State.

THE CONSTITUTION OF THE UNITED STATES

Editor's note: The conflicting, capricious, frequently unjust legislative acts of the states vis-a-vis each other and the union were one of the major problems the convention had been called to consider. Its principal solution, of course, was to grant overriding power to the national Government as legislator and executor of the "Supreme Law."

Throughout Article IV, however, the convention continued to specify areas where supervision by the national Congress would be a bridle on unilateral action by the states. The "Full Faith and Credit" paragraph and the first clause of Section 2—"Privileges and Immunities"—derived from the Articles of Confederation. The former underwent several revisions; the latter was accepted without argument. The admission of new states (Section 3) had been contemplated in Randolph's original resolutions. And even as the convention debates went on, the Congress of the Confederation passed an ordinance providing for the creation of five new states from the Northwest Territory. There was concern about the terms and conditions under which new states might enter the Union, but no doubt as to the national Government's position as final arbiter.

REPUBLICAN FORM OF GOVERNMENT GUARANTEED TO EACH STATE / July 18

The sixteenth resolution, "That the republican constitution and its existing laws ought to be guaranteed to each state by the United States," being considered, Mr. Gouverneur Morris thought the resolution very objectionable.

Mr. Wilson: The object is merely to secure the states against dangerous commotions, insurrections, and rebellions.

Mr. Mason: If the General Government should have no right to suppress rebellions against particular states, it will be in a bad situation indeed. As rebellions against itself originate in and against individual states, it must remain a passive spectator of its own subversion.

Mr. Randolph: The resolution has two objects—first, to secure a republican government; second, to suppress domestic commotions.

Mr. Madison moved to substitute, "that the constitutional authority of the states shall be guaranteed to them, respectively, against domestic as well as foreign violence."

Dr. McClurg seconded the motion.

Mr. Houston was afraid of perpetuating the existing constitutions of the states. That of Georgia was a very bad one and he hoped would be revised and amended. It may also be difficult for the General Government to decide between contending parties, each of which claim the sanction of the Constitution.

Mr. L. Martin was for leaving the states to suppress rebellions themselves.

Mr. Gorham thought it strange that a rebellion should be known to exist in the empire and the General Government should be restrained from interposing to subdue it. At this rate, an enterprising citizen might erect the standard of monarchy in a particular state, might gather together partisans from all quarters, might extend his views from state to state and threaten to establish a tyranny over the whole—and the General Government be compelled to remain an inactive witness of its own destruction. With regard to different parties in a state, as long as they confine their disputes to words, they will be harmless to the General Government and to each other. If they appeal to the sword, it will then be necessary for the General Government to interpose and put an end to it.

Mr. Carroll: Some such provision is essential. Every state ought to wish for it.

Mr. Randolph moved to add as an amendment to the motion, "and that no state be at liberty to form any other than a republican government."

Mr. Madison seconded the motion.

Mr. Rutledge thought it unnecessary to insert any guaranty. No doubt could be entertained but that Congress had the authority, if they had the means, to co-operate with any state in subduing a rebellion. It was in the nature of the thing.

Mr. Wilson moved "that a republican form of government shall be guaranteed to each state, and that each state shall be protected against foreign and domestic violence."

Mr. Madison and Mr. Randolph withdrew their propositions, and on the question for agreeing to Mr. Wilson's motion, it was unanimously agreed "that a republican form of government shall be guaranteed to each state."

Adjourned.

TWO SENATORS PER STATE APPROVED / *July 23*

Mr. Gouverneur Morris and Mr. King moved that the representation in the second branch consist of members from each state, who shall vote *per capita.*

Mr. Ellsworth said he had always approved of voting in that mode.

Mr. Gouverneur Morris moved to fill the blank with *three.* He wished the Senate to be a pretty numerous body. If two members only should be allowed to each state and a majority be made a quorum, the power would be lodged in fourteen members, which was too small a number for such a trust.

Mr. Gorham preferred two to three members for the blank. A small number was most convenient for deciding on peace and war, and so forth, which he expected would be vested in the second branch. The number of states will also increase. Kentucky, Vermont, the Province of Maine, and Franklin will probably soon be added to the present number. He presumed, also, that some of the largest states would be divided. The strength of the General Government will be not in the largeness, but the smallness of the states.

Mr. Mason thought three from each state, including new states, would make the second branch too numerous. Besides other objections, the additional expense ought always to form one, where it was not absolutely necessary.

Mr. Williamson: If the number be too great, the distant states will not be on an equal footing with the nearer states. The latter can more easily send and support their ablest citizens. He approved of the voting *per capita.*

The question for filling the blank with "three" defeated, 8 to 1.

The question for filling it with "two" was unanimously agreed to.

Mr. L. Martin was opposed to voting per capita as departing from the idea of the states being represented in the second branch.

Mr. Carroll was not struck with any particular objection against the

mode, but he did not wish so hastily to make so material an innova-   *185*
tion.

The question on the whole motion, namely, "the second branch to consist of two members from each state and to vote per capita," was approved, 9 to 1.

Congress in General

CHAPTER TWO

Powers and Limitations *189*

• Article I, Section 7: All Bills for raising Revenue shall originate in the House of Representatives; but the Senate may propose or concur with Amendments as on other Bills.
• Article I, Section 8: The Congress shall have Power . . . : To borrow Money on the credit of the United States; . . . To coin Money, regulate the Value thereof, and of foreign Coin, and fix the Standard of Weights and Measures; To provide for the Punishment of counterfeiting the Securities and current Coin of the United States. THE CONSTITUTION OF THE UNITED STATES

THE QUESTION OF ORIGINATING MONEY BILLS / *June 13*

Mr. Gerry moved to restrain the senatorial branch from originating money bills. The other branch was more immediately the representatives of the people, and it was a maxim that the people ought to hold the purse strings. If the Senate should be allowed to originate such bills, they would repeat the experiment till chance should furnish a set of representatives in the other branch who will fall into their snares.

Mr. Butler saw no reason for such a discrimination. We were always following the British constitution when the reason of it did not apply. There was no analogy between the House of Lords and the body proposed to be established. If the Senate should be degraded by any such discriminations, the best men would be apt to decline serving in it in favor of the other branch. And it will lead the latter into the practice of tacking other clauses to money bills.

Mr. Madison observed that the commentators on the British constitution had not yet agreed on the reason of the restriction on the House of Lords in money bills. Certain it was there could be no similar reason in the case before us. The Senate would be the representatives of the people as well as the first branch. If they should have any dangerous influence over it, they would easily prevail on some member of the latter to originate the bill they wished to be passed. As the Senate would be generally a more capable set of men, it would be wrong to disable them from any preparation of the business, especially of that which was most important and, in our republics, worse prepared than any other. The gentleman in pursuance of his principle ought to carry the restraint to the amendment as well as the originating of money bills, since an addition of a given sum would be equivalent to a distinct proposition of it.

Mr. King differed from Mr. Gerry and concurred in the objections to the proposition.

Mr. Read favored the proposition, but would not extend the restraint to the case of amendments.

Mr. Pinckney thinks the question premature. If the Senate should be formed on the same proportional representation as it stands at present, they should have equal power; otherwise, if a different principle should be introduced.

Mr. Sherman: As both branches must concur, there can be no danger whichever way the Senate may be formed. We establish two branches in order to get more wisdom, which is particularly needed in the finance business. The Senate bear their share of the taxes and are also the representatives of the people. "What a man does by another, he does by himself" is a maxim. In Connecticut, both branches can originate in all cases, and it has been found safe and convenient. Whatever might have been the reason of the rule as to the House of Lords, it is clear that no good arises from it now even there.

Gen. Pinckney: This distinction prevails in South Carolina and has been a source of pernicious disputes between the two branches. The Constitution is now evaded by informal schedules of amendments handed from the Senate to the other house.

Mr. Williamson wishes for a question, chiefly to prevent rediscussion. The restriction will have one advantage: It will oblige some member in the lower branch to move, and people can then mark him.

The question for excepting money bills as proposed by Mr. Gerry defeated, 7 to 3.

| July 6

The first clause relating to the originating of money bills was then resumed.

Mr. Gouverneur Morris was opposed to a restriction of this right in either branch, considered merely in itself and as unconnected with the point of representation in the second branch. It will disable the second branch from proposing its own money plans and giving the people an opportunity of judging by comparison of the merits of those proposed by the first branch.

Mr. Wilson could see nothing like a concession here on the part of the smaller states. If both branches were to say yes or no, it was of little consequence which should say yes or no first, which last. If either was indiscriminately to have the right of originating, the reverse of the report would, he thought, be most proper; since it was a maxim that the least numerous body was the fittest for deliberation, the most numerous for decision. He observed that this discrimination had been transcribed from the British into several American constitutions. But he was persuaded that on examination of the American experiments, it would be found to be a "trifle light as air." Nor could he ever discover the advantage of it in the parliamentary history of Great Britain. He hoped if there was any advantage in the privilege that it would be pointed out.

Mr. Williamson thought that if the privilege were not common to both branches, it ought rather to be confined to the second as the bills in that case would be more narrowly watched than if they originated with the branch having most of the popular confidence.

Mr. Mason: The consideration which weighed with the committee was that the first branch would be the immediate representatives of the people, the second would not. Should the latter have the power of giving away the people's money, they might soon forget the source from whence they received it. We might soon have an aristocracy. He had been much concerned at the principles which had been advanced by some gentlemen, but had the satisfaction to find they did not generally prevail. He was a friend to proportional representation in both branches, but supposed that some points must be yielded for the sake of accommodation.

Mr. Wilson: If he had proposed that the second branch should have an independent disposal of public money, the observations of Col. Mason would have been a satisfactory answer. But nothing could be farther from what he had said. His question was how is the power of the first branch increased or that of the second diminished by giving the proposed privilege to the former? Where is the difference in which branch it begins if both must concur in the end?

Mr. Gerry would not say that the concession was a sufficient one on the part of the small states. But he could not but regard it in the light of a concession. It would make it a constitutional principle that the second branch were not possessed of the confidence of the people in money matters, which would lessen their weight and influence. In the next place, if the second branch were dispossessed of the privilege, they would be deprived of the opportunity which their continuance in office three times as long as the first branch would give them, of making three successive essays in favor of a particular point.

Mr. Pinckney thought it evident that the concession was wholly on one side, that of the large states; the privilege of originating money bills being of no account.

Mr. Gouverneur Morris had waited to hear the good effects of the restriction. As to the alarm sounded of an aristocracy, his creed was that there never was, nor ever will be, a civilized society without an aristocracy. His endeavor was to keep it as much as possible from doing mischief. The restriction, if it has any real operation, will deprive us of the services of the second branch in digesting and proposing money bills, of which it will be more capable than the first branch. It will take away the responsibility of the second branch, the great security for good behavior. It will always leave a plea as to an obnoxious money bill that it was disliked, but could not be constitutionally amended, nor safely rejected. It will be a dangerous source of disputes between the two houses. We should either take the British constitution altogether or make one for ourselves. The executive there has dissolved two houses as the only cure for such disputes. Will our executive be able to apply such a remedy? Every law, directly or indirectly, takes money out of the pockets of the people. Again, what use may be made of such a privilege in case of great emergency! Suppose an enemy at the door and money instantly and absolutely necessary for repelling him, may not the popular branch avail itself of this duress to extort concessions from the Senate destructive of the Constitution itself? He illustrated this danger by the example of the Long Parliament's expedients for subverting the House of Lords; concluding on the whole that the restriction would be either useless or pernicious.

Dr. Franklin did not mean to go into a justification of the report; but as it had been asked what would be the use of restraining the second branch from meddling with money bills, he could not but remark that it was always of importance that the people should know who had disposed of their money and how it had been disposed of. It was a maxim that those who feel can best judge. This end would, he thought, be best attained if money affairs were to be confined to the immediate representatives of the people. This was his inducement to concur in the report. As to the danger or difficulty that might arise from a negative in the second branch where the people would not be proportionally represented, it might easily be got over by declaring that there should be no such negative, or if that will not do, by declaring that there shall be no such branch at all.

Mr. Martin said that it was understood in the committee that the difficulties and disputes which had been apprehended should be guarded against in the detailing of the plan.

Mr. Wilson: The difficulties and disputes will increase with the attempts to define and obviate them. Queen Anne was obliged to dissolve her Parliament in order to terminate one of these obstinate disputes between the two houses. Had it not been for the mediation of the crown, no one can say what the result would have been. The point is still *sub judice* in England. He approved of the principles laid down by the honorable president[1] (Dr. Franklin), his colleague, as to the expediency of keeping the people informed of their money affairs, but thought they would know as much and be as well satisfied in one way as in the other.

Gen. Pinckney was astonished that this point should have been considered as a concession. He remarked that the restriction as to money bills had been rejected on the merits singly considered by eight states against three, and that the very states which now called it a concession were then against it as nugatory or improper in itself.

/ July 14

Mr. Rutledge proposed to reconsider the two propositions touching the originating of money bills in the first, and the equality of votes in the second, branch.

Mr. Sherman was for the question on the whole at once. It was, he said, a conciliatory plan; it had been considered in all its parts, a great deal of time had been spent upon it, and if any part should now be altered, it would be necessary to go over the whole ground again.

Mr. L. Martin urged the question on the whole. He did not like many parts of it. He did not like having two branches, nor the inequality of votes in the first branch. He was willing, however, to make trial of the plan rather than do nothing.

Mr. Wilson traced the progress of the report through its several stages, remarking that when on the question concerning an equality of votes the house was divided, our constituents, had they voted as their representatives did, would have stood as two-thirds against the equality and one-third only in favor of it. This fact would ere long be known, and it would appear that this fundamental point has been carried by one-third against two-thirds. What hopes will our constituents entertain when they find that the essential principles of justice have been violated in the outset of the government? As to the privilege of originating money bills, it was not considered by any as of much moment, and by many as improper in itself. He hoped both clauses would be reconsidered. The equality of votes was a point of such critical importance that every opportunity ought to be allowed for discussing and collecting the mind of the convention upon it.

Mr. L. Martin denies that there were two-thirds against the equality

---

[1] President of the State of Pennsylvania.

of votes. The states that please to call themselves large are the weakest in the Union. Look at Massachusetts—look at Virginia—are they efficient states? He was for letting a separation take place if they desired it. He had rather there should be two confederacies than one founded on any other principle than an equality of votes, in the second branch at least.

Mr. Wilson was not surprised that those who say that a minority does more than a majority should say the minority is stronger than the majority. He supposed the next assertion will be that they are richer also, though he hardly expected it would be persisted in when the states shall be called on for taxes and troops.

Mr. Gerry also animadverted on Mr. L. Martin's remarks on the weakness of Massachusetts. He favored the reconsideration with a view, not of destroying the equality of votes, but of providing that the states should vote per capita, which, he said, would prevent the delays and inconveniences that had been experienced in Congress and would give a national aspect and spirit to the management of business. He did not approve of a reconsideration of the clause relating to money bills. It was of great consequence. It was the cornerstone of the accommodation. If any member of the convention had the exclusive privilege of making propositions, would anyone say that it would give him no advantage over other members? The report was not altogether to his mind, but he would agree to it as it stood, rather than throw it out altogether.

/ August 13

Article 4, Section 5, being reconsidered, Mr. Randolph moved that the clause be altered so as to read: "Bills for raising money for the purpose of revenue, or for appropriating the same, shall originate in the House of Representatives; and shall not be so amended or altered by the Senate as to increase or diminish the sum to be raised, or change the mode of levying it, or the object of its appropriation." He would not repeat his reasons, but barely remind the members from the smaller states of the compromise by which the larger states were entitled to this privilege.

Mr. Mason: This amendment removes all the objections urged against the section as it stood at first. By specifying purposes of revenue, it obviated the objection that the section extended to all bills under which money might incidentally arise. By authorizing amendments in the Senate, it got rid of the objections that the Senate could not correct errors of any sort and that it would introduce into the House of

Representatives the practice of tacking foreign matter to money bills. *195* These objections being removed, the arguments in favor of the proposed restraint on the Senate ought to have their full force. First, the Senate did not represent the people, but the states in their political character. It was improper, therefore, that it should tax the people. The reason was the same against their doing it as it had been against Congress doing it. Secondly, nor was it in any respect necessary in order to cure the evils of our republican system. He admitted that notwithstanding the superiority of the republican form over every other, it had its evils. The chief ones were the danger of the majority oppressing the minority and the mischievous influence of demagogues. The General Government of itself will cure them. As the states will not concur at the same time in their unjust and oppressive plans, the General Government will be able to check and defeat them, whether they result from the wickedness of the majority or from the misguidance of demagogues. Again, the Senate is not, like the House of Representatives, chosen frequently and obliged to return frequently among the people. They are to be chosen by the states for six years, will probably settle themselves at the seat of government, will pursue schemes for their own aggrandisement, will be able by wearying out the House of Representatives and taking advantage of their impatience at the close of a long session, to extort measures for that purpose. If they should be paid, as he expected would be yet determined and wished to be so, out of the national treasury, they will, particularly, extort an increase of their wages. A bare negative was a very different thing from that of originating bills. The practice in England was in point. The House of Lords does not represent or tax the people, because they are not elected by the people. If the Senate can originate, they will in the recess of the legislative sessions hatch their mischievous projects for their own purposes and have their money bills cut and dried (to use a common phrase) for the meeting of the House of Representatives. He compared the case to Poyning's law and signified that the House of Representatives might be rendered by degrees, like the Parliament of Paris, the mere depository of the decrees of the Senate. As to the compromise, so much had passed on that subject that he would say nothing about it. He did not mean by what he had said to oppose the permanency of the Senate. On the contrary, he had no repugnance to an increase of it, or to allowing it a negative, though the Senate was not by its present constitution entitled to it. But in all events, he would contend that the purse strings should be in the hands of the representatives of the people.

Mr. Wilson was himself directly opposed to the equality of vote granted to the Senate by its present constitution. At the same time, he wished not to multiply the vices of the system. He did not mean to enlarge on a subject which had been so much canvassed, but would remark, as an insuperable objection against the proposed restriction of money bills to the House of Representatives, that it would be a source of perpetual contentions where there was no mediator to decide them. The President here could not, like the executive magistrate in England, interpose by a prorogation or dissolution. This restriction had been found pregnant with altercation in every state where the constitution had established it. The House of Representatives will insert other things in money bills, and by making them conditions of each other destroy the deliberate liberty of the Senate. He stated the case of a preamble to a money bill sent up by the House of Commons in the reign of Queen Anne to the House of Lords, in which the conduct of the misplaced ministry who were to be impeached before the Lords was condemned—the Commons thus extorting a premature judgment without any hearing of the parties to be tried, and the House of Lords being thus reduced to the poor and disgraceful expedient of opposing to the authority of a law a protest on their journals against its being drawn into precedent. If there was anything like Poyning's law in the present case, it was in the attempt to vest the exclusive right of originating in the House of Representatives, and so far he was against it. He should be equally so if the right were to be exclusively vested in the Senate. With regard to the purse strings, it was to be observed that the purse was to have two strings, one of which was in the hands of the House of Representatives, the other in those of the Senate. Both houses must concur in untying, and of what importance could it be which untied first, which last? He could not conceive it to be any objection to the Senate's preparing the bills that they would have leisure for that purpose and would be in the habits of business. War, commerce, and revenue were the great objects of the General Government. All of them are connected with money. The restriction in favor of the House of Representatives would exclude the Senate from originating any important bills whatever.

Mr. Gerry considered this as a part of the plan that would be much scrutinized. Taxation and representation are strongly associated in the minds of the people and they will not agree that any but their immediate representatives shall meddle with their purses. In short, the acceptance of the plan will inevitably fail if the Senate be not restrained from originating money bills.

Mr. Gouverneur Morris: All the arguments suppose the right to originate and to tax to be exclusively vested in the Senate. The effects

commented on may be produced by a negative only in the Senate.
They can tire out the other house and extort their concurrence in
favorite measures as well by withholding their negative as by adhering
to a bill introduced by themselves.

Mr. Madison thought if the substitute offered by Mr. Randolph for
the original section is to be adopted, it would be proper to allow the
Senate at least so to amend as to diminish the sums to be raised. Why
should they be restrained from checking the extravagance of the
other house? One of the greatest evils incident to republican government was the spirit of contention and faction. The proposed substitute
which in some respects lessened the objections against the section had
a contrary effect with respect to this particular. It laid a foundation for
new difficulties and disputes between the two houses. The word *revenue* was ambiguous. In many acts, particularly in the regulation of
trade, the object would be twofold. The raising of revenue would be
one of them. How could it be determined which was the primary or
predominant one, or whether it was necessary that revenue should be
the sole object in exclusion even of other incidental effects? When the
contest was first opened with Great Britain, their power to regulate
trade was admitted, their power to raise revenue rejected. An accurate
investigation of the subject afterwards proved that no line could be
drawn between the two cases. The words *amend* or *alter* form an
equal source of doubt and altercation. When an obnoxious paragraph shall be sent down from the Senate to the House of Representatives, it will be called an origination under the name of an amendment.
The Senate may actually couch extraneous matter under that name.
In these cases, the question will turn on the degree of connection between the matter and object of the bill, and the alteration or amendment offered to it. Can there be a more fruitful source of dispute, or a
kind of dispute more difficult to be settled? His apprehensions on this
point were not conjectural. Disputes had actually flowed from this
source in Virginia, where the Senate can originate no bill. The words
"so as to *increase* or *diminish* the sum to be raised" were liable to
the same objections. In levying indirect taxes, which it seemed to be
understood were to form the principal revenue of the new government, the sum to be raised would be increased or diminished by a
variety of collateral circumstances influencing the consumption in general—the consumption of foreign or of domestic articles—of this or
that particular species of articles—and even by the mode of collection,
which may be closely connected with the productiveness of a tax. The
friends of the section had argued its necessity from the permanency of
the Senate. He could not see how this argument applied. The Senate

was not more permanent now than in the form it bore in the original propositions of Mr. Randolph and at the time when no objection whatever was hinted against its originating money bills. Or if in consequence of a loss of the present question, a proportional vote in the Senate should be reinstated, as has been urged as the indemnification, the permanency of the Senate will remain the same. If the right to originate be vested exclusively in the House of Representatives, either the Senate must yield against its judgment to that House—in which case the utility of the check will be lost—or the Senate will be inflexible and the House of Representatives must adapt its money bill to the views of the Senate, in which case the exclusive right will be of no avail. As to the compromise of this so much had been said, he would make a single observation. There were five states which had opposed the equality of votes in the Senate, namely, Massachusetts, Pennsylvania, Virginia, North Carolina, and South Carolina. As a compensation for the sacrifice extorted from them on this head, the exclusive origination of money bills in the other house had been tendered. Of the five states, a majority, namely, Pennsylvania, Virginia, and South Carolina, have uniformly voted against the proposed compensation on its own merits as rendering the plan of government still more objectionable. Massachusetts has been divided. North Carolina alone has set a value on the compensation and voted on that principle. What obligation then can the small states be under to concur against their judgments in reinstating the section?

Mr. Dickinson: Experience must be our only guide. Reason may mislead us. It was not reason that discovered the singular and admirable mechanism of the English constitution. It was not reason that discovered, or ever could have discovered, the odd and, in the eyes of those who are governed by reason, the absurd mode of trial by jury. Accidents probably produced these discoveries and experience has given a sanction to them. This is then our guide. And has not experience verified the utility of restraining money bills to the immediate representatives of the people? Whence the effect may have proceeded, he could not say—whether from the respect with which this privilege inspired the other branches of government to the House of Commons, or from the turn of thinking it gave to the people at large with regard to their rights—but the effect was visible and could not be doubted. Shall we oppose to this long experience the short experience of eleven years which we had ourselves on this subject? As to disputes, they could not be avoided anyway. If both houses should originate, each would have a different bill to which it would be attached and for which it would contend. He observed that all the prejudices of the people would be offended by refusing this exclusive privilege to the House of Representatives, and these prejudices should never be disregarded by us when no essential purpose was to be served. When this plan goes forth, it will be attacked by the popular leaders. Aristocracy will be the watchword, the Shibboleth, among its adversaries. Eight states have inserted in their constitutions the exclusive right of originating money bills in favor of the popular branch of the legislature. Most of them, however, allowed the other branch to amend. This, he thought, would be proper for us to do.

Mr. Randolph regarded this point as of such consequence that as he valued the peace of this country he would press the adoption of it. We had numerous and monstrous difficulties to combat. Surely we ought not to increase them. When the people behold in the Senate the countenance of an aristocracy and in the President the form at least of a little monarch, will not their alarms be sufficiently raised without taking from their immediate representatives a right which has been so long appropriated to them? The executive will have more influence over the Senate than over the House of Representatives. Allow the Senate to originate in this case and that influence will be sure to mix itself in their deliberations and plans. The declaration of war, he conceived, ought not to be in the Senate composed of twenty-six men only, but rather in the other house. In the other house ought to be placed the origination of the means of war. As to commercial regulations which may involve revenue, the difficulty may be avoided by restraining the definition to bills for the mere or sole purpose of raising revenue. The Senate will be more likely to be corrupt than the House of Representatives and should, therefore, have less to do with money matters. His principal object, however, was to prevent popular objections against the plan and to secure its adoption.

Mr. Rutledge: The friends of this motion are not consistent in their reasoning. They tell us that we ought to be guided by the long experience of Great Britain and not our own experience of eleven years, and yet they themselves propose to depart from it. The House of Commons not only have the exclusive right of originating, but the Lords are not allowed to alter or amend a money bill. Will not the people say that this restriction is but a mere tub to the whale? They cannot but see that it is of no real consequence and will be more likely to be displeased with it as an attempt to bubble them than to impute it to a watchfulness over their rights. For his part, he would prefer giving the exclusive right to the Senate if it was to be given exclusively at all. The Senate, being more conversant in business and having more leisure, will digest the bills much better, and as they are to have no effect till examined and approved by the House of Representatives, there can be no possible danger. These clauses in the constitutions of the states had been put in through a blind adherence to the British model. If the work was to be done over now, they would be omitted. The experiment in South Carolina, where the Senate cannot originate or amend money bills, has shown that it answers no good purpose and produces the very bad one of continually dividing and heating the two houses. Sometimes, indeed, if the matter of the amendment of the Senate is pleasing to the other house, they wink at the encroachment; if it be displeasing, then the Constitution is appealed to. Every session is distracted by altercations on this subject. The practice now becoming frequent is for the Senate not to make formal amendments, but to send down a schedule of the alterations which will procure the bill their assent.

Mr. Carroll: The most ingenious men in Maryland are puzzled to define the case of money bills or explain the Constitution on that point, though it seemed to be worded with all possible plainness and precision. It is a source of continual difficulty and squabble between the two houses.

Mr. McHenry mentioned an instance of extraordinary subterfuge to get rid of the apparent force of the Constitution.

The question on the first part of the motion as to the exclusive originating of money bills in the House of Representatives defeated, 7 to 4.

The question on originating by the House of Representatives and amending by the Senate defeated, 7 to 4.

The question on the last clause of Article 4, Section 5, "No money shall be drawn from the public treasury but in pursuance of appropriations *that shall originate in the House of Representatives," defeated, 10 to 1.*

CREDIT BILLS ELIMINATED / August 16

Mr. Gouverneur Morris moved to strike out "and emit bills on the credit of the United States." If the United States had credit, such bills would be unnecessary; if they had not, unjust and useless.

Mr. Butler seconds the motion.

Mr. Madison: Will it not be sufficient to prohibit the making them a tender? This will remove the temptation to emit them with unjust views, and promissory notes in that shape may in some emergencies be best.

Mr. Gouverneur Morris: Striking out the words will leave room still for notes of a *responsible* minister, which will do all the good without the mischief. The moneyed interest will oppose the plan of government if paper emissions be not prohibited.

Mr. Gorham was for striking out without inserting any prohibition. If the words stand, they may suggest and lead to the measure.

Mr. Mason had doubts on the subject. Congress, he thought, would not have the power unless it were expressed. Though he had a mortal hatred of paper money, yet as he could not foresee all emergencies, he was unwilling to tie the hands of the legislature. He observed that the late war could not have been carried on had such a prohibition existed.

Mr. Gorham: The power, as far as it will be necessary or safe, is involved in that of borrowing.

Mr. Mercer was a friend to paper money, though in the present state and temper of America, he should neither propose nor approve of such a measure. He was consequently opposed to a prohibition of it altogether. It will stamp suspicion on the government to deny it a discretion on this point. It was impolitic, also, to excite the opposition of all those who were friends to paper money. The people of property would be sure to be on the side of the plan, and it was impolitic to purchase their further attachment with the loss of the opposite class of citizens.

Mr. Ellsworth thought this a favorable moment to shut and bar the door against paper money. The mischiefs of the various experiments which had been made were now fresh in the public mind and had excited the disgust of all the respectable part of America. By withholding the power from the new government, more friends of influence would be gained to it than by almost anything else. Paper money can in no case be necessary. Give the government credit and other resources will offer. The power may do harm, never good.

Mr. Randolph, notwithstanding his antipathy to paper money, could not agree to strike out the words, as he could not foresee all the occasions that might arise.

Mr. Wilson: It will have a most salutary influence on the credit of the United States to remove the possibility of paper money. This expedient can never succeed whilst its mischiefs are remembered, and as long as it can be resorted to, it will be a bar to other resources.

Mr. Butler remarked that paper was a legal tender in no country in Europe. He was urgent for disarming the government of such a power.

Mr. Mason was still averse to tying the hands of the legislature altogether. If there was no example in Europe, as just remarked, it might be observed, on the other side, that there was none in which the government was restrained on this head.

Mr. Read thought the words, if not struck out, would be as alarming
as the mark of the beast in Revelation.

Mr. Langdon had rather reject the whole plan than retain the three
words "and emit bills."

The motion for striking out passed, 9 to 2.

The clause for borrowing money was agreed to unanimously.

• **Article I, Section 8: The Congress shall have Power to . . . provide for the
common Defence and general Welfare of the United States; . . . To define and
punish Piracies and Felonies committed on the high Seas, and Offences against
the Law of Nations; To declare War, grant Letters of Marque and Reprisal,
and make Rules concerning Captures on Land and Water; To raise and support
Armies, but no Appropriation of Money to that Use shall be for a longer Term
than two Years; To provide and maintain a Navy; To make Rules for the
Government and Regulation of the land and naval Forces; . . . To exercise
exclusive Legislation in all Cases whatsoever . . . over all Places purchased by
the Consent of the Legislature of the State in which the Same shall be, for the
Erection of Forts, Magazines, Arsenals, dock-Yards, and other needful Buildings.**

THE CONSTITUTION OF THE UNITED STATES

WAR POWERS DISCUSSED / *August 17*

On the clause, "to make war," Mr. Pinckney opposed the vesting this
power in the legislature. Its proceedings were too slow. It would meet
but once a year. The House of Representatives would be too numerous for such deliberations. The Senate would be the best depository,
being more acquainted with foreign affairs and most capable of
proper resolutions. If the states are equally represented in the Senate
so as to give no advantage to the large states the power will, notwithstanding, be safe, as the small have their all at stake in such cases
as well as the large states. It would be singular for one authority to
make war and another peace.

Mr. Butler: The objections against the legislature lie in a great
degree against the Senate. He was for vesting the power in the President, who will have all the requisite qualities and will not make war
but when the nation will support it.

Mr. Madison and Mr. Gerry moved to insert "declare," striking out
"make," war, leaving to the executive the power to repel sudden at-
tacks.

Mr. Sherman thought it stood very well. The executive should be

able to repel, and not to commence, war. "Make" is better than "de-   *203*
clare," the latter narrowing the power too much.

Mr. Gerry never expected to hear in a republic a motion to empower
the executive alone to declare war.

Mr. Ellsworth: There is a material difference between the cases of
making war and making peace. It should be more easy to get out of
war than into it. War, also, is a simple and overt declaration; peace,
attended with intricate and secret negotiations.

Mr. Mason was against giving the power of war to the executive, because (he was) not safely to be trusted with it, or to the Senate, because (it was) not so constructed as to be entitled to it. He was for
clogging, rather than facilitating war, but for facilitating peace. He
preferred "declare" to "make."

*Motion to insert "declare" in place of "make" was agreed to,
8 to 1.*

Mr. Pinckney's motion to strike out the whole clause was disagreed
to without call of states.

Mr. Butler moved to give the legislature the power of peace, as they
were to have that of war.

Mr. Gerry seconds him. Eight senators may possibly exercise
the power if vested in that body, and fourteen if all should be present,
and may, consequently, give up part of the United States. The Senate
are more liable to be corrupted by an enemy than the whole
legislature.

*On the motion for adding "and peace" after "war," it was unan-
imously negatived. Adjourned.*

POWER TO RAISE ARMIES DEBATED / *August 18*

Mr. Gorham moved to add "and support" after "raise."

*Agreed to unanimously, and then the clause was agreed to unani-
mously, as amended.*

Mr. Gerry took notice that there was no check here against standing
armies in time of peace. The existing Congress is so constructed that it
cannot of itself maintain an army. This would not be the case under
the new system. The people were jealous on this head, and great opposition to the plan would spring from such an omission. He suspected
that preparations of force were now making against it. He thought an
army dangerous in time of peace and could never consent to a power
to keep up an indefinite number. He proposed that there should not
be kept up in time of peace more than _____ thousand troops. His
idea was that the blank should be filled with two or three thousand.

Instead of "to build and equip fleets," "to provide and maintain a navy" was agreed to as a more convenient definition of the power.

A clause "to make rules for the government and regulation of the land and naval forces" was added from the existing Articles of Confederation.

Mr. L. Martin and Mr. Gerry now regularly moved: "Provided that in time of peace the army shall not consist of more than _____ thousand men."

Gen. Pinckney asked whether no troops were ever to be raised until an attack should be made on us.

Mr. Gerry: If there be no restriction, a few states may establish a military government.

Mr. Williamson reminded him of Mr. Mason's motion for limiting the appropriation of revenue as the best guard in this case.

Mr. Langdon saw no room for Mr. Gerry's distrust of the representatives of the people.

Mr. Dayton: Preparations for war are generally made in time of peace, and a standing force of some sort may, for aught we know, become unavoidable. He should object to no restrictions consistent with these ideas.

The motion of Mr. Martin and Mr. Gerry was disagreed to.

• Article I, Section 8: The Congress shall have Power . . . To provide for calling forth the Militia to execute the Laws of the Union, suppress Insurrections and repel Invasions; To provide for organizing, arming, and disciplining, the Militia, and for governing such Part of them as may be employed in the Service of the United States, reserving to the States respectively, the Appointment of the Officers, and the Authority of training the Militia according to the discipline prescribed by Congress; . . . .

• Article II, Section 2: The President shall be Commander in Chief of the Army and Navy of the United States, and of the Militia of the several States, when called into the actual Service of the United States.

THE CONSTITUTION OF THE UNITED STATES

QUESTION OF MILITIA RENEWS
CONTROVERSY OVER STATES' RIGHTS / *August 18*

Mr. Mason moved as an additional power "to make laws for the regulation and discipline of the militia of the several states, reserving to the states the appointment of the officers." He considered uniformity as necessary in the regulation of the militia throughout the Union.

Gen. Pinckney mentioned a case during the war in which a dissimilarity in the militia of different states had produced the most serious mischiefs. Uniformity was essential. The states would never keep up a proper discipline of the militia.

Mr. Ellsworth was for going as far in submitting the militia to the General Government as might be necessary, but thought the motion of Mr. Mason went too far. He moved "that the militia should have the same arms and exercise and be under rules established by the General Government when in actual service of the United States, and when states neglect to provide regulations for militia, it should be regulated and established by the Legislature of the United States." The whole authority over the militia ought by no means to be taken away from the states, whose consequence would pine away to nothing after such a sacrifice of power. He thought the general authority could not sufficiently pervade the Union for such a purpose, nor could it accommodate itself to the local genius of the people. It must be vain to ask the states to give the militia out of their hands.

Mr. Sherman seconds the motion.

Mr. Dickinson: We are come now to a most important matter—that of the sword. His opinion was that the states never would, nor ought to, give up all authority over the militia. He proposed to restrain the general power to one fourth part at a time, which by rotation would discipline the whole militia.

Mr. Butler urged the necessity of submitting the whole militia to the general authority, which had the care of the general defense.

Mr. Mason had suggested the idea of a select militia. He was led to think that would be, in fact, as much as the General Government could advantageously be charged with. He was afraid of creating insuperable objections to the plan. He withdrew his original motion and moved a power "to make laws for regulating and disciplining the militia, not exceeding one tenth part in any one year, and reserving the appointment of officers to the states."

Gen. Pinckney renewed Mr. Mason's original motion. For a part to be under the general and a part under the state governments would be an incurable evil. He saw no room for such distrust of the General Government.

Mr. Langdon seconds Gen. Pinckney's renewal. He saw no more reason to be afraid of the General Government than of the state governments. He was more apprehensive of the confusion of the different authorities on this subject than of either.

Mr. Madison thought the regulation of the militia naturally appertaining to the authority charged with the public defense. It did not seem in its nature to be divisible between two distinct authorities. If the states would trust the General Government with a power over the public treasure, they would from the same consideration of necessity grant it the direction of the public force. Those who had a full view of the public situation would from a sense of the danger guard against it. The states would not be separately impressed with the general situation, nor have the due confidence in the concurrent exertions of each other.

Mr. Ellsworth considered the idea of a select militia as impracticable, and if it were not, it would be followed by a ruinous declension of the great body of the militia. The states would never submit to the same militia laws. Three or four shillings, as a penalty, will enforce obedience better in New England than forty lashes in some other places.

Mr. Pinckney thought the power such a one as could not be abused and that the states would see the necessity of surrendering it. He had, however, but a scanty faith in militia. There must be also a real military force. This alone can effectually answer the purpose. The United States had been making an experiment without it, and we see the consequence in their rapid approaches toward anarchy.

Mr. Sherman took notice that the states might want their militia for defense against invasions and insurrections and for enforcing obedience to their laws. They will not give up this point. In giving up that of taxation, they retain a concurrent power of raising money for their own use.

Mr. Gerry thought this the last point remaining to be surrendered. If it be agreed to by the convention, the plan will have as black a mark as was set on Cain. He had no such confidence in the General Government as some gentlemen possessed, and believed it would be found that the states have not.

Mr. Mason thought there was great weight in the remarks of Mr. Sherman and moved an exception to his motion, "of such part of the militia as might be required by the states for their own use."

Mr. Read doubted the propriety of leaving the appointment of the militia officers to the states. In some states they are elected by the legislatures; in others, by the people themselves. He thought at least an appointment by the state executives ought to be insisted on.

Question for committing to the grand committee passed.

/ August 23

Mr. Ellsworth and Mr. Sherman moved to postpone the second clause in favor of the following: "To establish a uniformity of arms, exercise,

and organization for the militia, and to provide for the government of
them when called into the service of the United States."

The object of this proposition was to refer the plan for the militia to the General Government, but to leave the execution of it to the state governments.

Mr. Langdon said he could not understand the jealousy expressed by some gentlemen. The general and state governments were not enemies to each other, but different institutions for the good of the people of America. As one of the people, he could say, "The national Government is mine, the state government is mine. In transferring power from one to the other, I only take out of my left hand what it cannot so well use and put it into my right hand where it can be better used."

Mr. Gerry thought it was rather taking out of the right hand and putting it into the left. Will any man say that liberty will be as safe in the hands of eighty or a hundred men taken from the whole continent as in the hands of two or three hundred taken from a single state?

Mr. Dayton was against so absolute a uniformity. In some states there ought to be a greater proportion of cavalry than in others. In some place, rifles would be most proper, in others muskets, and so forth.

Gen. Pinckney preferred the clause reported by the committee, extending the meaning of it to the cases of fines, and so forth.

Mr. Madison: The primary object is to secure an effectual discipline of the militia. This will no more be done if left to the states separately than the requisitions have been hitherto paid by them. The states neglect their militia now, and the more they are consolidated into one nation, the less each will rely on its own interior provisions for its safety and the less prepare its militia for that purpose; in like manner, as the militia of a state would have been still more neglected than it has been if each county had been independently charged with the care of its militia. The discipline of the militia is evidently a national concern and ought to be provided for in the national Constitution.

Mr. L. Martin was confident that the states would never give up the power over the militia, and that if they were to do so, the militia would be less attended to by the general than by the state governments.

Mr. Randolph asked what danger there could be that the militia could be brought into the field and made to commit suicide on themselves. This is a power that cannot from its nature be abused, unless, indeed, the whole mass should be corrupted. He was for trammeling the General Government whenever there was danger, but here there could be none. He urged this as an essential point, observing that the militia were everywhere neglected by the state legislatures, the members of which courted popularity too much to enforce a proper discipline. Leaving the appointment of officers to the states protects the people against every apprehension that could produce murmur.

The question on Mr. Ellsworth's motion was defeated, 10 to 1.

A motion was then made to recommit the second clause, which was negatived.

The question to agree to the first part of the clause, namely, "To make laws for organizing, arming, and disciplining the militia, and for governing such part of them as may be employed in the service of the United States," was defeated, 9 to 2.

Mr. Madison moved to amend the next part of the clause so as to read "reserving to the states, respectively, the appointment of the officers under the rank of general officers."

Mr. Sherman considered this as absolutely inadmissible. He said that if the people should be so far asleep as to allow the most influential officers of the militia to be appointed by the General Government, every man of discernment would rouse them by sounding the alarm to them.

Mr. Gerry: Let us at once destroy the state governments, have an executive for life, or hereditary, and a proper Senate, and then there would be some consistency in giving full powers to the General Government; but as the states are not to be abolished, he wondered at the attempts that were made to give powers inconsistent with their existence. He warned the convention against pushing the experiment too far. Some people will support a plan of vigorous government at every risk; others of a more democratic cast will oppose it with equal determination, and a civil war may be produced by the conflict.

Mr. Madison: As the greatest danger is that of disunion of the states, it is necessary to guard against it by sufficient powers to the common government, and as the greatest danger to liberty is from large standing armies, it is **best to** prevent them by an effectual provision for a good militia.

Mr. Madison's motion defeated, 8 to 3.

On the question to agree to the "reserving to the states the appointment of the officers," it was agreed to unanimously.

The question on the clause "and the authority of training the militia according to the discipline prescribed by the United States" passed, 7 to 4.

• Article I, Section 8: The Congress shall have Power to lay and collect Taxes, Duties, Imposts and Excises . . . ; but all Duties, Imposts and Excises shall be uniform throughout the United States; . . . .

THE CONSTITUTION OF THE UNITED STATES

TAX POWERS DEBATED / August 16

Mr. Mason urged the necessity of connecting with the powers levying taxes, duties, and so forth, the prohibition in Article 6, Section 4, "that no tax should be laid on exports." He was unwilling to trust to its being done in a future article. He hoped the northern states did not mean to deny the southern this security. It would hereafter be as desirable to the former when the latter should become the most populous. He professed his jealousy for the productions of the southern or, as he called them, the staple states. He moved to insert the following amendment:

"Provided, that no tax, duty, or imposition shall be laid by the legislature of the United States on articles exported from any state."

Mr. Sherman had no objection to the proviso here other than that it would derange the parts of the report, as made by the committee, to take them in such an order.

Mr. Rutledge: It being of no consequence in what order points are decided, he should vote for the clause as it stood, but on condition that the subsequent part relating to Negroes should also be agreed to.

Mr. Gouverneur Morris considered such a proviso as inadmissible anywhere. It was so radically objectionable that it might cost the whole system the support of some members. He contended that it would not in some cases be equitable to tax imports without taxing exports, and that taxes on exports would be often the most easy and proper of the two.

Mr. Madison: First, the power of laying taxes on exports is proper in itself, and as the states cannot with propriety exercise it separately, it ought to be vested in them collectively. Secondly, it might with particular advantage be exercised with regard to articles in which America was not rivaled in foreign markets, as tobacco, and so forth; the contract between the French farmers-general and Mr. Morris, stipulating that if taxes should be laid in America on the export of tobacco they should be paid by the farmers, showed that it was understood by them that the price would be thereby raised in America and, consequently, the taxes be paid by the European consumer. Thirdly, it would be unjust to the states whose produce was exported by their neighbors to leave it subject to be taxed by the latter. This was a grievance which had already filled New Hampshire, Connecticut, New Jersey, Delaware, and North Carolina with loud complaints, as it related to imports, and they would be equally authorized by taxes by the states on exports. Fourthly, the southern states, being most in danger and most needing naval protection, could the less complain if the burden should be somewhat heaviest on them. And finally, we are not providing for the present moment only, and time will equalize the situation of the states in this matter. He was for these reasons against the motion.

Mr. Williamson considered the clause proposed against taxes on exports as reasonable and necessary.

Mr. Ellsworth was against taxing exports, but thought the prohibition stood in the most proper place and was against deranging the order reported by the committee.

Mr. Wilson was decidedly against prohibiting general taxes on exports. He dwelt on the injustice and impolicy of leaving New Jersey, Connecticut, and so forth, any longer subject to the exactions of their commercial neighbors.

Mr. Gerry thought the legislature could not be trusted with such a power. It might ruin the country. It might be exercised partially, raising one and depressing another part of it.

Mr. Gouverneur Morris: However the legislative power may be formed, it will, if disposed, be able to ruin the country. He considered the taxing of exports to be in many cases highly politic. Virginia has found her account in taxing tobacco. All countries having peculiar articles tax the exportation of them—as France, her wines and brandies. A tax here on lumber would fall on the West Indies and punish their restrictions on our trade. The same is true of livestock and, in some degree, of flour. In case of a dearth in the West Indies, we may extort what we please. Taxes on exports are a necessary source of revenue. For a long time the people of America will not have money to pay direct taxes. Seize and sell their effects and you push them into revolts.

Mr. Mercer was strenuous against giving Congress power to tax exports. Such taxes are impolitic, as encouraging the raising of articles not meant for exportation. The states had now a right, where their situation permitted, to tax both the imports and the exports of their uncommercial neighbors. It was enough for them to sacrifice one half of it. It had been said the southern states had most need of naval protection. The reverse was the case. Were it not for promoting the carrying trade of the northern states, the southern states could let

the trade go into foreign bottoms, where it would not need our pro- 211
tection. Virginia by taxing her tobacco had given an advantage to
that of Maryland.

Mr. Sherman: To examine and compare the states in relation to imports and exports will be opening a boundless field. He thought the
matter had been adjusted, and that imports were to be subject, and
exports not, to be taxed. He thought it wrong to tax exports, except
it might be such articles as ought not to be exported. The complexity
of the business in America would render an equal tax on exports impracticable. The oppression of the uncommercial states was guarded
against by the power to regulate trade between the states. As to compelling foreigners, that might be done by regulating trade in general.
The government would not be trusted with such a power. Objections
are most likely to be excited by considerations relating to taxes and
money. A power to tax exports would shipwreck the whole.

Mr. Carroll was surprised that any objection should be made to an
exception of exports from the power of taxation.

It was finally agreed that the question concerning exports should lie
over for the place in which the exception stood in the report—Maryland alone voting against it.

· Article VI: All Debts contracted and Engagements entered into, before the
Adoption of this Constitution, shall be as valid against the United States under
this Constitution, as under the Confederation.

THE CONSTITUTION OF THE UNITED STATES

Editor's note: Two days after the convention conferred on Congress
the basic power to tax, Messrs. Rutledge, Charles Pinckney, Gerry, and
King pointed out that no clause provided for payment of the debt
already contracted during the Revolution. The delegates were agreed
that the new government should fulfill the obligations contracted in
the course of the conflict that had made its existence possible. They
were uncertain, however, how sweeping their promises to creditors
should be. After considerable debate, they left the rights of creditors
exactly as they had been under the Confederation, but declared (in
Article VI) the government's intention to recognize past obligations,
and thus affirm its integrity.

· Article I, Section 9: . . . No Tax or Duty shall be laid on Articles exported from
any State.

No Preference shall be given by any Regulation of Commerce or Revenue to the Ports of one State over those of another: nor shall Vessels bound to, or from, one State, be obliged to enter, clear, or pay Duties in another.

• Article I, Section 8: The Congress shall have Power . . . To regulate Commerce with foreign Nations, and among the several States, and with the Indian Tribes.

THE CONSTITUTION OF THE UNITED STATES

TAX ON EXPORTS PROHIBITED / August 21

Article 7, Section 4, was then taken up.

Mr. Langdon: By this section the states are left at liberty to tax exports. New Hampshire, therefore, with other non-exporting states will be subject to be taxed by the states exporting its produce. This could not be admitted. It seems to be feared that the northern states will oppress the trade of the southern. This may be guarded against by requiring the concurrence of two-thirds, or three-fourths of the legislature in such cases.

Mr. Ellsworth: It is best as it stands. The power of regulating trade between the states will protect them against each other. Should this not be the case, the attempts of one to tax the produce of another passing through its hands will force a direct exportation and defeat themselves. There are solid reasons against Congress taxing exports. First, it will discourage industry, as taxes on imports discourage luxury. Secondly, the produce of different states is such as to prevent uniformity in such taxes. There are indeed but a few articles that could be taxed at all, as tobacco, rice, and indigo, and a tax on these alone would be partial and unjust. Thirdly, the taxing of exports would engender incurable jealousies.

Mr. Williamson: Though North Carolina has been taxed by Virginia by a duty on twelve thousand hogsheads of her tobacco through Virginia, yet he would never agree to this power. Should it take place, it would destroy the last hope of the adoption of the plan.

Mr. Gouverneur Morris: These local considerations ought not to impede the general interest. There is great weight in the argument that the exporting states will tax the produce of their uncommercial neighbors. The power of regulating the trade between Pennsylvania and New Jersey will never prevent the former from taxing the latter. Nor will such a tax force a direct exportation from New Jersey. The advantages possessed by a large trading city outweigh the disadvantage of a moderate duty and will retain the trade in that channel. If no tax can be laid on exports, an embargo cannot be laid, though in time of war such a measure may be of critical importance. *213* Tobacco, lumber, and livestock are three objects belonging to different states of which great advantage might be made by a power to tax exports. To these may be added ginseng (an aromatic Chinese herb) and meats for ships, by which a tax might be thrown on other nations. The idea of supplying the West Indies with lumber from Nova Scotia is one of the many follies of Lord Sheffield's pamphlet. The state of the country also will change and render duties on exports—as skins, beaver, and other peculiar raw materials—politic in the view of encouraging American manufactures.

Mr. Butler was strenuously opposed to a power over exports as unjust and alarming to the staple states.

Mr. Langdon suggested a prohibition on the states from taxing the produce of other states exported from their harbors.

Mr. Dickinson: The power of taxing exports may be inconvenient at present, but it must be of dangerous consequence to prohibit it with respect to all articles, and forever. He thought it would be better to except particular articles from the power.

Mr. Sherman: It is best to prohibit the national legislature in all cases. The states will never give up all power over trade. An enumeration of particular articles would be difficult, invidious, and improper.

Mr. Madison: As we ought to be governed by national and permanent views, it is a sufficient argument for giving the power over exports, that a tax, though it may not be expedient at present, may be so hereafter. A proper regulation of exports may, and probably will be necessary hereafter, and for the same purposes as the regulation of imports, namely, for revenue, domestic manufactures, and procuring equitable regulations from other nations. An embargo may be of absolute necessity and can alone be effectuated by the general authority. The regulation of trade between state and state cannot effect, more than indirectly, to hinder a state from taxing its own exports, by authorizing its citizens to carry their commodities freely into a neighboring state which might decline taxing exports in order to draw into its channel the trade of its neighbors. As to the fear of disproportionate burdens on the more exporting states, it might be remarked that it was agreed on all hands that the revenue would principally be drawn from trade, and as only a given revenue would be needed, it was not material whether all should be drawn wholly from imports or half from those and half from exports. The imports and exports must be pretty nearly equal in every state and relatively the same among the different states.

Mr. Ellsworth did not conceive an embargo by the Congress interdicted by this section.

Mr. McHenry conceived that power to be included in the power of
war.

Mr. Wilson: Pennsylvania exports the produce of Maryland, New
Jersey, and Delaware and will, by and by, when the River Delaware
is opened, export for New York. In favoring the general power over
exports, therefore, he opposed the particular interest of his state. He
remarked that the power had been attacked by reasoning which could
only have held good in case the General Government had been compelled, instead of authorized, to lay duties on exports. To deny this
power is to take from the common government half the regulation of
trade. It was his opinion that a power over exports might be more effectual than that over imports in obtaining beneficial treaties of commerce.

Mr. Gerry was strenuously opposed to the power over exports. It
might be made use of to compel the states to comply with the will of
the General Government and to grant it any new powers which might
be demanded. We have given it more power already than we know
how will be exercised. It will enable the General Government to oppress the states as much as Ireland is oppressed by Great Britain.

Mr. Fitzsimmons would be against a tax on exports to be laid immediately, but was for giving a power of laying the tax when a proper
time may call for it. This would certainly be the case when America
should become a manufacturing country. He illustrated his argument
by the duties in Great Britain on wool and other products.

Mr. Mason: If he were for reducing the states to mere corporations,
as seemed to be the tendency of some arguments, he should be for subjecting their exports, as well as imports, to a power of general taxation. He went on a principle often advanced, and in which he concurred, that a majority, when interested, will oppress the minority.
This maxim had been verified by our own legislature (of Virginia).
If we compare the states in this point of view, the eight northern states
have an interest different from the five southern states and have, in
one branch of the legislature, thirty-six votes against twenty-nine, and
in the other in the proportion of eight against five. The southern
states had, therefore, ground for their suspicions. The case of exports
was not the same with that of imports. The latter were the same
throughout the states; the former very different. As to tobacco, other
nations do raise it and are capable of raising it as well as Virginia.
The impolicy of taxing that article had been demonstrated by the experiment of Virginia.

Mr. Clymer remarked that every state might reason with regard to 215 its particular productions in the same manner as the southern states. The middle states may apprehend an oppression of their wheat, flour, provisions, and so forth, and with more reason, as these articles were exposed to a competition in foreign markets not incident to tobacco, rice, and so forth. They may apprehend also combinations against them between the eastern and southern states as much as the latter can apprehend them between the eastern and middle. He moved as a qualification of the power of taxing exports that it should be restrained to regulations of trade by inserting after the word "duty," Article 7, Section 4, the words "for the purpose of revenue."

Mr. Clymer's motion defeated, 8 to 3.

Question on Article 7, Section 4, "no tax shall be laid on exports," passed, 7 to 4.

REGULATION OF COMMERCE / August 29

Mr. Pinckney moved to postpone the report in favor of the following proposition: "That no act of the legislature for the purpose of regulating the commerce of the United States with foreign powers, among the several states, shall be passed without the assent of two-thirds of the members of each house."

He remarked that there were five distinct commercial interests. 1. The fisheries and West India trade which belonged to the New England states. 2. The interest of New York lay in a free trade. 3. Wheat and flour, the staples of the two middle states (New Jersey and Pennsylvania). 4. Tobacco, the staple of Maryland and Virginia, and partly of North Carolina. 5. Rice and indigo, the staples of South Carolina and Georgia. These different interests would be a source of oppressive regulations if no check to a bare majority should be provided. States pursue their interests with less scruple than individuals. The power of regulating commerce was a pure concession on the part of the southern states. They did not need the protection of the northern states at present.

Mr. Martin seconded the motion.

Gen. Pinckney said it was the true interest of the southern states to have no regulation of commerce, but considering the loss brought on the commerce of the eastern states by the Revolution, their liberal conduct toward the views of South Carolina, and the interest the weak southern states had in being united with the strong eastern states, he thought it proper that no fetters should be imposed on the power of making commercial regulations, and that his constituents, though prejudiced against the eastern states, would be reconciled to this liberality. He had himself, he said, prejudices against the eastern states before he came here, but would acknowledge that he had found them as liberal and candid as any men whatever.

Mr. Clymer: The diversity of commercial interest of necessity creates difficulties which ought not to be increased by unnecessary restrictions. The northern and middle states will be ruined if not enabled to defend themselves against foreign regulations.

Mr. Sherman, alluding to Mr. Pinckney's enumeration of particular interests as requiring a security against abuse of the power, observed that the diversity was of itself a security, adding that to require more than a majority to decide a question was always embarrassing, as had been experienced in cases requiring the votes of nine states in Congress.

Mr. Pinckney replied that his enumeration meant the five minute interests. It still left the two great divisions of northern and southern interests.

Mr. Gouverneur Morris opposed the object of the motion as highly injurious. Preferences to American ships will multiply them till they can carry the southern produce cheaper than it is now carried. A navy was essential to security, particularly of the southern states, and can only be had by a navigation act encouraging American bottoms and seamen. In those points of view, then, alone, it is the interest of the southern states that navigation acts should be facilitated. Shipping, he said, was the worst and most precarious kind of property and stood in need of public patronage.

Mr. Williamson was in favor of making two-thirds, instead of a majority, requisite as more satisfactory to the southern people. No useful measure, he believed, had been lost in Congress for want of nine votes. As to the weakness of the southern states, he was not alarmed on that account. The sickliness of their climate for invaders would prevent their being made an object. He acknowledged that he did not think the motion requiring two-thirds necessary in itself, because if a majority of the northern states should push their regulations too far, the southern states would build ships for themselves, but he knew the southern people were apprehensive on this subject and would be pleased with the precaution.

Mr. Spaight was against the motion. The southern states could at any time save themselves from oppression by building ships for their own use.

Mr. Butler differed from those who considered the rejection of the motion as no concession on the part of the southern states. He considered the interest of these and of the eastern states to be as different as the interests of Russia and Turkey. Being, notwithstanding, desirous of conciliating the affections of the eastern states, he should vote against requiring two-thirds instead of a majority.

Mr. Mason: If the government is to be lasting, it must be founded in the confidence and affections of the people and must be so constructed as to obtain these. The majority will be governed by their interests. The southern states are the minority in both houses. Is it to be expected that they will deliver themselves, bound hand and foot, to the eastern states and enable them to exclaim in the words of Cromwell on a certain occasion, "the Lord hath delivered them into our hands"?

Mr. Wilson took notice of the several objections and remarked that if every peculiar interest was to be secured, unanimity ought to be required. The majority, he said, would be no more governed by interest than the minority. It was surely better to let the latter be bound hand and foot than the former. Great inconveniences had, he contended, been experienced in Congress from the Article of Confederation requiring nine votes in certain cases.

Mr. Madison went into a pretty full view of the subject. He observed that the disadvantage to the southern states from a navigation act lay chiefly in a temporary rise of freight, attended, however, with an increase of southern as well as northern shipping—with the emigration of northern seamen and merchants to the southern states—and with a removal of the existing and injurious retaliations among the states on each other. The power of foreign nations to obstruct our retaliating measures on them by a corrupt influence, would also be less if a majority should be made competent than if two-thirds of each house should be required to legislate acts in this case. An abuse of the power would be qualified with all these good effects. But he thought an abuse was rendered improbable by the provision of two branches—by the independence of the Senate, by the negative of the executive, by the interest of Connecticut and New Jersey, which were agricultural, not commercial states, by the interior interest, which was also agricultural in the most commercial states, and by the accession of western states, which would be altogether agricultural. He added that the southern states would derive an essential advantage in the general security afforded by the increase of our maritime strength. He stated the vulnerable situation of them all and of Virginia in particular. The increase of the coasting trade and of seamen would also be favorable to the southern states by increasing the consumption of their produce. If the wealth of the eastern should in a still greater proportion be augmented, that wealth would contribute the more to the public wants and be otherwise a national benefit.

Mr. Rutledge was against the motion of his colleague. It did not follow from a grant of the power to regulate trade that it would be abused. At the worst, a navigation act could bear hard a little while only on the southern states. As we are laying the foundation for a great empire, we ought to take a permanent view of the subject and not look at the present moment only. He reminded the house of the necessity of securing the West India trade to this country. That was the great object and a navigation act was necessary for obtaining it.

Mr. Randolph said that there were features so odious in the Constitution as it now stands that he doubted whether he should be able to agree to it. A rejection of the motion would complete the deformity of the system. He took notice of the argument in favor of giving the power over trade to a majority, drawn from the opportunity foreign powers would have of obstructing retaliatory measures if two-thirds were made requisite. He did not think there was weight in that consideration. The difference between a majority and two-thirds did not afford room for such an opportunity. Foreign influence would also be more likely to be exerted on the President, who could require three-fourths by his negative. He did not mean, however, to enter into the merits. What he had in view was merely to pave the way for a declaration—which he might be hereafter obliged to make if an accumulation of obnoxious ingredients should take place—that he could not give his assent to the plan.

Mr. Gorham: If the government is to be so fettered as to be unable to relieve the eastern states, what motive can they have to join in it and thereby tie their own hands from measures which they could otherwise take for themselves? The eastern states were not led to strengthen the Union by fear for their own safety. He deprecated the consequences of disunion, but if it should take place, it was the southern part of the continent that had most reason to dread them. He urged the improbability of a combination against the interest of the southern states, the different situations of the northern and middle states being a security against it. It was, moreover, certain that foreign ships would never be altogether excluded, especially those of nations in treaty with us.

The report of the committee for striking out Section 6, requiring two-thirds of each house to pass a navigation act, was then agreed to.

Editor's note: The Committee of Detail overlooked or ignored the 219
new government's relations with the Indian tribes of America when
it offered its draft Constitution on August 6. Under the Articles of
Confederation, Indian affairs were the responsibility of Congress, but,
as in most matters, the rights of the states actually took precedence,
and the regulation of the Indian trade—and the Indians—bore no
relation to national interest or policy.

On August 18, Madison urged that unrestricted jurisdiction over
Indian affairs be among the enumerated powers of the new Congress.
His motion was reworked and reworded in committee, and eventually
the commerce clause of the Constitution simply declared that Congress could regulate commerce with foreign nations, among the states,
"and with the Indian Tribes."

• Article III, Section 3: Treason against the United States, shall consist only in
levying War against them, or, in adhering to their Enemies, giving them Aid
and Comfort. No Person shall be convicted of Treason unless on the Testimony
of two Witnesses to the same overt Act, or on Confession in open Court.

The Congress shall have Power to declare the Punishment of Treason, but no
Attainder of Treason shall work Corruption of Blood, or Forfeiture except during
the Life of the Person attainted.

• Article IV, Section 2: . . . A Person charged in any State with Treason, Felony,
or other Crime, who shall flee from Justice, and be found in another State,
shall on Demand of the executive Authority of the State from which he fled,
be delivered up, to be removed to the State having Jurisdiction of the Crime.

THE CONSTITUTION OF THE UNITED STATES

POWER TO DEFINE TREASON GRANTED / *August 20*

Article 7, Section 2, concerning treason, was then taken up.

Mr. Madison thought the definition too narrow. It did not appear
to go as far as the statute of Edward III. He did not see why more
latitude might not be left to the legislature. It would be as safe as in
the hands of state legislatures and it was inconvenient to bar a discretion which experience might enlighten and which might be applied
to good purposes as well as be abused.

Mr. Mason was for pursuing the statute of Edward III.

Mr. Gouverneur Morris was for giving to the Union an exclusive
right to declare what should be treason. In case of a contest between
the United States and a particular state, the people of the latter must,

under the disjunctive terms of the clause, be traitors to one or other authority.

Mr. Randolph thought the clause defective in adopting the words "in adhering" only. The British statute adds "giving them aid and comfort," which had a more extensive meaning.

Mr. Ellsworth considered the definition as the same in fact with that of the statute.

Mr. Gouverneur Morris: "Adhering" does not go so far as "giving aid and comfort," or the latter words may be restrictive of "adhering." In either case the statute is not pursued.

Mr. Wilson held "giving aid and comfort" to be explanatory, not operative words, and that it was better to omit them.

Mr. Dickinson thought the addition of "giving aid and comfort" unnecessary and improper, being too vague and extending too far. He wished to know what was meant by the "testimony of two witnesses"—whether they were to be witnesses to the same overt act or to different overt acts. He thought, also, that proof of an overt act ought to be expressed as essential in the case.

Dr. Johnson considered "giving aid and comfort" as explanatory of "adhering," and that something should be inserted in the definition concerning overt acts. He contended that treason could not be both against the United States and individual states, being an offense against the sovereignty, which can be but one in the same community.

Mr. Madison remarked that "and" before "in adhering" should be changed into "or"; otherwise both offenses, of "levying war," and of "adhering to the enemy," might be necessary to constitute treason. He added that as the definition here was of treason against the United States, it would seem that the individual states would be left in possession of a concurrent power, so far as to define and punish treason, particularly against themselves, which might involve double punishment.

Mr. Wilson and Dr. Johnson moved that "or any of them" after "United States" be struck out in order to remove the embarrassment, which was agreed to unanimously.

Mr. Madison: This has not removed the embarrassment. The same act might be treason against the United States as here defined and against a particular state according to its laws.

Mr. Ellsworth: There can be no danger to the general authority from this, as the laws of the United States are to be paramount.

Dr. Johnson was still of opinion there could be no treason against a particular state. It could not even at present as the Confederation now stands, the sovereignty being in the Union; much less can it be under the proposed system.

Mr. Mason: The United States will have a qualified sovereignty only. The individual states will retain a part of the sovereignty. An act may be treason against a particular state which is not so against the United States. He cited the rebellion of (Nathaniel) Bacon in Virginia as an illustration of the doctrine.

Dr. Johnson: That case would amount to treason against the sovereign—the supreme sovereign, the United States.

Mr. King observed that the controversy relating to treason might be of less magnitude than was supposed as the legislature might punish capitally under other names than treason.

Mr. Gouverneur Morris and Mr. Randolph wished to substitute the words of the British statute and moved to postpone Article 7, Section 2, in order to consider the following substitute:

"Whereas it is essential to the preservation of liberty to define precisely and exclusively what shall constitute the crime of treason, it is therefore ordained, declared, and established that if a man do levy war against the United States within their territories, or be adherent to the enemies of the United States within the said territories, giving them aid and comfort within their territories or elsewhere, and thereof be provably attainted of open deed, by the people of his condition, he shall be adjudged guilty of treason."

Question was defeated, 8 to 2.

It was then moved to strike out "against the United States" after "treason," so as to define treason generally, and this question passed, 8 to 2.

It was then moved to insert after "two witnesses," the words "to the same overt act."

Dr. Franklin wished this amendment to take place. Prosecutions for treason were generally virulent and perjury too easily made use of against innocence.

Mr. Wilson: Much may be said on both sides. Treason may sometimes be practiced in such a manner as to render proof extremely difficult, as in a traitorous correspondence with an enemy.

The question as to "same overt act" passed, 8 to 3.

Mr. King moved to insert before the word "power," the word "sole," giving the United States the exclusive right to declare the punishment of treason.

Mr. Broom seconds the motion.

Mr. Wilson: In cases of a general nature, treason can only be against the United States, and in such they should have the sole right to declare the punishment; yet in many cases it may be otherwise. The subject was, however, intricate, and he distrusted his present judgment on it.

Mr. King: This amendment results from the vote defining treason generally by striking out "against the United States," which excludes any treason against particular states. These may, however, punish offenses, as high misdemeanors.

Question for inserting the word "sole" was defeated, 6 to 5.

Mr. Wilson: The clause is ambiguous now. "Sole" ought either to have been inserted, or "against the United States" to be reinstated.

Mr. King: No line can be drawn between levying war and adhering to the enemy against the United States and against an individual state. Treason against the latter must be so against the former.

Mr. Sherman: Resistance against the laws of the United States, as distinguished from resistance against the laws of a particular state, forms the line.

Mr. Ellsworth: The United States are sovereign on one side of the line dividing the jurisdictions, the states on the other. Each ought to have power to defend their respective sovereignties.

Mr. Dickinson: War or insurrection against a member of the Union must be so against the whole body, but the Constitution should be made clear on this point.

The clause was reconsidered, and then Mr. Wilson and Mr. Ellsworth moved to reinstate "against the United States" after "treason."

Question passed, 6 to 5.

Mr. Madison was not satisfied with the footing on which the clause now stood. As treason against the United States involves treason against particular states, and vice versa, the same act may be twice tried and punished by the different authorities.

Mr. Gouverneur Morris viewed the matter in the same light.

It was moved and seconded to amend the sentence to read "Treason against the United States shall consist only in levying war against them, or in adhering to their enemies," which was agreed to.

Mr. Mason moved to insert the words "giving them aid and comfort," as restrictive of "adhering to their enemies." The latter, he thought, would be otherwise too indefinite. This motion was agreed to, Connecticut, Delaware, and Georgia only being in the negative.

Mr. L. Martin moved to insert after conviction "or on confession in open court."

Question—the negative states thinking the words superfluous—was agreed to, 7 to 3.

• Article IV, Section 2: . . . No Person held to Service or Labour in one State, **223** under the Laws thereof, escaping into another, shall, in Consequence of any Law or Regulation therein, be discharged from such Service or Labour, but shall be delivered up on Claim of the Party to whom such Service or Labour may be due. THE CONSTITUTION OF THE UNITED STATES

Editor's note: This, the famous Fugitive Slave Clause, developed during the convention's discussion of treason. Article IV, Section 2, had established the obligation of the states to return any fugitive from justice to his state of origin. The southern states then wanted a paragraph to provide for the return of runaway slaves, as well. The clause above was inserted to stipulate this. It was considered a major victory for the South. Minor changes in wording were made later, but the clause was agreed to without dissent on August 29.

• Article I, Section 9: . . . No Bill of Attainder or ex post facto Law shall be passed.
• Article I, Section 10: No State shall . . . pass any Bill of Attainder, ex post facto Law, ... THE CONSTITUTION OF THE UNITED STATES

EX POST FACTO LAWS PROHIBITED / *August 22*

Mr. Gerry and Mr. McHenry moved to insert after the second section, Article 7, the clause following, to wit, "The legislature shall pass no bill of attainder, nor any ex post facto law."

Mr. Gerry urged the necessity of this prohibition which, he said, was greater in the national than the state legislature, because the number of members in the former being fewer, they were on that account the more to be feared.

Mr. Gouverneur Morris thought the precaution as to ex post facto laws unnecessary, but essential as to bills of attainder.

Mr. Ellsworth contended that there was no lawyer, no civilian, who would not say that ex post facto laws were void of themselves. It cannot then be necessary to prohibit them.

Mr. Wilson was against inserting anything in the Constitution as to ex post facto laws. It will bring reflections on the Constitution and proclaim that we are ignorant of the first principles of legislation or are constituting a government that will be so.

The question being divided, the first part of the motion relating to bills of attainder was agreed to unanimously.

On the second part relating to ex post facto laws Mr. Carroll remarked that experience overruled all other calculations. It had proved that in whatever light they might be viewed by civilians or others the state legislatures had passed them, and they had taken effect.

Mr. Wilson: If these prohibitions in the state constitutions have no effect it will be useless to insert them in this Constitution. Besides, both sides will agree to the principle, but will differ as to its application.

Mr. Williamson: Such a prohibitory clause is in the Constitution of North Carolina, and though it has been violated, it has done good there and may do good here, because the judges can take hold of it.

Dr. Johnson thought the clause unnecessary and implying an improper suspicion of the national legislature.

Mr. Rutledge was in favor of the clause.

Question for inserting the prohibition of ex post facto laws passed, 7 to 3.

• Article I, Section 9: The Migration or Importation of such Persons as any of the States now existing shall think proper to admit, shall not be prohibited by the Congress prior to the Year one thousand eight hundred and eight, but a Tax or duty may be imposed on such Importation, not exceeding ten dollars for each Person. THE CONSTITUTION OF THE UNITED STATES

IMPORTATION OF SLAVES DEBATED / *August 21*

Mr. L. Martin proposed to vary Article 7, Section 4, so as to allow a prohibition or tax on the importation of slaves. In the first place, as five slaves are to be counted as three freemen in the apportionment of representatives, such a clause would leave an encouragement to this traffic. In the second place, slaves weakened one part of the Union which the other parts were bound to protect; the privilege of importing them was therefore unreasonable. And in the third place, it was inconsistent with the principles of the Revolution and dishonorable to the American character to have such a feature in the Constitution.

Mr. Rutledge did not see how the importation of slaves could be encouraged by this section. He was not apprehensive of insurrections and would readily exempt the other states from the obligation to protect the southern against them. Religion and humanity had nothing to do with this question. Interest alone is the governing principle with nations. The true question at present is whether the southern states shall or shall not be parties to the Union. If the northern states consult their interest, they will not oppose the increase of slaves, which will increase the commodities of which they will become the carriers.

Mr. Ellsworth was for leaving the clause as it stands. Let every state import what it pleases. The morality or wisdom of slavery are considerations belonging to the states themselves. What enriches a part enriches the whole, and the states are the best judges of their particular interest. The old Confederation had not meddled with this point, and he did not see any greater necessity for bringing it within the policy of the new one.

Mr. Pinckney: South Carolina can never receive the plan if it prohibits the slave trade. In every proposed extension of the powers of Congress, that state has expressly and watchfully excepted that of meddling with the importation of Negroes. If the states be all left at liberty on this subject, South Carolina may perhaps by degrees do of herself what is wished, as Virginia and Maryland already have done.

Adjourned.

| August 22

In convention. Article 7, Section 4, was resumed.

Mr. Sherman was for leaving the clause as it stands. He disapproved of the slave trade; yet as the states were now possessed of the right to import slaves, as the public good did not require it to be taken from them, and as it was expedient to have as few objections as possible to the proposed scheme of government, he thought it best to leave the matter as we find it. He observed that the abolition of slavery seemed to be going on in the United States, and that the good sense of the several states would probably by degrees complete it. He urged on the convention the necessity of dispatching its business.

Mr. Mason: This infernal traffic originated in the avarice of British merchants. The British Government constantly checked the attempts of Virginia to put a stop to it. The present question concerns not the importing states alone, but the whole Union. The evil of having slaves was experienced during the late war. Had slaves been treated as they might have been by the enemy, they would have proved dangerous instruments in their hands. But their folly dealt by the slaves as it did by the Tories. He mentioned the dangerous insurrections of the slaves in Greece and Sicily and the instructions given by Cromwell to the commissioners sent to Virginia to arm the servants and slaves in case other means of obtaining its submission should fail. Maryland and Virginia, he said, had already prohibited the importation of slaves ex pressly. North Carolina had done the same in substance. All this would be in vain if South Carolina and Georgia be at liberty to import. The western people are already calling out for slaves for their new lands and will fill that country with slaves if they can be got through South Carolina and Georgia. Slavery discourages arts and manufactures. The poor despise labor when performed by slaves. They prevent the emigration of whites, who really enrich and strengthen a country. They produce the most pernicious effect on manners. Every master of slaves is born a petty tyrant. They bring the judgment of Heaven on a country. As nations cannot be rewarded or punished in the next world, they must be in this. By an inevitable chain of causes and effects, Providence punishes national sins by national calamities. He lamented that some of our eastern brethren had from a lust of gain embarked in this nefarious traffic. As to the states being in possession of the right to import, this was the case with many other rights now to be properly given up. He held it essential in every point of view that the General Government should have power to prevent the increase of slavery.

Mr. Ellsworth, as he had never owned a slave, could not judge of the effects of slavery on character. He said, however, that if it was to be considered in a moral light, we ought to go further and free those already in the country. As slaves also multiply so fast in Virginia and Maryland, it is cheaper to raise than import them, whilst in the sickly rice swamps foreign supplies are necessary; if we go no further than is urged, we shall be unjust toward South Carolina and Georgia. Let us not intermeddle. As population increases, poor laborers will be so plenty as to render slaves useless. Slavery in time will not be a speck in our country. Provision is already made in Connecticut for abolishing it. And the abolition has already taken place in Massachusetts. As to the danger of insurrections from foreign influence, that will become a motive to kind treatment of the slaves.

Mr. Pinckney: If slavery be wrong, it is justified by the example of all the world. He cited the case of Greece, Rome, and other ancient states; the sanction given by France, England, Holland, and other modern states. In all ages, one-half of mankind have been slaves. If the southern states were let alone, they will probably of themselves stop importations. He would himself, as a citizen of South Carolina, vote for it. An attempt to take away the right, as proposed, will produce serious objections to the Constitution, which he wished to see adopted.

Gen. Pinckney declared it to be his firm opinion that if he and all his colleagues were to sign the Constitution and use their personal influence, it would be of no avail toward obtaining the assent of their constituents. South Carolina and Georgia cannot do without slaves. As to Virginia, she will gain by stopping the importations. Her slaves will rise in value and she has more than she wants. It would be unequal to require South Carolina and Georgia to confederate on such unequal terms. He said the royal assent before the Revolution had never been refused to South Carolina as to Virginia. He contended that the importation of slaves would be for the interest of the whole Union. The more slaves, the more produce to employ the carrying trade, the more consumption also, and the more of this, the more revenue for the common treasury. He admitted it to be reasonable that slaves should be dutied like other imports, but should consider a rejection of the clause as an exclusion of South Carolina from the Union.

Mr. Baldwin had conceived national objects alone to be before the convention, not such as, like the present, were of a local nature. Georgia was decided on this point. That state has always hitherto supposed a general government to be the pursuit of the central states, who wished to have a vortex for everything, that her distance would preclude her from equal advantage, and that she could not prudently purchase it by yielding national powers. From this it might be understood in what light she would view an attempt to abridge one of her favorite prerogatives. If left to herself, she may probably put a stop to the evil. As one ground for this conjecture, he took notice of the sect of _____, which he said was a respectable class of people who carried their ethics beyond the mere equality of men, extending their humanity to the claims of the whole animal creation.

Mr. Wilson observed that if South Carolina and Georgia were themselves disposed to get rid of the importation of slaves in a short time, as had been suggested, they would never refuse to unite because the importation might be prohibited. As the section now stands, all articles imported are to be taxed. Slaves alone are exempt. This is, in fact, a bounty on that state.

Mr. Gerry thought we had nothing to do with the conduct of the states as to slaves, but ought to be careful not to give any sanction to it.

Mr. Dickinson considered it as inadmissible on every principle of honor and safety that the importation of slaves should be authorized to the states by the Constitution. The true question was, whether the national happiness would be promoted or impeded by the importation, and this question ought to be left to the national Government, not to the states particularly interested. If England and France permit slavery, slaves are at the same time excluded from both those kingdoms. Greece and Rome were made unhappy by their slaves. He could not believe that the southern states would refuse to confederate on the account apprehended, especially as the power was not likely to be immediately exercised by the General Government.

Mr. Williamson stated the law of North Carolina on the subject, to wit, that it did not directly prohibit the importation of slaves. It imposed a duty of five pounds on each slave imported from Africa, ten pounds on each from elsewhere, and fifty pounds on each from a state licensing manumission. He thought the southern states could not be members of the Union if the clause should be rejected, and that it was wrong to force anything down not absolutely necessary and which any state must disagree to.

Mr. King thought the subject should be considered in a political light only. If two states will not agree to the Constitution as stated on one side, he could affirm with equal belief on the other that great and equal opposition would be experienced from the other states. He remarked on the exemption of slaves from duty whilst every other import was subjected to it as an inequality that could not fail to strike the commercial sagacity of the northern and middle states.

Mr. Langdon was strenuous for giving the power to the General Government. He could not with a good conscience leave it with the states, who could then go on with the traffic without being restrained by the opinions here given that they will themselves cease to import slaves.

Gen. Pinckney thought himself bound to declare candidly that he did not think South Carolina would stop her importations of slaves in any short time, but only stop them occasionally as she now does. He moved to commit the clause that slaves might be made liable to an equal tax with other imports, which he thought right, and which would remove one difficulty that had been started.

Mr. Rutledge: If the convention thinks that North Carolina, South Carolina, and Georgia will ever agree to the plan, unless their right to import slaves be untouched, the expectation is vain. The people of those states will never be such fools as to give up so important an interest. He was strenuous against striking out the section and seconded the motion of Gen. Pinckney for a commitment.

Mr. Gouverneur Morris wished the whole subject to be committed, including the clauses relating to taxes on exports and to a navigation act. These things may form a bargain among the northern and southern states.

Mr. Butler declared that he never would agree to the power of taxing exports.

Mr. Sherman said it was better to let the southern states import slaves than to part with them if they made that a *sine qua non*. He was opposed to a tax on slaves imported, as making the matter worse, because it implied they were property. He acknowledged that if the power of prohibiting the importation should be given to the General Government, it would be exercised He thought it would be its duty to exercise the power.

Mr. Read was for the commitment, provided the clause concerning taxes on exports should also be committed.

Mr. Sherman observed that that clause had been agreed to and, therefore, could not be committed.

Mr. Randolph was for committing in order that some middle ground might, if possible, be found. He could never agree to the clause as it stands. He would sooner risk the Constitution. He dwelt on the dilemma to which the convention was exposed. By agreeing to the clause, it would revolt the Quakers, the Methodists, and many others in the states having no slaves. On the other hand, two states might be lost to the Union. Let us then, he said, try the chance of a commitment.

Question for committing the remaining part of Sections 4 and 5 of Article 7 passed, 7 to 3.

SLAVE IMPORTS FORBIDDEN AFTER 1808 / *August 25*

The report of the committee of eleven being taken up, Gen. Pinckney moved to strike out the words "the year eighteen hundred," as the year limiting the importation of slaves, and to insert the words "the year eighteen hundred and eight."

Mr. Gorham seconded the motion.

Mr. Madison: Twenty years will produce all the mischief that can be apprehended from the liberty to import slaves. So long a term will be more dishonorable to the American character than to say nothing about it in the Constitution.

Motion passed, 7 to 4.

Mr. Gouverneur Morris was for making the clause read at once: "The importation of slaves into North Carolina, South Carolina, and Georgia shall not be prohibited."

This, he said, would be most fair and would avoid the ambiguity by which under the power with regard to naturalization, the liberty reserved to the states might be defeated. He wished it to be known, also, that this part of the Constitution was a compliance with those states. If the change of language, however, should be objected to by the members from those states, he should not urge it.

Mr. Mason was not against using the term, "slaves," but against naming North Carolina, South Carolina, and Georgia, lest it should give offense to the people of those states.

Mr. Sherman liked a description better than the terms proposed, which had been declined by the old Congress and were not pleasing to some people.

Mr. Clymer concurred with Mr. Sherman.

Mr. Williamson said that both in opinion and practice he was against slavery, but thought it more in favor of humanity from a view of all circumstances to let in South Carolina and Georgia on those terms than to exclude them from the Union.

Mr. Gouverneur Morris withdrew his motion.

Mr. Dickinson wished the clause to be confined to the states which had not themselves prohibited the importation of slaves, and for that purpose moved to amend the clause so as to read: "The importation of slaves into such of the states as shall permit the same shall not be prohibited by the legislature of the United States until the year 1808," which was disagreed to.

The first part of the report was then agreed to, amended as follows: "The migration or importation of such persons as the several states not existing shall think proper to admit shall not be prohibited by the legislature prior to the year 1808."

Mr. Baldwin, in order to restrain and more explicitly define "the average duty," moved to strike out of the second part the words "average of the duties laid on imports," and insert "common impost on articles not enumerated," which was agreed to unanimously.

Mr. Sherman was against this second part as acknowledging men to be property by taxing them as such under the character of slaves.

Mr. King and Mr. Langdon considered this as the price of the first part.

Gen. Pinckney admitted that it was so.

Mr. Mason: Not to tax will be equivalent to a bounty on the importation of slaves.

Mr. Gorham thought that Mr. Sherman should consider the duty not as implying that slaves are property, but as a discouragement to the importation of them.

Mr. Gouverneur Morris remarked that as the clause now stands, it implies that the legislature may tax freemen imported.

Mr. Sherman in answer to Mr. Gorham observed that the smallness of the duty showed revenue to be the object, not the discouragement of the importation.

Mr. Madison thought it wrong to admit in the Constitution the

idea that there could be property in men. The reason of duties did not
hold, as slaves are not, like merchandise, consumed.

Mr. Mason, in answer to Mr. Gouverneur Morris: The provision as
it stands was necessary for the case of convicts in order to prevent the
introduction of them.

It was finally agreed to make the clause read, "but a tax or duty
may be imposed on such importation, not exceeding ten dollars for
each person," and then the second part as amended was agreed to.

POWER TO VETO STATE LAWS PROHIBITED / *June 8*

In committee of the whole. On a reconsideration of the clause giving
the national legislature a negative on such laws of the states as might
be contrary to the Articles of Union or treaties with foreign nations,
Mr. Pinckney moved "that the national legislature should have authority to negative all laws which they should judge to be improper."
He urged that such a universality of the power was indispensably necessary to render it effectual; that the states must be kept in due subordination to the nation; that if the states were left to act of themselves in any case, it would be impossible to defend the national prerogatives, however extensive they might be on paper; that the Acts
of Congress had been defeated by this means, nor had foreign treaties
escaped repeated violations; that this universal negative was in fact
the cornerstone of an efficient national government; that under the
British Government, the negative of the crown had been found beneficial, and the states are more one nation now than the colonies were
then.

Mr. Madison seconded the motion. He could not but regard an indefinite power to negative legislative acts of the states as absolutely
necessary to a perfect system. Experience had evinced a constant tendency in the states to encroach on the Federal authority, to violate national treaties, to infringe the rights and interests of each other, to
oppress the weaker party within their respective jurisdictions. A negative was the mildest expedient that could be devised for preventing
these mischiefs. The existence of such a check would prevent attempts
to commit them. Should no such precaution be engrafted, the only
remedy would be in an appeal to coercion. Was such a remedy eligible? Was it practicable? Could the national resources, if exerted to
the utmost, enforce a national decree against Massachusetts, abetted
perhaps by several of her neighbors? It would not be possible. A small
proportion of the community in a compact situation acting on the de-

fensive and at one of its extremities might at any time bid defiance to the national authority. Any government for the United States, formed on the supposed practicability of using force against the unconstitutional proceedings of the states, would prove as visionary and fallacious as the government of Congress. The negative would render the use of force unnecessary. The states could of themselves pass no operative act, any more than one branch of a legislature, where there are two branches, can proceed without the other. But in order to give the negative this efficacy, it must extend to all cases. A discrimination would only be a fresh source of contention between the two authorities. In a word, to recur to the illustrations borrowed from the planetary system, this prerogative of the General Government is the great pervading principle that must control the centrifugal tendency of the states, which without it will continually fly out of their proper orbits and destroy the order and harmony of the political system.

Mr. Williamson was against giving a power that might restrain the states from regulating their internal police.

Mr. Gerry could not see the extent of such a power and was against every power that was not necessary. He thought a remonstrance against unreasonable acts of the states would restrain them. If it should not, force might be resorted to. He had no objection to authorize a negative to paper money and similar measures. When the Confederation was depending before Congress, Massachusetts was then for insetting the power of emitting paper money among the exclusive powers of Congress. He observed that the proposed negative would extend to the regulations of the militia—a matter on which the existence of the state might depend. The national legislature with such a power may enslave the states. Such an idea as this will never be acceded to. It has never been suggested or conceived among the people. No speculative projector—and there are enough of that character among us, in politics as well as in other things—has in any pamphlet or newspaper thrown out the idea. The states, too, have different interests and are ignorant of each other's interests. The negative, therefore, will be abused. New states, too, having separate views from the old states, will never come into the Union. They may even be under some foreign influence. Are they in such case to participate in the negative on the will of the other states?

Mr. Sherman thought the cases in which the negative ought to be exercised might be defined. He wished the point might not be decided till a trial at least should be made for that purpose.

Mr. Wilson would not say what modifications of the proposed power might be practicable or expedient. But, however novel it might appear, the principle of it, when viewed with a close and steady eye, is right. There is no instance in which the laws say that the individual should be bound in one case and at liberty to judge whether he will obey or disobey in another. The cases are parallel. Abuses of the power over the individual persons may happen, as well as over the individual states. Federal liberty is to the states what civil liberty is to private individuals and states are not more unwilling to purchase it by the necessary concession of their political sovereignty than the savage is to purchase civil liberty by the surrender of the personal sovereignty which he enjoys in a state of nature. A definition of the cases in which the negative should be exercised is impracticable. A discretion must be left on one side or the other. Will it not be most safely lodged on the side of the national Government? Among the first sentiments expressed in the first Congress, one was that Virginia is no more, that Massachusetts is no more, that Pennsylvania is no more, and so forth— we are now one nation of brethren; we must bury all local interests and distinctions. This language continued for some time. The tables at length began to turn. No sooner were the state governments formed than their jealousy and ambition began to display themselves. Each endeavored to cut a slice from the common loaf to add to its own morsel, till at length the Confederation became frittered down to the impotent condition in which it now stands. Review the progress of the Articles of Confederation through Congress and compare the first and last draft of it. To correct its vices is the business of this convention. One of its vices is the want of an effectual control in the whole over its parts. What danger is there that the whole will unnecessarily sacrifice a part? But reverse the case and leave the whole at the mercy of each part, and will not the general interest be continually sacrificed to local interests?

Mr. Dickinson deemed it impossible to draw a line between the cases proper and improper for the exercise of the negative. We must take our choice of two things. We must either subject the states to the danger of being injured by the power of the national Government, or the latter to the danger of being injured by that of the states. He thought the danger greater from the states. To leave the power doubtful would be opening another spring of discord, and he was for shutting as many of them as possible.

Mr. Bedford, in answer to his colleague's question, where would be the danger to the states from this power, would refer him to the smallness of his own state, which may be injured at pleasure without redress. It was meant, he found, to strip the small states of their equal right of suffrage. In this case, Delaware would have about one-ninetieth for its share in the general councils, whilst Pennsylvania and Virginia would possess one-third of the whole. Is there no difference of interests, no rivalship of commerce, of manufactures? Will not these large states crush the small ones whenever they stand in the way of their ambitious or interested views? This shows the impossibility of adopting such a system as that on the table, or any other founded on a change in the principle of representation. And, after all, if a state does not obey the law of the new system, must not force be resorted to as the only ultimate remedy in this as in any other system? It seems as if Pennsylvania and Virginia, by the conduct of their deputies, wished to provide a system in which they would have an enormous and monstrous influence. Besides, how can it be thought that the proposed negative can be exercised? Are the laws of the states to be suspended in the most urgent cases until they can be sent seven- or eight-hundred miles and undergo the deliberation of a body who may be incapable of judging of them? Is the national legislature, too, to sit continually, in order to revise the laws of the states?

Mr. Madison observed that the difficulties which had been stated were worthy of attention and ought to be answered before the question was put. The case of laws of urgent necessity must be provided for by some emanation of the power from the national Government into each state so far as to give a temporary assent at least. This was the practice in the royal colonies before the Revolution and would not have been inconvenient if the supreme power of negativing had been faithful to the American interest and had possessed the necessary information. He supposed that the negative might be very properly lodged in the Senate alone, and that the more numerous and expensive branch, therefore, might not be obliged to sit constantly. He asked Mr. Bedford what would be the consequence to the small states of a dissolution of the Union, which seemed likely to happen if no effectual substitute was made for the defective system existing, and he did not conceive any effectual system could be substituted on any other basis than that of a proportional suffrage. If the large states possessed the avarice and ambition with which they were charged, would the small ones in their neighborhood be more secure when all control of a general government was withdrawn?

Mr. Butler was vehement against the negative in the proposed extent as cutting off hope of equal justice to the distant states. The people there would not, he was sure, give it a hearing.

The next clause, "to negative all laws passed by the several states, contravening, in the opinion of the national legislature, the Articles of Union, or any treaties subsisting under the authority of the Union," was then taken up.

Mr. Gouverneur Morris opposed this power as likely to be terrible to the states and not necessary, if sufficient legislative authority should be given to the General Government.

Mr. Sherman thought it unnecessary, as the courts of the states would not consider as valid any law contravening the authority of the Union, and which the legislature would wish to be negatived.

Mr. L. Martin considered the power as improper and inadmissible. Shall all the laws of the states be sent up to the general legislature before they shall be permitted to operate?

Mr. Madison considered the negative on the laws of the states as essential to the efficacy and security of the General Government. The necessity of a general government proceeds from the propensity of the states to pursue their particular interests in opposition to the general interest. This propensity will continue to disturb the system unless effectually controlled. Nothing short of a negative on their laws will control it. They will pass laws which will accomplish their injurious objects before they can be repealed by the general legislature or set aside by the national tribunals. Confidence cannot be put in the state tribunals as guardians of the national authority and interests. In all the states, these are more or less dependent on the legislatures. In Georgia, they are appointed annually by the legislature. In Rhode Island, the judges who refused to execute an unconstitutional law were displaced and others substituted by the legislature, who would be the willing instruments of the wicked and arbitrary plans of their masters. A power of negativing the improper laws of the states is at once the most mild and certain means of preserving the harmony of the system. Its utility is sufficiently displayed in the British system. Nothing could maintain the harmony and subordination of the various parts of the empire, but the prerogative by which the crown stifles in the birth every act of every part tending to discord or encroachment. It is true, the prerogative is sometimes misapplied through ignorance or partiality to one particular part of the empire, but we have not the same reason to fear such misapplications in our system. As to the sending all laws up to the national legislature, that might be rendered unnecessary by some emanation of the power into the states, so far at least as to give a temporary effect to laws of immediate necessity.

Mr. Gouverneur Morris was more and more opposed to the negative. The proposal of it would disgust all the states. A law that ought to be negatived will be set aside in the judiciary department and, if that security should fail, may be repealed by a national law.

Mr. Sherman: Such a power involves a wrong principle, to wit, that a law of a state contrary to the Articles of the Union would, if not negatived, be valid and operative.

Mr. Pinckney urged the necessity of the negative.

Motion to give legislature veto power over state laws defeated, 7 to 3.

/ August 23

Mr. Charles Pinckney moved to add, as an additional power to be vested in the legislature of the United States, "to negative all laws passed by the several states, interfering, in the opinion of the legislature, with the general interests and harmony of the Union, provided that two-thirds of the members of each house assent to the same."

This principle, he observed, had formerly been agreed to. He considered the precaution as essentially necessary. The objection drawn from the predominance of the large states had been removed by the equality established in the Senate.

Mr. Broom seconded the proposition.

Mr. Sherman thought it unnecessary, the laws of the General Government being supreme and paramount to the state laws according to the plan as it now stands.

Mr. Madison proposed that it should be committed. He had been from the beginning a friend to the principle, but thought the modification might be made better.

Mr. Mason wished to know how the power was to be exercised. Are all laws whatever to be brought up? Is no road or bridge to be established without the sanction of the general legislature? Is this to sit constantly in order to receive and revise the state laws? He did not mean by these remarks to condemn the expedient, but he was apprehensive that great objections would lie against it.

Mr. Williamson thought it unnecessary, and having been already decided, a revival of the question was a waste of time.

Mr. Wilson considered this as the keystone wanted to complete the wide arch of government we are raising. The power of self-defense had been urged as necessary for the state governments. It was equally necessary for the General Government. The firmness of judges is not of itself sufficient. Something further is requisite. It will be better to pre-

vent the passage of an improper law than to declare it void 237
when passed.

Mr. Rutledge: If nothing else, this alone would damn, and ought
to damn, the Constitution. Will any state ever agree to be bound hand
and foot in this manner? It is worse than making mere corporations
of them, whose bylaws would not be subject to this shackle.

Mr. Ellsworth observed that the power contended for would require either that all laws of the state legislature should, previously to
their taking effect, be transmitted to the general legislature or be re-
pealable by the latter, or that the state executives should be appointed
by the General Government and have a control over the state laws. If
the last was meditated, let it be declared.

Mr. Pinckney declared that he thought the state executives ought to
be so appointed with such a control and that it would be so provided
if another convention should take place.

Mr. Gouverneur Morris did not see the utility or practicability of
the proposition of Mr. Pinckney, but wished it to be referred to the
consideration of a committee.

Mr. Langdon was in favor of the proposition. He considered it as
resolvable into the question whether the extent of the national Constitution was to be judged of by the general or the state governments.

The question for commitment defeated, 6 to 5.

Mr. Pinckney then withdrew his proposition.

• Article I, Section 8: The Congress shall have Power . . . To establish a uniform
Rule of Naturalization, and uniform Laws on the subject of Bankruptcies
throughout the United States; To establish Post Offices and post Roads; To
promote the Progress of Science and useful Arts, by securing for limited Times
to Authors and Inventors the exclusive Right to their respective Writings and
Discoveries; To constitute Tribunals inferior to the supreme Court; . . . To
make all Laws which shall be necessary and proper for carrying into Execution
the foregoing Powers, and all other Powers vested by this Constitution in the
Government of the United States, or in any Department or Officer thereof.

• Article I, Section 9: . . . The Privilege of the Writ of Habeas Corpus shall
not be suspended, unless when in Cases of Rebellion or Invasion the public
Safety may require it. . . . No Money shall be drawn from the Treasury, but
in Consequence of Appropriations made by Law; and a regular Statement and
Account of the Receipts and Expenditures of all public Money shall be published
from time to time. . . . No Title of Nobility shall be granted by the United
States: And no Person holding any Office of Profit or Trust under them, shall,

without the Consent of the Congress, accept of any present, Emolument, Office, or Title, of any kind whatever, from any King, Prince, or foreign State.

THE CONSTITUTION OF THE UNITED STATES

Editor's note: It is interesting that a number of congressional powers and limitations considered today to be of bed-rock importance entered the Constitution with little or no debate or dissent. The fact is, however, that it was the conditions under which a truly national union of the states could be achieved that represented the unexplored territory of the convention and spurred the delegates to the greatest exertions. How the integrity of the states could be preserved in relation to their larger or smaller neighbors was a greater problem than the propositions by which all would be governed when this was settled.

Actually, there were many precedents in the Articles of Confederation and the various state constitutions for the powers of Congress. Thus, when the Committee of Detail presented its draft Constitution to the convention on August 6, it contained many items derived from these sources, as well as from the convention debates to that point. The committee also introduced a few ideas arising from its own deliberations.

On August 16 and 17, the convention accepted without particular comment the committee recommendations that Congress establish a uniform rule of naturalization, establish a postal system and post roads, and constitute inferior courts. On August 20, the "Necessary and Proper" clause, under which Congress could legislate to execute its powers, was passed without dissent.

The uniform bankruptcy law was proposed by Charles Pinckney during discussion of the "Full Faith and Credit" paragraph and eventually accepted early in September.

The protection of creative "Writings and Discoveries" by copyright and patent was originally suggested by Madison and Pinckney in August and incorporated into the text of the Constitution in September.

Limitations on congressional authority also were recommended by the Committee of Detail, among them the prohibition against the granting of noble titles (actually a restraint on "the United States," rather than on Congress) and against acceptance by Federal personnel of privileges or rewards of any kind from foreign powers. This was an effort aimed particularly at protecting the diplomatic corps from foreign pressures and influences.

Pinckney, on August 28, urged adoption of the "Habeas Corpus" clause of the Massachusetts Constitution, which, however, permitted suspension of the privilege "on the most urgent occasions" and for as long as twelve months. Others felt the right should be inviolable. Gouverneur Morris proposed the wording that ultimately was adopted.

Suffrage and Qualifications

• Article I, Section 2: . . . the Electors [for the House of Representatives] in each State shall have the Qualifications requisite for Electors of the most numerous Branch of the State Legislature.[1]

THE CONSTITUTION OF THE UNITED STATES

THE RIGHT OF SUFFRAGE DISCUSSED / August 7

Mr. Ellsworth thought the qualifications of the electors stood on the most proper footing. The right of suffrage was a tender point and strongly guarded by most of the state constitutions. The people will not readily subscribe to the national Constitution if it should subject them to be disfranchised. The states are the best judges of the circumstances and temper of their own people.

Mr. Mason: The force of habit is certainly not attended to by those gentlemen who wish for innovations on this point. Eight or nine states have extended the right of suffrage beyond the freeholders. What will the people there say if they should be disfranchised? A power to alter the qualifications would be a dangerous power in the hands of the legislature.

Mr. Butler: There is no right of which the people are more jealous than that of suffrage. Abridgments of it tend to the same revolution as in Holland where they have at length thrown all power into the hands of the senates, who fill up vacancies themselves and form a rank of aristocracy.

Mr. Dickinson had a very different idea of the tendency of vesting the right of suffrage in the freeholders of the country. He considered them as the best guardians of liberty and the restriction of the right to them as a necessary defense against the dangerous influence of those multitudes without property and without principle with which our country, like all others, will in time abound. As to the unpopularity of the innovation, it was in his opinion chimerical. The great

---

[1] The suffrage was enlarged by the Fourteenth Amendment (1868), granting the right to vote to all citizens (including Negroes), and by the Nineteenth Amendment (1920), granting the same right to women.

mass of our citizens is composed at this time of freeholders and will be pleased with it.

Mr. Ellsworth: How shall the freehold be defined? Ought not every man who pays a tax to vote for the representative who is to levy and dispose of his money? Shall the wealthy merchants and manufacturers who will bear a full share of the public burdens not be allowed a voice in the imposition of them? Taxation and representation ought to go together.

Mr. Gouverneur Morris: He had long learned not to be the dupe of words. The sound of aristocracy, therefore, had no effect upon him. It was the thing, not the name, to which he was opposed, and one of his principal objections to the Constitution as it is now before us is that it threatens the country with an aristocracy. The aristocracy will grow out of the House of Representatives. Give the votes to people who have no property and they will sell them to the rich, who will be able to buy them. We should not confine our attention to the present moment. The time is not distant when this country will abound with mechanics and manufacturers who will receive their bread from their employers. Will such men be the secure and faithful guardians of liberty? Will they be the impregnable barrier against aristocracy? He was as little duped by the association of the words "taxation and representation." The man who does not give his vote freely is not represented. It is the man who dictates the vote. Children do not vote. Why? Because they want prudence, because they have no will of their own. The ignorant and the dependent can be as little trusted with the public interest. He did not conceive the difficulty of defining "freeholders" to be insuperable, still less that the restriction could be unpopular. Nine-tenths of the people are at present freeholders, and these will certainly be pleased with it. As to merchants and others, if they have wealth, and value the right, they can acquire it. If not, they don't deserve it.

Mr. Mason: We all feel too strongly the remains of ancient prejudices and view things too much through a British medium. A freehold is the qualification in England, and hence it is imagined to be the only proper one. The true idea in his opinion was that every man having evidence of attachment to, and permanent common interest with, the society ought to share in all its rights and privileges. Was this qualification restrained to freeholders? Does no other kind of property but land evidence a common interest in the proprietor? Does nothing besides property mark a permanent attachment? Ought the merchant, the moneyed man, the parent of a number of children, whose fortunes are to be pursued in his own country, to be viewed as suspicious characters and unworthy to be trusted with the common rights of their fellow citizens?

Mr. Madison: The right of suffrage is certainly one of the fundamental articles of republican government and ought not to be left to be regulated by the legislature. A gradual abridgment of this right has been the mode in which aristocracies have been built on the ruins of popular forms. Whether the constitutional qualification ought to be a freehold would with him depend much on the probable reception such a change would meet with in the states where the right was now exercised by every description of people. In several of the states, a freehold was now the qualification. Viewing the subject in its merits alone, the freeholders of the country would be the safest depositories of republican liberty. In future times, a great majority of the people will not only be without landed, but any other sort of property. These will either combine under the influence of their common situation—in which case the rights of property and the public liberty will not be secure in their hands—or what is more probable, they will become the tools of opulence and ambition—in which case there will be equal danger on another side. The example of England has been misconceived (by Col. Mason). A very small proportion of the representatives are there chosen by freeholders. The greatest part are chosen by the cities and boroughs, in many of which the qualification of suffrage is as low as it is in any one of the United States, and it was in the boroughs and cities, rather than the counties, that bribery most prevailed and the influence of the crown on elections was most dangerously exerted.

Dr. Franklin: It is of great consequence that we should not depress the virtue and public spirit of our common people, of which they displayed a great deal during the war and which contributed principally to the favorable issue of it. He related the honorable refusal of the American seamen, who were carried in great numbers into the British prisons during the war, to redeem themselves from misery or to seek their fortunes by entering on board the ships of the enemies to their country, contrasting their patriotism with a contemporary instance in which the British seamen made prisoners by the Americans readily entered on the ships of the latter on being promised a share of the prizes that might be made out of their own country. This proceeded, he said, from the different manner in which the common people were treated in America and Great Britain. He did not think that the elected had any right, in any case, to narrow the privileges of the electors. He quoted as arbitrary the British statute setting forth the danger of tumultuous meetings and under that pretext narrowing the right of suffrage to persons having freeholds of a certain value, observing that this statute was soon followed by another under the succeeding Parliament subjecting the people who had no votes to peculiar labors and hardships. He was persuaded, also, that such a restriction as was proposed would give great uneasiness in the populous states. The sons of a substantial farmer, not being themselves freeholders, would not be pleased at being disfranchised, and there are a great many persons of that description.

Mr. Mercer: The Constitution is objectionable in many points, but in none more than the present. He objected to the footing on which the qualification was put, but particularly to the mode of election by the people. The people cannot know and judge of the characters of candidates. The worst possible choice will be made. He quoted the case of the Senate in Virginia as an example in point. The people in towns can unite their votes in favor of one favorite and by that means always prevail over the people of the country, who, being dispersed, will scatter their votes among a variety of candidates.

Mr. Rutledge thought the idea of restraining the right of suffrage to the freeholders a very unadvised one. It would create division among the people and make enemies of all those who should be excluded.

NON-FREEHOLDERS PERMITTED TO VOTE / August 8

In convention. Article 4, Section 1, being under consideration, Mr. Mercer expressed his dislike of the whole plan and his opinion that it never could succeed.

Mr. Gorham: He had never seen any inconvenience from allowing such as were not freeholders to vote, though it had long been tried. The elections in Philadelphia, New York, and Boston, where the merchants and mechanics vote, are at least as good as those made by freeholders only. The case in England was not accurately stated yesterday (by Mr. Madison). The cities and large towns are not the seat of crown influence and corruption. These prevail in the boroughs, and not on account of the right which those who are not freeholders have to vote, but of the smallness of the number who vote. The people have been long accustomed to this right in various parts of America and will never allow it to be abridged. We must consult their rooted prejudices if we expect their concurrence in our propositions.

Mr. Mercer did not object so much to an election by the people at large, including such as were not freeholders, as to their being left to make their choice without any guidance. He hinted that candidates ought to be nominated by the state legislatures. **243**

On the question for agreeing to Article 4, Section 1, it passed.

"CERTAIN PERSONS" DISQUALIFIED FOR OFFICE / July 26

Mr. Mason moved, "That the Committee of Detail be instructed to receive a clause, requiring certain qualifications of landed property, and citizenship of the United States, in members of the national legislature, and disqualifying persons having unsettled accounts with, or being indebted to, the United States, from being members of the national legislature."

He observed that persons of the latter descriptions had frequently got into the state legislatures in order to promote laws that might shelter their delinquencies and that this evil had crept into Congress if report was to be regarded.

Mr. Pinckney seconded the motion.

Mr. Gouverneur Morris: If qualifications are proper, he would prefer them in the electors rather than the elected. As to debtors of the United States, they are but few. As to persons having unsettled accounts, he believed them to be pretty many. He thought, however, that such a discrimination would be both odious and useless and, in many instances, unjust and cruel. The delay of settlement had been more the fault of the public than of the individuals. What will be done with those patriotic citizens who have lent money or services or property to their country without having been yet able to obtain a liquidation of their claims? Are they to be excluded?

Mr. Gorham was for leaving to the legislature the providing against such abuses as had been mentioned.

Mr. Mason mentioned the parliamentary qualifications adopted in the reign of Queen Anne, which, he said, had met with universal approbation.

Mr. Madison had witnessed the zeal of men having accounts with the public to get into the legislatures for sinister purposes. He thought, however, that if any precaution were taken for excluding them, the one proposed by Col. Mason ought to be remodeled. It might be well to limit the exclusion to persons who had received money from the public and had not accounted for it.

Mr. Gouverneur Morris: It was a precept of great antiquity, as well as of high authority, that we should not be righteous overmuch. He thought we ought to be equally on our guard against being wise overmuch. The proposed regulation would enable the government to exclude particular persons from office as long as they pleased. He mentioned the case of the Commander-in-Chief's presenting his account for secret services, which, he said, was so moderate that everyone was astonished at it and so simple that no doubt could arise on it. Yet, had the auditor been disposed to delay the settlement, how easily he might have effected it, and how cruel would it be in such a case to keep a distinguished and meritorious citizen under a temporary disability and disfranchisement. He mentioned this case merely to illustrate the objectionable nature of the proposition. He was opposed to such minutious regulations in a constitution. The parliamentary qualifications quoted by Col. Mason had been disregarded in practice and were but a scheme of the landed against the moneyed interest.

Mr. Pinckney and Gen. Pinckney moved to insert by way of amendment the words "judiciary and executive," so as to extend the qualifications to those departments, which was agreed to unanimously.

Mr. Gerry thought the inconvenience of excluding a few worthy individuals who might be public debtors or have unsettled accounts ought not to be put in the scale against the public advantages of the regulation, and that the motion did not go far enough.

Mr. King observed that there might be great danger in requiring landed property as a qualification, since it might exclude the moneyed interest whose aids may be essential, in particular emergencies, to the public safety.

Mr. Dickinson was against any recital of qualifications in the Constitution. It was impossible to make a complete one, and a partial one would by implication tie up the hands of the legislature from supplying the omissions. The best defense lay in the freeholders, who were to elect the legislature. Whilst this resource should remain pure, the public interest would be safe. If it ever should be corrupt, no little expedients would repel the danger. He doubted the policy of interweaving into a republican constitution a veneration for wealth. He had always understood that a veneration for poverty and virtue were the objects of republican encouragement. It seemed improper that any man of merit should be subjected to disabilities in a republic, where merit was understood to form the great title to public trust, honors, and rewards.

Mr. Gerry: If property be one object of government, provisions to secure it cannot be improper.

Mr. Madison moved to strike out the word "landed" before the word "qualifications." If the proposition should be agreed to, he wished the committee to be at liberty to report the best criterion they could

devise. Landed possessions were no certain evidence of real wealth. 245
Many enjoyed them to a great extent who were more in debt than
they were worth. The unjust laws of the states had proceeded more
from this class of men than any others. It had often happened that
men who had acquired landed property on credit got into the legislatures with a view of promoting an unjust protection against their creditors. In the next place, if a small quantity of land should be made the
standard, it would be no security; if a large one, it would exclude the
proper representatives of those classes of citizens who were not land-
holders. It was politic as well as just that the interests and rights of
every class should be duly represented and understood in the public
councils. It was a provision everywhere established that the country
should be divided into districts and representatives taken from each,
in order that the legislative assembly might equally understand and
sympathize with the rights of the people in every part of the community. It was not less proper that every class of citizens should have an
opportunity of making its rights be felt and understood in the public
councils. The three principal classes into which our citizens were divisible were the landed, the commercial, and the manufacturing. The
second and third class bear, as yet, a small proportion to the first.
The proportion, however, will daily increase. We see in the populous
countries of Europe now what we shall be hereafter. These classes
understand much less of each other's interests and affairs than men of
the same class inhabiting different districts. It is particularly requisite,
therefore, that the interests of one or two of them should not be left
entirely to the care or impartiality of the third. This must be the case
if landed qualifications should be required; few of the mercantile and
scarcely any of the manufacturing class choosing, whilst they continue
in business, to turn any part of their stock into landed property. For
these reasons he wished, if it were possible, that some other criterion than the mere possession of land should be devised. He concurred with Mr. Gouverneur Morris in thinking that qualifications
in the electors would be much more effectual than in the elected. The
former would discriminate between real and ostensible property in
the latter, but he was aware of the difficulty of forming any uniform
standard that would suit the different circumstances and opinions prevailing in the different states.

Mr. Gouverneur Morris seconded the motion.

Motion for striking out "landed" approved, 10 to 1.

*Mr. Mason's proposition as to "qualification of property and citizen-
ship" approved, 8 to 3.*

The second part, for disqualifying debtors and persons having unsettled accounts, being under consideration, Mr. Carroll moved to strike out "having unsettled accounts."

Mr. Gorham seconded the motion, observing that it would put the commercial and manufacturing part of the people on a worse footing than others, as they would be most likely to have dealings with the public.

Mr. L. Martin: If these words should be struck out and the remaining words concerning debtors retained, it will be (to) the interest of the latter class to keep their accounts unsettled as long as possible.

Mr. Wilson was for striking them out. They put too much power in the hands of the auditors, who might combine with rivals in delaying settlements in order to prolong the disqualifications of particular men. We should consider that we are providing a constitution for future generations and not merely for the peculiar circumstances of the moment. The time has been and will again be when the public safety may depend on the voluntary aids of individuals, which will necessarily open accounts with the public, and when such accounts will be a characteristic of patriotism. Besides, a partial enumeration of cases will disable the legislature from disqualifying odious and dangerous characters.

Mr. Langdon was for striking out the whole clause for the reasons given by Mr. Wilson. So many exclusions, he thought, too, would render the system unacceptable to the people.

Mr. Gerry: If the arguments used today were to prevail, we might have a legislature composed of public debtors, pensioners, placemen, and contractors. He thought the proposed disqualifications would be pleasing to the people. They will be considered as a security against unnecessary or undue burdens being imposed on them.

He moved to add "pensioners" to the disqualified characters, which was disapproved, 7 to 3; North Carolina remained divided on the issue.

Mr. Gouverneur Morris: The last clause relating to public debtors will exclude every importing merchant. Revenue will be drawn, it is foreseen, as much as possible from trade. Duties, of course, will be bonded and the merchants will remain debtors to the public. He repeated that it had not been so much the fault of individuals as of the public that transactions between them had not been more generally liquidated and adjusted. At all events, to draw from our short and scanty experience rules that are to operate through succeeding ages does not savor much of real wisdom.

The question for striking out "persons having unsettled accounts with the United States" approved, 9 to 2.

Mr. Ellsworth was for disagreeing to the remainder of the clause disqualifying public debtors and for leaving to the wisdom of the legislature and the virtue of the citizens the task of providing against such evils. Is the smallest as well as the largest debtor to be excluded? Then every arrear of taxes will disqualify. Besides, how is it to be known to the people when they elect, who are or are not public debtors? The exclusion of pensioners and placemen in England is founded on a consideration not existing here. As persons of that sort are dependent on the crown, they tend to increase its influence.

Mr. Pinckney said he was at first a friend to the proposition for the sake of the clause relating to qualifications of property, but he disliked the exclusion of public debtors. It went too far. It would exclude persons who had purchased confiscated property or should purchase western territory of the public, and might be some obstacle to the sale of the latter.

Question for agreeing to the clause disqualifying public debtors defeated, 9 to 2.

RESIDENCE REQUIREMENTS / *August 8*

Article 4, Section 2, was then taken up.

Mr. Mason was for opening a wide door for emigrants, but did not choose to let foreigners and adventurers make laws for us and govern us. Citizenship for three years was not enough for ensuring that local knowledge which ought to be possessed by the representative. This was the principal ground of his objection to so short a term. It might also happen that a rich foreign nation, for example, Great Britain, might send over her tools, who might bribe their way into the legislature for insidious purposes. He moved that "seven" years, instead of "three," be inserted.

Mr. Gouverneur Morris seconded the motion, and on the question, all the states agreed to it, except Connecticut.

Mr. Sherman moved to strike out the word "resident" and insert "inhabitant," as less liable to misconstruction.

Mr. Madison seconded the motion. Both were vague, but the latter least so in common acceptation and would not exclude persons absent occasionally for a considerable time on public or private business. Great disputes had been raised in Virginia concerning the meaning of residence as a qualification of representatives, which were determined more according to the affection or dislike to the man in question than to any fixed interpretation of the word.

Mr. Wilson preferred "inhabitant."

Mr. Gouverneur Morris was opposed to both and for requiring nothing more than a freehold. He quoted great disputes in New York occasioned by these terms which were decided by the arbitrary will of the majority. Such a regulation is not necessary. People rarely choose a nonresident. It is improper, and in the first branch the people at large, not the states, are represented.

Mr. Rutledge urged and moved that a residence of seven years should be required in the state wherein the member should be elected. An emigrant from New England to South Carolina or Georgia would know little of its affairs and could not be supposed to acquire a thorough knowledge in less time.

Mr. Read reminded him that we were now forming a national Government, and such a regulation would correspond little with the idea that we were one people.

Mr. Wilson enforced the same consideration.

Mr. Madison suggested the case of new states in the west which could have, perhaps, no representation on that plan.

Mr. Mercer: Such a regulation would present a greater alienship than existed under the old federal system. It would interweave local prejudices and state distinctions in the very Constitution which is meant to cure them. He mentioned instances of violent disputes raised in Maryland concerning the term "residence."

Mr. Ellsworth thought seven years of residence was by far too long a term, but that some fixed term of previous residence would be proper. He thought one year would be sufficient, but seemed to have no objection to three years.

Mr. Dickinson proposed that it should read "inhabitant actually resident for _____ years." This would render the meaning less indeterminate.

Mr. Wilson: If a short term should be inserted in the blank, so strict an expression might be construed to exclude the members of the legislature, who could not be said to be actual residents in their states whilst at the seat of the General Government.

Mr. Mercer: It would certainly exclude men who had once been inhabitants and returning from residence elsewhere to resettle in their original state, although a want of the necessary knowledge could not in such cases be presumed.

Mr. Mason thought seven years too long, but would never agree to part with the principle. It is a valuable principle. He thought it a defect in the plan that the representatives would be too few to bring with them all the local knowledge necessary. If residence be not required, rich men of neighboring states may employ with success the

means of corruption in some particular district and thereby get into
the public councils after having failed in their own states. This is the
practice in the boroughs of England.

The question for inserting "inhabitant" in place of "resident" was
agreed to unanimously.

Mr. Ellsworth and Mr. Mason moved to insert "one year" for previous inhabitancy.

Mr. Williamson liked the report as it stood. He thought "resident"
a good enough term. He was against requiring any period of previous
residence. New residents, if elected, will be most zealous to conform to
the will of their constituents, as their conduct will be watched with a
more jealous eye.

*Article 4, Section 2, as amended in manner preceding, was agreed
to.*

· Article I, Section 6: . . . No Senator or Representative shall, during the Time for
which he was elected, be appointed to any civil Office under the Authority of
the United States, which shall have been created, or the Emoluments whereof
shall have been increased during such time; and no Person holding any Office
under the United States, shall be a Member of either House during his Continuance in Office. THE CONSTITUTION OF THE UNITED STATES

PLURAL OFFICE HOLDING / *August 14*

Article 6, Section 9, was taken up.

Mr. Pinckney argued that the making the members ineligible to offices was degrading to them, and the more improper, as their election into the legislature implied that they had the confidence of the
people; that it was inconvenient because the Senate might be supposed to contain the fittest men. He hoped to see that body become a
school of public ministers, a nursery of statesmen. That it was impolitic
because the legislature would cease to be a magnet to the first talents
and abilities. He moved to postpone the section in order to take up
the following proposition: "The members of each house shall be incapable of holding any office under the United States, for which they,
or any others for their benefit, receive any salary, fees, or emoluments
of any kind; and the acceptance of such office shall vacate their seats
respectively."

Gen. Mifflin seconded the motion.

Mr. Mason ironically proposed to strike out the whole section as a
more effectual expedient for encouraging that exotic corruption which

might not otherwise thrive so well in the American soil, for completing that aristocracy which was probably in the contemplation of some among us, and for inviting into the legislative service those generous and benevolent characters who will do justice to each other's merit by carving out offices and rewards for it. In the present state of American morals and manners, few friends, it may be thought, will be lost to the plan by the opportunity of giving premiums to a mercenary and depraved ambition.

Mr. Mercer: It is a first principle in political science that whenever the rights of property are secured, an aristocracy will grow out of it. Elective governments also necessarily become aristocratic because the rulers, being few, can and will draw emoluments for themselves from the many. The governments of America will become aristocracies. They are so already. The public measures are calculated for the benefit of the governors, not of the people. The people are dissatisfied and complain. They change their rulers, and the public measures are changed, but it is only a change of one scheme of emolument to the rulers for another. The people gain nothing by it, but an addition of instability and uncertainty to their other evils. Governments can only be maintained by force or influence. The executive has not force; deprive him of influence by rendering the members of the legislature ineligible to executive offices and he becomes a mere phantom of authority. The aristocratic part will not even let him in for a share of the plunder. The legislature must and will be composed of wealth and abilities, and the people will be governed by a junta. The executive ought to have a council being members of both houses. Without such an influence, the war will be between the aristocracy and the people. He wished it to be between the aristocracy and the executive. Nothing else can protect the people against those speculating legislatures which are now plundering them throughout the United States.

Mr. Gerry read a resolution of the legislature of Massachusetts, passed before the Act of Congress recommending the convention, in which her deputies were instructed not to depart from the rotation established in the fifth article of the Confederation, nor to agree, in any case, to give to the members of Congress a capacity to hold offices under the government. This, he said, was repealed in consequence of the Act of Congress with which the state thought it proper to comply in an unqualified manner. The sense of the state, however, was still the same. He could not think with Mr. Pinckney that the disqualification was degrading. Confidence is the road to tyranny. As to ministers and ambassadors, few of them were necessary. It is the opinion of a great many that they ought to be discontinued on our part, that none may be sent among us, and that source of influence shut up. If the Senate were to appoint ambassadors, as seemed to be intended, they will multiply embassies for their own sakes. He was not so fond of those productions as to wish to establish nurseries for them. If they are once appointed, the House of Representatives will be obliged to provide salaries for them whether they approve of the measures or not. If men will not serve in the legislature without a prospect of such offices, our situation is deplorable indeed. If our best citizens are actuated by such mercenary views, we had better choose a single despot at once. It will be more easy to satisfy the rapacity of one than of many. According to the idea of one gentleman (Mr. Mercer), our government, it seems, is to be a government of plunder. In that case, it certainly would be prudent to have but one, rather than many, to be employed in it. We cannot be too circumspect in the formation of this system. It will be examined on all sides and with a very suspicious eye. The people who have been so lately in arms against Great Britain for their liberties will not easily give them up. He lamented the evils existing at present under our governments, but imputed them to the faults of those in office, not to the people. The misdeeds of the former will produce a critical attention to the opportunities afforded by the new system to like or greater abuses. As it now stands, it is as complete an aristocracy as ever was framed. If great powers should be given to the Senate, we shall be governed in reality by a junta, as has been apprehended. He remarked that it would be very differently constituted from Congress. In the first place, there will be but two deputies from each state; in Congress there may be seven and are generally five. In the second place, they are chosen for six years; those of Congress annually. In the third place, they are not subject to recall; those of Congress are. And finally, in Congress nine states are necessary for all great purposes; here eight persons will suffice. Is it to be presumed that the people will ever agree to such a system? He moved to render the members of the House of Representatives as well as of the Senate ineligible, not only during, but for one year after the expiration of their terms. If it should be thought that this will injure the legislature by keeping out of it men of abilities who are willing to serve in other offices, it may be required as a qualification for other offices that the candidate shall have served a certain time in the legislature.

Mr. Gouverneur Morris: Exclude the officers of the Army and Navy and you form a band having a different interest from, and opposed to, the civil power. You stimulate them to despise and reproach those "talking lords who dare not face the foe." Let this spirit be roused at the end of a war before your troops shall have laid down their arms.

and though the civil authority be "entrenched in parchment to the teeth," they will cut their way to it. He was against rendering the members of the legislature ineligible to offices. He was for rendering them eligible again after having vacated their seats by accepting office. Why should we not avail ourselves of their services if the people choose to give them their confidence? There can be little danger of corruption either among the people or the legislatures who are to be the electors. If they say, "We see their merits, we honor the men, we choose to renew our confidence in them," have they not a right to give them a preference and can they be properly abridged of it?

Mr. Williamson introduced his opposition to the motion by referring to the question concerning "money bills." That clause, he said, was dead. Its ghost, he was afraid, would, notwithstanding, haunt us. It had been a matter of conscience with him to insist on it as long as there was hope of retaining it. He had swallowed the vote of rejection with reluctance. He could not digest it. All that was said on the other side was that the restriction was not convenient. We have now got a House of Lords which is to originate money bills. To avoid another inconvenience, we are to have a whole legislature at liberty to cut out offices for one another. He thought a self-denying ordinance for ourselves would be more proper. Bad as the Constitution has been made by expunging the restriction on the Senate concerning money bills, he did not wish to make it worse by expunging the present section. He had scarcely seen a single corrupt measure in the legislature of North Carolina which could not be traced up to office-hunting.

Mr. Sherman: The Constitution should lay as few temptations as possible in the way of those in power. Men of abilities will increase as the country grows more populous and as the means of education are more diffused.

Mr. Pinckney: No state has rendered the members of the legislature ineligible to offices. In South Carolina, the judges are eligible into the legislature. It cannot be supposed, then, that the motion will be offensive to the people. If the state constitutions should be revised, he believed restrictions of this sort would be rather diminished than multiplied.

Mr. Wilson could not approve of the section as it stood and could not give up his judgment to any supposed objections that might arise among the people. He considered himself as acting and responsible for the welfare of millions not immediately represented in this house. He had also asked himself the serious question, what he should say to his constituents in case they should call upon him to tell them why he sacrificed his own judgment in a case where they authorized him to ex-

ercise it. Were he to own to them that he sacrificed it in order to flat-   253
ter their prejudices, he should dread the retort, "Did you suppose the
people of Pennsylvania had not good sense enough to receive a good
government?" Under this impression, he should certainly follow his
own judgment, which disapproved of the section. He would remark,
in addition to the objections urged against it, that as one branch of
the legislature was to be appointed by the legislatures of the states,
the other by the people of the states—as both are to be paid by the
states and to be appointable to state offices—nothing seemed to be
wanting to prostrate the national legislature, but to render its members ineligible to national offices and by that means take away its
power of attracting those talents which were necessary to give weight
to the government and to render it useful to the people. He was far
from thinking the ambition which aspired to offices of dignity and
trust an ignoble or culpable one. He was sure it was not politic to regard it in that light or to withhold from it the prospect of those rewards which might engage it in the career of public service. He observed that the state of Pennsylvania, which had gone as far as any
state into the policy of fettering power, had not rendered the members
of the legislature ineligible to offices of government.

Mr. Ellsworth did not think the mere postponement of the reward
would be any material discouragement of merit. Ambitious minds will
serve two years or seven years in the legislature for the sake of qualifying themselves for other offices. This he thought a sufficient security for
obtaining the services of the ablest men in the legislature; although
whilst members, they should be ineligible to public offices. Besides,
merit will be most encouraged when most impartially rewarded. If
rewards are to circulate only within the legislature, merit out of it
will be discouraged.

Mr. Mercer was extremely anxious on this point. What led to the
appointment of this convention? The corruption and mutability of
the legislative councils of the states. If the plan does not remedy these,
it will not recommend itself and we shall not be able in our private
capacities to support and enforce it, nor will the best part of our citizens exert themselves for the purpose. It is a great mistake to suppose
that the paper we are to propose will govern the United States. It is
the men whom it will bring into the government, and interest in maintaining it, that are to govern them. The paper will only mark out the
mode and the form. Men are the substance and must do the business.
All government must be by force or influence. It is not the King of
France, but 200,000 janizaries of power that govern that kingdom.
There will be no such force here; influence, then, must be substituted,

and he would ask whether this could be done if the members of the legislature should be ineligible to offices of state, whether such a disqualification would not determine all the most influential men to stay at home and prefer appointments within their respective states.

Mr. Wilson was by no means satisfied with the answer given by Mr. Ellsworth to the argument as to the discouragement of merit. The members must either go a second time into the legislature and disqualify themselves or say to their constituents, "We served you before only from the mercenary view of qualifying ourselves for offices, and having answered this purpose, we do not choose to be again elected."

Mr. Gouverneur Morris put the case of a war, and the citizen most capable of conducting it happening to be a member of the legislature. What might have been the consequence of such a regulation at the commencement or even in the course of the late contest for our liberties?

Mr. Pinckney's motion defeated.

Mr. Gouverneur Morris moved to insert after "office," "except offices in the Army or Navy, but in that case their offices shall be vacated."

Mr. Broom seconds him.

Mr. Randolph had been and should continue uniformly opposed to the striking out of the clause as opening a door for influence and corruption. No arguments had made any impression on him, but those which related to the case of war and a co-existing incapacity of the fittest commanders to be employed. He admitted great weight in these and would agree to the exception proposed by Mr. G. Morris.

Mr. Butler and Mr. Pinckney urged a general postponement of Article 6, Section 9, till it should be seen what powers would be vested in the Senate, when it would be more easy to judge of the expediency of allowing the officers of state to be chosen out of that body.

Organization of the Congress

• Article I, Section 2: . . . The House of Representatives shall chuse their Speaker and other Officers; and shall have the sole Power of Impeachment.

• Article I, Section 3: . . . The Vice President of the United States shall be President of the Senate, but shall have no Vote, unless they be equally divided. The Senate shall chuse their other Officers, and also a President pro tempore, in the Absence of the Vice President, or when he shall exercise the Office of President of the United States.

• Article I, Section 4: The Times, Places and Manner of holding Elections for Senators and Representatives, shall be prescribed in each State by the Legislature thereof; but the Congress may at any time by Law make or alter such Regulations, except as to the Places of chusing Senators.

The Congress shall assemble at least once in every Year, and such Meeting shall be on the first Monday in December, unless they shall by Law appoint a different Day.[1]

• Article I, Section 5: Each House shall be the Judge of the Elections, Returns and Qualifications of its own Members, and a Majority of each shall constitute a Quorum to do Business; but a smaller Number may adjourn from day to day, and may be authorized to compel the Attendance of absent Members, in such Manner, and under such Penalties as each House may provide.

Each House may determine the Rules of its Proceedings, punish its Members for disorderly Behaviour, and, with the Concurrence of two thirds, expel a Member. . . . Neither House, during the Session of Congress, shall, without the Consent of the other, adjourn for more than three days, nor to any other Place than that in which the two Houses shall be sitting.

THE CONSTITUTION OF THE UNITED STATES

TIME OF MEETING / *August 7*

Mr. Madison wished to know the reasons of the committee for fixing by the Constitution the time of meeting for the legislature, and suggested that it be required only that one meeting at least should be held every year, leaving the time to be fixed or varied by law.

Mr. Gouverneur Morris moved to strike out the sentence. It was improper to tie down the legislature to a particular time or even to require a meeting every year. The public business might not require it.

Mr. Pinckney concurred with Mr. Madison.

Mr. Gorham: If the time be not fixed by the Constitution, disputes will arise in the legislature and the states will be at a loss to adjust thereto the times of their elections. In the New England states, the annual time of meeting had been long fixed by their charters and constitutions, and no inconvenience had resulted. He thought it necessary that there should be one meeting at least every year as a check on the executive department.

Mr. Ellsworth was against striking out the words. The legislature will not know till they are met whether the public interest required their meeting or not. He could see no impropriety in fixing the day, as the convention could judge of it as well as the legislature.

---

[1] Superseded by Twentieth Amendment (1933).

Mr. Wilson thought on the whole it would be best to fix the day. Mr. King could not think there would be a necessity for a meeting every year. A great vice in our system was that of legislating too much. The most numerous objects of legislation belong to the states. Those of the national legislature were but few. The chief of them were commerce and revenue. When these should be once settled, alterations would be rarely necessary and easily made.

Mr. Madison thought if the time of meeting should be fixed by a law, it would be sufficiently fixed and there would be no difficulty then, as had been suggested, on the part of the states in adjusting their elections to it. One consideration appeared to him to militate strongly against fixing a time by the Constitution. It might happen that the legislature might be called together by the public exigencies and finish their session but a short time before the annual period. In this case, it would be extremely inconvenient to reassemble so quickly and without the least necessity. He thought one annual meeting ought to be required, but did not wish to make two unavoidable.

Mr. Mason thought the objections against fixing the time insuperable, but that an annual meeting ought to be required as essential to the preservation of the Constitution. The extent of the country will supply business, and if it should not, the legislature, besides legislative, is to have inquisitorial powers, which cannot safely be long kept in a state of suspension.

Mr. Sherman was decided for fixing the time, as well as for frequent meetings of the legislative body. Disputes and difficulties will arise between the two houses and between both and the states if the time be changeable. Frequent meetings of Parliament were required at the revolution in England as an essential safeguard of liberty. So also are annual meetings in most of the American charters and constitutions. There will be business enough to require it. The western country and the great extent and varying state of our affairs in general will supply objects.

Mr. Randolph was against fixing any day irrevocably, but as there was no provision made anywhere in the Constitution for regulating the periods of meeting, and some precise time must be fixed until the legislature shall make provision, he could not agree to strike out the words altogether. Instead of which, he moved to add the words following: "unless a different day shall be appointed by law."

Motion passed, 8 to 2.

Mr. Gouverneur Morris moved to strike out "December" and insert "May." It might frequently happen that our measures ought to be influenced by those in Europe, which were generally planned during the winter, and of which intelligence would arrive in the spring.   *257*

Mr. Madison seconded the motion. He preferred May to December because the latter would require the traveling to and from the seat of government in the most inconvenient seasons of the year.

Mr. Wilson: The winter is the most convenient season for business.

Mr. Ellsworth: The summer will interfere too much with private business, that of almost all the probable members of the legislature being more or less connected with agriculture.

Mr. Randolph: The time is of no great moment now as the legislature can vary it. On looking into the constitutions of the states, he found that the times of their elections (with which the elections of the national representatives would no doubt be made to coincide) would suit better with December than May, and it was advisable to render our innovations as little incommodious as possible.

Motion defeated, 8 to 2.

Mr. Read moved to insert after the word "Senate," the words "subject to the negative to be hereafter provided." His object was to give an absolute negative to the executive. He considered this as so essential to the Constitution, to the preservation of liberty, and to the public welfare that his duty compelled him to make the motion.

Motion defeated.

Mr. Rutledge: Although it is agreed on all hands that an annual meeting of the legislature should be made necessary, yet that point seems not to be free from doubt as the clause stands. On this suggestion, "once at least in every year" was inserted.

Article 3, with the foregoing alterations, was agreed to and is as follows: "The legislative power shall be vested in a Congress, to consist of two separate and distinct bodies of men, a House of Representatives and a Senate. The legislature shall meet at least once in every year; and such meeting shall be on the first Monday in December, unless a different day shall be appointed by law."

• Article I, Section 6: The Senators and Representatives shall receive a Compensation for their Services, to be ascertained by Law, and paid out of the Treasury of the United States.   THE CONSTITUTION OF THE UNITED STATES

SALARIES / *August 14*

Mr. Ellsworth moved that the pay be fixed at five dollars, or the present value thereof, per day during their attendance and for every thirty miles in traveling to and from Congress.

Mr. Strong preferred four dollars, leaving the states at liberty to make additions.

Motion was defeated, 9 to 2.

Mr. Dickinson proposed that the wages of the members of both houses should be required to be the same.

Mr. Broom seconded him.

Mr. Gorham: This would be unreasonable. The Senate will be detained longer from home, will be obliged to remove their families, and in time of war, perhaps, to sit constantly. Their allowance should certainly be higher. The members of the senates in the states are allowed more than those of the other house.

Mr. Dickinson withdrew his motion.

It was then moved and unanimously agreed to amend the section by adding that the rate of pay was "to be ascertained by law."

/ August 14

Article 6, Section 10, was then taken up "that members be paid by their respective states."

Mr. Ellsworth said that in reflecting on this subject, he had been satisfied that too much dependence on the states would be produced by this mode of payment. He moved to strike it out and insert "that they should be paid out of the treasury of the United States an allowance not exceeding ———— dollars per day, or the present value thereof."

Mr. Gouverneur Morris remarked that if the members were to be paid by the states, it would throw an unequal burden on the distant states which would be unjust as the legislature was to be a national assembly. He moved that the payment be out of the national treasury, leaving the quantum to the discretion of the national legislature. There could be no reason to fear that they would overpay themselves.

Mr. Butler contended for payment by the states, particularly in the case of the Senate, who will be so long out of their respective states that they will lose sight of their constituents unless dependent on them for their support.

Mr. Langdon was against payment by the states. There would be some difficulty in fixing the sum, but it would be unjust to oblige the distant states to bear the expense of their members in traveling to and from the seat of government.

Mr. Madison: If the House of Representatives is to be chosen biennially, and the Senate to be constantly dependent on the legislatures, which are chosen annually, he could not see any chance for that stability in the General Government, the want of which was a principal evil in the state governments. His fear was that the organization of the government, supposing the Senate to be really independent for six years, would not effect our purpose. It was nothing more than a combination of the peculiarities of two of the state governments which separately had been found insufficient. The Senate was formed on the model of that of Maryland, the revisionary check on that of New York. What the effect of a union of these provisions might be could not be foreseen. The enlargement of the sphere of the government was indeed a circumstance which he thought would be favorable, as he had on several occasions undertaken to show. He was, however, for fixing, at least two extremes not to be exceeded by the national legislature in the payment of themselves.

Mr. Gerry: There are difficulties on both sides. The observation of Mr. Butler has weight in it. On the other side, the state legislatures may turn out the senators by reducing their salaries. Such things have been practiced.

Mr. Mason: It has not yet been noticed that the clause as it now stands makes the House of Representatives also dependent on the state legislatures, so that both houses will be made the instruments of the politics of the states, whatever they may be.

Mr. Broom could see no danger in trusting the general legislature with the payment of themselves. The state legislatures had this power, and no complaint had been made of it.

Mr. Sherman was not afraid that the legislature would make their own wages too high, but too low, so that men ever so fit could not serve unless they were at the same time rich. He thought the best plan would be to fix a moderate allowance to be paid out of the national treasury and let the states make such additions as they might judge fit. He moved that five dollars per day be the sum, any further emoluments to be added by the states.

Mr. Carroll had been much surprised at seeing this clause in the report. The dependence of both houses on the state legislatures is complete, especially as the members of the former are eligible to state offices. The states can now say, "If you do not comply with our wishes, we will starve you; if you do, we will reward you." The new government in this form was nothing more than a second edition of Congress in two volumes instead of one and, perhaps, with very few amendments.

Mr. Dickinson took it for granted that all were convinced of the necessity of making the General Government independent of the prejudices, passions, and improper views of the state legislatures. The contrary of this was effected by the section as it stands. On the other hand, there were objections against taking a permanent standard, as wheat, which had been suggested on a former occasion, as well as against leaving the matter to the pleasure of the national legislature. He proposed that an act should be passed every twelve years by the national legislature settling the quantum of their wages. If the General Government should be left dependent on the state legislatures, it would be happy for us if we had never met in this room.

Mr. Ellsworth was not unwilling himself to trust the legislature with authority to regulate their own wages, but well knew that an unlimited discretion for that purpose would produce strong, though perhaps not insuperable, objections. He thought changes in the value of money provided for his motion in the words "or the present value thereof."

Mr. L. Martin: As the Senate is to represent the states, the members of it ought to be paid by the states.

Mr. Carroll: The Senate was to represent and manage the affairs of the whole and not to be the advocates of state interests. They ought not then to be dependent on, nor paid by, the states.

Question for paying the members of the legislature out of the national treasury passed, 9 to 2.

• Article I, Section 6: . . . They [Senators and Representatives] shall in all Cases, except Treason, Felony and Breach of the Peace, be privileged from Arrest during their Attendance at the Session of their respective Houses, and in going to and returning from the same; and for any Speech or Debate in either House, they shall not be questioned in any other Place.

THE CONSTITUTION OF THE UNITED STATES

Editor's note: This was in the honorable tradition of British parliamentary freedom and was a part of several state constitutions, as well as the Articles of Confederation. It was accepted without debate on August 10.

QUORUM / *August 10*

Article 6, Section 3, was then taken up.

Mr. Gorham contended that less than a majority in each house should be made a quorum; otherwise great delay might happen in business and great inconvenience from the future increase of numbers

Mr. Mercer was also for less than a majority. So great a number will put it in the power of a few by seceding at a critical moment to introduce convulsions and endanger the government. Examples of secession have already happened in some of the states. He was for leaving it to the legislature to fix the quorum as in Great Britain, where the requisite number is small and no inconvenience has been experienced.

Mr. Mason: This is a valuable and necessary part of the plan. In this extended country, embracing so great a diversity of interests, it would be dangerous to the distant parts to allow a small number of members of the two houses to make laws. The central states could always take care to be on the spot, and by meeting earlier than the distant ones or wearying their patience and outstaying them, could carry such measures as they pleased. He admitted that inconveniences might spring from the secession of a small number, but he had also known good produced by an apprehension of it. He had known a paper emission prevented by that cause in Virginia. He thought the Constitution as now molded was founded on sound principles and was disposed to put into it extensive powers. At the same time, he wished to guard against abuses as much as possible. If the legislature should be able to reduce the number at all, it might reduce it as low as it pleased and the United States might be governed by a junta. A majority of the number which had been agreed on was so few that he feared it would be made an objection against the plan.

Mr. King admitted there might be some danger of giving an advantage to the central states, but was of opinion that the public inconvenience, on the other side, was more to be dreaded.

Mr. Gouverneur Morris moved to fix the quorum at thirty-three members in the House of Representatives and fourteen in the Senate. This is a majority of the present number and will be a bar to the legislature. Fix the number low and they will generally attend, knowing that advantage may be taken of their absence. The secession of a small number ought not to be suffered to break a quorum. Such events in the states may have been of little consequence. In the national councils, they may be fatal. Besides other mischiefs, if a few can break up a quorum, they may seize a moment when a particular part of the continent may be in need of immediate aid to extort, by threatening a secession, some unjust and selfish measure.

Mr. Mercer seconded the motion.

Mr. King said he had just prepared a motion which, instead of fixing the numbers proposed by Mr. Gouverneur Morris as quorums, made those the lowest numbers, leaving the legislature at liberty to increase them or not. He thought the future increase of members would render a majority of the whole extremely cumbersome.

Mr. Mercer agreed to substitute Mr. King's motion in place of Mr. Morris'.

Mr. Ellsworth was opposed to it. It would be a pleasing ground of confidence to the people that no law or burden could be imposed on them by a few men. He reminded the movers that the Constitution proposed to give such a discretion with regard to the number of representatives that a very inconvenient number was not to be apprehended. The inconvenience of secessions may be guarded against by giving to each house an authority to require the attendance of absent members.

Mr. Wilson concurred in the sentiments of Mr. Ellsworth.

Mr. Gerry seemed to think that some further precautions than merely fixing the quorum might be necessary. He observed that as seventeen would be a majority of a quorum of thirty-three and eight of fourteen, questions might by possibility be carried in the House of Representatives by two large states and in the Senate by the same states with the aid of two small ones. He proposed that the number for a quorum in the House of Representatives should not exceed fifty, nor be less than thirty-three, leaving the intermediate discretion to the legislature.

Mr. King: As the quorum could not be altered without the concurrence of the President, by less than two-thirds of each house, he thought there could be no danger in trusting the legislature.

Mr. Carroll: This would be no security against the continuance of the quorums at thirty-three and fourteen when they ought to be increased.

Motion defeated.

RIGHT OF EXPULSION / *August 10*

Mr. Madison observed that the right of expulsion (Article 6, Section 6) was too important to be exercised by a bare majority of a quorum and in emergencies of faction might be dangerously abused. He moved that "with the concurrence of two-thirds" might be inserted between "may" and "expel."

Mr. Randolph and Mr. Mason approved the idea.

Mr. Gouverneur Morris: This power may be safely trusted to a majority. To require more, may produce abuses on the side of the minority. A few men from factious motives may keep in a member who ought to be expelled.

Mr. Carroll thought that the concurrence of two-thirds, at least, ought to be required.

On the question requiring two-thirds in cases of expelling a member, ten states were in the affirmative, Pennsylvania divided.

Article 6, Section 6, as thus amended, was then agreed to unanimously.

• Article I, Section 5: . . . Each House shall keep a Journal of its Proceedings, and from time to time publish the same, excepting such Parts as may in their Judgment require Secrecy; and the Yeas and Nays of the Members of either House on any question shall, at the Desire of one fifth of those Present, be entered on the Journal.   THE CONSTITUTION OF THE UNITED STATES

JOURNAL OF PROCEEDINGS / *August 11*

In convention. Mr. Madison and Mr. Rutledge moved "that each house shall keep a Journal of its proceedings and shall publish the same from time to time, except such part of the proceedings of the Senate, when acting not in its legislative capacity, as may be judged by that house to require secrecy."

Mr. Mercer: This implies that other powers than legislative will be given to the Senate, which he hoped would not be given.

Mr. Madison and Mr. Rutledge's motion was disagreed to by all the states except Virginia.

Mr. Gerry and Mr. Sherman moved to insert after the words "publish them," the following, "except such as relate to treaties and military operations." Their object was to give each house a discretion in such cases.

Motion defeated.

Mr. Ellsworth: As the clause is objectionable in so many shapes, it may as well be struck out altogether. The legislature will not fail to publish their proceedings from time to time. The people will call for it if it should be improperly omitted.

Mr. Wilson thought the expunging of the clause would be very improper. The people have a right to know what their agents are doing or have done, and it should not be in the option of the legislature to conceal their proceedings. Besides, as this is a clause in the existing Confederation, not retaining it would furnish the adversaries of the reform with a pretext by which weak and suspicious minds may be easily misled.

Mr. Mason thought it would give a just alarm to the people to make a conclave of their legislature.

Mr. Sherman thought the legislature might be trusted in this case, if in any.

On the question on the first part of the section, down to "publish them," inclusive, it was agreed to.

On the question on the words to follow, to wit, "except such parts thereof as may in their judgment require secrecy," motion carried.

• Article I, Section 8: The Congress shall have Power . . . To exercise exclusive Legislation in all Cases whatsoever, over such District (not exceeding ten Miles square) as may, by Cession of particular States, and the Acceptance of Congress, become the Seat of the Government of the United States, and to exercise like Authority over all Places purchased by the Consent of the Legislature of the State in which the Same shall be, for the Erection of Forts, Magazines, Arsenals, dock-Yards, and other needful Buildings; . . . .

THE CONSTITUTION OF THE UNITED STATES

THE SEAT OF GOVERNMENT / *July 26*

Mr. Mason observed that it would be proper, as he thought, that some provision should be made in the Constitution against choosing for the seat of the General Government the city or place at which the seat of any state government might be fixed. There were two objections against having them at the same place, which, without mentioning others, required some precaution on the subject. The first was that it tended to produce disputes concerning jurisdiction. The second and principal one was that the intermixture of the two legislatures tended to give a provincial tincture to the national deliberations. He moved that the committee be instructed to receive a clause to prevent the seat of the national Government being in the same city or town with the seat of the government of any state longer than until the necessary public buildings could be erected.

Mr. Alexander Martin seconded the motion.

Mr. Gouverneur Morris did not dislike the idea, but was apprehensive that such a clause might make enemies of Philadelphia and New York, which had expectations of becoming the seat of the General Government.

Mr. Langdon approved the idea also, but suggested the case of a state moving its seat of government to the national seat after the erection of the public buildings.

Mr. Gorham: The precaution may be evaded by the national legislature by delaying to erect the public buildings.

Mr. Gerry conceived it to be the general sense of America that neither the seat of a state government, nor any large commercial city, should be the seat of the General Government.

Mr. Williamson liked the idea, but knowing how much the passions of men were agitated by this matter was apprehensive of turning them against the system. He apprehended also that an evasion might be practiced in the way hinted by Mr. Gorham.

Mr. Pinckney thought the seat of a state government ought to be avoided, but that a large town or its vicinity would be proper for the seat of the General Government.

Mr. Mason did not mean to press the motion at this time, nor to excite any hostile passions against the system. He was content to withdraw the motion for the present.

/ August 11

Mr. King remarked that the section authorized the two houses to adjourn to a new place. He thought this inconvenient. The mutability of place had dishonored the Federal Government and would require as strong a cure as we could devise. He thought a law, at least, should be made necessary to a removal of the seat of government.

Mr. Madison viewed the subject in the same light and joined with Mr. King in a motion requiring a law.

Mr. Gouverneur Morris proposed the additional alteration by inserting the words "during the session."

Mr. Spaight: This will fix the seat of government at New York. The present Congress will convene them there in the first instance, and they will never be able to remove, especially if the President should be a northern man.

Mr. Gouverneur Morris: Such a distrust is inconsistent with all government.

Mr. Madison supposed that a central place for the seat of government was so just and would be so much insisted on by the House of Representatives that, though a law should be made requisite for the purpose, it could and would be obtained.

The necessity of a central residence of the government would be much greater under the new than old government. The members of the new government would be more numerous. They would be taken more from the interior parts of the states; they would not, like members of the present Congress, come so often from the distant states by water. As the powers and objects of the new government would be far greater than heretofore, more private individuals would have business calling them to the seat of it and it was more necessary that the government should be in that position from which it could contemplate with the most equal eye and sympathize most equally with every part of the nation. These considerations, he supposed, would extort a removal, even if a law were made necessary. But in order to quiet suspicions both within and without doors, it might not be amiss to authorize the two houses by a concurrent vote to adjourn at their first meeting to the most proper place and to require thereafter the sanction of a law to their removal.

Motion defeated.

Editor's note: A week later (August 18), Madison moved that the congressional powers include the authority to legislate for the as yet undetermined seat of national Government. The Committee of Detail did not incorporate the motion in its draft, but in September, after some rewording to restrain the government from too-free exercise of its power, it was accepted. From this, of course, stems the congressional regulation of the District of Columbia.

The House and Senate

CHAPTER THREE

The House of Representatives 271

• Article I, Section 2: The House of Representatives shall be composed of Members chosen every second Year by the People of the several States, and the Electors in each State shall have the Qualifications requisite for Electors of the most numerous Branch of the State Legislature. . . .

When vacancies happen in the Representation from any State, the Executive Authority thereof shall issue Writs of Election to fill such Vacancies.

THE CONSTITUTION OF THE UNITED STATES

TERM OF OFFICE DEBATED / *June 12*

Mr. Sherman and Mr. Ellsworth moved to fill the blank left in the fourth resolution for the periods of electing the members of the first branch with the words "every year"—Mr. Sherman observing that he did it in order to bring on some question.

Mr. Rutledge proposed "every two years."

Mr. Jenifer proposed "every three years," observing that the too great frequency of elections rendered the people indifferent to them and made the best men unwilling to engage in so precarious a service.

Mr. Madison seconded the motion for three years. Instability is one of (the) great vices of our republics to be remedied. Three years will be necessary in a government so extensive for members to form any knowledge of the various interests of the states to which they do not belong and of which they can know but little from the situation and affairs of their own. One year will be almost consumed in preparing for, and traveling to and from, the seat of national business.

Mr. Gerry: The people of New England will never give up the point of annual elections. They know of the transition made in England from triennial to septennial elections and will consider each an innovation here as the prelude to a like usurpation. He considered annual elections as the only defense of the people against tyranny. He was as much against a triennial house as against an hereditary executive.

Mr. Madison observed that if the opinions of the people were to be our guide, it would be difficult to say what course we ought to take. No member of the convention could say what the opinions of his constituents were at this time; much less could he say what they would think if possessed of the information and lights possessed by the members here, and still less, what would be their way of thinking six or twelve months hence. We ought to consider what was right and neces-

272   sary in itself for the attainment of a proper government. A plan adjusted to this idea will recommend itself. The respectability of this convention will give weight to their recommendation of it. Experience will be constantly urging the adoption of it, and all the most enlightened and respectable citizens will be its advocates. Should we fall short of the necessary and proper point, this influential class of citizens will be turned against the plan and little support in opposition to them can be gained to it from the unreflecting multitude.

Mr. Gerry repeated his opinion that it was necessary to consider what the people would approve. This had been the policy of all legislators. If the reasoning of Mr. Madison were just, and we supposed a limited monarchy the best form in itself, we ought to recommend it, though the genius of the people was decidedly adverse to it, and having no hereditary distinctions among us, we were destitute of the essential materials for such an innovation.

The question for the triennial election of the first branch was passed, 7 to 4.

TWO-YEAR TERM APPROVED / *June 21*

The election of the first branch "for the term of three years" being considered, Mr. Randolph moved to strike out "three years" and insert "two years." He was sensible that annual elections were a source of great mischiefs in the states; yet it was the want of such checks against the popular intemperance as were now proposed that rendered them so mischievous. He would have preferred annual to biennial, but for the extent of the United States and the inconvenience which would result from them to the representatives of the extreme parts of the empire. The people were attached to frequency of elections. All the constitutions of the states, except that of South Carolina, had established annual elections.

Mr. Dickinson: The idea of annual elections was borrowed from the ancient usage of England, a country much less extensive than ours. He supposed biennial would be inconvenient. He preferred triennial and, in order to prevent the inconvenience of an entire change of the whole number at the same moment, suggested a rotation by an annual election of one-third.

Mr. Ellsworth was opposed to three years, supposing that even one year was preferable to two years. The people were fond of frequent elections and might be safely indulged in one branch of the legislature. He moved for "one year."

Mr. Strong seconded and supported the motion.

The World of
the Founding Fathers

The land was rich in resources beyond the
dreams of the most visionary,
and the people were determined to develop it
through the exercise of personal liberty

t-revolutionary America was largely unsettled; farmland covered most of the civilized area.

Sophisticated amusements—some with a moral included—were imported from Europe.

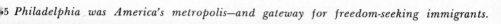
5 Philadelphia was America's metropolis—and gateway for freedom-seeking immigrants.

George Washingt[on]
gentleman planter, [was]
summoned from Virgi[nia]
to be inaugura[ted]
President in New Y[ork.]
Schuylkill River could [be]
crossed at Gray's Fer[ry]

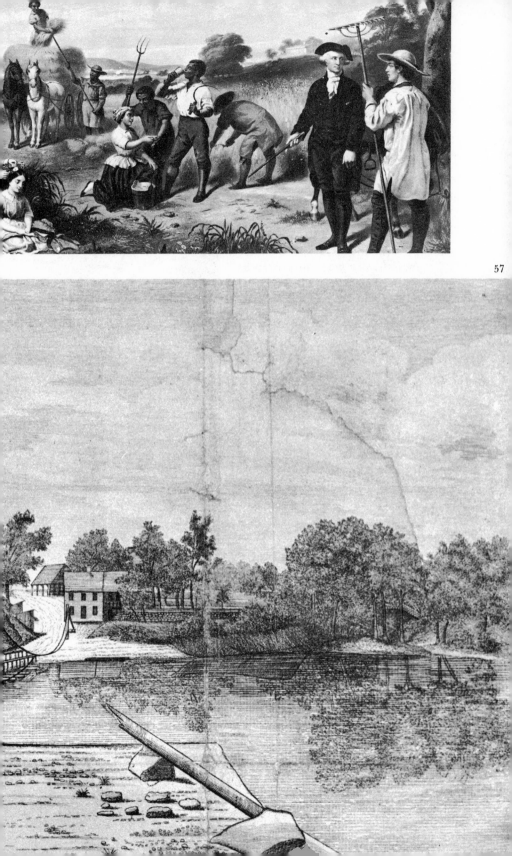

*New York, the nation's first
capital, was a flourishing center of
production and commerce.
Duncan Phyfe built his famous
furniture on Fulton Street (below),
not far from the first presidential
mansion at 1 Cherry Street (right).*

58 59

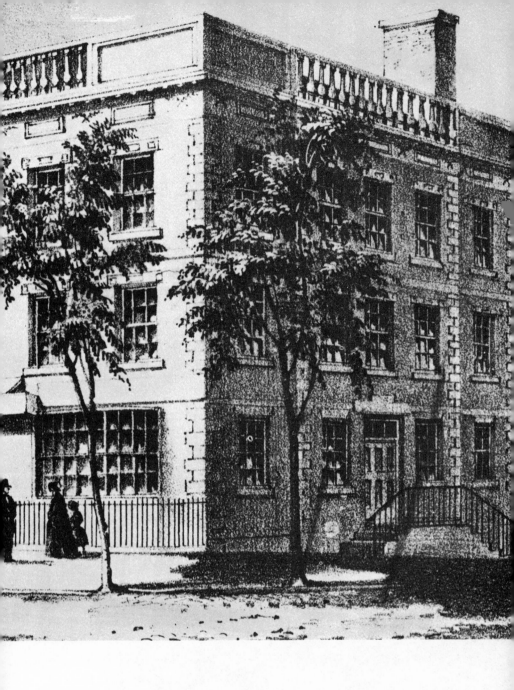

60 *A church, a general store, and a school formed the core of the rural village*

d New England. The clean lines of the church steeple dominated the landscape.

61

This 1782 check was payable in dollars, the monetary unit agreed to by the Continental Co

Philad:ᵃ 18

Cashier of the Bank

Pay to Clement
or bearer Eight hundred & fift
and 82/90

Owen

857 82/90 Dollars.

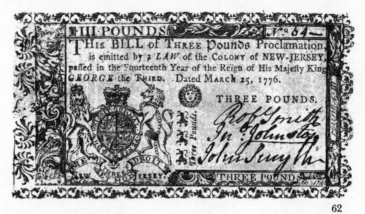

III POUNDS   Nº 64

This BILL of Three Pounds Proclamation is emitted by a LAW of the Colony of NEW-JERSEY, passed in the Fourteenth Year of the Reign of His Majesty King GEORGE the Third. Dated March 25, 1776.

THREE POUNDS.

THREE POUNDS.

NEW JERSEY.

62

British currency was used throughout the Thirteen Colonies. The three-pound note is dated three months before the Declaration of Independence.

63

THIRTY SHILLINGS.
'Tis *Death* to counterfeit.

Burlington in NEW-JERSEY,
Printed by Isaac Collins, 1776.

After the break with England, dollars were circulated, but British money persisted for a time.

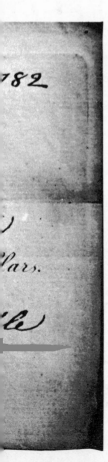

782

llars.

le

UNITED STATES   DOL

No. 22667   Fifty Dollars.

THE Bearer is entitled to receive FIFTY Spanish milled DOLLARS, or an equal Sum in Gold or Silver, according to a Resolution of Congress of the 14th January, 1779.

PERENNIS.

50 Dollars.

64

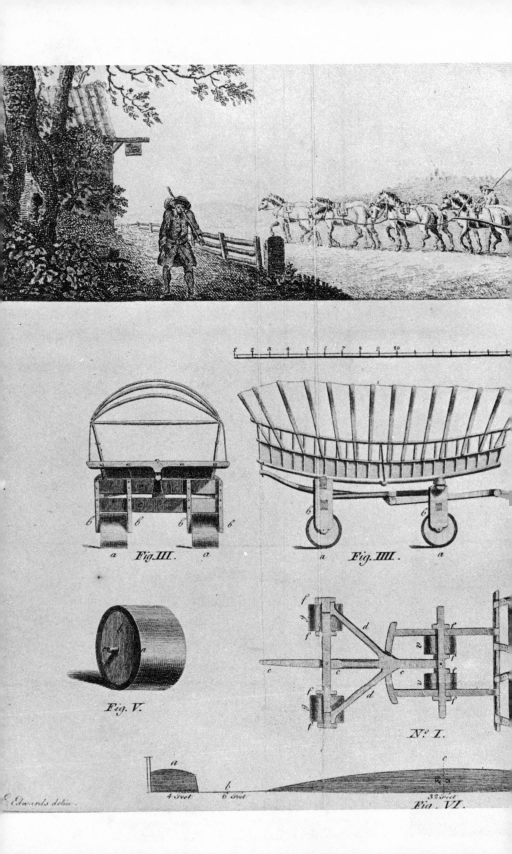

Fig.III.

Fig.IIII.

Fig.V.

N.º I.

Fig. VI.

G. Edwards delin.

The scow-shaped, wide-wheeled covered wagon, originally built to haul farm produce to the city, soon became the prime transportation of settlers to the lands of the West.

65

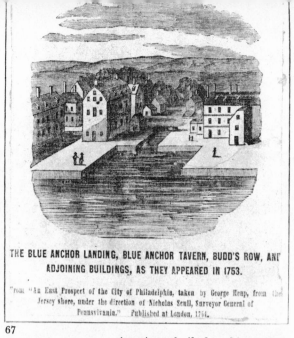

66

THE BLUE ANCHOR LANDING, BLUE ANCHOR TAVERN, BUDD'S ROW, AND ADJOINING BUILDINGS, AS THEY APPEARED IN 1753.

From "An East Prospect of the City of Philadelphia, taken by George Heap, from the Jersey shore, under the direction of Nicholas Scull, Surveyor General of Pennsylvania." Published at London, 1754.

67

Americans built fine ships to carry their exotic products—furs, pitch, indigo, lumber, whiskey—to foreign markets, and a navy to protect them.

68

69

A rear view of the State House in Philadelphia, as it appeared in 1799, twelve years after the Constitutional Convention.

Mr. Wilson, being for making the first branch an effectual representation of the people at large, preferred an annual election of it. This frequency was most familiar and pleasing to the people. It would not be more inconvenient to them than triennial elections, as the people in all the states have annual meetings with which the election of the national representatives might be made to coincide. He did not conceive that it would be necessary for the national legislature to sit constantly, perhaps not half, perhaps not one-fourth, of the year.

Mr. Madison was persuaded that annual elections would be extremely inconvenient, and apprehensive that biennial would be too much so; he did not mean inconvenient to the electors, but to the representatives. They would have to travel seven or eight hundred miles from the distant parts of the Union and would probably not be allowed even a reimbursement of their expenses. Besides, none of those who wished to be re-elected would remain at the seat of government, confiding that their absence would not effect them. The members of Congress had done this with few instances of disappointment. But as the choice was here to be made by the people themselves who would be much less complaisant to individuals and much more susceptible of impressions from the presence of a rival candidate, it must be supposed that the members from the most distant states would travel backwards and forwards at least as often as the elections should be repeated. Much was to be said also on the time requisite for new members (who would always form a large proportion) to acquire that knowledge of the affairs of the states in general, without which their trust could not be usefully discharged.

Mr. Sherman preferred annual elections, but would be content with biennial. He thought the representatives ought to return home and mix with the people. By remaining at the seat of government they would acquire the habits of the place, which might differ from those of their constituents.

Mr. Mason observed that the states being differently situated, such a rule ought to be formed as would put them nearly as possible on a level. If elections were annual, the middle states would have a great advantage over the extreme ones. He wished them to be biennial, and the rather as in that case they would coincide with the periodical elections of South Carolina as well as of the other states.

Mr. Hamilton urged the necessity of three years. There ought to be neither too much nor too little dependence on the popular sentiments. The checks in the other branches of the government would be but feeble and would need every auxiliary principle that could be interwoven. The British House of Commons were elected septennially;

274 yet the democratic spirit of the constitution had not ceased. Frequency of elections tended to make the people listless to them and to facilitate the success of little cabals. This evil was complained of in all the states. In Virginia, it had been lately found necessary to force the attendance and voting of the people by severe regulations.

The question of a three-year-term eliminated, the motion for "two years" was then inserted.

QUESTION OF RE-ELIGIBILITY DEBATED / *June 22*

Mr. Gorham moved to strike out the last member of the third resolution, concerning ineligibility of members of the first branch to office during the term of their membership and for one year after. He considered it unnecessary and injurious. It was true abuses had been displayed in Great Britain, but no one could say how far they might have contributed to preserve the due influence of the government, nor what might have ensued in case the contrary theory had been tried.

Mr. Butler opposed it. This precaution against intrigue was necessary. He appealed to the example of Great Britain, where men get into Parliament that they might get offices for themselves or their friends. This was the source of the corruption that ruined their government.

Mr. King thought we were refining too much. Such a restriction on the members would discourage merit. It would also give a pretext to the executive for bad appointments, as he might always plead this as a bar to the choice he wished to have made.

Mr. Wilson was against fettering elections and discouraging merit. He suggested also a fatal consequence in time of war of rendering perhaps the best commanders ineligible, appealed to our situation during the late war, and indirectly leading to a recollection of the appointment of the Commander-in-Chief out of Congress.

Mr. Mason was for shutting the door at all events against corruption. He enlarged on the venality and abuses in this particular in Great Britain and alluded to the multiplicity of foreign embassies by Congress. The disqualification he regarded as a cornerstone in the fabric.

Mr. Hamilton: There are inconveniences on both sides. We must take man as we find him, and if we expect him to serve the public, must interest his passion in doing so. A reliance on pure patriotism had been the source of many of our errors. He thought the remark of Mr. Gorham a just one. It was impossible to say what would be the effect in Great Britain of such a reform as had been urged. It was known that one of the ablest politicians (Mr. Hume) had pronounced all that influence on the side of the crown, which went under the name of corruption, an essential part of the weight which maintained the equilibrium of the Constitution.

Proposal to strike out "ineligibility" of representatives defeated by an equal division of the votes, 4 to 4.

275

/ June 23

Mr. Madison renewed his motion, yesterday made and waived, to render the members of the first branch "ineligible during their term of service, and for one year after, to such offices only as should be established, or the emolument augmented, by the legislature of the United States during the time of their being members." He supposed that the unnecessary creation of offices and increase of salaries were most experienced, and that if the door was shut against them, it might properly be left open for the appointment of members to other offices as an encouragement to the legislative service.

Mr. Alexander Martin seconded the motion.

Mr. Butler: The amendment does not go far enough and would be easily evaded.

Mr. Rutledge was for preserving the legislature as pure as possible by shutting the door against appointments of its own members to office, which was one source of its corruption.

Mr. Mason: The motion of my colleague is but a partial remedy for the evil. He appealed to him as a witness of the shameful partiality of the Legislature of Virginia to its own members. He enlarged on the abuses and corruption in the British Parliament connected with the appointment of its members. He could not suppose that a sufficient number of citizens could not be found who would be ready without the inducement of eligibility to offices to undertake the legislative service. Genius and virtue, it may be said, ought to be encouraged. Genius, for aught he knew, might, but that virtue should be encouraged by such a species of venality was an idea that at least had the merit of being new.

Mr. King remarked that we were refining too much in this business, and that the idea of preventing intrigue and solicitation of offices was chimerical. You say that no member shall himself be eligible to any office. Will this restrain him from availing himself of the same means which would gain appointments for himself, to gain them for his son, his brother, or any other object of his partiality? We were losing, therefore, the advantages on one side without avoiding the evils on the other.

Mr. Wilson supported the motion. The proper cure, he said, for corruption in the legislature was to take from it the power of appointing to offices. One branch of corruption would, indeed, remain—that of creating unnecessary offices or gaining unnecessary salaries—and for that the amendment would be a proper remedy. He animadverted on the impropriety of stigmatizing with the name of venality the laudable ambition of rising into the honorable offices of the government —an ambition most likely to be felt in the early and most incorrupt period of life, and which all wise and free governments had deemed it sound policy to cherish, not to check. The members of the legislature have, perhaps, the hardest and least profitable task of any who engage in the service of the state. Ought this merit to be made a disqualification?

Mr. Sherman observed that the motion did not go far enough. It might be evaded by the creation of a new office, the translation to it of a person from another office, and the appointment of a member of the legislature to the latter. A new embassy might be established to a new court and an ambassador taken from another in order to create a vacancy for a favorite member. He admitted that inconveniences lay on both sides. He hoped there would be sufficient inducements to the public service without resorting to the prospect of desirable offices and, on the whole, was rather against the motion of Mr. Madison.

Mr. Gerry thought there was great weight in the objection of Mr. Sherman. He added, as another objection against admitting the eligibility of members in any case, that it would produce intrigues of ambitious men for displacing proper officers in order to create vacancies for themselves. In answer to Mr. King, he observed that although members, if disqualified themselves, might still intrigue and cabal for their sons, brothers, and so forth, yet as their own interests would be dearer to them than those of their nearest connections, it might be expected they would go to greater lengths to promote them.

Mr. Madison had been led to this motion as a middle ground between an eligibility in all cases and an absolute disqualification. He admitted the probable abuses of an eligibility of the members to offices, particularly within the gift of the legislature. He had witnessed the partiality of such bodies to their own members, as had been remarked of the Virginia assembly by his colleague (Mr. Mason). He appealed, however, to him in turn to vouch another fact not less notorious in Virginia—that the backwardness of the best citizens to engage in the legislative service gave but too great success to unfit char-

THE HOUSE AND SENATE

acters. The question was not to be viewed on one side only. The advantages and disadvantages on both ought to be fairly compared. The objects to be aimed at were to fill all offices with the fittest characters and to draw the wisest and most worthy citizens into the legislative service. If, on one hand, public bodies were partial to their own members, on the other, they were as apt to be misled by taking characters on report, or the authority of patrons and dependents. All who had been concerned in the appointment of strangers on those recommendations must be sensible of this truth. Nor would the partialities of such bodies be obviated by disqualifying their own members. Candidates for office would hover round the seat of government, or be found among the residents there, and practice all the means of courting the favor of the members. A great proportion of the appointments made by the states were evidently brought about in this way. In the General Government, the evil must be still greater, the characters of distant states being much less known throughout the United States than those of the distant parts of the same state. The elections by Congress had generally turned on men living at the seat of the Federal Government or in its neighborhood. As to the next object, the impulse to the legislative service was evinced by experience to be in general too feeble with those best qualified for it. This inconvenience would also be more felt in the national Government than in the state governments, as the sacrifices required from the distant members would be much greater and the pecuniary provisions probably more disproportionate. It would therefore be impolitic to add fresh objections to the legislative service by an absolute disqualification of its members. The point in question was whether this would be an objection with the most capable citizens. Arguing from experience, he concluded that it would. The Legislature of Virginia would probably have been without many of its best members if in that situation they had been ineligible to Congress, to the government, and other honorable offices of the state.

Mr. Butler thought characters fit for office would never be unknown.

Mr. Mason: If the members of the legislature are disqualified, still the honors of the state will induce those who aspire to them to enter that service as the field in which they can best display and improve their talents and lay the train for their subsequent advancement.

Mr. Jenifer remarked that in Maryland the senators, chosen for five years, could hold no other office, and that this circumstance gained them the greatest confidence of the people.

Madison's motion of ineligibility for one year after expiration of term defeated, 8 to 2.

• Article I, Section 2: . . . No Person shall be a Representative who shall not have attained to the Age of twenty-five Years, and been seven Years a Citizen of the United States, and who shall not, when elected, be an Inhabitant of that State in which he shall be chosen.   THE CONSTITUTION OF THE UNITED STATES

AGE QUALIFICATION / June 22

Mr. Mason moved to insert "twenty-five years of age as a qualification for the members of the first branch." He thought it absurd that a man today should not be permitted by the law to make a bargain for himself, and tomorrow should be authorized to manage the affairs of a great nation. It was the more extraordinary as every man carried with him in his own experience a scale for measuring the deficiency of young politicians; since he would, if interrogated, be obliged to declare that his political opinions at the age of twenty-one were too crude and erroneous to merit an influence on public measures. It had been said that Congress had proved a good school for our young men. It might be so for anything he knew, but if it were, he chose that they should bear the expense of their own education.

Mr. Wilson was against abridging the rights of election in any shape. It was the same thing whether this were done by disqualifying the objects of choice or the persons choosing. The motion tended to damp the efforts of genius and of laudable ambition. There was no more reason for incapacitating youth than age, where the requisite qualifications were found. Many instances might be mentioned of signal services rendered in high stations to the public before the age of twenty-five. The present Mr. Pitt and Lord Bolingbroke were striking instances.

Twenty-five-year age qualification for service in the houses was approved, 7 to 3.

PROPERTY QUALIFICATION / August 10

In convention. Article 6, Section 2, was taken up.

Mr. Pinckney: The committee, as he had conceived, were instructed to report the proper qualifications of property for the members of the national legislature, instead of which they have referred the task to the national legislature itself. Should it be left on this footing, the first legislature will meet without any particular qualifications of property, and if it should happen to consist of rich men, they might fix such qualifications as may be too favorable to the rich; if of poor men, an opposite extreme might be run into. He was opposed to the establish-

ment of an undue aristocratic influence in the Constitution, but he
thought it essential that the members of the legislature, the executive,
and the judges should be possessed of competent property to make
them independent and respectable. It was prudent when such great
powers were to be trusted, to connect the prudent tie of property with
that of reputation in securing a faithful administration. The legislature would have the fate of the nation put into their hands. The
President would also have a very great influence on it. The judges
would not only have important causes between citizen and citizen, but also where foreigners are concerned. They will even be the
umpires between the United States and individual states as well as
between one and another. Were he to fix the quantum of property
which should be required, he should not think of less than one-hun-
dred-thousand dollars for the President, half of that sum for each of
the judges, and in like proportion for the members of the national legislature. He would, however, leave the sums blank. His motion was
that the President of the United States, the judges, and members of
the legislature should be required to swear that they were respectively possessed of a clear, unincumbered estate to the amount of
_____ in the case of the President, and so forth.

Mr. Rutledge seconded the motion, observing that the committee
had reported no qualifications because they could not agree on any
among themselves, being embarrassed by the danger, on one side, of
displeasing the people by making them high and, on the other, of rendering them nugatory by making them low.

Mr. Ellsworth: The different circumstances of different parts of the
United States and the probable difference between the present and
future circumstances of the whole render it improper to have either
uniform or fixed qualifications. Make them so high as to be useful in
the southern states and they will be inapplicable to the eastern states.
Suit them to the latter and they will serve no purpose in the former.
In like manner, what may be accommodated to the existing state of
things among us may be very inconvenient in some future state of
them. He thought for these reasons that it was better to leave this matter to the legislative discretion than to attempt a provision for it in
the Constitution.

Dr. Franklin expressed his dislike to everything that tended to de-
base the spirit of the common people. If honesty was often the compan-
ion of wealth, and if poverty was exposed to peculiar temptation, it
was not less true that the possession of property increased the desire
of more property. Some of the greatest rogues he was ever acquainted
with were the richest rogues. We should remember the character which

the Scripture requires in rulers, that they should be men hating cov-etousness. This Constitution will be much read and attended to in Europe, and if it should betray a great partiality to the rich, will not only hurt us in the esteem of the most liberal and enlightened men there, but discourage the common people from removing to this country.

The motion of Mr. Pinckney was rejected by so general a "no" that the states were not called.

Mr. Madison was opposed to the section as vesting an improper and dangerous power in the legislature. The qualifications of electors and elected were fundamental articles in a republican government and ought to be fixed by the Constitution. If the legislature could regulate those of either, it can by degrees subvert the Constitution. A republic may be converted into an aristocracy or oligarchy as well by limiting the number capable of being elected as the number authorized to elect. In all cases where the representatives of the people will have a personal interest distinct from that of their constituents, there was the same reason for being jealous of them as there was for relying on them with full confidence when they had a common interest. This was one of the former cases. It was as improper as to allow them to fix their own wages or their own privileges. It was a power, also, which might be made subservient to the views of one faction against another. Qualifications founded on artificial distinctions may be devised by the stronger in order to keep out partisans of a weaker faction.

Mr. Ellsworth admitted that the power was not unexceptionable, but he could not view it as dangerous. Such a power with regard to the electors would be dangerous because it would be much more liable to abuse.

Mr. Gouverneur Morris moved to strike out "with regard to property," in order to leave the legislature entirely at large.

Mr. Williamson: This would surely never be admitted. Should a majority of the legislature be composed of any particular description of men—of lawyers, for example—which is no improbable supposition, the future elections might be secured to their own body.

Mr. Madison observed that the British Parliament possessed the power of regulating the qualifications both of the electors and the elected, and the abuse they had made of it was a lesson worthy of our attention. They had made the changes in both cases subservient to their own views or to the views of political or religious parties.

Mr. Rutledge was opposed to leaving the power to the legislature. He proposed that the qualifications should be the same as for members of the state legislatures.

Mr. Wilson thought it would be best on the whole to let the section   281
go out. A uniform rule would probably never be fixed by the legislature, and this particular power would constructively exclude every
other power of regulating qualifications.
*Proposal to allow legislature to set its own qualifications for mem-
bership defeated, 7 to 3.*

CITIZENSHIP QUALIFICATION / *August 13*

In convention. Article 4, Section 2, being reconsidered, Mr. Wilson
and Mr. Randolph moved to strike out "seven years" and insert "four
years" as the requisite term of citizenship to qualify for the House of
Representatives. Mr. Wilson said it was very proper the electors should
govern themselves by this consideration, but unnecessary and improper
that the Constitution should chain them down to it.

Mr. Gerry wished that in future the eligibility might be confined to
natives. Foreign powers will intermeddle in our affairs and spare no
expense to influence them. Persons having foreign attachments will be
sent among us and insinuated into our councils in order to be made
instruments for their purposes. Everyone knows the vast sums laid out
in Europe for secret services. He was not singular in these ideas. A
great many of the most influential men in Massachusetts reasoned in
the same manner.

Mr. Williamson moved to insert "nine years" instead of "seven." He
wished this country to acquire, as fast as possible, national habits.
Wealthy emigrants do more harm by their luxurious examples than
good by the money they bring with them.

Mr. Hamilton was in general against embarrassing the government
with minute restrictions. There was, on one side, the possible danger
that had been suggested. On the other side, the advantage of encouraging foreigners was obvious and admitted. Persons in Europe
of moderate fortunes will be fond of coming here, where they will be
on a level with the first citizens. He moved that the section be so altered as to require merely "citizenship and inhabitancy." The right
of determining the rule of naturalization will then leave a discretion
to the legislature on this subject which will answer every purpose.

Mr. Madison seconded the motion. He wished to maintain the character of liberality which had been professed in all the constitutions
and publications of America. He wished to invite foreigners of merit
and republican principles among us. America was indebted to emigration for her settlement and prosperity. That part of America which
had encouraged them most had advanced most rapidly in population,

agriculture, and the arts. There was a possible danger, he admitted, that men with foreign predilections might obtain appointments, but it was by no means probable that it would happen in any dangerous degree. For the same reason that they would be attached to their native country, our own people would prefer natives of this country to them. Experience proved this to be the case. Instances were rare of a foreigner being elected by the people within any short space after his coming among us. If bribery was to be practiced by foreign powers, it would not be attempted among the electors, but among the elected, and among natives having full confidence of the people, not among strangers, who would be regarded with a jealous eye.

Mr. Wilson cited Pennsylvania as a proof of the advantage of encouraging emigrations. It was perhaps the youngest settlement (except Georgia) on the Atlantic, yet it was at least among the foremost in population and prosperity. He remarked that almost all the general officers of the Pennsylvania line of the late army were foreigners, and no complaint had ever been made against their fidelity or merit. Three of her deputies to the convention (Mr. R. Morris, Mr. Fitzsimmons, and himself) were also not natives. He had no objection to Col. Hamilton's motion and would withdraw the one made by himself.

Mr. Butler was strenuous against admitting foreigners into our public councils.

Hamilton's motion was defeated, 7 to 4.

Williamson's motion to insert "nine years" instead of "seven" defeated, 8 to 3.

Mr. Gouverneur Morris moved to add to the end of the section (Article 4, Section 2) a proviso that the limitation of seven years should not affect the rights of any person now a citizen.

Mr. Mercer seconded the motion. It was necessary, he said, to prevent a disfranchisement of persons who had become citizens under the faith and according to the laws and Constitution from their actual level in all respects with natives.

Mr. Rutledge: It might as well be said that all qualifications are disfranchisements and that to require the age of twenty-five years was a disfranchisement. The policy of the precaution was as great with regard to foreigners now citizens as to those who are to be naturalized in future.

Mr. Sherman: The United States have not invited foreigners, nor pledged their faith that they should enjoy equal privileges with native citizens. The individual states alone have done this. The former, therefore, are at liberty to make any discriminations they may judge requisite.

Mr. Gorham: When foreigners are naturalized, it would seem as if they stand on an equal footing with natives. He doubted, then, the propriety of giving a retrospective force to the restriction.

Mr. Madison animadverted on the peculiarity of the doctrine of Mr. Sherman. It was a subtlety by which every national engagement might be evaded. By parity of reason, whenever our public debts or foreign treaties become inconvenient, nothing more would be necessary to relieve us from them than to remodel the Constitution. It was said that the United States, as such, have not pledged their faith to the naturalized foreigners and, therefore, are not bound. Be it so, and that the states alone are bound. Who are to form the new Constitution by which the condition of that class of citizens is to be made worse than the other class? Are not the states the agents? Will they not be the members of it? Did they not appoint this convention? Are not they to ratify its proceedings? Will not the new Constitution be their act? If the new Constitution then violates the faith pledged to any description of people, will not the makers of it, will not the states, be the violaters? To justify the doctrine, it must be said that the states can get rid of the obligation by revising the Constitution, though they could not do it by repealing the law under which foreigners held their privileges. He considered this a matter of real importance. It would expose us to the reproaches of all those who should be affected by it, reproaches which would soon be echoed from the other side of the Atlantic and would unnecessarily enlist among the adversaries of the reform a very considerable body of citizens. We should moreover reduce every state to the dilemma of rejecting it or of violating the faith pledged to a part of its citizens.

Mr. Gouverneur Morris considered the case of persons under twenty-five years of age as very different from that of foreigners. No faith could be pleaded by the former in bar of the regulation. No assurance had ever been given that persons under that age should be in all cases on a level with those above it. But with regard to foreigners among us, the faith had been pledged that they should enjoy the privileges of citizens. If the restriction as to age had been confined to natives and had left foreigners under twenty-five years of age eligible in this case, the discrimination would have been an equal injustice on the other side.

Mr. Pinckney remarked that the laws of the states had varied much the terms of naturalization in different parts of America and contended that the United States could not be bound to respect them on such an occasion as the present. It was a sort of recurrence to first principles.

Mr. Mason was struck, not like Mr. Madison, with the peculiarity, but the propriety, of the doctrine of Mr. Sherman. The states have formed different qualifications themselves for enjoying different rights of citizenship. Greater caution would be necessary in the outset of the government than afterwards. All the great objects would then be provided for. Everything would be then set in motion. If persons among us attached to Great Britain should work themselves into our councils, a turn might be given to our affairs, and particularly to our commercial regulations, which might have pernicious consequences. The great houses of British merchants would spare no pains to insinuate the instruments of their views into the government.

Mr. Wilson read the clause in the Constitution of Pennsylvania giving to foreigners, after two years' residence, all the rights whatsoever of citizens, combined it with the Article of Confederation making the citizens of one state citizens of all, inferred the obligation Pennsylvania was under to maintain the faith thus pledged to her citizens of foreign birth and the just complaint which her failure would authorize. He observed, likewise, that the princes and states of Europe would avail themselves of such breach of faith to deter their subjects from emigrating to the United States.

Mr. Mercer enforced the same idea of a breach of faith.

Mr. Baldwin could not enter into the force of the arguments against extending the disqualification to foreigners now citizens. The discrimination of the place of birth was not more objectionable than that of age which all had concurred in the propriety of.

Question on the proviso of Mr. Gouverneur Morris in favor of foreigners now citizens defeated, 6 to 5.

The section (Article 4, Section 2) as formerly amended was then agreed to.

Mr. Wilson moved that in Article 5, Section 3, "nine years" be reduced to "seven," which was disagreed to, and Article 5, Section 3, was then confirmed, 8 to 3.

• Article I, Section 2: Representatives and direct Taxes shall be apportioned among the several States which may be included within this Union, according to their respective Numbers, [which shall be determined by adding to the whole Number of free Persons,[1] including those bound to Service for a Term of Years, and excluding Indians not taxed, three fifths of all other Persons].[2] The actual Enumeration shall be made within three Years after the first Meeting of the Congress of the United States, and within every subsequent Term of ten Years, in such Manner as they shall by Law direct. The Number of Representatives shall

[1] Modified by the 14th Amendment (1868).
[2] Superseded by the 14th Amendment.

not exceed one for every thirty Thousand, but each State shall have at Least one Representative; and until such enumeration shall be made, the State of New Hampshire shall be entitled to chuse three; Massachusetts eight; Rhode-Island and Providence Plantations one; Connecticut five; New York six; New Jersey four; Pennsylvania eight; Delaware one; Maryland six; Virginia ten; North Carolina five; South Carolina five; and George three.[3]
• Article I, Section 9: . . . No Capitation, or other direct, Tax shall be laid, unless in Proportion to the Census or Enumeration herein before directed to be taken. THE CONSTITUTION OF THE UNITED STATES

285

NUMBER OF MEMBERS / July 10

Mr. King reported from the committee yesterday appointed "that the states at the first meeting of the general legislature should be represented by sixty-five members in the following proportions, to wit: New Hampshire, by three; Massachusetts, eight; Rhode Island, one; Connecticut, five; New York, six; New Jersey, four; Pennsylvania, eight; Delaware, one; Maryland, six; Virginia, ten; North Carolina, five; South Carolina, five; Georgia, three.

Mr. Rutledge moved that New Hampshire be reduced from three to two members. Her numbers did not entitle her to three, and it was a poor state.

Gen. Pinckney seconds the motion.

Mr. King: New Hampshire has probably more than 120,000 inhabitants and has an extensive country of tolerable fertility. Its inhabitants may, therefore, be expected to increase fast. He remarked that the four eastern states, having 800,000 souls, have one-third fewer representatives than the four southern states, having not more than 700,000 souls, rating the blacks as five for three. The eastern people will advert to these circumstances and be dissatisfied. He believed them to be very desirous of uniting with their southern brethern, but did not think it prudent to rely so far on that disposition as to subject them to any gross inequality. He was fully convinced that the question concerning a difference of interests did not lie where it had hitherto been discussed, between the great and small states, but between the

---

[3] It is interesting to note the change of the number of representatives from that day to this: New Hampshire, three (now two); Massachusetts, eight (now twelve); Rhode Island, one (now two); Connecticut, five (now six); New York, six (now forty); New Jersey, four (now fifteen); Pennsylvania, eight (now twenty-seven); Delaware, one (now one); Maryland, six (now eight); Virginia, ten (now ten); North Carolina, five (now eleven); South Carolina, five (now six); Georgia, three (now ten).

southern and eastern. For this reason he had been ready to yield something in the proportion of representatives for the security of the southern. No principle would justify the giving them a majority. They were brought as near an equality as was possible. He was not averse to giving them a still greater security, but did not see how it could be done.

Gen. Pinckney: The report before it was committed was more favorable to the southern states than as it now stands. If they are to form so considerable a minority, and the regulation of trade is to be given to the General Government, they will be nothing more than overseers for the northern states. He did not expect the southern states to be raised to a majority of representatives, but wished them to have something like an equality. At present, by the alterations of the committee in favor of the northern states, they are removed farther from it than they were before. One member, indeed, had been added to Virginia, which he was glad of, as he considered her a southern state. He was glad also that the members of Georgia were increased.

Mr. Williamson was not for reducing New Hampshire from three to two, but for reducing some others. The southern interest must be extremely endangered by the present arrangement. The northern states are to have a majority in the first instance and the means of perpetuating it.

Mr. Dayton observed that the line between northern and southern interest had been improperly drawn; that Pennsylvania was the dividing state, there being six on each side of her.

Gen. Pinckney urged the reduction, dwelt on the superior wealth of the southern states and insisted on its having its due weight in the government.

Mr. Gouverneur Morris regretted the turn of the debate. The states, he found, had many representatives on the floor. Few, he feared, were to be deemed the representatives of America. He thought the southern states have by the report more than their share of weight. If the southern states are to supply money, the northern states are to spill their blood. Besides, the probable revenue to be expected from the southern states has been greatly overrated. He was against reducing New Hampshire.

Mr. Randolph was opposed to a reduction of New Hampshire, not because she had a full title to three members, but because it was in his contemplation, first, to make it the duty instead of leaving it to the discretion of the legislature to regulate the representation by a periodical census; secondly, to require more than a bare majority of votes in the legislature in certain cases, and particularly in commercial cases.

Gen. Pinckney and Mr. Alexander Martin moved that six representatives instead of five be allowed to North Carolina. **287**
Question defeated, 7 to 3.
Gen. Pinckney and Mr. Butler made the same motion in favor of South Carolina.
Question defeated, 7 to 4.
Gen. Pinckney and Mr. Houston moved that Georgia be allowed four instead of three representatives, urging the unexampled celerity of its population.
Question defeated, 7 to 4.

/ July 10

Mr. Madison moved that the number allowed to each state be doubled. A majority of a quorum of sixty-five members was too small a number to represent the whole inhabitants of the United States. They would not possess enough of the confidence of the people and would be too sparsely taken from the people to bring with them all the local information which would be frequently wanted. Double the number will not be too great, even with the future additions from the new states. The additional expense was too inconsiderable to be regarded in so important a case, and as far as the augmentation might be unpopular, on that score the objection was overbalanced by its effect on the hopes of a greater number of the popular candidates.

Mr. Ellsworth urged the objection of expense and that the greater the number, the more slowly would the business proceed, and the less probably be decided as it ought at last. He thought the number of representatives too great in most of the state legislatures, and that a large number was less necessary in the general legislature than in those of the states, as its business would relate to a few great national objects only.

Mr. Sherman would have preferred fifty to sixty-five. The great distance they will have to travel will render their attendance precarious and will make it difficult to prevail on a sufficient number of fit men to undertake the service. He observed that the expected increase from new states also deserved consideration.

Mr. Gerry was for increasing the number beyond sixty-five. The larger the number, the less the danger of their being corrupted. The people are accustomed to, and fond of, a numerous representation and will consider their rights as better secured by it. The danger of excess in the number may be guarded against by fixing a point within which the numbers shall always be kept.

Mr. Mason admitted that the objection drawn from the consideration of expense had weight both in itself and as the people might be
affected by it. But he thought it outweighed by the objections against
the smallness of the number. Thirty-eight will, he supposes, as being
a majority of sixty-five, form a quorum. Twenty will be a majority
of thirty-eight. This was certainly too small a number to make laws
for America. They would neither bring with them all the necessary
information relative to various local interests, nor possess the necessary confidence of the people. After doubling the number, the laws
might still be made by so few as almost to be objectionable on that account.

Mr. Read was in favor of the motion. Two of the states (Delaware
and Rhode Island) would have but a single member if the aggregate
number should remain at sixty-five, and in case of accident to either
of these, one state would have no representative present to give explanations or informations of its interests or wishes. The people would
not place their confidence in so small a number. He hoped the objects
of the General Government would be much more numerous than
seemed to be expected by some gentlemen and that they would become more and more so. As to the new states, the highest number of
representatives for the whole might be limited, and all danger of excess thereby prevented.

Mr. Rutledge opposed the motion. The representatives were too
numerous in all the states. The full number allotted to the states may
be expected to attend, and the lowest possible quorum should not,
therefore, be considered. The interests of their constituents will urge
their attendance too strongly for it to be omitted, and he supposed
the general legislature would not sit more than six or eight weeks in
the year.

Question for doubling the number defeated, 9 to 2.

*On the question for agreeing to the apportionment of representa-
tives as amended by the last committee, it passed in the affirmative.*

CENSUS AND REPRESENTATION / *July 10*

Mr. Broom gave notice to the house that he had concurred with a reserve to himself of an intention to claim for his state an equal voice in
the second branch, which he thought could not be denied after this
concession of the small states as to the first branch.

Mr. Randolph moved as an amendment to the report of the committee of five "that in order to ascertain the alterations in the population and wealth of the several states, the legislature should be required

to cause a census and estimate to be taken within one year after its 289 first meeting and every _____ years thereafter, and that the legislature arrange the representation accordingly."

Mr. Gouverneur Morris opposed it as fettering the legislature too much. Advantage may be taken of it in time of war or the apprehension of it by new states to extort particular favors. If the mode was to be fixed for taking a census, it might certainly be extremely inconvenient; if unfixed, the legislature may use such a mode as will defeat the object and perpetuate the inequality. He was always against such shackles on the legislature. They had been found very pernicious in most of the state constitutions. He dwelt much on the danger of throwing such a preponderance into the western scale, suggesting that in time the western people would outnumber the Atlantic states. He wished, therefore, to put it in the power of the latter to keep a majority of votes in their own hands. It was objected, he said, that if the legislature are left at liberty, they will never readjust the representation. He admitted that this was possible, but he did not think it probable unless the reasons against a revision of it were very urgent, and in this case it ought not to be done.

It was moved to postpone the proposition of Mr. Randolph in order to take up the following: "that the committee of eleven, to whom was referred the report of the committee of five on the subject of representation, be requested to furnish the convention with the principles on which they grounded the report," which was disagreed to, South Carolina alone voting in the affirmative.

/ July 11

In convention. Mr. Randolph's motion requiring the legislature to take a periodical census for the purpose of redressing inequalities in the representation was resumed.

Mr. Sherman was against shackling the legislature too much. We ought to choose wise and good men and then confide in them.

Mr. Mason: The greater the difficulty we find in fixing a proper rule of representation, the more unwilling ought we to be to throw the task from ourselves on the general legislature. He did not object to the conjectural ratio which was to prevail in the outset, but considered a revision from time to time according to some permanent and precise standard as essential to the fair representation required in the first branch. According to the present population of America, the northern part of it had a right to preponderate and he could not deny it. But he wished it not to preponderate hereafter, when the reason no longer continued. From the nature of man, we may be sure that those who have power in their hands will not give it up while they can retain it. On the contrary, we know that they will always, when they can, rather increase it. If the southern states, therefore, should have three-fourths of the people of America within their limits, the northern will hold fast the majority of representatives. One-fourth will govern the three-fourths. The southern states will complain, but they may complain from generation to generation without redress. Unless some principle, therefore, which will do justice to them hereafter, shall be inserted in the Constitution, disagreeable as the declaration was to him, he must declare he could neither vote for the system here, nor support it in his state. Strong objections had been drawn from the danger to the Atlantic interests from new western states. Ought we to sacrifice what we know to be right in itself, lest it should prove favorable to states which are not yet in existence? If the western states are to be admitted into the Union as they arise, they must, he would repeat, be treated as equals and subjected to no degrading discriminations. They will have the same pride and other passions which we have, and will either not unite with or will speedily revolt from, the Union if they are not in all respects placed on an equal footing with their brethren. It has been said they will be poor and unable to make equal contributions to the general treasury. He did not know but that in time they would be both more numerous and more wealthy than their Atlantic brethren. The extent and fertility of their soil made this probable, and though Spain might for a time deprive them of the natural outlet for their productions, yet she will, because she must, finally yield to their demands. He urged that numbers of inhabitants, though not always a precise standard of wealth, was sufficiently so for every substantial purpose.

Mr. Williamson was for making it a duty of the legislature to do what was right and not leaving it at liberty to do or not to do it. He moved that Mr. Randolph's proposition be postponed in order to consider the following: "that in order to ascertain the alterations that may happen in the population and wealth of the several states, a census shall be taken of the free white inhabitants and three-fifths of those of other descriptions on the first year after this government shall have been adopted and every _____ year thereafter, and that the representation be regulated accordingly."

Mr. Randolph agreed that Mr. Williamson's proposition should stand in place of his. He observed that the ratio fixed for the first meeting was a mere conjecture; that it placed the power in the hands of that part of America which could not always be entitled to it; that this power would not be voluntarily renounced, and that it was consequently the duty of the convention to secure its renunciation when justice might so require by some constitutional provisions. If equality between great and small states be inadmissible because in that case unequal numbers of constituents would be represented by equal numbers of votes, was it not equally inadmissible that a larger and more populous district of America should hereafter have less representation than a smaller and less populous district? If a fair representation of the people be not secured, the injustice of the government will shake it to its foundations. What relates to suffrage is justly stated by the celebrated Montesquieu as a fundamental article in republican governments. If the danger suggested by Mr. Gouverneur Morris be real, of advantage being taken of the legislature in pressing moments, it was an additional reason for tying their hands in such a manner that they could not sacrifice their trust to momentary considerations. Congress have pledged the public faith to new states that they shall be admitted on equal terms. They never would, nor ought to, accede on any other. The census must be taken under the direction of the general legislature. The states will be too much interested to take an impartial one for themselves.

Mr. Butler and Gen. Pinckney insisted that blacks be included in the rule of representation equally with the whites, and for that purpose moved the words "three-fifths" be struck out.

Mr. Gerry thought that three-fifths of them was, to say the least, the full proportion that could be admitted.

Mr. Gorham: This ratio was fixed by Congress as a rule of taxation. Then it was urged by the delegates representing the states having slaves that the blacks were still more inferior to freemen. At present, when the ratio of representation is to be established, we are assured that they are equal to freemen. The arguments on the former occasion had convinced him that three-fifths was pretty near the just proportion and he should vote according to the same opinion now.

Mr. Butler insisted that the labor of a slave in South Carolina was as productive and valuable as that of a freeman in Massachusetts; that as wealth was the great means of defense and utility to the nation, they were equally valuable to it with freemen, and that, consequently, an equal representation ought to be allowed for them in a government which was instituted principally for the protection of property and was itself to be supported by property.

Mr. Mason could not agree to the motion notwithstanding it was favorable to Virginia, because he thought it unjust. It was certain that the slaves were valuable, as they raised the value of land, increased the exports and imports and, of course, the revenue, would supply the means of feeding and supporting an army, and might, in cases of emergency, become themselves soldiers. As in these important respects they were useful to the community at large, they ought not to be excluded from the estimate of representation. He could not, however, regard them as equal to freemen and could not vote for them as such. He added, as worthy of remark, that the southern states have this peculiar species of property over and above the other species of property common to all the states.

Mr. Williamson reminded Mr. Gorham that if the southern states contended for the inferiority of blacks to whites when taxation was in view, the eastern states, on the same occasion, contended for their equality. He did not, however, either then or now concur in either extreme, but approved of the ratio of three-fifths.

Mr. Butler's motion for considering blacks as equal to whites in apportionment or representation defeated, 7 to 3.

Editor's note: The prohibition against a "Capitation"—or poll —tax has proved to be academic. The requirement that it be apportioned according to the census has made it too bulky and impractical to apply and, in any case, the section was superseded by the Sixteenth (income tax) Amendment. Nevertheless, it is interesting to note that two Eighteenth Century concerns were very much involved here. First was the surrender of states' rights in granting Congress the power to levy such a tax at all. It clearly showed the convention's determination that the new government should not be weakened by an inability to press for revenue from every source. And second was the old worry about the balance between small and large states. Tying the tax to population was, in part, a look into the future when the westward movement would create new states, perhaps more populous than wealthy. The propertied East was making sure that tax burdens would be proportional.

PERIODIC CENSUS APPROVED / *July 11*

Mr. Gouverneur Morris said he had several objections to the proposition of Mr. Williamson. In the first place, it fettered the legislature too much. In the second place, it would exclude some states altogether who would not have a sufficient number to entitle them to a single representation. In the third place, it will not consist with the resolution passed on Saturday last authorizing the legislature to adjust the representation from time to time on the principles of population and wealth, nor with the principles of equity. If slaves were to be considered as inhabitants, not as wealth, then the said resolution would not be pursued; if as wealth, then why is no other wealth but slaves included? These objections may perhaps be removed by amendments. His great objection was that the number of inhabitants was not a proper standard of wealth. The amazing difference between the comparative numbers and wealth of different countries rendered all reasoning superfluous on the subject. Numbers might with greater propriety be deemed a measure of strength than of wealth; yet the late defense made by Great Britain against her numerous enemies proved in the clearest manner that it is entirely fallacious even in this respect.

Mr. King thought there was great force in the objections of Mr. Gouverneur Morris. He would, however, accede to the proposition for the sake of doing something.

Mr. Rutledge contended for the admission of wealth in the estimate by which representation should be regulated. The western states will not be able to contribute in proportion to their numbers; they should not, therefore, be represented in that proportion. The Atlantic states will not concur in such a plan. He moved that "at the end of _____ years after the first meeting of the legislature, and of every _____ years thereafter, the legislature shall proportion the representation according to the principles of wealth and population."

Mr. Sherman thought the number of people alone the best rule for measuring wealth as well as representation, and that if the legislature were to be governed by wealth, they would be obliged to estimate it by numbers. He was at first for leaving the matter wholly to the discretion of the legislature, but he had been convinced by the observations of Mr. Randolph and Mr. Mason that the periods and the rule of revising the representation ought to be fixed by the Constitution.

Mr. Read thought the legislature ought not to be too much shackled. It would make the Constitution, like religious creeds, embarrassing to those bound to conform to it, and more likely to produce dissatisfaction and schism than harmony and union.

Mr. Mason objected to Mr. Rutledge's motion as requiring of the legislature something too indefinite and impracticable and leaving them a pretext for doing nothing.

Mr. Wilson had himself no objection to leaving the legislature entirely at liberty, but considered wealth as an impracticable rule.

Mr. Gorham: If the convention, who are comparatively so little biased by local views, are so much perplexed, how can it be expected that the legislature hereafter, under the full bias of those views, will be able to settle a standard? He was convinced by the arguments of others and his own reflections that the convention ought to fix some standard or other.

Mr. Gouverneur Morris: The arguments of others and his own reflections had led him to a very different conclusion. If we cannot agree on a rule that will be just at this time, how can we expect to find one that will be just in all times to come? Surely those who come after us will judge better of things present than we can of things future. He could not persuade himself that numbers would be a just rule at any time. The remarks of Mr. Mason relative to the western country had not changed his opinion on that head. Among other objections, it must be apparent they would not be able to furnish men equally enlightened to share in the administration of our common interests. The busy haunts of men, not the remote wilderness, was the proper school of political talents. If the western people get the power into their hands, they will ruin the Atlantic interests. The back members are always most averse to the best measures. He mentioned the case of Pennsylvania formerly. The lower part of the state had the power in the first instance. They kept it in their own hands and the country was the better for it. Another objection with him against admitting the blacks into the census was that the people of Pennsylvania would revolt at the idea of being put on a footing with slaves. They would reject any plan that was to have such an effect. Two objections had been raised against leaving the adjustment of the representation from time to time to the discretion of the legislature. The first was they would be unwilling to revise it at all. The second, that by referring to wealth, they would be bound by a rule which, if willing, they would be unable to execute. The first objection distrusts their fidelity. But if their duty, their honor, and their oaths will not bind them, let us not put into their hands our liberty and all our other great interests; let us have no government at all. In the second place, if these ties will bind them, we need not distrust the practicability of the rule. It was followed in part by the committee in the apportionment of representatives yesterday reported to the house. The best course that could be taken would be to leave the interests of the people to the representatives of the people.

Mr. Madison was not a little surprised to hear this implicit confidence urged by a member who on all occasions had inculcated so strongly the political depravity of men and the necessity of checking one vice and interest by opposing to them another vice and interest. If the representatives of the people would be bound by the ties he had

mentioned what need was there for a Senate? What of a revisionary
power? But his reasoning was not only inconsistent with his former
reasoning, but with itself. At the same time that he recommended this
implicit confidence to the southern states in the northern majority,
he was still more zealous in exhorting all to a jealousy of a western
majority. To reconcile the gentleman with himself, it must be imagined that he determined the human character by the points of the
compass. The truth was that all men having power ought to be distrusted to a certain degree. The case of Pennsylvania had been mentioned where it was admitted that those who were possessed of the
power in the original settlement never admitted the new settlements
to a due share of it. England was a still more striking example. The
power there had long been in the hands of the boroughs—of the minority—who had opposed and defeated every reform which had been
attempted. Virginia was in a less degree another example. With regard to the western states, he was clear and firm in opinion that no
unfavorable distinctions were admissible either in point of justice or
policy. He thought also that the hope of contributions to the treasury
from them had been much underrated. Future contributions, it seemed
to be understood on all hands, would be principally levied on imports
and exports. The extent and fertility of the western soil would for a
long time give to agriculture a preference over manufactures. Trials
would be repeated till some articles could be raised from it that would
bear a transportation to places where they could be exchanged for imported manufactures. Whenever the Mississippi should be opened to
them (which would of necessity be the case as soon as their population would subject them to any considerable share of the public burden) imposts on their trade could be collected with less expense and
greater certainty than on that of the Atlantic states. In the meantime,
as their supplies must pass through the Atlantic states, their contributions would be levied in the same manner with those of the Atlantic
states. He could not agree that any substantial objection lay against
fixing numbers for the perpetual standard of representation. It was
said that representation and taxation were to go together; that taxation and wealth ought to go together; that population and wealth
were not measures of each other. He admitted that in different cli-
mates, under different forms of government, and in different stages of
civilization, the inference was perfectly just. He would admit that in
no situation numbers of inhabitants were an accurate measure of
wealth. He contended, however, that in the United States it was sufficiently so for the object in contemplation. Although their climate
varied considerably, yet, as the governments, the laws, and the man-

ners of all were nearly the same, and the intercourse between different parts perfectly free, population, industry, arts, and the value of labor would constantly tend to equalize themselves. The value of labor might be considered as the principal criterion of wealth and ability to support taxes, and this would find its level in different places where the intercourse should be easy and free with as much certainty as the value of money or any other thing. Wherever labor would yield most, people would resort till the competition should destroy the inequality. Hence it is that the people are constantly swarming from the more to the less populous places—from Europe to America, from the northern and middle parts of the United States to the southern and western. They go where land is cheaper, because there labor is dearer. If it be true that the same quantity of produce raised on the banks of the Ohio is of less value than on the Delaware, it is also true that the same labor will raise twice or thrice the quantity in the former that it will raise in the latter situation.

Mr. Mason agreed with Mr. G. Morris that we ought to leave the interests of the people to the representatives of the people, but the objection was that the legislature would cease to be the representatives of the people. It would continue no longer than the states now containing a majority of the people should retain that majority. As soon as the southern and western population should predominate, which must happen in a few years, the power would be in the hands of the minority and would never be yielded to the majority unless provided for by the Constitution.

Periodic census approved, 6 to 4.

/ July 12

In convention. Mr. Gouverneur Morris moved to add to the clause empowering the legislature to vary the representation according to the principles of wealth and numbers of inhabitants a proviso "that taxation shall be in proportion to representation."

Mr. Butler contended again that representation should be according to the full number of inhabitants, including all the blacks, admitting the justice of Mr. Gouverneur Morris' motion.

Mr. Mason also admitted the justice of the principle, but was afraid embarrassments might be occasioned to the legislature by it. It might drive the legislature to the plan of requisitions.

Mr. Gouverneur Morris admitted that some objections lay against his motion, but supposed they would be removed by restraining the rule to direct taxation. With regard to indirect taxes on exports and

imports and on consumption, the rule would be inapplicable. Notwithstanding what had been said to the contrary, he was persuaded
that the imports and consumption were pretty nearly equal throughout the Union.

Gen. Pinckney liked the idea. He thought it so just that it could
not be objected to, but foresaw that if the revision of the census was
left to the discretion of the legislature, it would never be carried into
execution. The rule must be fixed and the execution of it enforced
by the Constitution. He was alarmed at what was said by Mr. Gouverneur Morris yesterday concerning the Negroes. He was now again
alarmed at what had been thrown out concerning the taxing of exports. South Carolina has in one year exported to the amount of
600,000 pounds sterling, all which was the fruit of the labor of her
blacks. Will she be represented in proportion to this amount? She will
not. Neither ought she then to be subject to a tax on it. He hoped a
clause would be inserted in the system restraining the legislature from
taxing exports.

Mr. Wilson approved the principle, but could not see how it could
be carried into execution unless restrained to direct taxation.

Mr. Gouverneur Morris having so varied his motion by inserting
the word "direct," it passed unanimously as follows: "provided always that direct taxation ought to be proportioned to representation."

Mr. Davie said it was high time now to speak out. He saw that it
was meant by some gentlemen to deprive the southern states of any
share of representation for their blacks. He was sure that North Carolina would never confederate on any terms that did not rate them at
least as three-fifths. If the eastern states meant, therefore, to exclude
them altogether, the business was at an end.

Dr. Johnson thought that wealth and population were the true,
equitable rules of representation, but he conceived that these two
principles resolved themselves into one, population being the best
measure of wealth. He concluded, therefore, that the number of people ought to be established as the rule and that all descriptions, including blacks equally with the whites, ought to fall within the computation. As various opinions had been expressed on the subject, he
would move that a committee might be appointed to take them into
consideration and report them.

Mr. Gouverneur Morris: It had been said that it is high time to
speak out. As one member, he would candidly do so. He came here to
form a compact for the good of America. He was ready to do so with
all the states. He hoped and believed that all would enter into such a
compact. If they would not, he was ready to join with any states that

would. But as the compact was to be voluntary, it is in vain for the eastern states to insist on what the southern states will never agree to. It is equally vain for the latter to require what the other states can never admit, and he verily believed the people of Pennsylvania will never agree to a representation of Negroes. What can be desired by these states more than has been already proposed—that the legislature shall from time to time regulate representation according to population and wealth?

Gen. Pinckney desired that the rule of wealth should be ascertained and not left to the pleasure of the legislature and that property in slaves should not be exposed to danger under a government instituted for the protection of property.

The first clause in the report of the first grand committee was postponed.

Mr. Ellsworth, in order to carry into effect the principle established, moved to add to the last clause adopted by the house the words following: "and that the rule of contribution by direct taxation, for the support of the Government of the United States, shall be the number of white inhabitants and three-fifths of every other description, in the several states, until some other rule that shall more accurately ascertain the wealth of the several states can be devised and adopted by the legislature."

Mr. Butler seconded the motion in order that it might be committed.

Mr. Randolph was not satisfied with the motion. The danger will be revived that the ingenuity of the legislature may evade or pervert the rule so as to perpetuate the power where it shall be lodged in the first instance. He proposed in lieu of Mr. Ellsworth's motion "that in order to ascertain the alterations in representation that may be required from time to time by changes in the relative circumstances of the states, a census shall be taken within two years from the first meeting of the general legislature of the United States and once within the term of every _____ years afterwards of all the inhabitants in the manner and according to the ratio recommended by Congress in their resolution of the 18th of April, 1783 (rating the blacks at three-fifths of their number), and that the legislature of the United States shall arrange the representation accordingly." He urged strenuously that express security ought to be provided for including slaves in the ratio of representation. He lamented that such a species of property existed, but as it did exist, the holders of it would require this security. It was perceived that the design was entertained by some of excluding slaves altogether; the legislature, therefore, ought not to be left at liberty.

Mr. Ellsworth withdraws his motion and seconds that of Mr. Randolph.

Mr. Wilson observed that less umbrage would, perhaps, be taken against an admission of the slaves into the rule of representation if it should be so expressed as to make them indirectly only an ingredient in the rule by saying that they should enter into the rule of taxation, and as representation was to be according to taxation, the end would be equally attained. He accordingly moved and was seconded so to alter the last clause adopted by the house that, together with the amendment proposed, the whole should read as follows: "provided always that the representation ought to be proportioned according to direct taxation, and in order to ascertain the alterations in the direct taxation, which may be required from time to time by the changes in the relative circumstances of the states, *Resolved,* that a census be taken within two years from the first meeting of the Legislature of the United States and once within the term of every ———— years afterwards of all the inhabitants of the United States, in the manner and according to the ratio recommended by Congress in their resolution of the 18th of April, 1783, and that the Legislature of the United States shall proportion the direct taxation accordingly."

Mr. King: Although the amendment varies the aspect somewhat, he had still two powerful objections against tying down the legislature to the rule of numbers—first, they were at this time an uncertain index of the relative wealth of the states; secondly, if they were a just index at this time, it cannot be supposed always to continue so. He was far from wishing to retain any unjust advantage whatever in one part of the Republic. If justice was not the basis of the connection, it could not be of long duration. He must be shortsighted indeed who does not foresee that whenever the southern states shall be more numerous than the northern, they can and will hold a language that will awe them into justice. If they threaten to separate now in case injury shall be done them, will their threats be less urgent or effectual when force shall back their demands? Even in the intervening period there will be no point of time at which they will not be able to say, Do us justice, or we will separate. He urged the necessity of placing confidence to a certain degree in every government and did not conceive that the proposed confidence as to a periodical readjustment of the representation exceeded that degree.

Mr. Pinckney moved to amend Mr. Randolph's motion so as to make "blacks equal to the whites in the ratio of representation." This, he urged, was nothing more than justice. The blacks are the laborers, the peasants, of the southern states. They are as productive of pecuniary resources as those of the northern states. They add equally to the wealth and, considering money as the sinew of war, to the strength of the nation. It will also be politic with regard to the northern states, as taxation is to keep pace with representation.

Gen. Pinckney moves to insert six years, instead of two, as the period, computing from the first meeting of the legislature, within which the first census should be taken.

Question for inserting six years instead of "two" in the proposition of Mr. Wilson, it passed, 5 to 4.

REAPPORTIONMENT BASED ON POPULATION / July 13

On the motion of Mr. Randolph, the vote of Monday last authorizing the legislature to adjust from time to time the representation upon the principles of wealth and numbers of inhabitants was reconsidered by common consent in order to strike out "wealth" and adjust the resolution to that requiring periodical revisions according to the number of whites and three-fifths of the blacks. The motion was in the words following:

"But, as the present situation of the states may probably alter in the number of their inhabitants, that the Legislature of the United States be authorized from time to time to apportion the number of representatives; and, in case any of the states shall hereafter be divided, or any two or more states united, or new states created within the limits of the United States, the Legislature of the United States shall possess authority to regulate the number of representatives in any of the foregoing cases upon the principle of their number of inhabitants, according to the provisions hereafter mentioned."

Mr. Gouverneur Morris opposed the alteration as leaving still an incoherence. If Negroes were to be viewed as inhabitants and the revision was to proceed on the principle of numbers of inhabitants, they ought to be added in their entire number and not in proportion of three-fifths. If as property, the word "wealth" was right, and striking it out would produce the very inconsistency which it was meant to get rid of. The train of business and the late turn which it had taken had led him, he said, into deep meditation on it, and he would candidly state the result. A distinction had been set up and urged between the northern and southern states. He had hitherto considered this doctrine as heretical. He still thought the distinction groundless. He sees, however, that it is persisted in and the southern gentlemen will not be satisfied unless they see the way open to their gaining a majority in the public councils. The consequence of such a transfer of power from the maritime to the interior and landed interest will, he foresees, be such an oppression to commerce that he shall be obliged to vote for the vicious principle of equality in the second branch in order to provide some defense for the northern states against it. But to come more to the point, either this distinction is fictitious or real; if fictitious, let it be dismissed and let us proceed with due confidence. If it be real, instead of attempting to blend incompatible things, let us at once take a friendly leave of each other. There can be no end of demands for security if every particular interest is to be entitled to it. The eastern states may claim it for their fishery and for other objects, as the southern states claim it for their peculiar objects. In this struggle between the two ends of the Union, what part ought the middle states in point of policy take? To join their eastern brethren according to his ideas. If the southern states get the power into their hands and be joined, as they will be, with the interior country, they will inevitably bring on a war with Spain for the Mississippi. This language is already held. The interior country, having no property nor interest exposed on the sea, will be little affected by such a war. He wished to know what security the northern and middle states will have against this danger. It has been said that North Carolina, South Carolina, and Georgia only, will in a little time have a majority of the people of America. They must in that case include the great interior country, and everything was to be apprehended from their getting the power into their hands.

Mr. Butler: The security the southern states want is that their Negroes may not be taken from them, which some gentlemen within or without doors have a very good mind to do. It was not supposed that North Carolina, South Carolina, and Georgia would have more people than all the other states, but many more relatively to the other states than they now have. The people and strength of America are evidently bearing southwardly and southwestwardly.

Mr. Wilson: If a general declaration would satisfy any gentleman, he had no indisposition to declare his sentiments. Conceiving that all men, wherever placed, have equal rights and are equally entitled to confidence, he viewed without apprehension the period when a few states should contain the superior number of people. The majority of people, wherever found, ought in all questions to govern the minority. If the interior country should acquire this majority, it will not only have the right, but will avail itself of it, whether we will or no. This jealousy misled the policy of Great Britain with regard to America. The fatal maxims espoused by her were that the colonies were growing too fast and that their growth must be stinted in time. What were the consequences? First, enmity on our part, then actual separation.

301

Like consequences will result on the part of the interior settlements if like jealousy and policy be pursued on ours. Further, if numbers be not a proper rule, why is not some better rule pointed out? No one has yet ventured to attempt it. Congress have never been able to discover a better. No state, as far as he had heard, had suggested any other. In 1783, after elaborate discussion of a measure of wealth, all were satisfied then, as they now are, that the rule of numbers does not differ much from the combined rule of numbers and wealth. Again, he could not agree that property was the sole or primary object of government and society. The cultivation and improvement of the human mind was the most noble object. With respect to this object, as well as to other personal rights, numbers were surely the natural and precise measure of representation. And with respect to property, they could not vary much from the precise measure. In no point of view, however, could the establishment of numbers as the rule of representation in the first branch vary his opinion as to the impropriety of letting a vicious principle into the second branch.

Question to strike out "wealth" and to make the change as moved by Mr. Randolph passed, 9 to 0.

Mr. Read moved to insert after the word "divided," "or enlarged by addition of territory," which was agreed to.

• Article I, Section 6: The Senators and Representatives shall receive a Compensation for their Services, to be ascertained by Law, and paid out of the Treasury of the United States. . . . No Senator or Representative shall, during the Time for which he was elected, be appointed to any civil Office under the Authority of the United States, which shall have been created, or the Emoluments whereof shall have been encreased during such time; and no Person holding any Office under the United States, shall be a Member of either House during his Continuance in Office.

THE CONSTITUTION OF THE UNITED STATES

NATIONAL TREASURY TO PAY SALARIES / *June 12*

The words "liberal compensation for members" being considered, Mr. Madison moved to insert the words "and fixed." He observed that it would be improper to leave the members of the national legislature to be provided for by the state legislature, because it would create an improper dependence, and to leave them to regulate their own wages was an indecent thing and might in time prove a dangerous one. He thought wheat, or some other article of which the average price throughout a reasonable period preceding might be settled in some convenient mode, would form a proper standard.

Mr. Mason seconded the motion, adding that it would be improper for other reasons to leave the wages to be regulated by the states. First, the different states would make different provision for their representatives, and an inequality would be felt among them, whereas he thought they ought to be in all respects equal; secondly, the parsimony of the states might reduce the provision so low that as had already happened in choosing delegates to Congress, the question would be, not who were most fit to be chosen, but who were most willing to serve.

Inserting the words "and fixed" passed, 8 to 3.

Dr. Franklin said he approved of the amendment just made for rendering the salaries as fixed, as possible, but disliked the word "liberal." He would prefer the word "moderate," if it was necessary to substitute any other. He remarked the tendency of abuses, in every case, to grow of themselves when once begun, and related very pleasantly the progression in ecclesiastical benefices, from the first departure from the gratuitous provision for the apostles to the establishment of the papal system. The word "liberal" was struck out.

Motion of Mr. Pierce that the wages should be paid out of the national treasury passed, 8 to 3.

In convention. The clause in the third resolution, "to receive fixed stipends, to be paid out of the national treasury," being considered, Mr. Ellsworth moved to substitute payment by the states out of their own treasuries, observing that the manners of different states were very different in the style of living and in the profits accruing from the exercise of like talents. What would be deemed, therefore, a reasonable compensation in some states, in others would be very unpopular, and might impede the system of which it made a part.

Mr. Williamson favored the idea. He reminded the house of the prospect of new states to the westward. They would be too poor, would pay little into the common treasury, and would have a different interest from the old states. He did not think, therefore, that the latter ought to pay the expense of men who would be employed in thwarting their measures and interests.

Mr. Gorham wished not to refer the matter to the state legislatures, who were always paring down salaries in such a manner as to keep out of office men most capable of executing the functions of them. He thought, also, it would be wrong to fix the compensation by the Constitution, because we could not venture to make it as liberal as it ought to be without exciting an enmity against the whole plan. Let the national legislature provide their own wages from time to time as the state legislatures do. He had not seen this part of their power abused, nor did he apprehend an abuse of it.

Mr. Randolph said he feared we were going too far in consulting popular prejudices. Whatever respect might be due to them in lesser matters or in cases where they formed the permanent character of the people, he thought it neither incumbent on, nor honorable for, the convention to sacrifice right and justice to that consideration. If the states were to pay the members of the national legislature, a dependence would be created that would vitiate the whole system. The whole nation has an interest in the attendance and services of the members. The national treasury, therefore, is the proper fund for supporting them.

Mr. King urged the danger of creating a dependence on the states by leaving to them the payment of the members of the national legislature. He supposed it would be best to be explicit as to the compensation to be allowed. A reserve on that point, or a reference to the national legislature of the quantum, would excite greater opposition than any sum that would be actually necessary or proper.

Mr. Sherman contended for referring both the quantum and the payment of it to the state legislatures.

Mr. Wilson was against fixing the compensation, as circumstances would change and call for a change of the amount. He thought it of great moment that the members of the national Government should be left as independent as possible of the state governments in all respects.

Mr. Madison concurred in the necessity of preserving the compensations for the national Government independent on the state governments, but at the same time approved of fixing them by the Constitution, which might be done by taking a standard which would not vary with circumstances. He disliked particularly the policy suggested by Mr. Williamson, of leaving the members from the poor states beyond the mountains to the precarious and parsimonious support of their constituents. If the western states hereafter arising should be admitted into the Union, they ought to be considered as equals and as brethren. If their representatives were to be associated in the common councils, it was of common concern that such provisions should be made as would invite the most capable and respectable characters into service.

Mr. Hamilton apprehended inconvenience from fixing the wages. He was strenuous against making the national council dependent on the legislative rewards of the states. Those who pay are the masters of those who are paid. Payment by the states would be unequal, as the distant states would have to pay for the same term of attendance and

more days in traveling to and from the seat of government. He ex-
patiated emphatically on the difference between the feelings and
views of the people and the governments of the states arising from
the personal interest and official inducements which must render the
latter unfriendly to the General Government.

Mr. Wilson moved that the salaries of the first branch "be ascertained by the national legislature and be paid out of the national
treasury."

Mr. Madison thought the members of the legislature too much interested (in) their own compensation. It would be indecent to put their
hands into the public purse for the sake of their own pockets.

*Question, "Shall the salaries of the first branch be ascertained by the
national legislature?" defeated, 7 to 2.*

/ June 22

On the question for striking out "national treasury," as moved by Mr.
Ellsworth, Mr. Hamilton renewed his opposition to it. He pressed the
distinction between the state governments and the people. The former
would be the rivals of the General Government. The state legislatures
ought not, therefore, to be the paymasters of the latter.

Mr. Ellsworth: If we are jealous of the state governments, they will
be so of us. If on going home I tell them we gave the General Government such powers because we could not trust you, will they adopt it?
And without their approbation it is a nullity.

*The question passed in the negative, 5 to 4; New York and Georgia
were divided.*

On a question for substituting "adequate compensation" in place of
"fixed stipends," it was agreed to; the friends of the latter being willing
that the practicability of fixing the compensation should be considered hereafter in forming the details.

It was then moved by Mr. Butler that a question be taken on both
points jointly, to wit, "adequate compensation to be paid out of the
national treasury." It was objected to as out of order, the parts having
been separately decided on. The president referred the question of
order to the house and it was determined to be in order.

*The question on the sentence was then postponed by South
Carolina, in right of the state.*

• Article I, Section 3: The Senate of the United States shall be composed of two Senators from each State, [chosen by the Legislature thereof,] [1] for six Years; and each Senator shall have one Vote.   THE CONSTITUTION OF THE UNITED STATES

QUESTION OF LENGTH OF TERM / *June 12*

Mr. Spaight moved to fill the blank for the duration of the appointments to the second branch of the national legislature with the words "seven years."

Mr. Sherman thought seven years too long. He grounded his opposition, he said, on the principle that if they did their duty well, they would be re-elected, and if they acted amiss, an earlier opportunity should be allowed for getting rid of them. He preferred five years, which would be between the terms of the first branch and of the executive.

Mr. Pierce proposed three years. Seven years would raise an alarm. Great mischiefs have arisen in England from their septennial act, which was reprobated by most of their patriotic statesmen.

Mr. Randolph was for the term of seven years. The democratic licentiousness of the state legislatures proved the necessity of a firm Senate. The object of this second branch is to control the democratic branch of the national legislature. If it be not a firm body, the other branch, being more numerous and coming immediately from the people, will overwhelm it. The Senate of Maryland, constituted on like principles, had been scarcely able to stem the popular torrent. No mischief can be apprehended, as the concurrence of the other branch, and in some measure of the executive, will in all cases be necessary. A firmness and independence may be the more necessary, also, in this branch, as it ought to guard the Constitution against encroachments of the executive, who will be apt to form combinations with the demagogues of the popular branch.

Mr. Madison considered seven years as a term by no means too long. What we wished was to give to the government that stability which was everywhere called for and which the enemies of the republican form alleged to be inconsistent with its nature. He was not afraid of giving too much stability by the term of seven years. His fear was that the popular branch would still be too great an overmatch for it. It

---

[1] Superseded by the Seventeenth Amendment (1913).

was to be much lamented that we had so little experience to guide us. 307
The Constitution of Maryland was the only one that bore any analogy
to this part of the plan. In no instance had the Senate of Maryland
created just suspicions of danger from it. In some instances, perhaps, it
may have erred by yielding to the House of Delegates. In every instance of their opposition to the measures of the House of Delegates,
they had had with them the suffrages of the most enlightened and impartial people of the other states, as well as of their own. In the states
where the senates were chosen in the same manner as the other
branches of the legislature and held their seats for four years, the institution was found to be no check whatever against the instabilities
of the other branches. He conceived it to be of great importance that a
stable and firm government, organized in the republican form, should
be held out to the people. If this be not done, and the people be left
to judge of this species of government by the operations of the defective
systems under which they now live, it is much to be feared the time is
not distant when, in universal disgust, they will renounce the blessing which they have purchased at so dear a rate and be ready for any
change that may be proposed to them.

*Question for "seven years" as the term for the second branch passed,
8 to 1.*

/ June 26

Mr. Gorham moved to fill the blank with "six years," one-third of the
members to go out every second year.

Mr. Wilson seconded the motion.

Gen. Pinckney opposed six years, in favor of four years. The states,
he said, had different interests. Those of the southern, and of South
Carolina in particular, were different from the northern. If the senators should be appointed for a long term, they would settle in the state
where they exercised their functions, and would in a little time be
rather the representatives of that, than of the state appointing them.

Mr. Read moved that the term be nine years. This would admit of
a very convenient rotation, one-third going out triennially. He would
still prefer "during good behavior," but being little supported in that
idea, he was willing to take the longest term that could be obtained.

Mr. Broom seconded the motion.

MADISON ARGUES FOR A LONG TERM /

Mr. Madison: In order to judge of the form to be given to this institution, it will be proper to take a view of the ends to be served by it.

These were, first, to protect the people against their rulers; secondly, to protect the people against the transient impressions into which they themselves might be led. A people deliberating in a temperate moment and with the experience of other nations before them on the plan of government most likely to secure their happiness would first be aware that those charged with the public happiness might betray their trust. An obvious precaution against this danger would be to divide the trust between different bodies of men who might watch and check each other. In this way they would be governed by the same prudence which has prevailed in organizing the subordinate departments of government, where all business liable to abuses is made to pass through separate hands, the one being a check on the other. It would next occur to such a people that they themselves were liable to temporary errors through want of information as to their true interest, and that men chosen for a short term and employed but a small portion of that in public affairs might err from the same cause. This reflection would naturally suggest that the government be so constituted as that one of its branches might have an opportunity of acquiring a competent knowledge of the public interests. Another reflection equally becoming a people on such an occasion would be that they themselves as well as a numerous body of representatives were liable to err also from fickleness and passion. A necessary fence against this danger would be to select a portion of enlightened citizens whose limited number and firmness might seasonably interpose against impetuous counsels. It ought finally to occur to a people deliberating on a government for themselves that as different interests necessarily result from the liberty meant to be secured, the major interest might under sudden impulses be tempted to commit injustice on the minority. In all civilized countries, the people fall into different classes having a real or supposed difference of interests. There will be creditors and debtors, farmers, merchants, and manufacturers. There will be particularly the distinction of rich and poor. It was true as had been observed (by Mr. Pinckney), we had not among us those hereditary distinctions of rank which were a great source of the contests in the ancient governments as well as the modern states of Europe, nor those extremes of wealth or poverty which characterize the latter. We cannot, however, be regarded even at this time as one homogeneous mass in which everything that affects a part will affect in the same manner the whole. In framing a system which we wish to last for ages, we should not lose sight of the changes which ages will produce. An increase of population will of necessity increase the proportion of those who will labor under all the hardships of life and secretly sigh for a more equal distribution of its blessings. These may in time outnumber those who are placed above the feelings of indigence. According to the equal laws of suffrage, the power will slide into the hands of the former. No agrarian attempts have yet been made in this country, but symptoms of a leveling spirit, as we have understood, have sufficiently appeared in certain quarters to give notice of the future danger. How is this danger to be guarded against on republican principles? How is the danger in all cases of interested coalitions to oppress the minority to be guarded against? Among other means, by the establishment of a body in the government sufficiently respectable for its wisdom and virtue to aid on such emergencies the preponderance of justice by throwing its weight into that scale. Such being the objects of the second branch in the proposed government, he thought a considerable duration ought to be given to it. He did not conceive that the term of nine years could threaten any real danger, but in pursuing his particular ideas on the subject, he should require that the long term allowed to the second branch should not commence till such a period of life as would render a perpetual disqualification to be re-elected little inconvenient either in a public or private view. He observed that as it was more than probable we were now digesting a plan which in its operation would decide forever the fate of republican government, we ought not only to provide every guard to liberty that its preservation could require, but be equally careful to supply the defects which our own experience had particularly pointed out.

SHERMAN FAVORS FREQUENT ELECTIONS /

Mr. Sherman: Government is instituted for those who live under it. It ought, therefore, to be so constituted as not to be dangerous to their liberties. The more permanency it has, the worse, if it be a bad government. Frequent elections are necessary to preserve the good behavior of rulers. They also tend to give permanency to the government by preserving that good behavior, because it insures their re-election. In Connecticut, elections have been very frequent, yet great stability and uniformity, both as to persons and measures, have been experienced from its original establishment to the present time—a period of more than a hundred and thirty years. He wished to have provision made for steadiness and wisdom in the system to be adopted, but he thought six or four years would be sufficient. He should be content with either.

Mr. Read wished it to be observed by the small states that it was their interest that we should become one people as much as possible; that state attachments should be extinguished as much as possible;

that the Senate should be so constituted as to have the feelings of citizens of the whole.

HAMILTON AGREES WITH MADISON /

Mr. Hamilton: He did not mean to enter particularly into the subject. He concurred with Mr. Madison in thinking we were now to decide forever the fate of republican government, and that if we did not give that form due stability and wisdom, it would be disgraced and lost among ourselves, disgraced and lost to mankind forever. He acknowledged himself not to think favorably of republican government, but addressed his remarks to those who did think favorably of it in order to prevail on them to tone their government as high as possible. He professed himself to be as zealous an advocate for liberty as any man whatever, and trusted he should be as willing a martyr to it, although he differed as to the form in which it was most eligible. He concurred also in the general observations of Mr. Madison on the subject, which might be supported by others if it were necessary. It was certainly true that nothing like an equality of property existed; that an inequality would exist as long as liberty existed, and that it would unavoidably result from that very liberty itself. This inequality of property constituted the great and fundamental distinction in society. When the tribunitial power had leveled the boundary between the patricians and plebeians, what followed? The distinction between rich and poor was substituted. He meant not, however, to enlarge on the subject. He rose principally to remark that Mr. Sherman seemed not to recollect that one branch of the proposed government was so formed as to render it particularly the guardians of the poorer orders of citizens, nor to have adverted to the true causes of the stability which had been exemplified in Connecticut. Under the British system, as well as the federal, many of the great powers appertaining to government —particularly all those relating to foreign nations—were not in the hands of the government there. Their internal affairs, also, were extremely simple owing to sundry causes, many of which were peculiar to that country. Of late the government had entirely given way to the people and had in fact suspended many of its ordinary functions in order to prevent those turbulent scenes which had appeared elsewhere. He asks Mr. Sherman whether the state at this time dare impose and collect a tax on the people? To these causes and not to the frequency of elections, the effect, as far as it existed, ought to be chiefly ascribed.

GERRY FAVORS A SHORT TERM /

Mr. Gerry wished we could be united in our ideas concerning a permanent government. All aim at the same end, but there are great differences as to the means. One circumstance, he thought, should be carefully attended to. There was not a one-thousandth part of our fellow citizens who were not against every approach toward monarchy, will they ever agree to a plan which seems to make such an approach? The convention ought to be extremely cautious in what they hold out to the people. Whatever plan may be proposed will be espoused with warmth by many out of respect to the quarter it proceeds from, as well as from an approbation of the plan itself. And if the plan should be of such a nature as to rouse a violent opposition, it is easy to foresee that discord and confusion will ensue, and it is even possible that we may become a prey to foreign powers. He did not deny the position of Mr. Madison that the majority will generally violate justice when they have an interest in so doing, but did not think there was any such temptation in this country. Our situation was different from that of Great Britain, and the great body of lands yet to be parceled out and settled would very much prolong the difference. Notwithstanding the symptoms of injustice which had marked many of our public councils, they had not proceeded so far as not to leave hopes that there would be a sufficient sense of justice and virtue for the purpose of government. He admitted the evils arising from a frequency of elections, and would agree to give the Senate a duration of four or five years. A longer term would defeat itself. It would never be adopted by the people.

NINE-YEAR TERM DEFEATED, SIX-YEAR TERM APPROVED /

Mr. Wilson did not mean to repeat what had fallen from others, but would add an observation or two which he believed had not yet been suggested. Every nation may be regarded in two relations—first, to its own citizens; secondly, to foreign nations. It is, therefore, not only liable to anarchy and tyranny within, but has wars to avoid and treaties to obtain from abroad. The Senate will probably be the depository of the powers concerning the latter objects. It ought, therefore, to be made respectable in the eyes of foreign nations. The true reason why Great Britain has not yet listened to a commercial treaty with us has been because she had no confidence in the stability or efficacy of our government. Nine years with a rotation will provide these desirable qualities and give our government an advantage in this respect over monarchy itself. In a monarchy, much must always depend on the temper of the man. In such a body, the personal character will be lost in the political. He would add another observation. The popular objection against appointing any public body for a long term was that it might by gradual encroachments prolong itself first into a body for life, and finally become a hereditary one. It would be a satisfactory answer to this objection that as one-third would go out triennially, there would be always three divisions holding their places from unequal times, and consequently acting under the influence of different views and different impulses.

Nine-year term, one-third to go out triennially, defeated, 8 to 3.

Six-year term, one-third to go out biennially, passed, 7 to 4.[1]

• **Article I, Section 3: . . . No Person shall be a Senator who shall not have attained to the Age of thirty Years, and been nine Years a Citizen of the United States, and who shall not, when elected, be an Inhabitant of that State for which he shall be chosen.** THE CONSTITUTION OF THE UNITED STATES

AGE QUALIFICATION / *June 12*

On the question for filling the blank with "thirty years" as the qualification for being elected senator, it was agreed to, 7 to 4.

COMPROMISE ON CITIZENSHIP QUALIFICATION / *August 9*

Article 5, Section 3, was then taken up.

Mr. Gouverneur Morris moved to insert fourteen instead of four-years' citizenship as a qualification for senators, urging the danger of admitting strangers into our public councils.

---

[1] Article I, Section 3: . . . Immediately after they shall be assembled in Consequence of the first Election, they shall be divided as equally as may be into three Classes. The Seats of the Senators of the first Class shall be vacated at the Expiration of the second Year, of the second Class at the Expiration of the fourth Year, and of the third Class at the Expiration of the sixth Year, so that one third may be chosen every second Year; [and if Vacancies happen by Resignation, or otherwise, during the Recess of the Legislature of any State, the Executive thereof may make temporary Appointments until the next Meeting of the Legislature, which shall then fill such Vacancies]. (The bracketed section was modified by the Seventeenth Amendment—Editor.)

Mr. Pinckney seconded him.

Mr. Ellsworth was opposed to the motion as discouraging meritorious aliens from emigrating to this country.

Mr. Pinckney: As the Senate is to have the power of making treaties and managing our foreign affairs, there is a peculiar danger and impropriety in opening its door to those who have foreign attachments. He quoted the jealousy of the Athenians on this subject, who made it death for any stranger to intrude his voice into their legislative proceedings.

Mr. Mason highly approved of the policy of the motion. Were it not that many, not natives of this country, had acquired great credit during the Revolution, he should be for restraining the eligibility into the Senate to natives.

Mr. Madison was not averse to some restrictions on this subject, but could never agree to the proposed amendment. He thought any restriction, however, in the Constitution unnecessary and improper: unnecessary, because the national legislature is to have the right of regulating naturalization and can by virtue thereof fix different periods of residence as conditions of enjoying different privileges of citizenship; improper, because it will put it out of the power of the national legislature, even by special acts of naturalization, to confer the full rank of citizens on meritorious strangers, and because it will discourage the most desirable class of people from emigrating to the United States. Should the proposed Constitution have the intended effect of giving stability and reputation to our government, great numbers of respectable Europeans, men who love liberty and wish to partake its blessings, will be ready to transfer their fortunes hither. All such would feel the mortification of being marked with suspicious incapacitations, though they should not covet the public honors. He was not apprehensive that any dangerous number of strangers would be appointed by the state legislatures if they were left at liberty to do so, nor that foreign powers would make use of strangers as instruments for their purposes. Their bribes would be expended on men whose circumstances would rather stifle than excite jealousy and watchfulness in the public.

Mr. Butler was decidedly opposed to the admission of foreigners without a long residence in the country. They bring with them, not only attachments to other countries, but ideas of government so distinct from ours that in every point of view they are dangerous. He acknowledged that if he himself had been called into public life within a short time after his coming to America, his foreign habits, opinions, and attachments would have rendered him an improper agent in public affairs. He mentioned the great strictness observed in Great Britain on this subject.

Dr. Franklin was not against a reasonable time, but should be very sorry to see anything like illiberality inserted in the Constitution. The people in Europe are friendly to this country. Even in the country with which we have been lately at war, we have now and had during the war, a great many friends, not only among the people at large, but in both houses of Parliament. In every other country in Europe, all the people are our friends. We found in the course of the Revolution that many strangers served us faithfully and that many natives took part against their country. When foreigners, after looking about for some other country in which they can obtain more happiness, give a preference to ours, it is a proof of attachment which ought to excite our confidence and affection.

Mr. Randolph did not know but it might be problematical whether emigrations to this country were, on the whole, useful or not, but he could never agree to the motion for disabling them for fourteen years to participate in the public honors. He reminded the convention of the language held by our patriots during the Revolution and the principles laid down in all our American constitutions. Many foreigners may have fixed their fortunes among us under the faith of these invitations. All persons under this description, with all others who would be affected by such a regulation, would enlist themselves under the banners of hostility to the proposed system. He would go as far as seven years, but no farther.

Mr. Wilson said he rose with feelings which were perhaps peculiar, mentioning the circumstance of his not being a native and the possibility, if the ideas of some gentlemen should be pursued, of his being incapacitated from holding a place under the very Constitution which he had shared in the trust of making. He remarked the illiberal complexion which the motion would give to the system, and the effect which a good system would have in inviting meritorious foreigners among us, and the discouragement and mortification they must feel from the degrading discrimination now proposed. He had himself experienced this mortification. On his removal into Maryland, he found himself from defect of residence under certain legal incapacities which never ceased to produce chagrin, though he assuredly did not desire, and would not have accepted, the offices to which they related. To be appointed to a place may be matter of indifference. To be incapable of being appointed is a circumstance grating and mortifying.

Mr. Gouverneur Morris: The lesson we are taught is that we should be governed as much by our reason and as little by our feelings as possible. What is the language of reason on this subject? That we should not be polite at the expense of prudence. There was a moderation in all things. It is said that some tribes of Indians carried their hospitality so far as to offer to strangers their wives and daughters. Was this a proper model for us? He would admit them to his house, he would invite them to his table, would provide for them comfortable lodgings, but would not carry the complaisance so far as to bed them with his wife. He would let them worship at the same altar, but did not choose to make priests of them. He ran over the privileges which emigrants would enjoy among us, though they should be deprived of that of being eligible to the great offices of government, observing that they exceeded the privileges allowed to foreigners in any part of the world, and that as every society from a great nation down to a club had the right of declaring the conditions on which new members should be admitted, there could be no room for complaint. As to those philosophical gentlemen, those citizens of the world as they called themselves, he owned he did not wish to see any of them in our public councils. He would not trust them. The men who can shake off their attachments to their own country can never love any other. These attachments are the wholesome prejudices which uphold all governments. Admit a Frenchman into your Senate, and he will study to increase the commerce of France; an Englishman, and he will feel an equal bias in favor of that of England. It has been said that the legislatures will not choose foreigners, at least improper ones. There was no knowing what legislatures would do. Some appointments made by them proved that everything ought to be apprehended from the cabals practiced on such occasions. He mentioned the case of a foreigner who left this state in disgrace and worked himself into an appointment from another to Congress.

The question on the motion of Mr. Gouverneur Morris to insert fourteen in place of four years defeated, 7 to 4.

On the question for thirteen years moved by Mr. Gouverneur Morris, it was negatived as above.

On ten years, moved by Gen. Pinckney, the votes were the same.

Dr. Franklin reminded the convention that it did not follow from an omission to insert the restriction in the Constitution that the persons in question would be actually chosen into the legislature.

Mr. Rutledge: Seven years of citizenship have been required for the House of Representatives. Surely a longer time is requisite for the Senate, which will have more power.

Mr. Williamson: It is more necessary to guard the Senate in this case than the other house. Bribery and cabal can be more easily practiced in the choice of the Senate, which is to be made by the legislatures, composed of a few men than of the House of Representatives, who will be chosen by the people.

Mr. Randolph will agree to nine years with the expectation that it will be reduced to seven if Mr. Wilson's motion to reconsider the vote fixing seven years for the House of Representatives should produce a reduction of that period.

Question for nine years passed, 6 to 4.

The term "resident" was struck out and "inhabitant" inserted.

• **Article I, Section 6: The Senators and Representatives shall receive a Compensation for their Services, to be ascertained by Law, and paid out of the Treasury of the United States.** THE CONSTITUTION OF THE UNITED STATES

SALARIES DISCUSSED / *June 26*

The clause of the fourth resolution, "to receive fixed stipends by which they may be compensated for their services," being considered, Gen. Pinckney proposed that no salary should be allowed. As this (the senatorial) branch was meant to represent the wealth of the country, it ought to be composed of persons of wealth, and if no allowance was to be made, the wealthy alone would undertake the service. He moved to strike out the clause.

Dr. Franklin seconded the motion. He wished the convention to stand fair with the people. There were in it a number of young men who would probably be of the Senate. If lucrative appointments should be recommended, we might be chargeable with having carved out places for ourselves.

The question was defeated, 6 to 5.

Mr. Williamson moved to change the expression into these words, to wit, "to receive a compensation for the devotion of their time to the public service." The motion was seconded by Mr. Ellsworth and agreed to by all the states except South Carolina. It seemed to be meant only to get rid of the word "fixed" and leave greater room for modifying the provision on this point.

Mr. Ellsworth moved to strike out "to be paid out of the national treasury" and insert "to be paid by their respective states." If the Senate was meant to strengthen the government, it ought to have the confidence of the states. The states will have an interest in keeping up a representation and will make such provision for supporting the members as will insure their attendance.

THE HOUSE AND SENATE

Mr. Madison considered this as a departure from a fundamental principle and subverting the end intended by allowing the Senate a duration of six years. They would, if this motion should be agreed to, hold their places during pleasure—during the pleasure of the state legislatures. One great end of institution was that being a firm, wise, and impartial body, it might not only give stability to the General Government in its operations on individuals, but hold an even balance among different states. The motion would make the Senate, like Congress, the mere agents and advocates of state interests and views instead of being the impartial umpires and guardians of justice and the general good. Congress had lately, by the establishment of a board with full powers to decide on the mutual claims between the United States and the individual states, fairly acknowledged themselves to be unfit for discharging this part of the business referred to them by the Confederation.

Mr. Dayton considered the payment of the Senate by the states as fatal to their independence. He was decided for paying them out of the national treasury.

Attempt to eliminate Senate compensation defeated, 6 to 5.

· Article II, Section 2: . . . He [the President] shall have Power, by and with the Advice and Consent of the Senate, to make Treaties, provided two thirds of the Senators present concur; and he shall nominate, and by and with the Advice and Consent of the Senate, shall appoint Ambassadors, other public Ministers and Consuls, ...   THE CONSTITUTION OF THE UNITED STATES

TREATY POWERS DEBATED / *August 15*

In convention. Article 6, Section 11, was agreed to. Article 6, Section 12, was then taken up.

Mr. Strong moved to amend the article so as to read: "Each House shall possess the right of originating all bills, except bills for raising money for the purposes of revenue, or for appropriating the same, and for fixing the salaries of the officers of the government, which shall originate in the House of Representatives; but the Senate may propose or concur with amendments, as in other cases."

Mr. Mason seconds the motion. He was extremely earnest to take this power from the Senate who, he said, could already sell the whole country by means of treaties.

Mr. Gorham urged the amendment as of great importance. The

Senate will first acquire the habit of preparing money bills and then the practice will grow into an exclusive right of preparing them.

Mr. Gouverneur Morris opposed it as unnecessary and inconvenient.

Mr. Williamson: Some think this restriction on the Senate essential to liberty; others think it of no importance. Why should not the former be indulged? He was for an efficient and stable government, but many would not strengthen the Senate if not restricted in the case of money bills. The friends of the Senate would, therefore, lose more than they would gain by refusing to gratify the other side. He moved to postpone the subject till the powers of the Senate should be gone over.

Mr. Rutledge seconds the motion.

Mr. Mercer should hereafter be against returning to a reconsideration of this section. He contended (alluding to Mr. Mason's observations) that the Senate ought not to have the power of treaties. This power belonged to the executive department, adding that treaties would not be final, so as to alter the laws of the land, till ratified by legislative authority. This was the case of treaties in Great Britain, particularly the late treaty of commerce with France.

Mr. Mason did not say that a treaty would repeal a law, but that the Senate by means of treaties might alienate territory, and so forth, without legislative sanction. The cessions of the British islands in the West Indies by treaty alone were an example. If Spain should possess herself of Georgia, therefore, the Senate might by treaty dismember the Union. He wished the motion to be decided now, that the friends of it might know how to conduct themselves.

Question for postponing Section 12 passed, 6 to 5.

/ August 23

Article 9, Section 1, being resumed, to wit, "The Senate of the United States shall have power to make treaties, and to appoint ambassadors and judges of the supreme court," Mr. Madison observed that the Senate represented the states alone, and that for this, as well as other obvious reasons, it was proper that the President should be an agent in treaties.

Mr. Gouverneur Morris did not know that he should agree to refer the making of treaties to the Senate at all, but for the present would move to add as an amendment to the section after "treaties," the following: "But no treaty shall be binding on the United States which is not ratified by law."

Mr. Madison suggested the inconvenience of requiring a legal rati- **319** fication of treaties to alliance for the purpose of war, and so forth.

Mr. Gorham: Many other disadvantages must be experienced if treaties of peace and all negotiations are to be previously ratified, and if not previously, the ministers would be at a loss how to proceed. What would be the case in Great Britain if the King were to proceed in this manner? American ministers must go abroad not instructed by the same authority (as will be the case with other ministers) which is to ratify their proceedings.

Mr. Gouverneur Morris: As to treaties of alliance, they will oblige foreign powers to send their ministers here; the very thing we should wish for. Such treaties could not be otherwise made if his amendment should succeed. In general, he was not solicitous to multiply and facilitate treaties. He wished none to be made with Great Britain till she should be at war. Then a good bargain might be made with her. So with other foreign powers. The more difficulty in making treaties, the more value will be set on them.

Mr. Wilson: In the most important treaties, the King of Great Britain, being obliged to resort to Parliament for the execution of them, is under the same fetters as the amendment of Mr. Morris will impose on the Senate. It was refused yesterday to permit even the legislature to lay duties on exports. Under the clause without the amendment, the Senate alone can make a treaty requiring all the rice of South Carolina to be sent to some one particular port.

Mr. Dickinson concurred in the amendment as most safe and proper, though he was sensible it was unfavorable to the little states, which would otherwise have an equal share in making treaties.

Dr. Johnson thought there was something of solecism in saying that the acts of a minister with plenipotentiary powers from one body should depend for ratification on another body. The example of the King of Great Britain was not parallel. Full and complete power was vested in him. If the Parliament should fail to provide the necessary means of execution, the treaty would be violated.

Mr. Gorham, in answer to Mr. Gouverneur Morris, said that negotiations on the spot were not to be desired by us, especially if the whole legislature is to have anything to do with treaties. It will be generally influenced by two or three men who will be corrupted by the ambassadors here. In such a government as ours, it is necessary to guard against the government itself being seduced.

Mr. Randolph, observing that almost every speaker had made objections to the clause as it stood, moved in order to a further consideration of the subject that the motion of Mr. Gouverneur Morris should be postponed.

On this question it was lost, the states being equally divided.
Gouverneur Morris' motion defeated, 8 to 1.

The several clauses of Article 9, Section 1, were then separately postponed after inserting "and other public ministers" next, after "ambassadors."

Mr. Madison hinted for consideration whether a distinction might not be made between different sorts of treaties; allowing the President and Senate to make treaties eventual, and of alliance for limited terms, and requiring the concurrence of the whole legislature in other treaties.

The first section of Article 9 was finally referred to the committee of five, and the house then adjourned.

/ September 7

The other parts of the same section were then agreed to.

The Fourth Section, to wit, "The President, by and with the advice and consent of the Senate, shall have power to make treaties," was then taken up.

Mr. Wilson moved to add after the word "Senate," the words "and House of Representatives." As treaties, he said, are to have the operation of laws, they ought to have the sanction of laws also. The circumstance of secrecy in the business of treaties formed the only objection, but this, he thought, so far as it was inconsistent with obtaining the legislative sanction, was outweighed by the necessity of the latter.

Mr. Sherman thought the only question that could be made was whether the power could be safely trusted to the Senate. He thought it could, and that the necessity of secrecy in the case of treaties forbade a reference of them to the whole legislature.

Mr. Fitzsimmons seconded the motion of Mr. Wilson.

The question was defeated, 10 to 1.

On the clause "He shall nominate," and so forth, "appoint ambassadors," and so forth, Mr. Wilson objected to the mode of appointing as blending a branch of the legislature with the executive. Good laws are of no effect without a good executive, and there can be no good executive without a responsible appointment of officers to execute. Responsibility is in a manner destroyed by such an agency of the Senate. He would prefer the council proposed by Mr. Mason, provided its advice should not be made obligatory by the President.

Mr. Pinckney was against joining the Senate in these appointments, except in the instances of ambassadors, who, he thought, ought not to be appointed by the President.

321

Mr. Gouverneur Morris said that as the President was to nominate, there would be responsibility, and as the Senate was to concur, there would be security. As Congress now make appointments, there is no responsibility.

Mr. Gerry: The idea of responsibility in the nomination to offices is chimerical. The President cannot know all characters and can therefore always plead ignorance.

Mr. King: As the idea of a council, proposed by Mr. Mason, has been supported by Mr. Wilson, he would remark that most of the inconvenience charged on the Senate are incident to a council of advice. He differed from those who thought the Senate would sit constantly. He did not suppose it was meant that all the minute officers were to be appointed by the Senate or any other original source, but the higher officers of the departments to which they belong. He was of the opinion, also, that the people would be alarmed at an unnecessary creation of new corps, which must increase the expense as well as influence of the government.

TWO-THIRDS TREATY
CONCURRENCE APPROVED / September 8

In convention. The last report of the committee of eleven was resumed.

Mr. King moved to strike out the exception of treaties of peace from the general clause requiring two-thirds of the Senate for making treaties.

Mr. Wilson wished the requisition of two-thirds to be struck out altogether. If the majority cannot be trusted, it was a proof, as observed by Mr. Gorham, that we were not fit for one society.

A reconsideration of the whole clause was agreed to.

Mr. Gouverneur Morris was against striking out the exception of treaties of peace. If two-thirds of the Senate should be required for peace, the legislature will be unwilling to make war for that reason on account of the fisheries or the Mississippi, the two great objects of the Union. Besides, if a majority of the Senate be for peace and are not allowed to make it, they will be apt to effect their purpose in the more disagreeable mode of negativing the supplies for the war.

Mr. Williamson remarked that treaties are to be made in the branch of the government where there may be a majority of the states without a majority of the people. Eight men may be a majority of a quorum and should not have the power to decide the conditions of peace. There would be no danger that the exposed states, as South Carolina or Georgia, would urge an improper war for the western territory.

Mr. Wilson: If two-thirds are necessary to make peace, the minority may perpetuate war against the sense of the majority.

Mr. Gerry enlarged on the danger of putting the essential rights of the Union in the hands of so small a number as a majority of the Senate representing perhaps not one-fifth of the people. The Senate will be corrupted by foreign influence.

Mr. Sherman was against leaving the rights established by the treaty of peace to the Senate, and moved to annex a proviso that no such rights should be ceded without the sanction of the legislature.

Mr. Gouverneur Morris seconded the ideas of Mr. Sherman.

Mr. Madison observed that it had been too easy in the present Congress to make treaties, although nine states were required for the purpose.

Question for striking out "except treaties of peace" passed, 8 to 3.

Mr. Rutledge and Mr. Gerry moved that "no treaty shall be made without the consent of two-thirds of all the members of the Senate," according to the example in the present Congress.

Mr. Gorham: There is a difference in the case, as the President's consent will also be necessary in the new Government.

Mr. Sherman moved that "no treaty shall be made without a majority of the whole number of the Senate." Mr. Gerry seconded him.

Mr. Williamson: This will be less security than two-thirds, as now required.

Mr. Sherman: It will be less embarrassing.

The question defeated, 6 to 5.

Mr. Madison moved that a quorum of the Senate consist of two-thirds of all the members.

Mr. Gouverneur Morris: This will put it in the power of one man to break up a quorum.

Mr. Madison: This may happen to any quorum.

The question defeated, 6 to 5.

Mr. Williamson and Mr. Gerry moved "that no treaty should be made without previous notice to the members and a reasonable time for their attending."

On the question, all the states voted no; except North Carolina, South Carolina, and Georgia.

On a question on the clause of the report of the committee of eleven, relating to treaties by two-thirds of the Senate, all the states voted aye; except Pennsylvania, New Jersey, and Georgia.

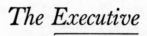

The Executive

CHAPTER FOUR

• Article II, Section 1: The executive Power shall be vested in a President of the United States of America.   THE CONSTITUTION OF THE UNITED STATES

SINGLE OR PLURAL EXECUTIVE? / *June 1*

The committee of the whole proceeded to the seventh resolution (of Randolph's original fifteen) "that a national executive be instituted, to be chosen by the national legislature for the term of _____ years, and so forth, to be ineligible thereafter to possess the executive powers of Congress, and so forth."

Mr. Pinckney was for a vigorous executive, but was afraid the executive powers of the Congress might extend to peace and war, which would render the executive a monarchy of the worst kind, to wit, an elective one.

Mr. Wilson moved that the executive consist of a single person. Mr. C. Pinckney seconded the motion to read "that a national executive to consist of a single person be instituted."

A considerable pause ensuing and the chairman asking if he should put the question, Dr. Franklin observed that it was a point of great importance and wished that the gentlemen would deliver their sentiments on it before the question was put.

Mr. Rutledge animadverted on the shyness of gentlemen on this and other subjects. He said it looked as if they supposed themselves precluded by having frankly disclosed their opinions from afterwards changing them, which he did not take to be at all the case. He said he was for vesting the executive power in a single person, though he was not for giving him the power of war and peace. A single man would feel the greatest responsibility and administer the public affairs best.

Mr. Sherman said he considered the executive magistracy as nothing more than an institution for carrying the will of the legislature into effect, that the person or persons ought to be appointed by, and accountable to, the legislature only, which was the depository of the supreme will of the society. As they were the best judges of the business which ought to be done by the executive department and, consequently, of the number necessary from time to time for doing it, he wished the number might not be fixed, but that the legislature should be at liberty to appoint one or more as experience might dictate.

Mr. Wilson preferred a single magistrate as giving most energy, dispatch, and responsibility to the office. He did not consider the prerogatives of the British monarchs as a proper guide in defining the executive powers. Some of these prerogatives were of a legislative nature, among others, that of war and peace. The only powers he considered strictly executive were those of executing the laws and appointing officers not appertaining to, and appointed by, the legislature.

Mr. Gerry favored the policy of annexing a council to the executive in order to give weight and inspire confidence.

Mr. Randolph strenuously opposed a unity in the executive magistracy. He regarded it as the foetus of monarchy. We had, he said, no motive to be governed by the British government as our prototype. He did not mean, however, to throw censure on that excellent fabric. If we were in a situation to copy it, he did not know that he would be opposed to it, but the fixed genius of the people of America required a different form of government. He could not see why the great requisites for the executive department—vigor, dispatch, and responsibility—could not be found in three men as well as in one man. The executive ought to be independent. It ought, therefore, in order to support its independence, to consist of more than one.

Mr. Wilson said that unity in the executive, instead of being the foetus of monarchy, would be the best safeguard against tyranny. He repeated that he was not governed by the British model, which was inapplicable to the situation of this country, the extent of which was so great and the manners so republican that nothing but a great confederated republic would do for it.

Mr. Wilson's motion for a single magistrate was postponed by common consent, the committee seeming unprepared for any decision on it, and the first part of the clause agreed to, namely, "that a national executive be instituted."

Mr. Madison thought it would be proper, before a choice should be made between a unity and a plurality in the executive, to fix the extent of the executive authority; that as certain powers were in their nature executive and must be given to that department, whether administered by one or more persons, a definition of their extent would assist the judgment in determining how far they might be safely entrusted to a single officer. He accordingly moved that so much of the clause before the committee as related to the powers of the executive should be struck out, and that after the words "that a national executive ought to be instituted," there be inserted the words following: "with power to carry into effect the national laws, to appoint to offices in cases not otherwise provided for, and to execute such other powers,

'not legislative nor judiciary in their nature,' as may from time to   *329*
time be delegated by the national legislature."

The words "not legislative nor judiciary in their nature" were added to the proposed amendment in consequence of a suggestion by Gen. Pinckney that improper powers might otherwise be delegated.

Mr. Wilson seconded this motion.

Mr. Pinckney moved to amend the amendment by striking out the last member of it, namely, "and to execute such other powers, not legislative nor judiciary in their nature, as may from time to time be delegated." He said they were unnecessary, the object of them being included in the "power to carry into effect the national laws."

Mr. Randolph seconded the motion.

Mr. Madison did not know that the words were absolutely necessary, or even the preceding words, "to appoint to offices, and so forth," the whole being, perhaps, included in the first member of the proposition. He did not, however, see any inconvenience in retaining them, and cases might happen in which they might serve to prevent doubts and misconstructions.

Question postponed.

/ June 12

Mr. Rutledge and Mr. C. Pinckney moved that the blank for the number of persons in the executive be filled with the words, "one person." They supposed the reasons to be so obvious and conclusive in favor of one that no member would oppose the motion.

Mr. Randolph opposed it with great earnestness, declaring that he should not do justice to the country which sent him if he were silently to suffer the establishment of a unity in the executive department. He felt an opposition to it which he believed he should continue to feel as long as he lived. He urged first, that the permanent temper of the people was adverse to the very semblance of monarchy; secondly, that a unity was unnecessary, a plurality being equally competent to all the objects of the department; thirdly, that the necessary confidence would never be reposed in a single magistrate; fourthly, that the appointments would generally be in favor of some inhabitant near the center of the community, and consequently the remote parts would not be on an equal footing. He was in favor of three members of the executive, to be drawn from different portions of the country.

Mr. Butler contended strongly for a single magistrate as most likely to answer the purpose of the remote parts. If one man should be appointed, he would be responsible to the whole and would be impartial to its interests. If three or more should be taken from as many districts, there would be a constant struggle for local advantages. In military matters, this would be particularly mischievous. He said his opinion on this point had been formed under the opportunity he had had of seeing the manner in which a plurality of military heads distracted Holland when threatened with invasion by the imperial troops. One man was for directing the force to the defense of this part, another to that part of the country, just as he happened to be swayed by prejudice or interest.

Question postponed by vote of 6 to 4.

SINGLE EXECUTIVE APPROVED / *June 4*

In committee of the whole. The question was resumed on motion of Mr. Pinckney, seconded by Mr. Wilson, "Shall the blank for the number of the executive be filled with a single person?

Mr. Wilson was in favor of the motion. It had been opposed by the gentleman from Virginia (Mr. Randolph), but the arguments used had not convinced him. He observed that the objections of Mr. Randolph were leveled not so much against the measure itself as against its unpopularity. If he could suppose that it would occasion a rejection of the plan of which it should form a part, though the part were an important one, yet he would give it up rather than lose the whole. On examination, he could see no evidence of the alleged antipathy of the people. On the contrary, he was persuaded that it does not exist. All know that a single magistrate is not a king. One fact has great weight with him. All the thirteen states, though agreeing in scarce any other instance, agree in placing a single magistrate at the head of the government. The idea of three heads has taken place in none. The degree of power is indeed different, but there are no co-ordinate heads. In addition to his former reasons for preferring a unity, he would mention another. The tranquillity, not less than the vigor of the government, he thought, would be favored by it. Among three equal members, he foresaw nothing but uncontrolled, continued, and violent animosities, which would not only interrupt the public administration, but diffuse their poison through the other branches of government, through the states, and at length through the people at large. If the members were to be unequal in power, the principle of opposition to the unity was given up; if equal, the making them an odd number would not be a remedy. In courts of justice, there are two sides only to a question. In the legislative and executive departments, questions have commonly many sides. Each member, therefore, might *331* espouse a separate one, and no two agree.

Mr. Sherman: This matter is of great importance and ought to be well considered before it is determined. Mr. Wilson, he said, had observed that in each state a single magistrate was placed at the head of the government. It was so, he admitted, and properly so, and he wished the same policy to prevail in the Federal Government. But then it should be also remarked that in all the states there was a council of advice, without which the first magistrate could not act. A council he thought necessary to make the establishment acceptable to the people. Even in Great Britain, the King has a council and attracts the confidence of the people.

Mr. Williamson asks Mr. Wilson whether he means to annex a council.

Mr. Wilson means to have no council, which oftener serves to cover than prevent malpractices.

Mr. Gerry was at a loss to discover the policy of three members for the executive. It would be extremely inconvenient in many instances, particularly in military matters, whether relating to the militia, any army, or a navy. It would be a general with three heads.

Single executive approved, 7 to 3.

Term of Office

· Article 2, Section 1: . . . He [the President] shall hold his Office during the Term of four Years, ... THE CONSTITUTION OF THE UNITED STATES

DEBATE ON A SEVEN-YEAR TERM / *June 1*

Mr. Wilson moved that the blank for the term of duration should be filled with three years, observing at the same time that he preferred this short period on the supposition that a re-eligibility would be provided for.

Mr. Pinckney moved for seven years.

Mr. Sherman was for three years and against the doctrine of rotation as throwing out of office the men best qualified to execute its duties.

Mr. Mason was for seven years at least, and for prohibiting a re-eligibility as the best expedient both for preventing the effect of a false complaisance on the side of the legislature toward unfit characters and a temptation on the side of the executive to intrigue with the legislature for a reappointment.

Mr. Bedford was strongly opposed to so long a term as seven years. He begged the committee to consider what the situation of the country would be in case the first magistrate should be saddled on it for such a period, and it should be found on trial that he did not possess the qualifications ascribed to him, or should lose them after his appointment. An impeachment, he said, would be no cure for this evil, as an impeachment would reach misfeasance only, not incapacity. He was for a triennial election and for an ineligibility after a period of nine years.

The question for seven years passed, 5 to 4; Massachusetts divided its votes.

There being five ayes, four noes, and one divided, a question was asked whether a majority had voted in the affirmative. The president decided that it was an affirmative vote.

Motion for seven-year term passed, 5 to 4.

/ June 2

On the question for electing the executive by the national legislature for the term of seven years, it was agreed to, 8 to 2.

/ June 2

The question for making the executive "ineligible after seven years" was next taken and agreed to, 7 to 2.

DEBATE ON "DURING GOOD BEHAVIOR" / *July 17*

The clause "for the term of seven years" being resumed, Mr. Broom was for a shorter term since the executive magistrate was now to be re-eligible. Had he remained ineligible a second time, he should have preferred a longer term.

Dr. McClurg moved to strike out "seven years" and insert "during good behavior." By striking out the words declaring him not re-eligible, he was put into a situation that would keep him dependent forever on the legislature, and he conceived the independence of the executive to be equally essential with that of the judiciary department.

Mr. Gouverneur Morris seconded the motion. He expressed great pleasure in hearing it. This was the way to get a good government. His fear that so valuable an ingredient would not be attained had led him to take the part he had done. He was indifferent how the executive should be chosen, provided he held his place by this tenure.

Mr. Broom highly approved the motion. It obviated all his difficulties.

Mr. Sherman considered such a tenure as by no means safe or admissible. As the executive magistrate is now re-eligible, he will be on good behavior as far as will be necessary. If he behaves well, he will be continued; if otherwise, displaced in a succeeding election.

Mr. Madison: If it be essential to the preservation of liberty that the legislative, executive, and judiciary powers be separate, it is essential to a maintenance of the separation that they should be independent of each other. The executive could not be independent of the legislature if dependent on the pleasure of that branch for a reappointment. Why has it determined that the judges should not hold their places by such a tenure? Because they might be tempted to cultivate the legislature by an undue complaisance, and thus render the legislature the virtual expositor as well as the maker of the laws. In like manner, a dependence of the executive on the legislature would render it the executor as well as the maker of laws, and then, according to the observation of Montesquieu, tyrannical laws may be made that they may be executed in a tyrannical manner. There was an analogy between the executive and judiciary departments in several respects. The latter executed the laws in certain cases as the former did in others. The former expounded and applied them for certain purposes, as the latter did for others. The difference between them seemed to consist chiefly in two circumstances—first, the collective interest and security were much more in the power belonging to the executive than to the judiciary department; secondly, in the administration of the former, much greater latitude is left to opinion and discretion than in the administration of the latter. But if the second consideration proves that it will be more difficult to establish a rule sufficiently precise for trying the executive than the judges, and forms an objection to the same tenure of office, both considerations prove that it might be more dangerous to suffer a union between the executive and legislative powers than between the judiciary and legislative powers. He conceived it to be absolutely necessary to a well-constituted republic that the two first should be kept distinct and independent of each other. Whether the plan proposed by the motion was a proper one was another question, as it depended on the practicability of instituting a tribunal for impeachments as certain and as adequate in the one case as in the other. On the other hand, respect for the mover entitled his proposition to a fair hearing and discussion until a less objectionable expedient should be applied for guarding against a dangerous union of the legislative and executive departments.

Mr. Mason: This motion was made some time ago and negatived by a very large majority. He trusted that it would be again negatived. It would be impossible to define the misbehavior in such a manner as to subject it to a proper trial, and perhaps still more impossible to compel so high an offender holding his office by such a tenure to submit to a trial. He considered an executive during good behavior as a softer name only for an executive for life, and that the next would be an easy step to hereditary monarchy. If the motion should finally succeed, he might himself live to see such a revolution. If he did not, it was probable his children or grandchildren would. He trusted there were few men in the house who wished for it. No state, he was sure, had so far revolted from republican principles as to have the least bias in its favor.

Mr. Madison was not apprehensive of being thought to favor any step toward monarchy. The real object with him was to prevent its introduction. Experience had proved a tendency in our government to throw all power into the legislative vortex. The executives of the states are in general little more than ciphers; the legislatures, omnipotent. If no effectual check be devised for restraining the instability and encroachments of the latter, a revolution of some kind or other would be inevitable. The preservation of republican government, therefore, required some expedient for the purpose, but required evidently, at the same time, that in devising it the genuine principles of that form should be kept in view.

Mr. Gouverneur Morris was as little a friend to monarchy as any gentleman. He concurred in the opinion that the way to keep out monarchical government was to establish such a republican government as would make the people happy and prevent a desire of change.

Dr. McClurg was not so much afraid of the shadow of monarchy as to be unwilling to approach it, nor so wedded to republican government as not to be sensible of the tyrannies that had been and may be exercised under that form. It was an essential object with him to make the executive independent of the legislature, and the only mode left for effecting it after the vote destroying his ineligibility a second time was to appoint him during good behavior.

Question of establishing executive term "during good behavior" defeated, 6 to 4.

Question "Shall the executive continue for seven years?" passed in the negative, 5 to 3.

Mr. King was afraid we should shorten the term too much.

Mr. Gouverneur Morris was for a short term in order to avoid impeachments which would be otherwise necessary.

Mr. Butler was against the frequency of the election. Georgia and South Carolina were too distant to send electors often.

Mr. Ellsworth was for six years. If the elections be too frequent, the executive will not be firm enough. There must be duties which will make him unpopular for the moment. There will be *outs* as well as *ins*. His administration, therefore, will be attacked and misrepresented.

Mr. Williamson was for six years. The expense will be considerable and ought not to be unnecessarily repeated. If the elections are too frequent, the best men will not undertake the service, and those of an inferior character will be liable to be corrupted.

The question for six-year term passed, 9 to 1.

A FIFTEEN- OR TWENTY-YEAR TERM? / *July 24*

Mr. L. Martin, suspending his motion as to the ineligibility, moved "that the appointment of the executive shall continue for eleven years."

Mr. Gerry suggested fifteen years.

Mr. King, twenty years. This is the medium life of princes.

Mr. Davie, eight years.

Mr. Wilson: The difficulties and perplexities into which the house is thrown proceed from the election by the legislature, which he was sorry had been reinstated. The inconvenience of this mode was such that he would agree to almost any length of time in order to get rid of the dependence which must result from it. He was persuaded that the longest term would not be equivalent to a proper mode of election, unless it should be during good behavior. It seemed to be supposed that at a certain advance of life a continuance in office would cease to be agreeable to the officer as well as desirable to the public. Experience had shown in a variety of instances that both a capacity and inclination for public service existed in very advanced stages. He mentioned the instance of a doge of Venice who was elected after he was eighty years of age. The popes have generally been elected at very advanced periods, and yet in no case had a more steady or a better-concerted policy been pursued than in the court of Rome. If the executive should come into office at thirty-five years of age, which he presumes may happen, and his continuance should be fixed at fifteen years, at the age of fifty, in the very prime of life and with all the aid of experience, he must be cast aside like a useless hulk. What an irreparable loss would the British jurisprudence have sustained had the age of fifty been fixed there as the ultimate limit of capacity or readiness to serve the public. The great luminary, Lord Mansfield, held his seat for thirty years after his arrival at that age. Notwithstanding what had been done, he could not but hope that a better mode of election would yet be adopted, and one that would be more agreeable to the general sense of the house. That time might be given for further deliberation, he would move that the present question be postponed till tomorrow.

Mr. Broom seconded the motion to postpone.

Mr. Gerry: We seem to be entirely at a loss on this head. He would suggest whether it would not be advisable to refer the clause relating to the executive to the Committee of Detail to be appointed. Perhaps they will be able to hit on something that may unite the various opinions which have been thrown out.

SEVEN-YEAR TERM REINTRODUCED / July 26

In convention. Mr. Mason: In every stage of the question relative to the executive, the difficulty of the subject and the diversity of the opinions concerning it have appeared, nor have any of the modes of constituting that department been satisfactory. First, it has been proposed that the election should be made by the people at large; that is, that an act which ought to be performed by those who know most of eminent characters and qualifications should be performed by those who know least; secondly, that the election should be made by the legislatures of the states; thirdly, by the executives of the states. Against these modes, also, strong objections have been urged. Fourthly, it has been proposed that the election should be made by electors chosen by the people for that purpose. This was at first agreed to, but on further consideration has been rejected. Fifthly, since which, the mode of Mr. Williamson requiring each freeholder to vote for several candidates has been proposed. This seemed, like many other propositions, to carry a plausible face, but on closer inspection is liable to fatal objections. A popular election in any form, as Mr. Gerry has observed, would throw the appointment into the hands of the Cincinnati, a society for the members of which he had a great respect, but which he never wished to have a preponderating influence in the government. Sixthly, another expedient was proposed by Mr. Dickinson, which is liable to so palpable and material an inconvenience that he had little doubt of its being by this time rejected by himself. It would exclude every man who happened not to be popular within his own state, though the causes of his local unpopularity might be of such a nature as to recommend him to the states at large. Seventhly, among other expedients, a lottery has been introduced. But as the tickets do not appear to be in much demand, it will probably not be carried on and nothing, therefore, need be said on that subject. After reviewing all these various modes, he was led to conclude that an election by the national legislature, as originally proposed, was the best. If it was liable to objections, it was liable to fewer than any other. He conceived at the same time that a second election ought to be absolutely prohibited. Having for his primary object—for the polar star of his political conduct—the preservation of the rights of the people, he held it as an essential point, as the very palladium of civil liberty, that the great officers of state, and particularly the executive, should at fixed periods return to that mass from which they were at first taken in order that they may feel and respect those rights and interests which are again to be personally valuable to them. He concluded with moving that the constitution of the executive, as reported by the committee of the whole, be reinstated, "that the executive be appointed for seven years, and be ineligible a second time."

Mr. Davie seconded the motion.

Dr. Franklin: It seems to have been imagined by some that the returning to the mass of the people was degrading the magistrate. This, he thought, was contrary to republican principles. In free governments, the rulers are the servants and the people their superiors and sovereigns. For the former, therefore, to return among the latter was not to degrade, but to promote them. And it would be imposing an unreasonable burden on them to keep them always in a state of servitude and not allow them to become again one of the masters.

Mr. Mason's motion for a seven-year term and ineligibility for re-election passed, 7 to 3.

Mr. Gouverneur Morris was now against the whole paragraph. In answer to Mr. Mason's position that a periodical return of the great officers of the state into the mass of the people was the palladium of civil liberty, he would observe that on the same principle the judiciary ought to be periodically degraded—certain it was that the legislature ought, on every principle, yet no one had proposed or conceived that the members of it should be re-eligible. In answer to Dr. Franklin that a return into the mass of the people would be a promotion instead of degradation, he had no doubt that our executive, like most others, would have too much patriotism to shrink from the burden of his office, and too much modesty not to be willing to decline the promotion.

The whole resolution, as amended in the words following:

"That a national executive be instituted, to consist of a single person, to be chosen by the national legislature for the term of seven years, to be ineligible a second time, with power to carry into execution the national laws, to appoint to offices in cases not otherwise provided for, to be removable on impeachment and conviction of malpractice or neglect of duty, to receive a fixed compensation for the devotion of his time to the public service, to be paid out of the national treasury," passed, 6 to 3.

FOUR-YEAR TERM APPROVED / September 6

Mr. Spaight and Mr. Williamson moved to insert "seven" instead of "four" years for the term of the President.

Motion defeated, 8 to 3.

Mr. Spaight and Mr. Williamson then moved to insert "six" instead of "four."

Motion defeated, 9 to 2.

Four-year term approved, 10 to 1, North Carolina voting in the negative.

RE-ELIGIBILITY OF THE EXECUTIVE / July 19

In convention. On reconsideration of the vote rendering the executive re-eligible a second time, Mr. Martin moved to reinstate the words "to be ineligible a second time."

Mr. Gouverneur Morris: It is necessary to take into one view all that relates to the establishment of the executive, on the due formation of which must depend the efficacy and utility of the union among the present and future states. It has been a maxim in political science that republican government is not adapted to a large extent of country because the energy of the executive magistracy cannot reach the extreme parts of it. Our country is an extensive one. We must either, then, renounce the blessings of the Union or provide an executive with sufficient vigor to pervade every part of it. This subject was of so much importance that he hoped to be indulged in an extensive view of it. One great object of the executive is to control the legislature. The legislature will continually seek to aggrandize and perpetuate themselves and will seize those critical moments produced by war, invasion, or convulsion for that purpose. It is necessary, then, that the executive magistrate should be the guardian of the people, even of the lower classes, against legislative tyranny; against the great and the wealthy, who in the course of things will necessarily compose the legislative body. Wealth tends to corrupt the mind, to nourish its love of power, and to stimulate it to oppression. History proves this to be the spirit of the opulent. The check provided in the second branch was not meant as a check on legislative usurpations of power, but on the abuse of lawful powers, on the propensity of the first branch to legislate too much, to run into projects of paper money, and similar expedients. It is no check on legislative tyranny. On the contrary, it may favor it and, if the first branch can be seduced, may find the means of success. The executive, therefore, ought to be so constituted as to be the great protector of the mass of the people. It is the duty of the executive to appoint the officers and to command the forces of the republic—to appoint, first, ministerial officers for the administration of public affairs; secondly, officers for the dispensation of justice. Who will be the best judges whether these appointments be well made? The people at large, who will know, will see, will feel the effects of them. Again, who can judge so well of the discharge of military duties for the protection and security of the people as the people themselves, who are to be protected and secured? He finds, too, that the executive is not to be re-eligible. What effect will this have? In the first place, it will destroy the great incitement to merit public esteem by taking away the hope of being rewarded with a reappointment. It may give a dangerous turn to one of the strongest passions in the human breast. The love of fame is the great spring to noble and illustrious actions. Shut the civil road to glory, and he may be compelled to seek it by the sword. In the second place, it will tempt him to make the most of the short space of time allotted him to accumulate wealth and provide for his friends. In the third place, it will produce violations of the very Constitution it is meant to secure. In moments of pressing danger, the tried abilities and established character of a favorite magistrate will prevail over respect for the forms of the Constitution. The executive is also to be impeachable. This is a dangerous part of the plan. It will hold him in such dependence that he will be no check on the legislature, will not be a firm guardian of the people and of the public interest. He will be the tool of a faction, of some leading demagogue in the legislature. These, then, are the faults of the executive establishment as now proposed. Can no better establishment be devised? If he is to be the guardian of the people, let him be appointed by the people. If he is to be a check on the legislature, let him not be impeachable. Let him be of short duration that he may with propriety be re-eligible. It has been said that the candidates for this office will not be known to the people. If they be known to the legislature, they must have such notoriety and eminence of character that they cannot possibly be unknown to the people at large. It cannot be possible that a man shall have sufficiently distinguished himself to merit this high trust without having his character proclaimed by fame throughout the empire. As to the danger from an unimpeachable magistrate, he could not regard it as formidable. There must be certain great officers of state, a minister of finance, of war, of foreign affairs, and so forth. These, he presumes, will exercise their functions in subordination to the executive and will be amenable by impeachment to the public justice. Without these ministers, the executive can do nothing of consequence. He suggested a biennial election of the executive at the time of electing the first branch, and the executive to hold over so as to prevent any interregnum in the administration. An election by the people at large, throughout so great an extent of country, could not be influenced by those little combinations and those momentary lies which often decide popular elections within a narrow sphere. It will probably be objected that the election will be influenced by the members of the legislature, particularly of the first branch, and that it will be nearly the same thing with an election by the legislature itself. It could not be denied that such an influence would exist. But it might be answered that as the legislature or the candidates for it would be divided, the enmity of one part would counteract the friendship of another; that if the administration of the executive were good, it would be unpopular to oppose his re-election; if bad, it ought to be opposed, and a reappointment prevented, and lastly, that in every view this indirect dependence on the favor of the legislature could not be so mischievous as a direct dependence for his appointment. He saw no alternative for making the executive independent of the legislature, but either to give him his office for life or make him eligible by the people. Again, it might be objected that two years would be too short a duration. But he believes that as long as he (the President) should behave himself well he would be continued in his place. The extent of the country would secure his re-election against the factions and discontents of particular states. It deserved consideration, also, that such an ingredient in the plan would render it extremely palatable to the people. These were the general ideas which occurred to him on the subject and which led him to wish and move that the whole constitution of the executive might undergo reconsideration.

Mr. Randolph urged the motion of Mr. L. Martin for restoring the words making the executive ineligible a second time. If he ought to be independent, he should not be left under a temptation to court a reappointment. If he should be reappointable by the legislature, he will be no check on it. His revisionary power will be of no avail. He had always thought and contended, as he still did, that the danger apprehended by the little states was chimerical, but those who thought otherwise ought to be peculiarly anxious for the motion. If the executive be appointed, as has been determined by the legislature, he will probably be appointed either by joint ballot of both houses or be nominated by the first and appointed by the second branch. In either case, the large states will preponderate. If he is to court the same influence for his reappointment, will he not make his revisionary power and all the other functions of his administration subservient to the views of the large states? Besides, is there not great reason to apprehend that in case he should be re-eligible, a false complaisance in the legislature might lead them to continue an unfit man in office in preference to a fit one? It has been said that a constitutional bar to reappointment will inspire unconstitutional endeavors to perpetuate himself. It may be answered that his endeavors can have no effect unless the people be corrupt to such a degree as to render all precautions hopeless; to which may be added that this argument supposes him to be more powerful and dangerous than other arguments which have been used admit and, consequently, calls for stronger fetters on his authority. He thought an election by the legislature with an incapacity to be elected a second time would be more acceptable to the people than the plan suggested by Mr. Gouverneur Morris.

Mr. King did not like the ineligibility. He thought there was great force in the remark of Mr. Sherman that he who has proved himself most fit for an office ought not to be excluded by the Constitution from holding it. He would therefore prefer any other reasonable plan that could be substituted. He was much disposed to think that in such cases the people at large would choose wisely. There was indeed some difficulty arising from the improbability of a general concurrence of the people in favor of any one man. On the whole, he was of opinion that an appointment by electors chosen by the people for the purpose would be liable to fewest objections.

Mr. Paterson's ideas nearly coincided, he said, with those of Mr. King. He proposed that the executive should be appointed by electors, to be chosen by the states in a ratio that would allow one elector to the smallest, and three to the largest states.

Mr. Wilson: It seems to be the unanimous sense that the executive

342 should not be appointed by the legislature unless he be rendered ineligible a second time. He perceived with pleasure that the idea was gaining ground of an election, mediately or immediately, by the people.

Mr. Madison: If it be a fundamental principle of free government that the legislative, executive, and judiciary powers should be separately exercised, it is equally so that they be independently exercised. There is the same, and perhaps greater reason why the executive should be independent of the legislature than why the judiciary should. A coalition of the two former powers would be more immediately and certainly dangerous to public liberty. It is essential then that the appointment of the executive should either be drawn from some source, or held by some tenure that will give him a free agency with regard to the legislature. This could not be if he was to be appointable from time to time by the legislature. It was not clear that an appointment in the first instance, even with an ineligibility afterwards, would not establish an improper connection between the two departments. Certain it was that the appointment would be attended with intrigues and contentions that ought not to be unnecessarily admitted. He was disposed for these reasons to refer the appointment to some other source. The people at large was, in his opinion, the fittest in itself. It would be as likely as any that could be devised to produce an executive magistrate of distinguished character. The people generally could only know and vote for some citizen whose merits had rendered him an object of general attention and esteem. There was one difficulty, however, of a serious nature attending an immediate choice by the people. The right of suffrage was much more diffusive in the northern than the southern states, and the latter could have no influence in the election on the score of the Negroes. The substitution of electors obviated this difficulty and seemed, on the whole, to be liable to fewest objections.

Mr. Gerry: If the executive is to be elected by the legislature, he certainly ought not to be re-eligible. This would make him absolutely dependent. He was against a popular election. The people are uninformed and would be misled by a few designing men. He urged the expediency of an appointment of the executives by electors to be chosen by the state executives. The people of the states will then choose the first branch, the legislatures of the states the second branch of the national legislature, and the executives of the states the national executive. This, he thought, would form a strong attachment in the states to the national system. The popular mode of electing the chief magistrate would certainly be the worst of all. If he should be

so elected and should do his duty, he will be turned out for it like *343*
Governor Bowdoin in Massachusetts and President Sullivan in New
Hampshire.
Mr. L. Martin moved that the executive be ineligible a second time.
Mr. Williamson seconds the motion. He had no great confidence in
electors to be chosen for the special purpose. They would not be the
most respectable citizens, but persons not occupied in the high offices of
government. They would be liable to undue influence, which might
the more readily be practiced, as some of them will probably be in appointment six or eight months before the object of it comes on.
Mr. Ellsworth supposed any persons might be appointed electors,
except, solely, members of the national legislature.
*The question, "Shall he be ineligible a second time?" defeated,
8 to 2.*

RE-ELIGIBILITY RECONSIDERED / July 24

Mr. L. Martin and Mr. Gerry moved to reinstate the ineligibility of
the executive a second time.
Mr. Ellsworth: With many this appears a natural consequence of
his being elected by the legislature. It was not the case with him. The
executive, he thought, should be re-elected if his conduct proved him
worthy of it. And he will be more likely to render himself worthy of
it if he be rewardable with it. The most eminent characters also will
be more willing to accept the trust under this condition than if they
foresee a necessary degradation at a fixed period.
Mr. Gerry: That the executive should be independent of the legislature is a clear point. The longer the duration of his appointment,
the more will his dependence be diminished. It will be better then
for him to continue ten, fifteen, or even twenty years and be ineligible
afterwards.
Mr. King was for making him re-eligible. This is too great an advantage to be given up for the small effect it will have on his dependence, if impeachments are to lie. He considered these as rendering the
tenure during pleasure.
Motion suspended by Mr. L. Martin.

/ July 25

Mr. Pinckney moved "that the election by the legislature be qualified with a proviso that no person be eligible for more than six years in any twelve years." He thought this would have all the advantage and at the same time avoid in some degree the inconvenience of an absolute ineligibility a second time.

Mr. Mason approved the idea. It had the sanction of experience in the instance of Congress and some of the executives of the states. It rendered the executive as effectually independent as an ineligibility after his first election and opened the way at the same time for the advantage of his future services. He preferred on the whole the election by the national legislature; though candor obliged him to admit that there was great danger of foreign influence as had been suggested. This was the most serious objection with him that had been urged.

Mr. Butler: The two great evils to be avoided are cabal at home and influence from abroad. It will be difficult to avoid either if the election be made by the national legislature. On the other hand, the government should not be made so complex and unwieldy as to disgust the states. This would be the case if the election should be referred to the people. He liked best an election by electors chosen by the legislatures of the states. He was against a re-eligibility at all events. He was also against a ratio of votes in the states. An equality should prevail in this case. The reasons for departing from it do not hold in the case of the executive as in that of the legislature.

Mr. Gerry approved of Mr. Pinckney's motion as lessening the evil.

Mr. Gouverneur Morris was against a rotation in every case. It formed a political school in which we were always governed by the scholars and not by the masters. The evils to be guarded against in this case are: first, the undue influence of the legislature; secondly, instability of councils; thirdly, misconduct in office. To guard against the first, we run into the second evil. We adopt a rotation which produces instability of councils. To avoid Scylla, we fall into Charybdis. A change of men is ever followed by a change of measures. We see this fully exemplified in the vicissitudes among ourselves, particularly in the state of Pennsylvania. The self-sufficiency of a victorious party scorns to tread in the paths of their predecessors. Rehoboam will not imitate Solomon. Secondly, the rotation in office will not prevent intrigue and dependence on the legislature. The man in office will look forward to the period at which he will become re-eligible. The distance of the period, the improbability of such a protraction of his life, will be no obstacle. Such is the nature of man—formed by his benevolent Author, no doubt, for wise ends—that although he knows his existence to be limited to a span, he takes his measures as if he were to live forever. But taking another supposition, the inefficacy of the expedient will be manifest. If the magistrate does not look forward to his re-election to the executive, he will be pretty sure to keep in view the opportunity of his going into the legislature itself. He will have little objection then to an extension of power on a theater where he expects to act a distinguished part, and will be very unwilling to take any step that may endanger his popularity with the legislature, on his influence over which the figure he is to make will depend. Finally, to avoid the third evil, impeachments will be essential and, hence, an additional reason against an election by the legislature. He considered an election by the people as the best, by the legislature as the worst, mode. Putting both these aside, he could not but favor the idea of Mr. Wilson of introducing a mixture of lot. It will diminish, if not destroy, both cabal and dependence.

345

Mode of Election

· Article II, Section 1: He [the President] shall . . . together with the Vice President, chosen for the same Term, be elected, as follows

Each State shall appoint, in such Manner as the Legislature thereof may direct, a Number of Electors, equal to the whole Number of Senators and Representatives to which the State may be entitled in the Congress: but no Senator or Representative, or Person holding an Office of Trust or Profit under the United States, shall be appointed an Elector.

[The Electors shall meet in their respective States, and vote by Ballot for two Persons, of whom at least shall not be an Inhabitant of the same State with themselves. And they shall make a List of all the Persons voted for, and of the Number of Votes for each; which List they shall sign and certify, and transmit sealed to the Seat of the Government of the United States, directed to the President of the Senate. The President of the Senate shall, in the Presence of the Senate and House of Representatives, open all the Certificates, and the Votes shall then be counted. The Person having the greatest Number of Votes shall be the President, if such Number be a Majority of the whole Number of Electors appointed; . . . .][1]

The Congress may determine the Time of chusing the Electors, and the Day on which they shall give their Votes; which Day shall be the same throughout the United States.   THE CONSTITUTION OF THE UNITED STATES

---

[1] Superseded by the Twelfth Amendment (1804), which was modified by the Twentieth (1933).

The next clause in the seventh resolution relating to the mode of appointing, and the duration of the executive being under consideration, Mr. Wilson said he was almost unwilling to declare the mode which he wished to take place, being apprehensive that it might appear chimerical. He would say, however, at least, that in theory he was for election by the people. Experience, particularly in New York and Massachusetts, showed that an election of the first magistrate by the people at large was both a convenient and successful mode. The objects of choice in such cases must be persons whose merits have general notoriety.

Mr. Sherman was for the appointment by the legislature and for making him absolutely dependent on that body, as it was the will of that which was to be executed. An independence of the executive on the supreme legislature was in his opinion the very essence of tyranny, if there was any such thing.

Mr. Wilson renewed his declarations in favor of an appointment by the people. He wished to derive not only both branches of the legislature from the people without the intervention of the state legislatures, but the executive also, in order to make them as independent as possible of each other as well as of the states.

Mr. Mason favors the idea, but thinks it impracticable. He wishes, however, that Mr. Wilson might have time to digest it into his own form. The clause "to be chosen by the national legislature" was accordingly postponed.

Mr. Rutledge suggests an election of the executive by the second branch only of the national legislature.

The committee then rose, and the house adjourned.

Question postponed.

ELECTION BY THE LEGISLATURE DEFEATED / *June 2*

Mr. Wilson made the following motion, to be substituted for the mode proposed by Mr. Randolph's resolution, "that the executive magistracy shall be elected in the following manner:

'That the states be divided into ———— districts, and that the persons qualified to vote in each district for members of the first branch of the national legislature elect ———— members for their respective districts to be electors of the executive magistracy; that the said electors of the executive magistracy meet at ————, and they, or any ———— of them, so met, shall proceed to elect by ballot, but not out of their own body, _____ person _____ in whom the executive authority of the national government shall be vested.' "

Mr. Wilson repeated his arguments in favor of an election without the intervention of the states. He supposed, too, that this mode would produce more confidence among the people in the first magistrate than an election by the national legislature.

Mr. Gerry opposed the election by the national legislature. There would be a constant intrigue kept up for the appointment. The legislature and the candidates would bargain and play into one another's hands. Votes would be given by the former under promises or expectations from the latter of recompensing them by services to members of the legislature or their friends. He liked the principle of Mr. Wilson's motion, but feared it would alarm and give a handle to the state partisans as tending to supersede altogether the state authorities. He thought the community not yet ripe for stripping the states of their powers, even such as might not be requisite for local purposes. He was for waiting till the people should feel more the necessity of it. He seemed to prefer the taking the suffrages of the states instead of electors, or letting the legislatures nominate and the electors appoint. He was not clear that the people ought to act directly even in the choice of electors, being too little informed of personal characters in large districts and liable to deceptions.

Mr. Williamson could see no advantage in the introduction of electors chosen by the people, who would stand in the same relation to them as the state legislatures, whilst the expedient would be attended with great trouble and expense.

Wilson's motion defeated, 8 to 2; question resumed July 17.

ELECTION BY STATE GOVERNORS DEFEATED / *June 9*

In committee of the whole. Mr. Gerry, according to previous notice given by him, moved "that the national executive should be elected by the executives of the states, whose proportion of votes should be the same with that allowed to the states in the election of the Senate." If the appointment should be made by the national legislature, it would lessen that independence of the executive which ought to prevail, would give birth to intrigue and corruption between the executive and legislature previous to the election and to partiality in the executive afterwards to the friends who promoted him. Some other mode, therefore, appeared to him necessary. He proposed that of appointing by the state executives as most analogous to the principle observed in electing the other branches of the national government: the first branch being chosen by the people of the states, and the second, by the legislatures of the states, he did not see any objection against letting the executive be appointed by the executives of the states. He supposed the executives would be most likely to select the fittest men and that it would be their interest to support the man of their choice.

Mr. Randolph urged strongly the inexpediency of Mr. Gerry's mode of appointing the national executive. The confidence of the people would not be secured by it to the national magistrate. The small states would lose all chance of an appointment from within themselves. Bad appointments would be made, the executives of the states being little conversant with characters not within their own small spheres. The state executives, too, notwithstanding their constitutional independence, being in fact dependent on the state legislatures, will generally be guided by the views of the latter and prefer either favorites within the states, or such as it may be expected will be most partial to the interests of the state. A national executive thus chosen will not be likely to defend with becoming vigilance and firmness the national rights against state encroachments. Vacancies also must happen. How can these be filled? He could not suppose, either, that the executives would feel the interest in supporting the national executive which had been imagined. They will not cherish the great oak which is to reduce them to paltry shrubs.

Motion defeated, 9 to 0.

ELECTION BY LEGISLATURE RESUMED / *July 17*

The next clause, "to be chosen by the national legislature" being considered, Mr. Gouverneur Morris was pointedly against his (the President's) being so chosen. He will be the mere creature of the legislature if appointed and impeachable by that body. He ought to be elected by the people at large—by the freeholders of the country. That difficulties attend this mode, he admits, but they have been found superable in New York and in Connecticut and would, he believed, be found so in the case of an executive for the United States. If the people should elect, they will never fail to prefer some man of distinguished character or services; some man, if he might so speak, of Continental reputation. If the legislature elect, it will be the work of intrigue, of cabal, and of faction; it will be like the election of a pope by a conclave of cardinals; real merit will rarely be the title to the appointment. He moved to strike out "national legislature" and insert "citizens of the United States."

Mr. Sherman thought that the sense of the nation would be better expressed by the legislature than by the people at large. The latter will never be sufficiently informed of characters and, besides, will never give a majority of votes to any one man. They will generally vote for some man in their own state, and the largest state will have the best chance for the appointment. If the choice be made by the legislature, a majority of voices may be made necessary to constitute an election.

Mr. Wilson: Two arguments have been urged against an election of the executive magistrate by the people. The first is the example of Poland, where an election of the supreme magistrate is attended with the most dangerous commotions. The cases, he observed, were totally dissimilar. The Polish nobles have resources and dependents which enable them to appear in force and to threaten the republic as well as each other. In the next place, the electors all assemble at one place, which would not be the case with us. The second argument is that a majority of the people would never concur. It might be answered that the concurrence of a majority of the people is not a necessary principle of election, nor required as such in any of the states. But allowing the objection all its force, it may be obviated by the expedient used in Massachusetts where the legislature by a majority of voices decide in case a majority of the people do not concur in favor of one of the candidates. This would restrain the choice to a good nomination at least, and prevent in a great degree intrigue and cabal. A particular objection with him against an absolute election by the legislature was that the executive in that case would be too dependent to stand as the mediator between the intrigues and sinister views of the representatives and the general liberties and interests of the people.

Mr. Pinckney did not expect this question would again have been brought forward, an election by the people being liable to the most obvious and striking objections. They will be led by a few active and designing men. The most populous states, by combining in favor of the same individual, will be able to carry their points. The national legislature, being most immediately interested in the laws made by themselves, will be most attentive to the choice of a fit man to carry them properly into execution.

Mr. Gouverneur Morris: It is said that in case of an election by the people the populous states will combine and elect whom they please. Just the reverse. The people of such states cannot combine. If there be any combination, it must be among their representatives in the legislature. It is said the people will be led by a few designing men. This might happen in a small district. It can never happen throughout the continent. In the election of a governor of New York, it sometimes is the case in particular spots that the activity and intrigues of little partisans are successful, but the general voice of the state is never influenced by such artifices. It is said the multitude will be uninformed. It is true they would be uninformed of what passed in the legislative conclave if the election were to be made there, but they will not be uninformed of those great and illustrious characters which have merited their esteem and confidence. If the executive be chosen by the national legislature, he will not be independent of it, and if not independent, usurpation and tyranny on the part of the legislature will be the consequence. This was the case in England in the last century. It has been the case in Holland where their senates have engrossed all power. It has been the case everywhere. He was surprised that an election by the people at large should ever have been likened to the Polish election of the first magistrate. An election by the legislature will bear a real likeness to the election by the diet of Poland. The great must be the electors in both cases, and the corruption and cabal which are known to characterize the one would soon find their way into the other. Appointments made by numerous bodies are always worse than those made by single responsible individuals or by the people at large.

Mr. Mason: It is curious to remark the different language held at different times. At one moment we are told that the legislature is entitled to thorough confidence and to indefinite power. At another, that it will be governed by intrigue and corruption and cannot be trusted at all. But not to dwell on this inconsistency, he would observe that a government which is to last ought at least to be practicable. Would this be the case if the proposed election should be left to the people at large? He conceived it would be as unnatural to refer the choice of a proper character for chief magistrate to the people as it would be to refer a trial of colors to a blind man. The extent of the country renders it impossible that the people can have the requisite capacity to judge of the respective pretensions of the candidates.

Mr. Wilson could not see the contrariety stated by Col. Mason. The legislature might deserve confidence in some respects and distrust in others. In acts which were to affect them and their constituents precisely alike, confidence was due; in others, jealousy was warranted. In the appointment to great offices, where the legislature might feel many motives not common to the public, confidence was surely misplaced. This branch of business, it was notorious, was the most corruptly managed of any that had been committed to legislative bodies.

Mr. Williamson conceived that there was the same difference between an election in this case by the people and by the legislature as between an appointment by lot and by choice. There are at present distinguished characters who are known perhaps to almost every man. This will not always be the case. The people will be sure to vote for some man in their own state, and the largest state will be sure to succeed. This will not be Virginia, however. Her slaves will have no suffrage. As the salary of the executive will be fixed and he will not be eligible a second time, there will not be such a dependence on the legislature as has been imagined.

Question of election by the people defeated, 9 to 1.

Mr. L. Martin moved that the executive be chosen by electors appointed by the several legislatures of the individual states.

Motion defeated, 8 to 2.

Question on the words "to be chosen by the national legislature," passed unanimously in the affirmative. Question on the words "for the term of seven years," postponed.

"To carry into execution the national laws," agreed to.

"To appoint to offices in cases not otherwise provided for," agreed to.

"To be ineligible a second time"—Mr. Houston moved to strike out this clause.

Mr. Sherman seconds the motion.

Mr. Gouverneur Morris espoused the motion. The ineligibility proposed by the clause, as it stood, tended to destroy the great motive to good behavior, the hope of being rewarded by a reappointment. It was saying to him, "Make hay while the sun shines."

Question for striking out as moved by Mr. Houston passed, 6 to 4.

ELECTION BY SPECIAL ELECTORS APPROVED / *July 19*

Mr. Ellsworth moved to strike out the appointment by the national legislature and to insert "to be chosen by electors, appointed by the legislatures of the states in the following ratio, to wit: one for each state not exceeding two hundred thousand inhabitants; two for each above that number, and not exceeding three hundred thousand, and three for each state exceeding three hundred thousand."

Mr. Broom seconded the motion.

Mr. Rutledge was opposed to all the modes, except the appointment by the national legislature. He will be sufficiently independent if he be not re-eligible.

Mr. Gerry preferred the motion of Mr. Ellsworth to an appointment by the national legislature or by the people, though not to an appointment by the state executives. He moved that the electors proposed by Mr. Ellsworth should be twenty-five in number and allotted in the following proportion: to New Hampshire, one; Massachusetts, three; Rhode Island, one; Connecticut, two; New York, two; New Jersey, two; Pennsylvania, three; Delaware, one; Maryland, two; Virginia, three; North Carolina, two; South Carolina, two; Georgia, one.

The question as moved by Mr. Ellsworth being divided on the first part, "Shall the national executive be appointed by electors?" passed, 6 to 3. On the second part, "Shall the electors be chosen by the state legislatures?" passed, 8 to 2.

RATIO OF ELECTORS DECIDED / July 20

In convention. The proposed ratio of electors for appointing the executive, to wit, one for each state whose inhabitants do not exceed two hundred thousand, and so forth, being taken up, Mr. Madison observed that this would make in time all, or nearly all, the states equal, since there were few that would not in time contain the number of inhabitants entitling them to three electors; that this ratio ought either to be made temporary or so varied as that it would adjust itself to the growing population of the states.

Mr. Gerry moved that in the first instance the electors should be allotted to the states in the following ratio: to New Hampshire, one; Massachusetts, three; Rhode Island, one; Connecticut, two; New York, two; New Jersey, two; Pennsylvania, three; Delaware, one; Maryland, two; Virginia, three; North Carolina, two; South Carolina, two; Georgia, one.

Mr. Ellsworth moved that two electors be allotted to New Hampshire. Some rule ought to be pursued, and New Hampshire has more than a hundred thousand inhabitants. He thought it would be proper also to allot two to Georgia.

Mr. Broom and Mr. Martin moved to postpone Mr. Gerry's allotment of electors, leaving a fit ratio to be reported by the committee to be appointed for detailing the resolutions.

Mr. Houston seconded the motion of Mr. Ellsworth to add another elector to New Hampshire and Georgia.

Mr. Williamson moved as an amendment to Mr. Gerry's allotment of electors, in the first instance, that in future elections of the national executive, the number of electors to be appointed by the several states shall be regulated by their respective numbers of representatives in the first branch, pursuing, as nearly as may be, the present proportions.

Question on Mr. Gerry's ratio of electors passed, 6 to 4.

Mr. Williamson moved "that the electors of the executive should be paid out of the national treasury for the service to be performed by them." Justice required this, as it was a national service they were to render.

The motion was agreed to.

SPECIAL ELECTORS RECONSIDERED / July 24

In convention. The appointment of the executive by electors being reconsidered, Mr. Houston moved that he be appointed by the national legislature, instead of "electors appointed by the state legislatures," according to the last decision of the mode. He dwelt chiefly on the improbability that capable men would undertake the service of electors from the more distant states.

Mr. Spaight seconded the motion.

Mr. Gerry opposed it. He thought there was no ground to apprehend the danger urged by Mr. Houston. The election of the executive magistrate will be considered as of vast importance and will create great earnestness. The best men, the governors of the states, will not hold it derogatory from their character to be the electors. If the motion should be agreed to, it will be necessary to make the executive ineligible a second time in order to render him independent of the legislature, which was an idea extremely repugnant to his way of thinking.

Mr. Strong supposed that there would be no necessity if the executive should be appointed by the legislature to make him ineligible a second time, as new elections of the legislature will have intervened, and he will not depend for his second appointment on the same set of men that his first was received from. It had been suggested that gratitude for his past appointment would produce the same effect as dependence for his future appointment. He thought very differently. Besides, this objection would lie against the electors, who would be objects of gratitude as well as the legislature. It was of great importance not to make the government too complex, which would be the case if a new set of men, like the electors, should be introduced into it. He thought, also, that the first characters in the states would not feel sufficient motives to undertake the office of electors.

Mr. Williamson was for going back to the original ground to elect the executive for seven years and render him ineligible a second time. The proposed electors would certainly not be men of the first, nor even of the second grade in the states. These would all prefer a seat in the Senate or the other branch of the legislature. He did not like the unity in the executive. He had wished the executive power to be lodged in three men, taken from three districts into which the states should be divided. As the executive is to have a kind of veto on the laws and there is an essential difference of interests between the northern and southern states, particularly in the carrying trade, the power will be dangerous, if the executive is to be taken from part of the Union, to the part from which he is not taken. The case is different here from what it is in England where there is a sameness of interests throughout the kingdom. Another objection against a single magistrate is that he will be an elective king and will feel the spirit of one. He will spare no pains to keep himself in for life and will then lay a train for the succession of children. It was pretty certain, he thought, that we should at some time or other have a king, but he wished no precaution to be omitted that might postpone the event as long as possible. Ineligibility a second time appeared to him to be the best precaution. With this precaution he had no objection to a longer term than seven years. He would go as far as ten or twelve years.

Mr. Gerry moved that the legislatures of the states should vote by ballot for the executive in the same proportions as it had been proposed they should choose electors, and that in case a majority of the votes should not center on the same person, the first branch of the national legislature should choose two out of the four candidates having most votes, and out of these two the second branch should choose the executive.

Mr. Houston's motion that the executive be appointed by the national legislature passed, 7 to 4.

ELECTION BY LEGISLATURE RECONSIDERED / *July 24*

Mr. Wilson: As the great difficulty seems to spring from the mode of election, he would suggest a mode which had not been mentioned. It was that the executive be elected for six years by a small number, not more than fifteen, of the national legislature, to be drawn from it, not by ballot, but by lot, and who should retire immediately and make the election without separating. By this mode intrigue would be avoided in the first instance and the dependence would be diminished. This was not, he said, a digested idea and might be liable to strong objections.

Mr. Gouverneur Morris: Of all possible modes of appointment, that by the legislature is the worst. If the legislature is to appoint and to impeach or to influence the impeachment, the executive will be the mere creature of it. He had been opposed to the impeachment, but was now convinced that impeachment must be provided for if the appointment was to be of any duration. No man would say that an executive known to be in the pay of an enemy should not be removable in some way or other. He had been charged heretofore (by Mr. Mason) with inconsistency in pleading for confidence in the legislature on some occasions and urging a distrust on others. The charge was not well-founded. The legislature is worthy of unbounded confidence in some respects and liable to equal distrust in others. When their interest coincides precisely with that of their constituents, as happens in many of their acts, no abuse of trust is to be apprehended. When a strong personal interest happens to be opposed to the general interest, the legislature cannot be too much distrusted. In all public bodies, there are two parties. The executive will necessarily be more connected with one than with the other. There will be a personal interest, therefore, in one of the parties to oppose, as well as in the other to support, him. Much had been said of the intrigues that will be practiced by the executive to get into office. Nothing had been said on the other side of the intrigues to get him out of office. Some leader of a party will always covet his seat, will perplex his administration, will cabal with the legislature, till he succeeds in supplanting him. This was the way in which the King of England was got out—he meant the real king, the minister. This was the way in which Pitt (Lord Chatham) forced himself into place. Fox was for pushing the matter still farther. If he had carried his India bill, which he was very near doing, he would have made the minister the king in form almost as well as in substance. Our President will be the British minister; yet we are about to make him appointable by the legislature. Something has been said of the danger of monarchy; if a good government should not now be formed, if a good organization of the executive should not be provided, he doubted whether we should not have something worse than a limited monarchy. In order to get rid of the dependence of the executive on the legislature, the expedient of making him ineligible a second time had been devised. This was as much as to say we should give him the benefit of experience and then deprive ourselves of the use of it. But make him ineligible a second time and prolong his duration even to fifteen years, will he by any wonderful interposition of Providence at that period cease to be a man? No, he will be unwilling to quit his exaltation; the road to his object through the Constitution will be shut; he will be in possession of the sword; a civil war will ensue, and the commander of the victorious army, on whichever side, will be the despot of America. This consideration renders him particularly anxious that the executive should be properly constituted. The vice here would not, as in some other parts of the system, be curable. It is the most difficult of all, rightly to balance the executive. Make him too weak—the legislature will usurp his power. Make him too strong—he will usurp on the legislature. He preferred a short period, a re-eligibility, but a different mode of election. A long period would prevent an adoption of the plan. It ought to do so. He should himself be afraid to trust it. He was not prepared to decide on Mr. Wilson's mode of election just hinted by him. He thought it deserved consideration. It would be better that chance should decide than intrigue.

ELECTION BY LEGISLATURE DEFEATED / *July 25*

In convention. The clause relating to the executive being again under consideration, Mr. Ellsworth moved "that the executive be appointed by the legislature, except when the magistrate last chosen shall have continued in office the whole term for which he was chosen, and be re-eligible; in which case the choice shall be by electors appointed by the legislatures of the states for that purpose." By this means a deserving magistrate may be re-elected without making him dependent on the legislature.

Mr. Gerry repeated his remark that an election at all by the national legislature was radically and incurably wrong and moved "that the executive be appointed by the governors and presidents of the states, with advice of their councils, and where there are no councils, by electors chosen by the legislatures. The executives to vote in the following proportions, namely, ———."

Mr. Madison: There are objections against every mode that has been, or perhaps can be, proposed. The election must be made either by some existing authority under the national or state constitutions, or by some special authority derived from the people, or by the people themselves. The two existing authorities under the national Constitution would be the legislative and judiciary. The latter, he presumed, was out of the question. The former was, in his judgment, liable to insuperable objections. Besides the general influence of that mode on the independence of the executive, in the first place, the election of the chief magistrate would agitate and divide the legislature so much that the public interest would materially suffer by it. Public bodies are always apt to be thrown into contentions, but into more violent ones by such occasions than by any others. In the second place, the candidate would intrigue with the legislature, would derive his ap-

pointment from the predominant faction and be apt to render his ad-   *357*
ministration subservient to its views. In the third place, the ministers
of foreign powers would have, and would make use of, the opportunity
to mix their intrigues and influence with the election. Limited as the
powers of the executive are, it will be an object of great moment with
the great rival powers of Europe who have American possessions to
have at the head of our government a man attached to their respective
politics and interests. No pains, nor perhaps expense, will be spared to
gain from the legislature an appointment favorable to their wishes.
Germany and Poland are witnesses of this danger. In the former, the
election of the head of the empire, till it became in a manner hereditary, interested all Europe and was much influenced by foreign interference. In the latter, although the elective magistrate has very little
real power, his election has at all times produced the most eager interference of foreign princes and has, in fact, at length slid entirely into
foreign hands. The existing authorities in the states are the legislative,
executive, and judiciary. The appointment of the national executive
by the first was objectionable in many points of view, some of which
had been already mentioned. He would mention one which of itself
would decide his opinion. The legislatures of the states had betrayed
a strong propensity to a variety of pernicious measures. One object of
the national legislature was to control this propensity. One object of
the national executive, so far as it would have a negative on the laws,
was to control the national legislature, so far as it might be infected
with a similar propensity. Refer the appointment of the national
executive to the state legislatures and this controlling purpose may be
defeated. The legislatures can and will act with some kind of regular
plan and will promote the appointment of a man who will not oppose
himself to a favorite object. Should a majority of the legislatures at
the time of election have the same object, or different objects of the
same kind, the national executive would be rendered subservient to
them. An appointment by the state executives was liable, among other
objections, to this insuperable one, that being standing bodies they
could and would be courted and intrigued with by the candidates, by
their partisans, and by the ministers of foreign powers. The state judiciaries had not been, and he presumed would not be, proposed as a
proper source of appointment. The option before us then lay between
an appointment by electors chosen by the people and an immediate
appointment by the people. He thought the former mode free from
many of the objections which had been urged against it and greatly
preferable to an appointment by the national legislature. As the electors would be chosen for the occasion, would meet at once and pro-

ceed immediately to an appointment, there would be very little opportunity for cabal or corruption: As a further precaution, it might be required that they should meet at some place distinct from the seat of government and even that no person within a certain distance of the place at the time should be eligible. This mode, however, had been rejected so recently and by so great a majority that it probably would not be proposed anew. The remaining mode was an election by the people, or rather by the qualified part of them at large. With all its imperfections, he liked this best. He would not repeat either the general arguments for, or the objections against, this mode. He would only take notice of two difficulties which he admitted to have weight. The first arose from the disposition in the people to prefer a citizen of their own state and the disadvantage this would throw on the smaller states. Great as this objection might be, he did not think it equal to such as lay against every other mode which had been proposed. He thought, too, that some expedient might be hit upon that would obviate it. The second difficulty arose from the disproportion of qualified voters in the northern and southern states and the disadvantages which this mode would throw on the latter. The answer to this objection was, in the first place, that this disproportion would be continually decreasing under the influence of the republican laws introduced in the southern states and the more rapid increase of their population; in the second place, that local considerations must give way to the general interest. As an individual from the southern states, he was willing to make the sacrifice.

Mr. Ellsworth: The objection drawn from the different sizes of the states is unanswerable. The citizens of the largest states would invariably prefer the candidate within the state, and the largest states would invariably have the man.

Mr. Ellsworth's motion for election by legislature defeated, 7 to 4.

ELECTION BY THE PEOPLE RECONSIDERED / *July 25*

Mr. Williamson was sensible that strong objections lay against an election of the executive by the legislature and that it opened a door for foreign influence. The principal objection against an election by the people seemed to be the disadvantage under which it would place the smaller states. He suggested as a cure for this difficulty that each man should vote for three candidates; one of them, he observed, would be probably of his own state, the other two of some other states, and as probably of a small as a large one.

Mr. Gouverneur Morris liked the idea, suggesting as an amendment that each man should vote for two persons, one of whom at least should not be of his own state.

Mr. Madison also thought something valuable might be made of the suggestion with the proposed amendment of it. The second best man in this case would probably be the first in fact. The only objection which occurred was that each citizen, after having given his vote for his favorite fellow-citizen, would throw away his second on some obscure citizen of another state in order to ensure the object of his first choice. But it could hardly be supposed that the citizens of many states would be so sanguine of having their favorite elected as not to give their second vote with sincerity to the next object of their choice. It might, moreover, be provided in favor of the smaller states that the executive should not be eligible more than _____ times in _____ years from the same state.

Mr. Gerry: A popular election in this case is radically vicious. The ignorance of the people would put it in the power of some one set of men, dispersed through the Union and acting in concert, to delude them into any appointment. He observed that such a society of men existed in the order of the Cincinnati. They are respectable, united, and influential. They will, in fact, elect the chief magistrate in every instance if the election be referred to the people. His respect for the characters composing this society could not blind him to the danger and impropriety of throwing such a power into their hands.

Mr. Dickinson: As far as he could judge from the discussions which had taken place during his attendance, insuperable objections lay against an election of the executive by the national legislature, as also by the legislatures or executives of the states. He had long leaned toward an election by the people, which he regarded as the best and purest source. Objections, he was aware, lay against this mode, but not so great, he thought, as against the other modes. The greatest difficulty in the opinion of the house seemed to arise from the partiality of the states to their respective citizens. But might not this very partiality be turned to a useful purpose? Let the people of each state choose its best citizen. The people will know the most eminent characters of their own states, and the people of different states will feel an emulation in selecting those of whom they will have the greatest reason to be proud. Out of the thirteen names thus selected, an executive magistrate may be chosen either by the national legislature or by electors appointed by it.

• Article II, Section 1: . . . and if there be more than one who have such Majority, and have an equal Number of [Electoral] Votes, then the House of

Representatives shall immediately chuse by Ballot one of them for President; and if no Person have a Majority, then from the five highest on the List the said House shall in like Manner chuse the President. But in chusing the President, the Votes shall be taken by States, the Representation from each State having one Vote; A quorum for this Purpose shall consist of a Member or Members from two thirds of the States, and a Majority of all the States shall be necessary to a Choice. In every Case, after the Choice of the President, the Person having the greatest Number of Votes of the Electors shall be the Vice President. But if there should remain two or more who have equal Votes, the Senate shall chuse from them by Ballot the Vice President.[1]   THE CONSTITUTION OF THE UNITED STATES

SENATE'S ROLE IN
PRESIDENTIAL ELECTIONS / September 4

Mr. Gorham disapproved of making the next highest after the President the Vice President without referring the decision to the Senate, in case the next highest should have less than a majority of votes. As the regulation stands, a very obscure man with very few votes may arrive at that appointment.

Mr. Sherman said the object of this clause of the report of the committee was to get rid of the ineligibility which was attached to the mode of election by the legislature and to render the executive independent of the legislature. As the choice of the President was to be made out of the five highest, obscure characters were sufficiently guarded against in that case, and he had no objection to requiring the Vice President to be chosen in like manner where the choice was not decided by a majority in the first instance.

Mr. Madison was apprehensive that by requiring both the President and Vice President to be chosen out of the five highest candidates, the attention of the electors would be turned too much to making candidates, instead of giving their votes in order to a definitive choice. Should this turn be given to the business, the election would, in fact, be consigned to the Senate altogether. It would have the effect at the same time, he observed, of giving the nomination of the candidates to the largest states.

Mr. Gouverneur Morris concurred in and enforced the remarks of Mr. Madison.

Mr. Randolph and Mr. Pinckney wished for a particular explanation and discussion of the reasons for changing the mode of electing the executive.

---

[1] This section superseded by the Twelfth Amendment (1804), which was modified by the Twentieth (1933).

Mr. Gouverneur Morris said he would give the reasons of the committee and his own. The first was the danger of intrigue and faction if the appointment should be made by the legislature. The next was the inconvenience of an ineligibility required by that mode in order to lessen its evils. The third was the difficulty of establishing a court of impeachments, other than the Senate, which would not be so proper for the trial, nor the other branch for the impeachment of the President if appointed by the legislature. In the fourth place, nobody had appeared to be satisfied with an appointment by the legislature. In the fifth place, many were anxious even for an immediate choice by the people. And finally, the sixth reason was the indispensable necessity of making the executive independent of the legislature. As the electors would vote at the same time throughout the United States, and at so great a distance from each other, the great evil of cabal was avoided. It would be impossible also to corrupt them. A conclusive reason for making the Senate, instead of the Supreme Court, the judge of impeachments was that the latter was to try the President after the trial of the impeachment.

Mr. Mason confessed that the plan of the committee had removed some capital objections, particularly the danger of cabal and corruption. It was liable, however, to this strong objection, that nineteen times in twenty the President would be chosen by the Senate, an improper body for the purpose.

Mr. Butler thought the mode not free from objections, but much more so than an election by the legislature, where as in elective monarchies, cabal, faction, and violence would be sure to prevail.

Mr. Pinckney stated as objections to the mode, first, that it threw the whole appointment, in fact, into the hands of the Senate. Secondly, the electors will be strangers to the several candidates and, of course, unable to decide on their comparative merits. Thirdly, it makes the executive re-eligible, which will endanger the public liberty. Fourthly, it makes the same body of men which will, in fact, elect the President, his judges in case of an impeachment.

Mr. Williamson had great doubts whether the advantage of re-eligibility would balance the objection to such a dependence of the President on the Senate for his reappointment. He thought, at least, the Senate ought to be restrained to the two highest on the list.

Mr. Gouverneur Morris said the principal advantage aimed at was that of taking away the opportunity for cabal. The President may be made, if thought necessary, ineligible on this as well as on any other mode of election. Other inconveniences may be no less redressed on this plan than any other.

Mr. Baldwin thought the plan not so objectionable when well considered, as at first view. The increasing intercourse among the people of the states would render important characters less and less unknown, and the Senate would consequently be less and less likely to have the eventual appointment thrown into their hands.

Mr. Wilson: This subject has greatly divided the house and will also divide the people out-of-doors. It is in truth the most difficult of all on which we have had to decide. He had never made up an opinion on it entirely to his own satisfaction. He thought the plan, on the whole, a valuable improvement on the former. It gets rid of one great evil, that of cabal and corruption, and continental characters will multiply as we more and more coalesce, so as to enable the electors in every part of the Union to know and judge of them. It clears the way, also, for a discussion of the question of re-eligibility on its own merits, which the former mode of election seemed to forbid. He thought it might be better, however, to refer the eventual appointment to the legislature than to the Senate and to confine it to a smaller number than five of the candidates. The eventual election by the legislature would not open cabal anew, as it would be restrained to certain designated objects of choice and as these must have had the previous sanction of a number of the states; and if the election be made as it ought, as soon as the votes of the electors are opened and it is known that no one has a majority of the whole, there can be little danger of corruption. Another reason for preferring the legislature to the Senate in this business was that the House of Representatives will be so often changed as to be free from the influence and faction to which the permanence of the Senate may subject that branch.

Mr. Randolph preferred the former mode of constituting the executive, but if the change was to be made, he wished to know why the eventual election was referred to the Senate and not to the legislature? He saw no necessity for this and many objections to it. He was apprehensive, also, that the advantage of the eventual appointment would fall into the hands of the states near the seat of government.

Mr. Gouverneur Morris said the Senate was preferred because fewer could then say to the President, "You owe your appointment to us." He thought the President would not depend so much on the Senate for his reappointment as on his general good conduct.

The further consideration of the report was postponed at this time in order that each member might take a copy of the remainder of it.

The report made yesterday as to the appointment of the executive being then taken up, Mr. Pinckney renewed his opposition to the mode, arguing, first, that the electors will not have sufficient knowledge of the fittest men and will be swayed by an attachment to the eminent men of their respective states. Hence, secondly, the dispersion of the votes would leave the appointment with the Senate, and as the President's reappointment will thus depend on the Senate, he will be the mere creature of that body. Thirdly, he will combine with the Senate against the House of Representatives. Fourthly, this change in the mode of election was meant to get rid of the ineligibility of the President a second time, whereby he will become fixed for life under the auspices of the Senate.

Mr. Gerry did not object to this plan of constituting the executive in itself, but should be governed in his final vote by the powers that may be given to the President.

Mr. Rutledge was much opposed to the plan reported by the committee. It would throw the whole power into the Senate. He was also against a re-eligibility. He moved to postpone the report under consideration and take up the original plan of appointment by the legislature, to wit—"He shall be elected by joint ballot by the legislature, to which election a majority of the votes of the members present shall be required. He shall hold his office during the term of seven years, but shall not be elected a second time."

Mr. Mason admitted that there were objections to an appointment by the legislature as originally planned. He had not yet made up his mind, but would state his objections to the mode proposed by the committee. First, it puts the appointment, in fact, into the hands of the Senate, as it will rarely happen that a majority of the whole vote will fall on any one candidate, and as the existing President will always be one of the five highest, his reappointment will, of course, depend on the Senate. Secondly, considering the powers of the President and those of the Senate, if a coalition should be established between these two branches, they will be able to subvert the Constitution. The great objection with him would be removed by depriving the Senate of the eventual election. He accordingly moved to strike out the words "if such number be a majority of that of the electors."

Mr. Williamson seconded the motion. He could not agree to the clause without some such modification. He preferred making the highest, though not having a majority of the votes, President, to a reference of the matter to the Senate. Referring the appointment to the Senate lays a certain foundation for corruption and aristocracy.

Mr. Gouverneur Morris thought the point of less consequence than it was supposed on both sides. It is probable that a majority of the votes will fall on the same man; as each elector is to give two votes, more than one-fourth will give a majority. Besides, as one vote is to be given to a man out of the state, and as this vote will not be thrown away, half the votes will fall on characters eminent and generally known. Again, if the President shall have given satisfaction, the votes will turn on him, of course, and a majority of them will reappoint him without resort to the Senate. If he should be disliked, all disliking him would take care to unite their votes so as to ensure his being supplanted.

Mr. Mason: Those who think there is no danger of there not being a majority for the same person in the first instance ought to give up the point to those who think otherwise.

Mr. Sherman reminded the opponents of the new mode proposed that if the small states had the advantage in the Senate's deciding among the five highest candidates, the large states would have in fact the nomination of these candidates.

Motion to deny Senate a role in electing President defeated, 10 to 1.

ELECTION BY LEGISLATURE DEFEATED AGAIN / September 5

Mr. Wilson moved to strike out "Senate" and insert the word "legislature."

Mr. Madison considered it a primary object to render an eventual resort to any part of the legislature improbable. He was apprehensive that the proposed alteration would turn the attention of the large states too much to the appointment of candidates, instead of aiming at an effectual appointment of the officer, as the large states would predominate in the legislature, which would have the final choice out of the candidates. Whereas if the Senate (in which the small states predominate) should have the final choice, the concerted effort of the large states would be to make the appointment in the first instance conclusive.

Mr. Randolph: We have in some revolutions of this plan made a bold stroke for monarchy. We are now doing the same for an aristocracy. He dwelt on the tendency of such an influence in the Senate over the election of the President, in addition to its other powers, to convert that body into a real and dangerous aristocracy.

Mr. Dickinson was in favor of giving the eventual election to the legislature instead of the Senate. It was too much influence to be superadded to that body.

The question moved by Mr. Wilson defeated, 7 to 3.

ELECTION BY SENATE RECONSIDERED / September 6

In convention. Mr. King and Mr. Gerry moved to insert in the fourth clause of the report (September 4) after the words "may be entitled in the legislature," the words following, "But no person shall be appointed an elector who is a member of the legislature of the United States, or who holds any office of profit or trust under the United States," which passed.

Mr. Gerry proposed, as the President was to be elected by the Senate out of the five highest candidates, that if he should not at the end of his term be re-elected by a majority of the electors and no other candidate should have a majority, the eventual election should be made by the legislature. This, he said, would relieve the President from his particular dependence on the Senate for his continuance in office.

Mr. King liked the idea as calculated to satisfy particular members and promote unanimity and as likely to operate but seldom.

Mr. Read opposed it, remarking that if individual members were to be indulged, alterations would be necessary to satisfy most of them.

Mr. Williamson espoused it as a reasonable precaution against the undue influence of the Senate.

Mr. Sherman liked the arrangement as it stood, though he should not be averse to some amendments. He thought, he said, that if the legislature were to have the eventual appointment instead of the Senate, it ought to vote in that case by states—in favor of the small states, as the large states would have so great an advantage in nominating the candidates.

Mr. Gouverneur Morris thought favorably of Mr. Gerry's proposition. It would free the President from being tempted in naming to offices to conform to the will of the Senate and, thereby, virtually give the appointments to office to the Senate.

Mr. Wilson said that he had weighed carefully the report of the committee for remodeling the constitution of the executive, and on combining it with other parts of the plan he was obliged to consider the whole as having a dangerous tendency to aristocracy, as throwing a dangerous power into the hands of the Senate. They will have, in fact, the appointment of the President, and through his dependence on them the virtual appointment to offices, among others, (of) officers of the judiciary department. They are to make treaties and they are to try all impeachments. In allowing them thus to make the executive and judiciary appointments, to be the court of impeachments, and to make treaties which are to be laws of the land, the legislative, executive, and judiciary powers are all blended in one branch of the government. The power of making treaties involves the case of subsidies, and here, as an additional evil, foreign influence is to be dreaded. According to the plan as it now stands, the President will not be the man of the people as he ought to be, but the minion of the Senate. He cannot even appoint a tidewaiter (a customs official who supervises the landing of goods) without the Senate. He had always thought the Senate too numerous a body for making appointments to office. The Senate will, moreover, in all probability be in constant session. They will have high salaries. And with all these powers and the President in their interest, they will depress the other branch of the legislature and aggrandize themselves in proportion. Add to all this that the Senate sitting in conclave can, by holding up to their respective states various and improbable candidates, contrive so to scatter their votes as to bring the appointment of the President ultimately before themselves. Upon the whole, he thought the new mode of appointing the President with some amendments a valuable improvement, but he could never agree to purchase it at the price of the ensuing parts of the report, nor befriend a system of which they make a part.

Mr. Gouverneur Morris expressed his wonder at the observations of Mr. Wilson, so far as they preferred the plan in the printed report to the new modification of it before the house, and entered into a comparative view of the two with an eye to the nature of Mr. Wilson's objections to the last. By the first, the Senate, he observed, had a voice in appointing the President out of all the citizens of the United States; by this they were limited to five candidates, previously nominated to them, with a probability of being barred altogether by the successful ballot of the electors. Here, surely, was no increase of power. They are now to appoint judges nominated to them by the President. Before, they had the appointment without any agency whatever of the President. Here, again, was surely no additional power. If they are to make treaties, as the plan now stands, the power was the same in the printed plan. If they are to try impeachments, the judges must have been triable by them before. Wherein then lay the dangerous tendency of the innovations to establish an aristocracy in the Senate? As to the appointment of officers, the weight of sentiment in the house was opposed to the exercise of it by the President alone; though it was not the case with himself. If the Senate would act as was suspected in misleading the states into a fallacious disposition of their votes for a President, they would, if the appointment were withdrawn wholly from them, make such representations in their several states where they have influence as would favor the object of their partiality.

Mr. Williamson, replying to Mr. Morris, observed that the aristocratic complexion proceeds from the change in the mode of appointing the President, which makes him dependent on the Senate.

Mr. Clymer said that the aristocratic part to which he could never accede was that in the printed plan, which gave the Senate the power of appointing to offices.

Mr. Hamilton said that he had been restrained from entering into the discussions by his dislike of the scheme of government in general, but as he meant to support the plan to be recommended as better than nothing, he wished in this place to offer a few remarks. He liked the new modification on the whole better than that in the printed report. In this, the President was a monster, elected for seven years and ineligible afterwards, having great powers in appointments to office, and continually tempted, by this constitutional disqualification, to abuse them in order to subvert the government. Although he should be made re-eligible, still, if appointed by the legislature, he would be tempted to make use of corrupt influence to be continued in office. It seemed peculiarly desirable, therefore, that some other mode of election should be devised. Considering the different views of different states, and the different districts, northern, middle, and southern, he concurred with those who thought that the votes would not be concentered and that the appointment would, consequently, in the present mode devolve on the Senate. The nominaton to offices will give great weight to the President. Here then is a mutual connection and influence that will perpetuate the President and aggrandize both him and the Senate. What is to be the remedy? He saw none better than to let the highest number of ballots, whether a majority or not, appoint the President. What was the objection to this? Merely that too small a number might appoint. But as the plan stands, the Senate may take the candidate having the smallest number of votes and make him President.

Mr. Madison made a motion requiring two-thirds at least of the Senate to be present at the choice of a President.

Mr. Pinckney seconded the motion.

Mr. Gorham thought it a wrong principle to require more than a majority in any case. In the present, it might prevent for a long time any choice of a President.

Motion passed, 6 to 4.

Mr. Williamson suggested, as better than an eventual choice by the Senate, that this choice should be made by the legislature voting by states and not per capita.

Mr. Sherman suggested "the House of Representatives" as preferable to "the legislature," and moved accordingly to strike out the words "The Senate shall immediately choose," and so forth, and insert, "The House of Representatives shall immediately choose by ballot one of them for President, the members from each state having one vote."

Mr. Mason liked the latter mode best, as lessening the aristocratic influence of the Senate.

Mr. Sherman's motion passed, 10 to 1.

Mr. Gouverneur Morris suggested the idea of providing that in all cases the President in office should not be one of the five candidates, but be only re-eligible in case a majority of the electors should vote for him.

Mr. Madison remarked that as a majority of members would make a quorum in the House of Representatives, it would follow from the amendment of Mr. Sherman, giving the election to a majority of states, that the President might be elected by two states only, Virginia and Pennsylvania, which have eighteen members if these states alone should be present.

Motion that the eventual election of President, in case of an equality of the votes of the electors, be referred to the House of Representatives passed, 7 to 3.

Mr. King moved to add to the amendment of Mr. Sherman, "But a quorum for this purpose shall consist of a member or members from two-thirds of the states, and also of a majority of the whole number of the House of Representatives."

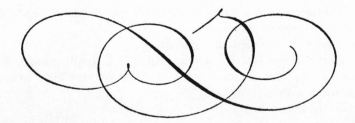

Historic Scenes and Documents

A band of foresighted patriots,
schooled in Eighteenth Century libertarian
thought, construct a philosophy and
a workable plan of freedom

Five colonial leaders, defining the abuses of tyranny, declare independence for all.

*Without dissent,
the Continental Congress
approves the assertion
of independence, a promise
of free government,
prepared in committee
by Jefferson. A number of
these same delegates
later attended the
Constitutional Convention.*

The Resolutions as Reported from a Committee of the whole in Convention on y: 13th June 1787.

1. Resolved that it is the Opinion of this Committee that _the_ a national Government _of the U.S._ ought to be established _consisting_ consisting of a supreme Legislative Judiciary and Executive.

2. Resolved that the national Legislature ought to consist of Two Branches.

3. Resolved that the Members of the first Branch of the national Legislature ought to be elected by the People of the several States for the Term of ~~Two~~ Three Years ~~to receive a~~ _to be of the age of 25 Years to receive a~~fixed~~ fixed Stipend, by which ~~they may be compensated for the devotion of~~ _adequate compensation for their Services_ ~~their time to publick Service~~ to be paid out the ~~national~~ _publick_ Treasury, to be ineligible to any Office established by a particular State, or under the authority of the United States (except those peculiarly belonging to the functions of the first Branch during the Term of Service _& the of the first Branch_ under the national Government for the Space of year after its Expiration.

4th. Resolved that the Members of the Second Branch of the national Legislature _of the U.S_ ought to be chosen by the individual Legislatures, to be of the Age of Thirty Years at least, to hold their Office for a Term sufficient to ensure their Independency namely Seven Years, to receive fixed Stipends by which they may be compensated for the devotion of their time to public Service

In the spring of 1787,
fifty-five Americans meet in
Philadelphia to revise
the Articles of Confederation.

Edmund Randolph, representing
the state of Virginia,
introduces his fifteen-point plan
for a new government.

Wednesday Aug. 22 in Convention

Art. VII. Sect. IIII. resumed

Mr Sherman was f[or]
the clause as it stands. He disapproved of t[he]
trade: yet as the States were now possess[ed]
right to import slaves, as the public goo[d]
require it to be taken from them, and [it is]
expedient to have as few objections as [possible]
to the proposed scheme of Government,
is best to leave the matter as we [find it]
that the abolition of slavery seem[s]
in the United States and that s[eve-]
ral States would probably by de g[rees]
urged on the Convention the neces[sity]
Colo. Mason. This infernal traf[fic]
avarice of British merchants. [The]
have certainly checked the attemp[t]
but [a] stop to it. The present quest[ion]
he importing States alone bu[t]

After three-and-a-half months of
debate, the Constitution is completed, but
some delegates, not yet satisfied, refuse
to sign it. Virginia's James Madison
has kept the only record of every debate.
At left, he notes a discourse by
Roger Sherman (see page 225 of the text). 75

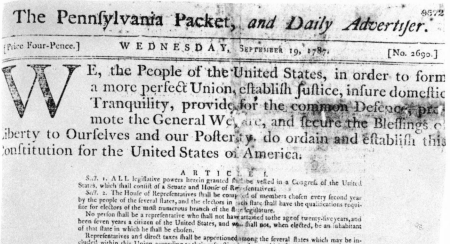

WE, the People of the United States, in order to form a more perfect Union, eſtabliſh juſtice, inſure domeſtic Tranquility, provide for the common Defence, promote the General Welfare, and ſecure the Bleſſings of Liberty to Ourſelves and our Poſterity, do ordain and eſtabliſh this Conſtitution for the United States of America.

ARTICLE I.

Sect. 1. ALL legiſlative powers herein granted ſhall be veſted in a Congreſs of the United States, which ſhall conſiſt of a Senate and Houſe of Repreſentatives.

Sect. 2. The Houſe of Repreſentatives ſhall be compoſed of members choſen every ſecond year by the people of the ſeveral ſtates, and the electors in each ſtate ſhall have the qualifications requiſite for electors of the moſt numerous branch of the ſtate legiſlature.

No perſon ſhall be a repreſentative who ſhall not have attained to the age of twenty-five years, and been ſeven years a citizen of the United States, and who ſhall not, when elected, be an inhabitant of that ſtate in which he ſhall be choſen.

Repreſentatives and direct taxes ſhall be apportioned among the ſeveral ſtates which may be included within this Union, according to their reſpective numbers, which ſhall be determined by adding to the whole number of free perſons, including thoſe bound to ſervice for a term of years, and excluding Indians not taxed, three-fifths of all other perſons. The actual enumeration ſhall be made within three years after the firſt meeting of the Congreſs of the United States, and within every ſubſequent term of ten years, in ſuch manner as they ſhall by law direct. The number of repreſentatives ſhall not exceed one for every thirty thouſand, but each ſtate ſhall have at leaſt one repreſentative; and until ſuch enumeration ſhall be made, the ſtate of New-Hampſhire ſhall be entitled to chuſe three, Maſſachuſetts eight, Rhode-Iſland and Providence Plantations one, Connecticut five, New-York ſix, New-Jerſey four, Pennſylvania eight, Delaware one, Maryland ſix, Virginia ten, North-Carolina five, South-Carolina five, and Georgia three.

When vacancies happen in the repreſentation from any ſtate, the Executive authority thereof ſhall iſſue writs of election to fill ſuch vacancies.

The Houſe of Repreſentatives ſhall chuſe their Speaker and other officers; and ſhall have the ſole power of impeachment.

Sect. 3. The Senate of the United States ſhall be compoſed of two ſenators from each ſtate, choſen by the legiſlature thereof, for ſix years; and each ſenator ſhall have one vote.

Immediately after they ſhall be aſſembled in conſequence of the firſt election, they ſhall be divided as equally as may be into three claſſes. The ſeats of the ſenators of the firſt claſs ſhall be vacated at the expiration of the ſecond year, of the ſecond claſs at the expiration of the fourth year, and of the third claſs at the expiration of the ſixth year, ſo that one-third may be choſen every ſecond year; and if vacancies happen by reſignation, or otherwiſe, during the receſs of the Legiſlature of any ſtate, the Executive thereof may make temporary appointments until the next meeting of the Legiſlature, which ſhall then fill ſuch vacancies.

No perſon ſhall be a ſenator who ſhall not have attained to the age of thirty years, and been nine years a citizen of the United States, and who ſhall not, when elected, be an inhabitant of that ſtate for which he ſhall be choſen.

The Vice-Preſident of the United States ſhall be Preſident of the ſenate, but ſhall have no vote, unleſs they be equally divided.

The Senate ſhall chuſe their other officers, and alſo a Preſident pro tempore, in the abſence of the Vice-Preſident, or when he ſhall exerciſe the office of Preſident of the United States.

The Senate ſhall have the ſole power to try all impeachments. When ſitting for that purpoſe, they ſhall be on oath or affirmation. When the Preſident of the United States is tried, the Chief Juſtice ſhall preſide: And no perſon ſhall be convicted without the concurrence of two-thirds of the members preſent.

Judgment in caſes of impeachment ſhall not extend further than to removal from office, and diſqualification to hold and enjoy any office of honor, truſt or profit under the United States; but the party convicted ſhall nevertheleſs be liable and ſubject to indictment, trial, judgment and puniſhment, according to law.

Sect. 4. The times, places and manner of holding elections for ſenators and repreſentatives, ſhall be preſcribed in each ſtate by the legiſlature thereof; but the Congreſs may at any time by law make or alter ſuch regulations, except as to the places of chuſing Senators.

The Congreſs ſhall aſſemble at leaſt once in every year, and ſuch meeting ſhall be on the firſt Monday in December, unleſs they ſhall by law appoint a different day.

Sect. 5. Each houſe ſhall be the judge of the elections, returns and qualifications of its own members, and a majority of each ſhall conſtitute a quorum to do buſineſs; but a ſmaller number may adjourn from day to day, and may be authoriſed to compel the attendance of abſent members, in ſuch manner, and under ſuch penalties as each houſe may provide.

Each houſe may determine the rules of its proceedings, puniſh its members for diſorderly behaviour, and, with the concurrence of two-thirds, expel a member.

Each houſe ſhall keep a journal of its proceedings, and from time to time publiſh the ſame, excepting ſuch parts as may in their judgment require ſecrecy; and the yeas and nays of the members of either houſe on any queſtion ſhall, at the deſire of one-fifth of thoſe preſent, be entered on the journal.

Neither houſe, during the ſeſſion of Congreſs, ſhall, without the conſent of the other, adjourn for more than three days, nor to any other place than that in which the two houſes ſhall be ſitting.

Sect. 6. The ſenators and repreſentatives ſhall receive a compenſation for their ſervices, to be aſcertained by law, and paid out of the treaſury of the United States. They ſhall in all caſes, except treaſon, felony and breach of the peace, be privileged from arreſt during their attendance at the ſeſſion of their reſpective houſes, and in going to and returning from the ſame; and for any ſpeech or debate in either houſe, they ſhall not be queſtioned in any other place.

No ſenator or repreſentative ſhall, during the time for which he was elected, be appointed to any civil office under the authority of the United States, which ſhall have been created, or the emoluments whereof ſhall have been encreaſed during ſuch time; and no perſon holding any office under the United States, ſhall be a member of either houſe during his continuance in office.

Sect. 7. All bills for raiſing revenue ſhall originate in the houſe of repreſentatives; but the ſenate may propoſe or concur with amendments as on other bills.

Every bill which ſhall have paſſed the houſe of repreſentatives and the ſenate, ſhall, before it become a law, be preſented to the preſident of the United States; if he approve he ſhall ſign it, but if not he ſhall return it, with his objections to that houſe in which it ſhall have originated, who ſhall enter the objections at large on their journal, and proceed to reconſider it. If after ſuch reconſideration two-thirds of that houſe ſhall agree to paſs the bill, it ſhall be ſent, together with the objections, to the other houſe, by which it ſhall likewiſe be reconſidered, and if approved by two-thirds of that houſe, it ſhall become a law. But in all ſuch caſes the votes of both houſes ſhall

On September 17, 1787, the convention is adjourned and the Constitution, born in secrecy, is made public. It proclaims that it has been designed to "secure the blessings of liberty" for all.

We the People of the United States, in insure domestic Tranquility, provide for the common defence, promote the general Welfare, and our Posterity, do ordain and establish this Constitution for the United States of America.

Article. I.

Section. 1. All legislative Powers herein granted shall be vested in a Congress of the United States, which shall consist of a Senate and House of Representatives.

Section. 2. The House of Representatives shall be composed of Members chosen every second Year by the People of the several States, and the Electors in each State shall have the Qualifications requisite for Electors of the most numerous Branch of the State Legislature.

No Person shall be a Representative who shall not have attained to the Age of twenty five Years, and been seven Years a Citizen of the United States, and who shall not, when elected, be an Inhabitant of that State in which he shall be chosen.

Representatives and direct Taxes shall be apportioned among the several States which may be included within this Union, according to their respective Numbers, which shall be determined by adding to the whole Number of free Persons, including those bound to Service for a Term of Years, and excluding Indians not taxed, three fifths of all other Persons. The actual Enumeration shall be made within three Years after the first Meeting of the Congress of the United States, and within every subsequent Term of ten Years, in such Manner as they shall by Law direct. The Number of Representatives shall not exceed one for every thirty Thousand, but each State shall have at Least one Representative; and until such enumeration shall be made, the State of New Hampshire shall be entitled to chuse three, Massachusetts eight, Rhode Island and Providence Plantations one, Connecticut five, New York six, New Jersey four, Pennsylvania eight, Delaware one, Maryland six, Virginia ten, North Carolina five, South Carolina five, and Georgia three.

When vacancies happen in the Representation from any State, the Executive Authority thereof shall issue Writs of Election to fill such Vacancies.

The House of Representatives shall chuse their Speaker and other Officers; and shall have the sole Power of Impeachment.

*Arguments for and against
the Constitution are heard now
in every state. From them emerges*
The Federalist, *a brilliant
defense of the document. Below
is Hamilton's outline of topics.*

79

*Buoyancy is th
of the day as ratific
accomplishe
York celebrates
parade and honors Har
invaluable contr
with a hug*

80

Order of Proceſſion

In Honor of the Conſtitution of the United States.

AT eight o'Clock on Wedneſday Morning the 23d of July, 10 Guns will fire, when the PROCESSION will parade and proceed by the following Route, viz : Down Broad-Way to Great-Dock-Street, thence through Hanover-Square, Queen, Chatham, Diviſion, and Arundel-Streets ; and from thence through Bullock-Street to Bayard's-Houſe.

No. 1.   2 Horſemen with Trumpets.
    2.   1 piece of Artillery.

No.	Firſt DIVISION.

No.		No.	
3	4 Foreſters in Frocks, carrying Axes.	12	A Band of Muſic.
4	Columbus in his Ancient Dreſs—on Horſeback.	13	Taylors.
5	6 Foreſters, &c.	14	Meaſurers of Grain.
6	A Plough.	15	Millers.
7	A Sower.	16	Inſpectors of Flour.
8	A Harrow.	17	Bakers.
9	Farmers.	18	Brewers.
10	United States Arms, borne by Col. White, ſupported	19	Diſtillers.
11	Gardeners. [by the Society of the Cincinnati.		

Second DIVISION.

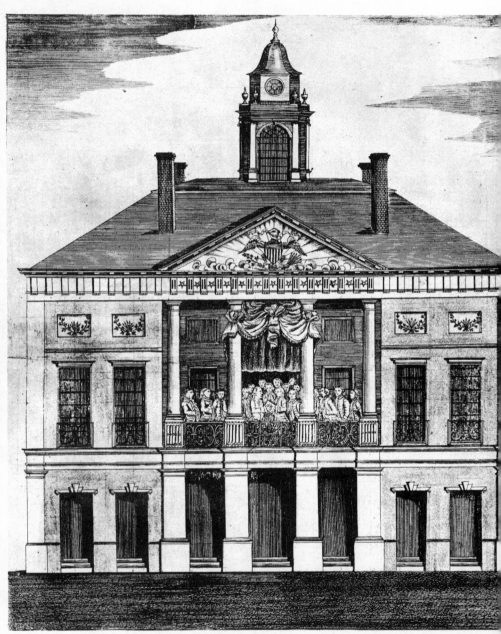

81

On the balcony of Federal Hall in New York City (
the first President of the newly created
States, George Washington, takes the oath of o
a brief and stirring ceremony. Later (righ
small chamber within, he reads his inaugural a

82

in war" and now "first
peace," Washington is
the unanimous choice
esident, for behind his
tocratic demeanor lies
epublican philosophy.

83

GEORGE WASHINGTON,

PRESIDENT *of the United States.*

1st Congress

—

J O H N   A D A M S,   Vice-President *of the United States.*

—

MEMBERS OF THE SENATE OF THE UNITED STATES.

Richard Baffett,   *Mr Bayard upper 2d street No 34*   William Samuel Johnfon,
Pierce Butler,   Samuel Johnfton,
Charles Carroll,   Rufus King,
Triftram Dalton,   *market ftreet*   John Langdon,
Philemon Dickinfon,   *above Congrefs Hall*   Richard Henry Lee,
Oliver Elfworth,   *3d ftreet No. 121*   Robert Morris,
Jonathan Elmer,   *pine ftreet 97*   William Maclay,
Theodore Fofter,   James Monroe,
William Few,   George Read,
James Gunn,   Caleb Strong,
John Henry,   Jofeph Stanton, jun.
Benjamin Hawkins,   *Corner of 5th & market ftreet*   Philip Schuyler,
Ralph Izard,   *2d ftreet New market No 211*   Paine Wingate,

---

MEMBERS OF THE HOUSE OF REPRESENTATIVES OF THE UNITED STATES.

FREDERICK AUGUSTUS MUHLENBERG, *Speaker.*

Fifher Ames,   Samuel Livermore,
John Baptift Afhe,   James Madifon, jun.
Abraham Baldwin,   George Mathews,
Egbert Benfon,   Andrew Moore,
Timothy Bloodworth,   Peter Muhlenberg,
Elias Boudinot,   John Page,
John Brown,   Jofiah Parker,
Edanus Burke,   George Partridge,
Lambert Cadwalader,   Jeremiah Van Renffelaer,
Daniel Carroll,   James Schureman,
George Clymer,   Thomas Scott,
Ifaac Coles,   Theodore Sedgwick,
Benjamin Contee,   Jofhua Seney,
Thomas Fitzfimons,   John Sevier,
William Floyd,   Roger Sherman,
Abiel Fofter,   Peter Silvefter,
George Gale,   Thomas Sinnickfon,
   William Smith, *(of Maryland),*
Nicholas Gilman,   William Smith, *(of South-Carolina),*
Benjamin Goodhue,   John Steele,
Samuel Griffin,   Michael Jenifer Stone,
Jonathan Grout,   Jonathan Sturges,
William B. Giles,   Thomas Sumpter,
Thomas Hartley,   George Thatcher,
John Hathorn,   Jonathan Trumbull,
Daniel Heifter,   Thomas Tuder Tucker,
Daniel Huger,   John Vining,
Benjamin Huntington,   Jeremiah Wadfworth,
James Jackfon,   Alexander White,
John Lawrance,   Henry Wynkoop,
Richard Bland Lee,   Hugh Williamfon,
George Leonard,

*Outstanding figures from
each state are elected to the first
Congress of the United States.
Eighteen of them also attended the
Constitutional Convention.*

Washington's death comes with the end
of the century. Jefferson eulogizes him:
"It may truly be said, that never did
nature and fortune combine more perfectly
to make a man great, and to place
him . . . in an everlasting remembrance."

• Article II, Section 1: The President shall, at stated Times, receive for his Services, a Compensation, which shall neither be encreased nor diminished during the Period for which he shall have been elected, and he shall not receive within that Period any other Emolument from the United States, or any of them.

THE CONSTITUTION OF THE UNITED STATES

FRANKLIN OPPOSES EXECUTIVE SALARY / *June 2*

Dr. Franklin moved that what related to the compensation for the services of the executive be postponed in order to substitute, "whose necessary expenses shall be defrayed, but who shall receive no salary, stipend, fee, or reward whatsoever for their services." He said that being very sensible of the effect of age on his memory, he had been unwilling to trust to that for the observations which seemed to support his motion and had reduced them to writing that he might with the permission of the committee read, instead of speaking them.

Mr. Wilson made an offer to read the paper, which was accepted.

The following is a literal copy of the paper:

"Sir: It is with reluctance that I rise to express a disapprobation of any one article of the plan for which we are so much obliged to the honorable gentleman (Randolph) who laid it before us. From its first reading, I have borne a good will to it and in general wished it success. In this particular of salaries to the executive branch, I happen to differ; and as my opinion may appear new and chimerical, it is only from a persuasion that it is right, and from a sense of duty, that I hazard it. The committee will judge of my reasons when they have heard them and their judgment may possibly change mine. I think I see inconveniences in the appointment of salaries; I see none in refusing them, but, on the contrary, great advantages.

"Sir, there are two passions which have a powerful influence on the affairs of men. These are ambition and avarice; the love of power and the love of money. Separately, each of these has great force in prompting men to action but when united in view of the same object, they have in many minds the most violent effects. Place before the eyes of such men a post of *honor,* that shall be at the same time a place of *profit,* and they will move heaven and earth to obtain it. The vast number of such places it is that renders the British government so tempestuous. The struggles for them are the true sources of all those factions which are perpetually dividing the nation, distracting its councils, hurrying sometimes into fruitless and mischievous wars, and often compelling a submission to dishonorable terms of peace.

"And of what kind are the men that will strive for this profitable pre-eminence, through all the bustle of cabal, the heat of contention, the infinite mutual abuse of parties, tearing to pieces the best of characters? It will not be the wise and moderate, the lovers of peace and good order, the men fittest for the trust. It will be the bold and the violent, the men of strong passions and indefatigable activity in their selfish pursuits. These will thrust themselves into your government and be your rulers. And these, too, will be mistaken in the expected happiness of their situation; for their vanquished competitors of the same spirit and from the same motives will perpetually be endeavoring to distress their administration, thwart their measures, and render them odious to the people.

"Besides these evils, sir, though we may set out in the beginning with moderate salaries, we shall find that such will not be of long continuance. Reasons will never be wanting for proposed augmentations. And there will always be a party for giving more to the rulers that the rulers may be able in return to give more to them. Hence, as all history informs us, there has been in every state and kingdom a constant kind of warfare between the governing and governed, the one striving to obtain more for its support, and the other to pay less. And this has alone occasioned great convulsions, actual civil wars, ending either in dethroning of the princes or enslaving of the people. Generally, indeed, the ruling power carries its point, the revenues of princes constantly increasing; and we see that they are never satisfied, but always in want of more. The more the people are discontented with the oppression of taxes, the greater need the prince has of money to distribute among his partisans and pay the troops that are to suppress all resistance and enable him to plunder at pleasure. There is scarce a king in a hundred who would not, if he could follow the example of Pharaoh, get first all the people's money, then all their lands, and then make them and their children servants forever. It will be said that we don't propose to establish kings. I know it, but there is a natural inclination in mankind to kingly government. It sometimes relieves them from aristocratic domination. They had rather have one tyrant than five hundred. It gives more of the appearance of equality among citizens, and that they like. I am apprehensive, therefore, perhaps too apprehensive, that the government of these states may in future times end in a monarchy. But this catastrophe I think may be long delayed if in our proposed system we do not sow the seeds of contention, faction, and tumult by making our posts of honor places of profit. If we do,

I fear that though we do employ at first, a number, and not a single person, the number will in time be set aside; it will only nourish the fetus of a king, as the honorable gentleman from Virginia very aptly expressed it, and a king will the sooner be set over us.

"It may be imagined by some that this is a Utopian idea and that we can never find men to serve us in the executive department without paying them well for their services. I conceive this to be a mistake. Some existing facts present themselves to me which incline me to a contrary opinion. The high sheriff of a county in England is an honorable office, but it is not a profitable one. It is rather expensive and, therefore, not sought for. But yet it is executed, and well executed, and usually by some of the principal gentlemen of the county. In France, the office of counselor or member of their judiciary parliament is more honorable. It is therefore purchased at a high price; there are, indeed, fees on the law proceedings which are divided among them, but these fees do not amount to more than three per cent on the sum paid for the place. Therefore, as legal interest is there at five per cent, they in fact pay two per cent for being allowed to do the judiciary business of the nation, which is at the same time entirely exempt from the burden of paying them any salaries for their services. I do not, however, mean to recommend this as an eligible mode for our judiciary department. I only bring the instance to show that the pleasure of doing good and serving their country, and the respect such conduct entitles them to, are sufficient motives with some minds to give up a great portion of their time to the public without the mean inducement of pecuniary satisfaction.

"Another instance is that of a respectable society who have made the experiment and practiced it with success more than one hundred years. I mean the Quakers. It is an established rule with them that they are not to go to law, but in their controversies they must apply to their monthly, quarterly, and yearly meetings. Committees of these sit with patience to hear the parties and spend much time in composing their differences. In doing this, they are supported by a sense of duty and the respect paid to usefulness. It is honorable to be so employed, but it is never made profitable by salaries, fees, or perquisites. And, indeed, in all cases of public service, the less the profit the greater the honor.

"To bring the matter nearer home: Have we not seen the greatest and most important of our offices, that of general of our armies, executed for eight years together, without the smallest salary, by a patriot whom I will not now offend by any other praise; and this through fatigues and distresses in common with the other brave men, his military friends and companions, and the constant anxieties peculiar to his station? And shall we doubt finding three or four men in all the United States with public spirit enough to bear sitting in peaceful council for perhaps an equal term, merely to preside over our civil concerns and see that our laws are duly executed? Sir, I have a better opinion of our country. I think we shall never be without a sufficient number of wise and good men to undertake and execute well and faithfully the office in question.

"Sir, the saving of the salaries that may at first be proposed is not an object with me. The subsequent mischiefs of proposing them are what I apprehend. And therefore it is that I move the amendment. If it is not seconded or accepted, I must be contented with the satisfaction of having delivered my opinion frankly and done my duty."

The motion was seconded by Mr. Hamilton, with the view, he said, merely of bringing so respectable a proposition before the committee, and which was besides enforced by arguments that had a certain degree of weight. No debate ensued and the proposition was postponed for the consideration of the members. It was treated with great respect, but rather for the author of it than from any apparent conviction of its expediency or practicability.

Dr. Franklin's no-salary proposal postponed.

• **Article II, Section 1: . . . No Person except a natural born Citizen, or a Citizen of the United States, at the time of the Adoption of this Constitution, shall be eligible to the Office of President; neither shall any Person be eligible to that Office who shall not have attained to the Age of thirty five Years, and been fourteen Years a Resident within the United States.**

THE CONSTITUTION OF THE UNITED STATES

Editor's note: No provision was made as to the age and citizenship qualifications for the President until August 22. In that version the words "in the whole" preceded the fourteen-year residence requirement. When the Committee of Style left this phrase out of its draft of September 12, it was felt that a change of meaning may have been intended, altering the necessity for the fourteen years of residence to be consecutive.

• **Article II, Section 1: . . . Before he [the President] enter on the Execution of his Office, he shall take the following Oath or Affirmation:—"I do solemnly swear**

(or affirm) that I will faithfully execute the Office of President of the United **373**
States, and will to the best of my Ability, preserve, protect and defend the Constitution of the United States." THE CONSTITUTION OF THE UNITED STATES

Editor's note: The grave and measured phrases of the presidential
oath were formulated by the Committee of Detail. Mason and Madison
urged the additional responsibility to "preserve, protect and defend"
the Constitution. The Committee of Style made no changes. During the
closing sessions, however, "to the best of my judgment and power" was
replaced by "to the best of my ability."

Powers and Controls

· Article II, Section 2: He [the President] shall have Power, by and with the
Advice and Consent of the Senate, to make Treaties, provided two thirds of the
Senators present concur; and he shall nominate, and by and with the Advice and
Consent of the Senate, shall appoint Ambassadors, other public Ministers and
Consults, ... THE CONSTITUTION OF THE UNITED STATES

* TREATY POWER / *September 7*

The Fourth Section: "The President, by and with the advice and consent of the Senate, shall have power to make treaties; but no treaty
shall be made without the consent of two-thirds of the members
present," being considered, and the last clause being before the house,
Mr. Wilson thought it objectionable to require the concurrence of
two-thirds, which puts it into the power of a minority to control the
will of a majority.

Mr. King concurred in the objection, remarking that as the executive was here joined in the business, there was a check which did not
exist in Congress where the concurrence of two-thirds was required.

Mr. Madison moved to insert after the word "treaty," the words
"except treaties of peace," allowing these to be made with less difficulty than other treaties.

It was agreed to unanimously.

Mr. Madison then moved to authorize a concurrence of two-thirds
of the Senate to make treaties of peace without the concurrence of
the President. The President, he said, would necessarily derive so

much power and importance from a state of war that he might be tempted, if authorized, to impede a treaty of peace.

Mr. Butler seconded the motion.

Mr. Gorham thought the security unnecessary, as the means of carrying on the war would not be in the hands of the President, but of the legislature.

Mr. Gouverneur Morris thought the power of the President in this case harmless and that no peace ought to be made without the concurrence of the President, who was the general guardian of the national interests.

Mr. Butler was strenuous for the motion as a necessary security against ambitious and corrupt Presidents. He mentioned the late perfidious policy of the stadtholder in Holland and the artifices of the Duke of Marlborough to prolong the war of which he had the management.

Mr. Gerry was of opinion that in treaties of peace a greater rather than a lesser proportion of votes was necessary than in other treaties. In treaties of peace the dearest interests will be at stake, as the fisheries, territories, and so forth. In treaties of peace, also, there is more danger to the extremities of the continent, of being sacrificed, than on any other occasion.

Mr. Williamson thought that treaties of peace should be guarded at least by requiring the same concurrence as in other treaties.

Motion to exclude treaties of peace from concurrence of the President defeated, 8 to 3.

• Article II, Section 2: . . . he [the President] shall have Power to grant Reprieves and Pardons for Offences against the United States, except in Cases of Impeachment. THE CONSTITUTION OF THE UNITED STATES

PARDONING POWER / September 15

Article 2, Section 2: "He shall have power to grant reprieves and pardons for offences against the United States," and so forth.

Mr. Randolph moved to except "cases of treason." The prerogative of pardon in these cases was too great a trust. The President may himself be guilty. The traitors may be his own instruments.

Mr. Mason supported the motion.

Mr. Gouverneur Morris had rather there should be no pardon for treason than let the power devolve on the legislature.

Mr. Wilson: Pardon is necessary for cases of treason and is best placed in the hands of the executive. If he be himself a party to the guilt, he can be impeached and prosecuted.

Mr. King thought it would be inconsistent with the constitutional separation of the executive and legislative powers to let the prerogative be exercised by the latter. A legislative body is utterly unfit for the purpose. They are governed too much by the passions of the moment. In Massachusetts, one assembly would have hung all the insurgents in that state; the next was equally disposed to pardon them all. He suggested the expedient of requiring the concurrence of the Senate in acts of pardon.

Mr. Madison admitted the force of objections to the legislature, but the pardon of treasons was so peculiarly improper for the President that he should acquiesce in the transfer of it to the former rather than leave it altogether in the hands of the latter. He would prefer to either an association of the Senate, as a council of advice, with the President.

Mr. Randolph could not admit the Senate into a share of the power. The great danger to liberty lay in a combination between the President and that body.

Mr. Mason: The Senate has already too much power. There can be no danger of too much lenience in legislative pardons, as the Senate must concur, and the President, moreover, can require two-thirds of both houses.

Motion to restrict the President's pardoning power defeated, 8 to 2.

• Article I, Section 7: Every Bill which shall have passed the House of Representatives and the Senate, shall, before it become a Law, be presented to the President of the United States; If he approve he shall sign it, but if not he shall return it, with his Objections to that House in which it shall have originated, who shall enter the Objections at large on their Journal, and proceed to reconsider it. If after such Reconsideration two thirds of that House shall agree to pass the Bill, it shall be sent, together with the Objections, to the other House, by which it shall likewise be reconsidered, and if approved by two thirds of that House, it shall become a Law. But in all such Cases the Votes of both Houses shall be determined by Yeas and Nays, and the Names of the Persons voting for and against the Bill shall be entered on the Journal of each House respectively. If any Bill shall not be returned by the President within ten Days (Sundays excepted) after it shall have been presented to him, the Same shall be a Law, in like Manner as if he had signed it, unless the Congress by their Adjournment prevent its Return, in which Case it shall not be a Law.

Every Order, Resolution, or Vote to which the Concurrence of the Senate and

House of Representatives may be necessary (except on a question of Adjournment) shall be presented to the President of the United States; and before the Same shall take Effect, shall be approved by him or, being disapproved by him, shall be repassed by two thirds of the Senate and House of Representatives, according to the Rules and Limitations prescribed in the Case of a Bill.

THE CONSTITUTION OF THE UNITED STATES

ABSOLUTE EXECUTIVE VETO DENIED / *June 4*

Mr. Gerry's proposition being now before the committee, Mr. Wilson and Mr. Hamilton move that the last part of it, namely, "which shall not be afterwards passed by ———— parts of each branch of the national legislature," be struck out, so as to give the executive an absolute negative on the laws. There was no danger, they thought, of such a power being too much exercised. It was mentioned by Mr. Hamilton that the King of Great Britain had not exerted his negative since the revolution.

Mr. Gerry sees no necessity for so great a control over the legislature as the best men in the community would be comprised in the two branches of it.

Dr. Franklin said he was sorry to differ from his colleague, for whom he had a very great respect, on any occasion, but he could not help it on this. He had had some experience of this check in the executive on the legislature under the proprietary government of Pennsylvania. The negative of the governor was constantly made use of to extort money. No good law whatever could be passed without a private bargain with him. An increase of his salary, or some donation, was always made a condition, till at last it became the regular practice to have orders in his favor, on the treasury, presented along with the bills to be signed, so that he might actually receive the former before he should sign the latter. When the Indians were scalping the western people and notice of it arrived, the concurrence of the governor in the means of self-defense could not be got till it was agreed that his estate should be exempted from taxation, so that the people were to fight for the security of his property, whilst he was to bear no share of the burden. This was a mischievous sort of check. If the executive was to have a council, such a power would be less objectionable. It was true, the King of Great Britain had not, as was said, exerted his negative since the revolution, but that matter was easily explained. The bribes and emoluments now given to the members of Parliament rendered it unnecessary, everything being done according to the will of the ministers. He was afraid if a negative should be given as proposed that more power and money would be demanded till at last enough would be got to influence and bribe the legislature into a complete subjection to the will of the executive.

Mr. Sherman was against enabling any one man to stop the will of the whole. No one man could be found so far above all the rest in wisdom. He thought we ought to avail ourselves of his wisdom in revising the laws, but not permit him to overrule the decided and cool opinions of the legislature.

Mr. Madison supposed that if a proper proportion of each branch should be required to overrule the objection of the executive, it would answer the same purpose as an absolute negative. It would rarely, if ever, happen that the executive, constituted as ours is proposed to be, would have firmness enough to resist the legislature, unless backed by a certain part of the body itself. The King of Great Britain, with all his splendid attributes, would not be able to withstand the unanimous and eager wishes of both houses of Parliament. To give such a prerogative would certainly be obnoxious to the temper of this country —its present temper at least.

Mr. Wilson believed, as others did, that this power would seldom be used. The legislature would know that such a power existed and would refrain from such laws as it would be sure to defeat. Its silent operation would therefore preserve harmony and prevent mischief. The case of Pennsylvania formerly was very different from its present case. The executive was not then, as now, to be appointed by the people. It will not in this case, as in the one cited, be supported by the head of a great empire, actuated by a different and sometimes opposite interest. The salary, too, is now proposed to be fixed by the Constitution, or if Dr. Franklin's idea should be adopted, all salary whatever interdicted. The requiring a large proportion of each house to overrule the executive check might do in peaceable times, but there might be tempestuous moments in which animosities may run high between the executive and legislative branches, and in which the former ought to be able to defend itself.

Mr. Butler had been in favor of a single executive magistrate, but could he have entertained an idea that a complete negative on the laws was to be given him, he certainly should have acted very differently. It had been observed that in all countries the executive power is in a constant course of increase. This was certainly the case in Great Britain. Gentlemen seemed to think that we had nothing to apprehend from an abuse of the executive power. But why might not a Catiline or a Cromwell arise in this country as well as in others?

Mr. Bedford was opposed to every check on the legislature, even the council of revision first proposed. He thought it would be sufficient to mark out in the Constitution the boundaries to the legislative authority, which would give all the requisite security to the rights of the other departments. The representatives of the people were the best judges of what was for their interest and ought to be under no external control whatever. The two branches would produce a sufficient control within the legislature itself.

Mr. Mason observed that a vote had already passed, he found,— he was out at the time—for vesting the executive powers in a single person. Among these powers was that of appointing to offices in certain cases. The probable abuses of a negative had been well explained by Dr. Franklin, as proved by experience the best of all tests. Will not the same door be opened here? The executive may refuse its assent to necessary measures till new appointments shall be referred to him, and having by degrees engrossed all these into his own hands, the American executive, like the British, will by bribery and influence save himself the trouble and odium of exerting his negative afterwards. We are, Mr. Chairman, going very far in this business. We are not indeed constituting a British government, but a more dangerous monarchy—an elective one. We are introducing a new principle into our system, and not necessary, as in the British government where the executive has greater rights to defend. Do gentlemen mean to pave the way to hereditary monarchy? Do they flatter themselves that the people will ever consent to such an innovation? If they do, I venture to tell them they are mistaken. The people never will consent. And do gentlemen consider the danger of delay and the still greater danger of a rejection, not for a moment, but forever, of the plan which shall be proposed to them?

Notwithstanding the oppression and injustice experienced among us from democracy, the genius of the people is in favor of it and the genius of the people must be consulted. He could not but consider the federal system as in effect dissolved by the appointment of this convention to devise a better one. And do gentlemen look forward to the dangerous interval between the extinction of an old and the establishment of a new government and to the scenes of confusion which may ensue? He hoped that nothing like a monarchy would ever be attempted in this country. A hatred to its oppressions had carried the people through the late Revolution. Will it not be enough to enable the executive to suspend offensive laws till they shall be coolly revised and the objections to them overruled by a greater majority than was required in the first instance? He never could agree to give up all the rights of the people to a single magistrate. If more than one had been fixed on, greater powers might have been entrusted to the executive. He hoped this attempt to give such powers would have its weight hereafter as an argument for increasing the number of the executive.

Dr. Franklin: A gentleman from South Carolina (Mr. Butler) a day or two ago called our attention to the case of the United Netherlands. He wished the gentleman had been a little fuller and had gone back to the original of that government. The people, being under great obligations to the Prince of Orange, whose wisdom and bravery had saved them, chose him for the stadtholder. He did very well. Inconveniences, however, were felt from his powers, which growing more and more oppressive, were at length set aside. Still, however, there was a party for the Prince of Orange, which descended to his son, who excited insurrections, spilled a great deal of blood, murdered the DeWitts, and got the powers revested in the stadtholder. Afterwards, another prince had power to excite insurrections and make the stadtholdership hereditary. And the present stadtholder is ready to wade through a bloody civil war to the establishment of a monarchy. Mr. Mason had mentioned the circumstance of appointing officers. He knew how that point would be managed. No new appointment would be suffered, as heretofore in Pennsylvania, unless it be referred to the executive, so that all profitable offices will be at his disposal. The first man put at the helm will be a good one. Nobody knows what sort may come afterwards. The executive will be always increasing here, as elsewhere, till it ends in a monarchy.

Absolute executive veto defeated, 10 to 0.

TWO-THIRDS OF
LEGISLATURE OVERRULES VETO / *June 4*

Mr. Butler moved that the resolution be altered so as to read, "Resolved, that the national executive have a power to suspend any legislative act for the term of _____ ."

Dr. Franklin seconded the motion.

Mr. Gerry observed that the power of suspending might do all the mischief dreaded from the negative of useful laws without answering the salutary purpose of checking unjust or unwise ones.

On a question for enabling two-thirds of each branch of the legislature to overrule the provisionary check, it passed in the affirmative, sub silentio, *and was inserted in the blank of Mr. Gerry's motion.*

Mr. Gerry's motion, which gave the executive alone, without the judiciary, the revisionary control on the laws unless overruled by two-thirds of each branch, passed, 8 to 2.

/ July 21

The tenth resolution, giving the executive a qualified veto, requiring two-thirds of each branch of the legislature to overrule it, was then agreed to unanimously.

THREE-FOURTHS OVERRULES VETO / *August 15*

Mr. Gouverneur Morris regretted that something like the proposed check could not be agreed to. He dwelt on the importance of public credit and the difficulty of supporting it without some strong barrier against the instability of legislative assemblies. He suggested the idea of requiring three-fourths of each house to *repeal* laws where the President should not concur. He had no great reliance on the revisionary power as the executive was now to be constituted (elected by Congress). The legislature will contrive to soften down the President. He recited the history of paper emissions and the perseverance of the legislative assemblies in repeating them with all the distressing effects of such measures before their eyes. Were the national legislature formed and a war was now to break out, this ruinous expedient would be again resorted to if not guarded against. Requiring three-fourths to repeal would, though not a complete remedy, prevent the hasty passage of laws and the frequency of those repeals which destroy faith in the public, and which are among our greatest calamities.

Mr. Dickinson was strongly impressed with the remark of Mr. Mercer as to the power of the judges to set aside the law. He thought no such power ought to exist. He was at the same time at a loss what expedient to substitute. The Justiciary of Aragon, he observed, became by degrees the lawgiver.

Mr. Gouverneur Morris suggested the expedient of an absolute negative in the executive. He could not agree that the judiciary, which was part of the executive, should be bound to say that a direct violation of the Constitution was law. A control over the legislature might have its inconveniences, but view the danger on the other side. The most virtuous citizens will often, as members of a legislative body, concur in measures which afterwards, in their private capacity, they will be ashamed of. Encroachments of the popular branch of the government ought to be guarded against. The Ephori at Sparta became

in the end absolute. The report of the council of censors in Pennsylvania points out the many invasions of the legislative department on
the executive, numerous as the latter is, within the short term of seven
years, and in a state where a strong party is opposed to the Constitution and watching every occasion of turning the public resentments
against it. If the executive be overturned by the popular branch, as
happened in England, the tyranny of one man will ensue. In Rome,
where the aristocracy overturned the throne, the consequence was different. He enlarged on the tendency of the legislative authority to
usurp on the executive and wished the section to be postponed in order to consider of some more effectual check than requiring two-thirds
only to overrule the negative of the executive.

Mr. Sherman: Can one man be trusted better than all the others, if
they all agree? This was neither wise nor safe. He disapproved of
judges meddling in politics and parties. We have gone far enough in
forming the negative as it now stands.

Mr. Carroll: When the negative to be overruled by two-thirds only
was agreed to, the quorum was not fixed. He remarked that as a majority was now to be the quorum, seventeen in the larger and eight
in the smaller house might carry points. The advantage that might
be taken of this seemed to call for greater impediments to improper
laws. He thought the controlling power, however, of the executive,
could not be well decided till it was seen how the formation of that
department would be finally regulated. He wished the consideration
of the matter to be postponed.

Mr. Gorham saw no end to these difficulties and postponements.
Some could not agree to the form of government before the powers
were defined. Others could not agree to the powers till it was seen how
the government was to be formed. He thought a majority as large
a quorum as was necessary. It was the quorum almost everywhere fixed
in the United States.

Mr. Wilson, after viewing the subject with all coolness and attention possible, was most apprehensive of a dissolution of the government from the legislature swallowing up all the other powers. He
remarked that the prejudices against the executive resulted from a
misapplication of the adage that the Parliament was the palladium of
liberty. Where the executive was really formidable, king and tyrant
were naturally associated in the minds of people, not legislature and
tyranny. But where the executive was not formidable, the two last
were most properly associated. After the destruction of the King in
Great Britain, a more pure and unmixed tyranny sprang up in the
Parliament than had been exercised by the monarch. He insisted that

we had not guarded against the danger on this side by a sufficient self-defensive power, either to the executive or judiciary department.

Mr. Rutledge was strenuous against postponing and complained much of the tediousness of the proceedings.

Mr. Ellsworth held the same language. We grow more and more skeptical as we proceed. If we do not decide soon, we shall be unable to come to any decision.

The question for postponement passed in the negative, only Delaware and Maryland being in the affirmative.

Mr. Williamson moved to change "two-thirds of each house" into "three-fourths," as requisite to overrule the dissent of the President. He saw no danger in this and preferred giving the power to the President alone to admitting the judges into the business of legislation.

Mr. Wilson seconds the motion, referring to and repeating the ideas of Mr. Carroll.

Motion for three-fourths, instead of two-thirds, passed, 6 to 4.

VETO OF BILLS / August 15

Mr. Madison, observing that if the negative of the President was confined to bills, it would be evaded by acts under the form and name of resolutions, votes, and so forth, proposed that "or resolve" should be added after "bill" in the beginning of Section 13, with an exception as to votes of adjournment, and so forth. *(After a short and rather confused conversation on the subject, the question was put and rejected, 8 to 3.)*

"Ten days, Sundays excepted," instead of "seven" were allowed to the President for returning bills with his objections; New Hampshire and Massachusetts, only, voting against it. The Thirteenth Section of Article 6, as amended, was then agreed to.

/ September 12

Mr. Williamson moved to reconsider the clause requiring three-fourths of each house to overrule the negative of the President, in order to strike out three-fourths and insert two-thirds. He had, he remarked, himself proposed three-fourths instead of two-thirds, but he had since been convinced that the latter proportion was the best. The former puts too much in the power of the President.

Mr. Sherman was of the same opinion, adding that the states would not like to see so small a minority, and the President, prevailing over the general voice. In making laws, regard should be had to the sense

of the people who are to be bound by them, and it was more probable
that a single man should mistake or betray this sense than the legislature.

Mr. Gouverneur Morris: Considering the difference between the
two proportions numerically, amounts, in one house to two members only and in the other to not more than five—according to the
numbers of which the legislature is at first to be composed. It is the
interest, moreover, of the distant states to prefer three-fourths, as they
will be oftenest absent and need the interposing check of the President. The excess, rather than the deficiency, of laws was to be dreaded.
The example of New York shows that two-thirds is not sufficient to
answer the purpose.

Mr. Hamilton added his testimony to the fact that two-thirds in
New York had been ineffectual, either where a popular object or a
legislative faction operated—of which he mentioned some instances.

Mr. Gerry: It is necessary to consider the danger on the other side
also. Two-thirds will be a considerable, perhaps a proper, security.
Three-fourths puts too much in the power of a few men. The primary
object of the revisionary check of the President is not to protect the
general interest, but to defend his own department. If three-fourths
be required, a few senators, having hopes from the nomination of the
President to offices, will combine with him and impede proper laws.
Making the Vice President speaker increases the danger.

Mr. Williamson was less afraid of too few than of too many laws.
He was, most of all, afraid that the repeal of bad laws might be rendered too difficult by requiring three-fourths to overcome the dissent
of the President.

Mr. Mason had always considered this as one of the most exceptionable parts of the system. As to the numerical argument of Mr. Gouverneur Morris, little arithmetic was necessary to understand that three-
fourths was more than two-thirds, whatever the numbers of the legislature might be. The example of New York depended on the real
merits of the laws. The gentlemen citing it had, no doubt, given their
own opinions, who could equally paint the abuses on the other side.
His leading view was to guard against too great an impediment to the
repeal of laws.

Mr. Gouverneur Morris dwelt on the danger to the public interest
from the instability of laws as the most to be guarded against. On the
other side, there could be little danger. If one man in office will not
consent where he ought, every fourth year another can be substituted. This term was not too long for fair experiments. Many good
laws are not tried long enough to prove their merit. This is often the

case with new laws opposed to old habits. The inspection laws of Virginia and Maryland, to which all are now so much attached, were unpopular at first.

Mr. Pinckney was warmly in opposition to three-fourths as putting a dangerous power in the hands of a few senators headed by the President.

Mr. Madison: When three-fourths was agreed to, the President was to be elected by the legislature and for seven years. He is now to be elected by the people and for four years. The object of the revisionary power is twofold: first, to defend the executive rights; secondly, to prevent popular or factious injustice. It was an important principle in this and in the state constitutions to check legislative injustice and encroachments. The experience of the states had demonstrated that their checks are insufficient. We must compare the danger from the strength of three-fourths. He thought on the whole, the former was the greater. As to the difficulty of repeals, it was probable that in doubtful cases the policy would soon take place of limiting the duration of laws, so as to require renewal, instead of repeal.

Motion to insert two-thirds in place of three-fourths passed, 6 to 4.

· Article II, Section 4: The President, Vice President and all civil Officers of the United States, shall be removed from Office on Impeachment for, and Conviction of, Treason, Bribery, or other high Crimes and Misdemeanors.

THE CONSTITUTION OF THE UNITED STATES

QUESTION OF IMPEACHMENT INTRODUCED / July 20

On the clause "to be removable on impeachment and conviction for malpractice or neglect of duty," Mr. Pinckney and Mr. Gouverneur Morris moved to strike out this part of the resolution. Mr. Pinckney observed he ought not to be impeachable whilst in office.

Mr. Davie: If he be not impeachable whilst in office, he will spare no efforts or means whatever to get himself re-elected. He considered this as an essential security for the good behavior of the executive.

Mr. Wilson concurred in the necessity of making the executive impeachable whilst in office.

Mr. Gouverneur Morris: He can do no criminal act without co-adjutors, who may be punished. In case he should be re-elected that will be a sufficient proof of his innocence. Besides, who is to impeach? Is the impeachment to suspend his functions? If it is not, the mischief will go on. If it is, the impeachment will be nearly equivalent to a displacement and will render the executive dependent on those who are to impeach.

Mr. Mason: No point is of more importance than that the right of impeachment should be continued. Shall any man be above justice? Above all, shall that man be above it who can commit the most extensive injustice? When great crimes were committed, he was for punishing the principal as well as the coadjutors. There had been so much debate and difficulty as to the mode of choosing the executive. He approved of that which had been adopted at first, namely, of referring the appointment to the national legislature. One objection against electors was the danger of their being corrupted by the candidates, and this furnished a peculiar reason in favor of impeachments whilst in office. Shall the man who has practiced corruption, and by that means procured his appointment in the first instance, be suffered to escape punishment by repeating his guilt?

Dr. Franklin was for retaining the clause as favorable to the executive. History furnishes one example only of a first magistrate being formally brought to public justice. Everybody cried out against this as unconstitutional. What was the practice before this in cases where the chief magistrate rendered himself obnoxious? Why, recourse was had to assassination, in which he was not only deprived of his life, but of the opportunity of vindicating his character. It would be the best way, therefore, to provide in the Constitution for the regular punishment of the executive where his misconduct should deserve it, and for his honorable acquittal where he should be unjustly accused.

Mr. Gouverneur Morris admits corruption and some few other offenses to be such as ought to be impeachable, but thought the cases ought to be enumerated and defined.

Mr. Madison thought it indispensable that some provision should be made for defending the community against the incapacity, negligence, or perfidy of the chief magistrate. The limitation of the period of his service was not a sufficient security. He might lose his capacity after his appointment. He might pervert his administration into a scheme of peculation or oppression. He might betray his trust to foreign powers. The case of the executive magistracy was very distinguishable from that of the legislature, or any other public body holding offices of limited duration. It could not be presumed that all or even the majority of the members of an assembly would either lose their capacity for discharging, or be bribed to betray, their trust. Besides the restraints of their personal integrity and honor, the difficulty of acting in concert for purposes of corruption was a security to the public. And if one or a few members only should be seduced, the soundness of the remaining members would maintain the integrity and fidelity of the body. In the case of the executive magistracy, which was to be administered by a single man, loss of capacity, or corruption, was more within the compass of probable events and either of them might be fatal to the republic.

Mr. Pinckney did not see the necessity of impeachments. He was sure they ought not to issue from the legislature, who would in that case hold them as a rod over the executive and by that means effectually destroy his independence. His revisionary power, in particular, would be rendered altogether insignificant.

Mr. Gerry urged the necessity of impeachments. A good magistrate will not fear them. A bad one ought to be kept in fear of them. He hoped the maxim would never be adopted here that the chief magistrate could do no wrong.

Mr. King expressed his apprehensions that an extreme caution in favor of liberty might enervate the government we were forming. He wished the house to recur to the primitive axiom that the three great departments of government should be separate and independent; that the executive and judiciary should be so as well as the legislative; that the executive should be so equally with the judiciary. Would this be the case if the executive should be impeachable? It had been said that the judiciary would be impeachable. But it should have been remembered at the same time that the judiciary hold their places not for a limited time, but during good behavior. It is necessary, therefore, that a form should be established for trying misbehavior. Was the executive to hold his place during good behavior? The executive was to hold his place for a limited time, like the members of the legislature. Like them, particularly the Senate, whose members would continue in appointment the same term of six years, he would periodically be tried for his behavior by his electors, who would continue or discontinue him in trust according to the manner in which he had discharged it. Like them, therefore, he ought to be subject to no intermediate trial by impeachment. He ought not to be impeachable unless he held his office during good behavior—a tenure which would be most agreeable to him provided an independent and effectual forum could be devised. But under no circumstances ought he to be impeachable by the legislature. This would be destructive of his independence and of the principles of the Constitution. He relied on the vigor of the executive as a great security for the public liberties.

Mr. Randolph: The propriety of impeachments was a favorite principle with him. Guilt, wherever found, ought to be punished. The executive will have great opportunities of abusing his power, particularly in time of war, when the military force, and in some respects the public money, will be in his hands. Should no regular punishment be provided, it will be irregularly inflicted by tumults and insurrections. He is aware of the necessity of proceeding with a cautious hand and of excluding, as much as possible, the influence of the legislature from the business. He suggested for consideration an idea which had fallen from Col. Hamilton of composing a forum out of the judges belonging to the states, and even of requiring some preliminary inquest whether just ground of impeachment existed.

Dr. Franklin mentioned the case of the Prince of Orange during the late war. An arrangement was made between France and Holland by which their two fleets were to unite at a certain time and place. The Dutch fleet did not appear. Everybody began to wonder at it. At length it was suspected that the stadtholder was at the bottom of the matter. This suspicion prevailed more and more. Yet, as he could not be impeached and no regular examination took place, he remained in his office; and strengthening his own party, as the party opposed to him became formidable, he gave birth to the most violent animosities and contentions. Had he been impeachable, a regular and peaceable inquiry would have taken place, and he would, if guilty, have been duly punished—if innocent, restored to the confidence of the public.

Mr. King remarked that the case of the stadtholder was not applicable. He held his place for life and was not periodically elected. In the former case, impeachments are proper to secure good behavior; in the latter, they are unnecessary, the periodical responsibility to electors being an equivalent security.

Mr. Wilson observed that if the idea were to be pursued, the senators who are to hold their places during the same term with the executive ought to be subject to impeachment and removal.

Mr. Pinckney apprehended that some gentlemen reasoned on a supposition that the executive was to have powers which would not be committed to him. He presumed that his powers would be so circumscribed as to render impeachments unnecessary.

Mr. Gouverneur Morris' opinion had been changed by the arguments used in the discussion. He was now sensible of the necessity of impeachments if the executive was to continue for any length of time in office. Our executive was not like a magistrate having a life interest, much less like one having an hereditary interest in his office. He may be bribed by a greater interest to betray his trust, and no one would say that we ought to expose ourselves to the danger of seeing the first magistrate in foreign pay without being able to guard against it by displacing him. One would think the King of England well secured against bribery. He has, as it were, a fee simple in the whole kingdom. Yet Charles II was bribed by Louis XIV. The executive ought, therefore, to be impeachable for treachery. Corrupting his electors and incapacity were other causes of impeachment. For the latter he should be punished, not as a man but as an officer, and punished only by degradation from his office. This magistrate is not the king, but the prime minister. The people are the king. When we make him amenable to justice, however, we should take care to provide some mode that will not make him dependent on the legislature.

The motion that the executive be removable on impeachments passed, 8 to 2.

CAUSES FOR IMPEACHMENT DEBATED / September 8

The clause referring to the Senate the trial of impeachments against the President for treason and bribery was taken up.

Mr. Mason: Why is the provision restrained to treason and bribery only? Treason, as defined in the Constitution, will not reach many great and dangerous offenses. Hastings is not guilty of treason. Attempts to subvert the Constitution may not be treason as above defined. As bills of attainder, which have saved the British constitution, are forbidden, it is the more necessary to extend the power of impeachments. He moved to add after "bribery," "or maladministration." Mr. Gerry seconded him.

Mr. Madison: So vague a term will be equivalent to a tenure during pleasure of the Senate.

Mr. Gouverneur Morris: It will not be put in force and can do no harm. An election of every four years will prevent maladministration.

Mr. Mason withdrew "maladministration" and substituted "other high crimes and misdemeanors against the state."

Mr. Madison objected to a trial of the President by the Senate, especially as he was to be impeached by the other branch of the legislature and for any act which might be called a misdemeanor. The President under these circumstances was made improperly dependent. He would prefer the Supreme Court for the trial of impeachments or, rather, a tribunal of which that should form a part.

Mr. Gouverneur Morris thought no other tribunal than the Senate could be trusted. The Supreme Court were too few in number and might be warped or corrupted. He was against a dependence of the executive on the legislature, considering the legislative tyranny the great danger to be apprehended; but there could be no danger that the Senate would say untruly, on their oaths, that the President was guilty of crimes or facts, especially as in four years he can be turned out.

389

Mr. Pinckney disapproved of making the Senate the Court of Impeachments as rendering the President too dependent on the legislature. If he opposes a favorite law, the two houses will combine against him and under the influence of heat and faction throw him out of office.

Mr. Williamson thought there was more danger of too much leniency than of too much rigor toward the President, considering the number of cases in which the Senate was associated with the President.

Mr. Sherman regarded the Supreme Court as improper to try the President, because the judges would be appointed by him.

Motion by Mr. Madison, to strike out the words "by the Senate," after the word "conviction," defeated, 9 to 2.

In the amendment of Col. Mason, just agreed to, the word "state," after the words "misdemeanors against," was struck out, and the words "United States" unanimously inserted in order to remove ambiguity.

On motion, the following: "The Vice President, and other civil officers of the United States shall be removed from office on impeachment and conviction, as aforesaid," was added to the clause on the subject of impeachments.

· Article I, Section 3: . . . The Senate shall have the sole Power to try all Impeachments. When sitting for that Purpose, they shall be on Oath or Affirmation. When the President of the United States is tried, the Chief Justice shall preside: And no Person shall be convicted without the Concurrence of two thirds of the Members present.

Judgment in Cases of Impeachment shall not extend further than to removal from Office, and disqualification to hold and enjoy any Office of honor, Trust or Profit under the United States: but the Party convicted shall nevertheless be liable and subject to Indictment, Trial, Judgment and Punishment, according to Law.

THE CONSTITUTION OF THE UNITED STATES

METHOD OF IMPEACHMENT AGREED UPON / *June 2*

Mr. Dickinson moved "that the executive be made removable by the national legislature on the request of a majority of the legislatures of individual states." It was necessary, he said, to place the power of removing somewhere. He did not like the plan of impeaching the great officers of state. He did not know how provision could be made for the removal of them in a better mode than that which he had proposed. He had no idea of abolishing the state governments, as some gentlemen seemed inclined to do. The happiness of this country, in his opinion, required considerable powers to be left in the hands of the states.

Mr. Bedford seconded the motion.

Mr. Sherman contended that the national legislature should have power to remove the executive at pleasure.

Mr. Mason: Some mode of displacing an unfit magistrate is rendered indispensable by the fallibility of those who choose, as well as by the corruptibility of the man chosen. He opposed decidedly the making the executive the mere creature of the legislature as a violation of the fundamental principle of good government.

Mr. Madison and Mr. Wilson observed that it would leave an equality of agency in the small with the great states; that it would enable a minority of the people to prevent the removal of an officer who had rendered himself justly criminal in the eyes of a majority; that it would open a door for intrigues against him in states where his administration, though just, might be unpopular, and might tempt him to pay court to particular states whose leading partisans he might fear, or wish to engage as his partisans. They both thought it bad policy to introduce such a mixture of the state authorities where their agency could be otherwise supplied.

Mr. Dickinson considered the business as so important that no man ought to be silent or reserved. He went into a discourse of some length, the sum of which was that the legislative, executive, and judiciary departments ought to be made as independent as possible, but that such an executive as some seemed to have in contemplation was not consistent with a republic; that a firm executive could only exist in a limited monarchy. In the British government itself, the weight of the executive arises from the attachments which the crown draws to itself and not merely from the force of its prerogatives. In place of these attachments, we must look out for something else. One source of stability is the double branch of the legislature. The division of the country into distinct states formed the other principal source of stability. This division ought therefore to be maintained and considerable powers to be left with the states. This was the ground of his consolation for the future fate of his country. Without this, and in case of a consolidation of the states into one great republic, we might read its fate in the history of smaller ones. A limited monarchy he considered as one of the best governments in the world. It was not certain that the same blessings were derivable from any other form. It was certain that equal blessings had never yet been derived from any of the republican forms. A limited monarchy, however, was out of the question. The spirit of the times, the state of our affairs, forbade the experiment, if it were desirable. Was it possible, moreover, in the nature of things to introduce it, even if these obstacles were less insuperable? A house of nobles was essential to such a government. Could these be created by a breath, or by a stroke of the pen? No. They were the growth of ages and could only arise under a complication of circumstances, none of which existed in this country. But though a form, the most perfect, perhaps, in itself, be unattainable, we must not despair. If ancient republics have been found to flourish for a moment only and then vanish forever, it only proves that they were badly constituted and that we ought to seek every remedy for their diseases. One of these remedies he conceived to be the accidental lucky division of this country into distinct states—a division which some seemed desirous to abolish altogether.

As to the point of representation in the national legislature, as it might affect states of different sizes, he said it must probably end in mutual concession. He hoped that each state would retain an equal voice, at least in one branch of the national legislature, and supposed the sums paid within each state would form a better ratio for the other branch than either the number of inhabitants or the quantum of property.

Motion to remove the executive on request of "a majority of the state legislatures" defeated, 9 to 1.

Mr. Williamson, seconded by Mr. Davie, moved to add to the last clause the words "and to be removable on impeachment and conviction of malpractice or neglect of duty," which was agreed to.

Vice President and "Cabinet"

• Article I, Section 3: The Vice President of the United States shall be President of the Senate, but shall have no Vote, unless they be equally divided.

THE CONSTITUTION OF THE UNITED STATES

TO PRESIDE OVER SENATE / *September 7*

The Third Section, "The Vice President shall be, ex officio, President of the Senate," being then considered, Mr. Gerry opposed this regulation. We might as well put the President himself at the head of the legislature. The close intimacy that must subsist between the President and Vice President makes it absolutely improper. He was against having any Vice President.

Mr. Gouverneur Morris: The Vice President then will be the first heir-apparent that ever loved his father. If there should be no Vice President, the President of the Senate would be temporary successor, which would amount to the same thing.

Mr. Sherman saw no danger in the case. If the Vice President were not to be President of the Senate, he would be without employment, and some member by being made President must be deprived of his vote, unless when an equal division of votes might happen in the Senate, which would be but seldom.

Mr. Randolph concurred in the opposition to the clause.

Mr. Williamson observed that such an officer as Vice President was not wanted. He was introduced merely for the sake of a valuable mode of election which required two to be chosen at the same time.

Mr. Mason thought the office of Vice President an encroachment on the rights of the Senate and that it mixed too much the legislative and the executive, which, as well as the judiciary department, ought to be kept as separate as possible. He took occasion to express his dislike of any reference whatever of the power to make appointments to either branch of the legislature. On the other hand, he was averse to vest so dangerous a power in the President alone. As a method for avoiding both, he suggested that a privy council of six members to the President should be established, to be chosen for six years by the Senate—two out of the eastern, two out of the middle, and two out of the southern quarters of the Union—and to go out in rotation, two every second year; the concurrence of the Senate to be required only in the appointment of ambassadors and in making treaties, which are more of a legislative nature. This would prevent the constant sitting of the Senate, which he thought dangerous, as well as keep the department separate and distinct. It would also save the expense of constant sessions of the Senate. He had, he said, always considered the Senate as too unwieldy and expensive for appointing officers, especially the smallest, such as tidewaiters, and so forth. He had not reduced his idea to writing, but it could be easily done if it should be found acceptable.

The question, "Shall the Vice President be, ex officio, President of the Senate?" passed, 8 to 2.

• Article II, Section 1: . . . In Case of the Removal of the President from Office, or of his Death, Resignation, or Inability to discharge the Powers and Duties of the said Office, the Same shall devolve on the Vice President, and the Congress may by Law provide for the Case of Removal, Death, Resignation or Inability, both of the President and Vice President, declaring what Officer shall then act as President, and such Officer shall act accordingly, until the Disability be removed, or a President shall be elected. THE CONSTITUTION OF THE UNITED STATES

Editor's note: The question of presidential succession arose during debate over the role of the Vice President. The convention and the Committee of Style made changes in the original version of August 6, and reversed each other's decisions several times, but both failed to clear up ambiguities in the language: When was the President disabled and who was to judge, and what powers exactly were to "devolve" on the Vice President? Although there was debate on these issues, the wording finally incorporated into the Constitution has, on several occasions in our history, caused confusion and grave consternation.

• Article II, Section 2: The President . . . may require the Opinion, in writing, of the principal Officer in each of the executive Departments, upon any Subject relating to the Duties of their respective Offices, ...

THE CONSTITUTION OF THE UNITED STATES

QUESTION OF AN EXECUTIVE COUNCIL / *September 7*

The clause, "and may require the opinion in writing of the principal officer in each of the executive departments, upon any subject relating to the duties of their respective offices," being before the house, Mr. Mason said that in rejecting a council to the President we were about to try an experiment on which the most despotic government had never ventured. The grand seignior himself had his divan. He moved to postpone the consideration of the clause in order to take up the following:

"That it be an instruction to the committee of the states to prepare a clause or clauses for establishing an executive council, as a council of state for the President of the United States; to consist of six members, two of which from the eastern, two from the middle, and two from the southern states; with a rotation and duration of office similar to those of the Senate; such council to be appointed by the legislature, or by the Senate."

Dr. Franklin seconded the motion. We seemed, he said, too much to fear cabals in appointments by a number and have too much confidence in those of single persons. Experience showed that caprice, the intrigues of favorites and mistresses, were, nevertheless, the means most prevalent in monarchies. Among instances of abuse in such modes of appointment, he mentioned the many bad governors appointed in Great Britain for the colonies. He thought a council would not only be a check on a bad President, but be a relief to a good one.

Mr. Gouverneur Morris: The question of a council was considered in the committee, where it was judged that the President, by persuading his council to concur in his wrong measures, would acquire their protection for them.

Mr. Wilson approved of a council in preference to making the Senate a party to appointments.

Mr. Dickinson was for a council. It would be a singular thing if the measures of the executive were not to undergo some previous discussion before the President.

Mr. Madison was in favor of the instruction to the committee proposed by Col. Mason.

Mr. Mason's motion for legislature to appoint an executive council defeated, 8 to 3.

On the question of authorizing the President to call for the opinions of the heads of departments in writing, it passed in the affirmative, only New Hampshire voting no.

The clause was then unanimously agreed to.

• Article II, Section 2: . . . The President shall have Power to fill up all Vacancies that may happen during the Recess of the Senate, by granting Commissions which shall expire at the End of their next Session.

• Article II, Section 3: He shall from time to time give to the Congress Information of the State of the Union, and recommend to their Consideration such Measures as he shall judge necessary and expedient; he may, on extraordinary Occasions, convene both Houses, or either of them, and in Case of Disagreement between them, with Respect to the Time of Adjournment, he may adjourn them to such Time as he shall think proper; he shall receive Ambassadors and other public Ministers; he shall take Care that the Laws be faithfully executed, and shall Commission all the officers of the United States.

THE CONSTITUTION OF THE UNITED STATES

Editor's note: Richard Dobbs Spaight of North Carolina, taking his text from the Constitution of South Carolina, proposed the presidential power to fill vacancies when the Senate was recessed, and it was accepted on September 7. Section 3 of Article II contained recommendations of the Committee of Detail which were adopted by the convention in August with only minor word changes.

The Judiciary

CHAPTER FIVE

Establishment and Appointment 399

• Article III, Section 1: The judicial Power of the United States, shall be vested in one supreme Court, and in such inferior Courts as the Congress may from time to time ordain and establish. THE CONSTITUTION OF THE UNITED STATES

CREATION OF A NATIONAL JUDICIARY / *June 4*

It was then moved and seconded to proceed to the consideration of the ninth resolution submitted by Mr. Randolph; when on motion to agree to the first clause, namely, "Resolved, that a national judiciary be established," it passed in the affirmative.

It was then moved and seconded to add these words to the first clause of the ninth resolution, namely, "to consist of one supreme tribunal and of one or more inferior tribunals," which passed in the affirmative.

The committee then rose and the house adjourned.

/ *June 5*

In committee of the whole. The words "one or more" were struck out before "inferior tribunals," as an amendment to the last clause of the ninth resolution. The clause "that the national judiciary be chosen by the national legislature" being under consideration, Mr. Wilson opposed the appointment of judges by the national legislature. Experience showed the impropriety of such appointments by numerous bodies. Intrigue, partiality, and concealment were the necessary consequences. A principal reason for unity in the executive was that officers might be appointed by a single responsible person.

Mr. Rutledge was by no means disposed to grant so great a power to any single person. The people will think we are leaning too much toward monarchy. He was against establishing any national tribunal, except a single supreme one. The state tribunals are most proper to decide in all cases in the first instance.

Dr. Franklin observed that two modes of choosing the judges had been mentioned—to wit, by the legislature and by the executive. He wished such other modes to be suggested as might occur to other gentlemen, it being a point of great moment. He would mention one which he had understood was practiced in Scotland. He then, in a brief and entertaining manner, related a Scotch mode in which the nomination proceeded from the lawyers, who always selected the ablest of the profession in order to get rid of him and share his practice among themselves. It was here, he said, the interest of the electors to make the best choice, which should always be made the case if possible.

QUESTION OF LOWER TRIBUNALS / *June 5*

Mr. Rutledge, having obtained a rule for reconsideration of the clause for establishing inferior tribunals under the national authority, now moved that that part of the clause in the ninth resolution should be expunged, arguing that the state tribunals might and ought to be left in all cases to decide in the first instance, the right of appeal to the supreme national tribunal being sufficient to secure the national rights and uniformity of judgments; that it was making an unnecessary encroachment on the jurisdiction of the states and creating unnecessary obstacles to their adoption of the new system.

Mr. Sherman seconded the motion.

Mr. Madison observed that unless inferior tribunals were dispersed throughout the republic with final jurisdiction in many cases, appeals would be multiplied to a most oppressive degree; that, besides, an appeal would not in many cases be a remedy. What was to be done after improper verdicts in state tribunals, obtained under the biased directions of a dependent judge or the local prejudices of an undirected jury? To remand the cause for a new trial would answer no purpose. To order a new trial at the supreme bar would oblige the parties to bring up their witnesses, though ever so distant from the seat of the court. An effective judiciary establishment commensurate to the legislative authority was essential. A government without a proper executive and judiciary would be the mere trunk of a body, without arms or legs to act or move.

Mr. Wilson opposed the motion on like grounds. He said the admiralty jurisdiction ought to be given wholly to the national government as it related to cases not within the jurisdiction of particular states, and to a scene in which controversies with foreigners would be most likely to happen.

Mr. Sherman was in favor of the motion. He dwelt chiefly on the supposed expensiveness of having a new set of courts when the existing state courts would answer the same purpose.

Mr. Dickinson contended strongly that if there was to be a national legislature, there ought to be a national judiciary, and that the former ought to have authority to institute the latter.

The question for Mr. Rutledge's motion to strike out "inferior tribunals" passed in the affirmative.

• Article II, Section 2: . . . he [the President] shall nominate, and by and with the Advice and Consent of the Senate, shall appoint . . . Judges of the supreme Court, and all other Officers of the United States, whose Appointments are not herein otherwise provided for, and which shall be established by Law: . . . .

THE CONSTITUTION OF THE UNITED STATES

EXECUTIVE NOMINATION
OF JUDICIARY DEBATED / *July 18*

The eleventh resolution, "That a national judiciary shall be established to consist of one supreme tribunal," agreed to unanimously.

On the clause, "the judges of which to be appointed by the second branch of the national legislature," Mr. Gorham would prefer an appointment by the second branch to an appointment by the whole legislature, but he thought even that branch too numerous and too little personally responsible to insure a good choice. He suggested that the judges be appointed by the executive with the advice and consent of the second branch in the mode prescribed by the Constitution of Massachusetts. This mode had been long practiced in that country and was found to answer perfectly well.

Mr. Wilson would still prefer an appointment by the executive, but if that could not be attained would prefer, in the next place, the mode suggested by Mr. Gorham. He thought it his duty, however, to move in the first instance "that the judges be appointed by the executive."

Mr. Gouverneur Morris seconded the motion.

Mr. L. Martin was strenuous for an appointment by the second branch. Being taken from all the states, it would be best informed of characters and most capable of making a fit choice.

Mr. Sherman concurred in the observations of Mr. Martin, adding that the judges ought to be diffused, which would be more likely to be attended to by the second branch than by the executive.

Mr. Mason: The mode of appointing the judges may depend in some degree on the mode of trying impeachments of the executive. If the judges were to form a tribunal for that purpose, they surely ought not to be appointed by the executive. There were insuperable objections, besides, against referring the appointment to the executive. He mentioned as one that as the seat of government must be in some one state and as the executive would remain in office for a considerable time—for four, five, or six years at least—he would insensibly form local and personal attachments within the particular state that would deprive equal merit elsewhere of an equal chance of promotion.

Mr. Gorham: As the executive will be responsible, in point of character at least, for a judicious and faithful discharge of his trust, he will be careful to look through all the states for proper characters. The senators will be as likely to form their attachments at the seat of government where they reside as the executive. If they cannot get the man of the particular state to which they may respectively belong, they will be indifferent to the rest. Public bodies feel no personal responsibility and give full play to intrigue and cabal. Rhode Island is a full illustration of the insensibility to character produced by a participation of numbers in dishonorable measures and of the length to which a public body may carry wickedness and cabal.

Mr. Gouverneur Morris supposed it would be improper for an impeachment of the executive to be tried before the judges. The latter would in such cases be drawn into intrigues with the legislature and an impartial trial would be frustrated. As they would be much about the seat of government, they might even be previously consulted, and arrangements might be made for a prosecution of the executive. He thought, therefore, that no argument could be drawn from the probability of such a plan of impeachments against the motion before the house.

Mr. Madison suggested that the judges might be appointed by the executive with the concurrence of one-third, at least, of the second branch. This would unite the advantage of responsibility in the executive with the security afforded in the second branch against any incautious or corrupt nomination by the executive.

Mr. Sherman was clearly for an election by the Senate. It would be composed of men nearly equal to the executive and would, of course, have, on the whole, more wisdom. They would bring into their deliberations a more diffusive knowledge of characters. It would be less easy for candidates to intrigue with them than with the executive magistrate. For these reasons, he thought there would be a better security for a proper choice in the Senate than in the executive.

Mr. Randolph: It is true that when the appointment of the judges was vested in the second branch an equality of votes had not been given to it. Yet he had rather leave the appointment there than give it to the executive. He thought the advantage of personal responsibility might be gained in the Senate by requiring the respective votes of the members to be entered on the journal. He thought, too, that the hope of receiving appointments would be more diffusive if they depended on the Senate, the members of which would be diffusively known, than if they depended on a single man, who could not be personally known to a very great extent, and, consequently, that opposition to the system would be so far weakened.

Mr. Bedford thought there were solid reasons against leaving the appointment to the executive. He must trust more to information than the Senate. It would put it in his power to gain over the larger states by gratifying them with a preference of their citizens. The responsibility of the executive, so much talked of, was chimerical. He could not be punished for mistakes.

Mr. Gorham remarked that the Senate could have no better information than the executive. They must, like him, trust to information from the members belonging to the particular state where the candidate resided. The executive would certainly be more answerable for a good appointment, as the whole blame of a bad one would fall on him alone. He did not mean that he would be answerable under any other penalty than that of public censure, which with honorable minds was a sufficient one.

Mr. Gorham moved "that the judges be nominated and appointed by the executive, by and with the advice and consent of the second branch, and every such nomination shall be made at least _____ days prior to such appointment." This mode, he said, had been ratified by the experience of a hundred-and-forty years in Massachusetts. If the appointment should be left to either branch of the legislature, it will be a mere piece of jobbing.

Mr. Gouverneur Morris seconded and supported the motion.

Mr. Sherman thought it less objectionable than an absolute appointment by the executive, but disliked it as too much fettering the Senate.

Mr. Madison moved "that the judges should be nominated by the executive, and such nomination should become an appointment if not disagreed to within _____ days by two-thirds of the second branch."

Mr. Gouverneur Morris seconded the motion.

By common consent, the consideration of it was postponed till to-morrow.

LEGISLATIVE NOMINATION DEBATED / *July 18*

The twelfth resolution, "That the national legislature be empowered to appoint inferior tribunals," being taken up, Mr. Butler could see no necessity for such tribunals. The state tribunals might do the business.

Mr. L. Martin concurred. They will create jealousies and oppositions in the state tribunals with the jurisdiction of which they will interfere.

Mr. Gorham: There are in the states already Federal courts with jurisdiction for trial of piracies committed on the seas. No complaints have been made by the states or the courts of the states. Inferior tribunals are essential to render the authority of the national legislature effectual.

Mr. Randolph observed that the courts of the states cannot be trusted with administration of the national laws. The objects of jurisdiction are such as will often place the general and local policy at variance.

Mr. Gouverneur Morris urged also the necessity of such a provision.

Mr. Sherman was willing to give the power to the legislature, but wished them to make use of the state tribunals whenever it could be done with safety to the general interest.

Mr. Mason thought many circumstances might arise, not now to be foreseen, which might render such a power absolutely necessary.

The twelfth resolution, empowering the national legislature to appoint inferior tribunals, passed unanimously.

Mr. Madison disliked the election of the judges by the legislature, or any numerous body. Besides the danger of intrigue and partiality, many of the members were not judges of the requisite qualifications. The legislative talents, which were very different from those of a judge, commonly recommended men to the favor of legislative assemblies. It was known, too, that the accidental circumstances of presence and absence, of being a member or not a member, had a very undue influence on the appointment. On the other hand, he was not satisfied with referring the appointment to the executive. He rather inclined to give it to the senatorial branch, as numerous enough to be confided in, as not so numerous as to be governed by the motives of the other branch, and as being sufficiently stable and independent to follow their deliberate judgments. He hinted this only and moved that the appointment by the legislature might be struck out and a blank left to be hereafter filled on maturer reflection.

Mr. Wilson seconds it.

Appointment of national judiciary by national legislature defeated, 9 to 2.

The motion made by Mr. Madison on the 18th of July and then postponed, "that the judges should be nominated by the executive, and such nominations become appointments, unless disagreed to by two-thirds of the second branch of the legislature," was now resumed.

Mr. Madison stated as his reasons for the motion—first, that it secured the responsibility of the executive, who would in general be more capable and likely to select fit characters than the legislature, or even the second branch of it, who might hide their selfish motives under the number concerned in the appointment; secondly, that in case of any flagrant partiality or error in the nomination, it might be fairly presumed that two-thirds of the second branch would join in putting a negative on it; thirdly, that as the second branch was very differently constituted when the appointment of the judges was formerly referred to it and was now to be composed of equal votes from all the states, the principle of compromise which had prevailed in other instances required in this that there should be a concurrence of two authorities, in one of which the people, in the other the states, should be represented. The executive magistrate would be considered as a national officer, acting for and equally sympathizing with every part of the United States. If the second branch alone should have this power, the judges might be appointed by a minority of the people, though by a majority of the states, which could not be justified on any principle, as their proceedings were to relate to the people rather than to the states, and as it would, moreover, throw the appointments entirely into the hands of the northern states, a perpetual ground of jealousy and discontent would be furnished to the southern states.

Mr. Pinckney was for placing the appointment in the second branch exclusively. The executive will possess neither the requisite knowledge of characters, nor confidence of the people for so high a trust.

Mr. Randolph would have preferred the mode of appointment proposed formerly by Mr. Gorham, as adopted in the Constitution of Massachusetts, but thought the motion depending so great an improvement of the clause, as it stands, that he anxiously wished it success. He laid great stress on the reponsibility of the executive as a security for fit appointments. Appointments by the legislatures have generally resulted from cabal, from personal regard, or some other consideration than a title derived from the proper qualifications. The same inconveniences will proportionally prevail if the appointments be referred to either branch of the legislature or to any other authority administered by a number of individuals.

Mr. Ellsworth would prefer a negative in the executive on a nomination by the second branch, the negative to be overruled by a concurrence of two-thirds of the second branch, to the mode proposed by the motion, but preferred an absolute appointment by the second branch to either. The executive will be regarded by the people with a jealous eye. Every power for augmenting unnecessarily his influence will be disliked. As he will be stationary, it was not to be supposed he could have a better knowledge of characters. He will be more open to caresses and intrigues than the Senate. The right to supersede his nomination will be ideal only. A nomination under such circumstances will be equivalent to an appointment.

Mr. Gouverneur Morris supported the motion. First, the states in their corporate capacity will frequently have an interest staked on the determination of the judges. As in the Senate the states are to vote, the judges ought not to be appointed by the Senate. Next to the impropriety of being judge in one's own cause is the appointment of the judge. Secondly, it had been said the executive would be uninformed of characters. The reverse was the truth. The Senate will be so. They must take the character of candidates from the flattering pictures drawn by their friends. The executive, in the necessary intercourse with every part of the United States required by the nature of his administration, will or may have the best possible information. Thirdly, it had been said that a jealousy would be entertained of the executive. If the executive can be safely trusted with the command of the army, there cannot surely be any reasonable ground of jealousy in the present case. He added that if the objections against an appointment of the executive by the legislature had the weight that had been allowed, there must be some weight in the objection to an appointment of the judges by the legislature, or by any part of it.

Mr. Gerry: The appointment of the judges, like every other part of the Constitution, should be so modeled as to give satisfaction both to the people and to the states. The mode under consideration will give satisfaction to neither. He could not conceive that the executive could be as well informed of characters throughout the Union as the Senate. It appeared to him, also, a strong objection that two-thirds of the Senate were required to reject a nomination of the executive. The Senate would be constituted in the same manner as Congress and the appointments of Congress have been generally good.

Mr. Madison observed that he was not anxious that two-thirds should be necessary to disagree to a nomination. He had given this form to his motion chiefly to vary it the more clearly from one which had just been rejected. He was content to obviate the objection last made and accordingly so varied the motion as to let a majority reject. **407** Mr. Mason found it his duty to differ from his colleagues in their opinions and reasonings on this subject. Notwithstanding the form of the proposition by which the appointment seemed to be divided between the executive and Senate, the appointment was substantially vested in the former alone. The false complaisance which usually prevails in such cases will prevent a disagreement to the first nominations. He considered the appointment by the executive as a dangerous prerogative. It might even give him an influence over the judiciary department itself. He did not think the difference of interest between the northern and southern states could be properly brought into this argument. It would operate and require some precautions in the case of regulating navigation, commerce, and imposts, but he could not see that it had any connection with the judiciary department.

Appointment by the Senate of presidentially nominated judges passed, 6 to 3.

· Article II, Section 2: . . . but the Congress may by Law vest the Appointment of such inferior Officers, as they think proper, in the President alone, in the Courts of Law, or in the Heads of Departments.

THE CONSTITUTION OF THE UNITED STATES

Editor's note: Requiring the "Advice and Consent" of the Senate for Presidential appointments seemed to some an improper weakening of the executive power. But the convention not only passed this section, but intensified it in September by the additional clause above to make sure the executive would not create official positions *not* provided for by the Congress.

· Article III, Section 1: . . . The Judges, both of the supreme and inferior Courts, shall hold their Offices during good Behaviour, ...

THE CONSTITUTION OF THE UNITED STATES

TO SERVE "DURING GOOD BEHAVIOUR" / *August 27*

Mr. Dickinson moved as an amendment to Article II, Section 2, after the words "good behaviour," the words, "Provided that they may be removed by the executive on the application by the Senate and House of Representatives."

Mr. Gerry seconded the motion.

Mr. Gouverneur Morris thought it a contradiction in terms to say that the judges should hold their offices during good behavior and yet be removable without a trial. Besides, it was fundamentally wrong to subject judges to so arbitrary an authority.

Mr. Sherman saw no contradiction or impropriety if this were made a part of the constitutional regulation of the judiciary establishment. He observed that a like provision was contained in the British statutes.

Mr. Rutledge: If the Supreme Court is to judge between the United States and particular states, this alone is an insuperable objection to the motion.

Mr. Wilson considered such a provision in the British government as less dangerous than here, the House of Lords and House of Commons being less likely to concur on the same occasions. Chief Justice Holt, he remarked, had successively offended, by his independent conduct, both houses of Parliament. Had this happened at the same time he would have been ousted. The judges would be in a bad situation if made to depend on any gust of faction which might prevail in the two branches of our government.

Mr. Randolph opposed the motion as weakening too much the independence of the judges.

Mr. Dickinson was not apprehensive that the legislature, composed of different branches, constructed on such different principles, would improperly unite for the purpose of displacing a judge.

On the question for agreeing to Mr. Dickinson's motion, it was negatived.

Legislature's power to remove judiciary defeated, 7 to 1.

Judicial tenure "during good behaviour" approved, 6 to 2.

· Article III, Section 1: . . . The Judges, . . . shall, at stated Times, receive for their Services, a Compensation, which shall not be diminished during their Continuance in Office.   THE CONSTITUTION OF THE UNITED STATES

TO RECEIVE FIXED SALARIES / *June 4*

The following clauses of the ninth resolution were agreed to: "to hold their offices during good behavior, and to receive punctually, at stated times, a fixed compensation for their services, in which no increase nor diminution shall be made so as to affect the persons actually in office at the time of such increase or diminution."

"To hold their offices during good behavior, and to receive fixed salaries"—agreed to unanimously.

"In which (salaries of judges) no increase or diminution shall be made so as to affect the persons actually in office at the time."

Mr. Gouverneur Morris moved to strike out "no increase." He thought the legislature ought to be at liberty to increase salaries as circumstances might require and that this would not create any improper dependence in the judges.

Dr. Franklin was in favor of the motion. Money may not only become plentier, but the business of the department may increase as the country becomes more populous.

Mr. Madison: The dependence will be less if the increase alone should be permitted, but it will be improper even so far to permit a dependence. Whenever an increase is wished by the judges, or may be in agitation in the legislature, an undue complaisance in the former may be felt toward the latter. If at such a crisis there should be in court suits to which leading members of the legislature may be parties, the judges will be in a situation which ought not to be suffered if it can be prevented. The variations in the value of money may be guarded against by taking, for a standard, wheat or some other thing of permanent value. The increase of business will be provided for by an increase of the number who are to do it. An increase of salaries may easily be so contrived as not to affect persons in office.

Mr. Gouverneur Morris: The value of money may not only alter, but the state of society may alter. In this event, the same quantity of wheat, the same value, would not be the same compensation. The amount of salaries must always be regulated by the manners and the style of living in a country. The increase of business cannot be provided for in the supreme tribunal in the way that has been mentioned. All the business of a certain description, whether more or less, must be done in that single tribunal. Additional labor alone in the judges can provide for additional business. Additional compensation, therefore, ought not to be prohibited.

Motion to prohibit increases in judicial salaries defeated, 6 to 2.

"Judicial Review"

• Article III, Section 2: The judicial Power shall extend to all Cases, in Law and Equity, arising under this Constitution, the Laws of the United States, and Treaties made, or which shall be made, under their Authority;—to all Cases affecting Ambassadors, other public Ministers and Consuls;—to all Cases of admiralty and maritime Jurisdiction;—to Controversies to which the United States shall be a Party;—to Controversies between two or more States;—between a State and Citizens of another State;[1]—between Citizens of different States,—between Citizens of the same State claiming Lands under Grants of different States, and between a State, or the Citizens thereof, and foreign States, Citizens or Subjects.

In all Cases affecting Ambassadors, other public Ministers and Consuls, and those in which a State shall be Party, the supreme Court shall have original Jurisdiction. In all the other Cases before mentioned, the supreme Court shall have appellate Jurisdiction, both as to Law and Fact, with such Exceptions, and under such Regulations as the Congress shall make.

THE CONSTITUTION OF THE UNITED STATES

A "COUNCIL OF REVISION" INTRODUCED / *June 4*

The first clause of the eighth resolution, relating to a council of revision, was next taken into consideration.

Mr. Gerry doubts whether the judiciary ought to form a part of it, as they will have a sufficient check against encroachments on their own department by their exposition of the laws, which involved a power of deciding on their constitutionality. In some states the judges had actually set aside laws as being against the constitution. This was done, too, with general approbation. It was quite foreign from the nature of their office to make them judges of the policy of public measures. He moves to postpone the clause in order to propose "that the national executive shall have a right to negative any legislative act which shall not be afterwards passed by _____ parts of each branch of the national legislature."

Mr. King seconded the motion, observing that the judges ought to be able to expound the law, as it should come before them free from the bias of having participated in its formation.

Mr. Wilson thinks neither the original proposition nor the amendment goes far enough. If the legislature, executive, and judiciary ought to be distinct and independent, the executive ought to have an absolute negative. Without such a self-defense, the legislature can at any moment sink into non-existence. He was for varying the proposition in such a manner as to give the executive and judiciary jointly an absolute negative.

---

[1] Limited by the 11th Amendment (1798)

The question to postpone in order to take Mr. Gerry's propo-   *411*
sition into consideration was agreed to.

JUDICIAL-EXECUTIVE VETO REJECTED / *June 6*

Mr. Wilson moved to reconsider the vote excluding the judiciary from a share in the revision of the laws and to add after "national executive," the words "with a convenient number of the national judiciary," remarking the expediency of re-enforcing the executive with the influence of that department.

Mr. Madison seconded the motion. He observed that the great difficulty in rendering the executive competent to its own defense arose from the nature of republican government, which could not give to an individual citizen that settled pre-eminence in the eyes of the rest, that weight of property, that personal interest against betraying the national interest, which appertain to an hereditary magistrate. In a republic, personal merit alone could be the ground of political exaltation, but it would rarely happen that this merit would be so pre-eminent as to produce universal acquiescence. The executive magistrate would be envied and assailed by disappointed competitors; his firmness, therefore, would need support. He would not possess those great emoluments from his station, nor that permanent stake in the public interest which would place him out of the reach of foreign corruption. He would stand in need, therefore, of being controlled as well as supported. An association of the judges in his revisionary function would both double the advantage and diminish the danger. It would also enable the judiciary department the better to defend itself against legislative encroachments. Two objections had been made: first, that the judges ought not to be subject to the bias which a participation in the making of laws might give in the exposition of them; secondly, that the judiciary department ought to be separate and distinct from the other great departments. The first objection had some weight, but it was much diminished by reflecting that a small proportion of the laws coming in question before a judge would be such wherein he had been consulted that a small part of this proportion would be so ambiguous as to leave room for his prepossessions, and that but a few cases would probably arise in the life of a judge under such ambiguous passages. How much good, on the other hand, would proceed from the perspicuity, the conciseness, and the systematic character, which the code of laws would receive from the judiciary talents. As to the second objection, it either had no weight or it applied with equal weight to the executive and to the judiciary revision of the laws. The maxim on which the objection was founded required a separation of the executive, as well as the judiciary, from the legislature and from each other. There would in truth, however, be no improper mixture of these distinct powers in the present case. In England, whence the maxim itself had been drawn, the executive had an absolute negative on the laws, and the supreme tribunal of justice (the House of Lords) formed one of the other branches of the legislature. In short, whether the object of the revisionary power was to restrain the legislature from encroaching on the other co-ordinate departments or on the rights of the people at large, or from passing laws unwise in their principle or incorrect in their form, the utility of annexing the wisdom and weight of the judiciary to the executive seemed incontestable.

Mr. Gerry thought the executive, whilst standing alone, would be more impartial than when he could be covered by the sanction and seduced by the sophistry of the judges.

Mr. King. If the unity of the executive was preferred for the sake of responsibility, the policy of it is as applicable to the revisionary as to the executive power.

Mr. Pinckney had been at first in favor of joining the heads of the principal departments, the secretary at war, of foreign affairs, and so forth, in the council of revision. He had, however, relinquished the idea from a consideration that these could be called on by the executive magistrate whenever he pleased to consult them. He was opposed to the introduction of the judges into the business.

Mr. Mason was for giving all possible weight to the revisionary institution. The executive power ought to be well secured against legislative usurpations on it. The purse and the sword ought never to get into the same hands, whether legislative or executive.

Mr. Dickinson: Secrecy, vigor, and dispatch are not the principal properties required in the executive. Important as these are, that of responsibility is more so, which can only be preserved by leaving it singly to discharge its functions. He thought, too, a junction of the judiciary to it involved an improper mixture of powers.

Mr. Wilson remarked that the responsibility required belonged to his executive duties. The revisionary duty was an extraneous one, calculated for collateral purposes.

Mr. Williamson was for substituting a clause requiring two-thirds for every effective act of the legislature in place of the revisionary provision.

Motion for joining the judges to the executive in the revisionary business defeated, 8 to 3.

Mr. Wilson moved as an amendment to the tenth resolution "that the supreme national judiciary should be associated with the executive in the revisionary power." This proposition had been before made and failed, but he was so confirmed by reflection in the opinion of its utility that he thought it incumbent on him to make another effort. The judiciary ought to have an opportunity of remonstrating against projected encroachments on the people as well as on themselves. It had been said that the judges, as expositors of the laws, would have an opportunity of defending their constitutional rights. There was weight in this observation, but this power of the judges did not go far enough. Laws may be unjust, may be unwise, may be dangerous, may be destructive, and yet may not be so unconstitutional as to justify the judges in refusing to give them effect. Let them have a share in the revisionary power and they will have an opportunity of taking notice of those characters of a law, and of counteracting by the weight of their opinions the improper views of the legislature.

Mr. Madison seconded the motion.

Mr. Gorham did not see the advantage of employing the judges in this way. As judges, they are not to be presumed to possess any peculiar knowledge of the mere policy of public measures. Nor can it be necessary as a security for their constitutional rights. The judges in England have no such additional provision for their defense, yet their jurisdiction is not invaded. He thought it would be best to let the executive alone be responsible and at most to authorize him to call on the judges for their opinions.

Mr. Ellsworth approved heartily of the motion. The aid of the judges will give more wisdom and firmness to the executive. They will possess a systematic and accurate knowledge of the laws which the executive cannot be expected always to possess. The law of nations, also, will frequently come into question. Of this the judges alone will have competent information.

Mr. Madison considered the object of the motion as of great importance to the mediated Constitution. It would be useful to the judiciary department by giving it an additional opportunity of defending itself against legislative encroachments. It would be useful to the executive by inspiring additional confidence and firmness in exerting the revisionary power. It would be useful to the legislature by the valuable assistance it would give in preserving a consistency, conciseness, perspicuity, and technical propriety in the laws—qualities peculiarly necessary and yet shamefully wanting in our republican codes. It would, moreover, be useful to the community at large, as an additional check against a pursuit of those unwise and unjust measures which constituted so great a portion of our calamities. If any solid objection could be urged against the motion, it must be on the supposition that it tended to give too much strength, either to the executive or judiciary. He did not think there was the least ground for this apprehension. It was much more to be apprehended that, notwithstanding this co-operation of the two departments, the legislature would still be an overmatch for them. Experience in all the states had evinced a powerful tendency in the legislature to absorb all power into its vortex. This was the real source of danger to the American constitutions and suggested the necessity of giving every defensive authority to the other departments that was consistent with republican principles.

Mr. Mason said he had always been a friend to this provision. It would give a confidence to the executive which he would not otherwise have and without which the revisionary power would be of little avail.

Mr. Gerry did not expect to see this point, which had undergone full discussion, again revived. The object, he conceived, of the revisionary power was merely to secure the executive department against legislative encroachment. The executive, therefore, who will best know and be ready to defend his rights, ought alone to have the defense of them. The motion was liable to strong objections. It was combining and mixing together the legislative and the other departments. It was establishing an improper coalition between the executive and judiciary departments. It was making statesmen of the judges and setting them up as the guardians of the rights of the people. He relied, for his part, on the representatives of the people as the guardians of their rights and interests. It was making the expositors of the laws, the legislators, which ought never to be done. A better expedient for correcting the laws would be to appoint, as had been done in Pennsylvania, a person or persons of proper skill to draw bills for the legislature.

Mr. Strong thought, with Mr. Gerry, that the power of making ought to be kept distinct from that of expounding the laws. No maxim was better established. The judges in exercising the function of expositors might be influenced by the part they had taken in passing the laws.

Mr. Gouverneur Morris: Some check being necessary on the legislature, the question is in what hands it should be lodged. On one side, it was contended that the executive alone ought to exercise it. He did not think that an executive appointed for six years and impeachable whilst in office would be a very effectual check. On the other side, it was urged that he ought to be re-enforced by the judiciary department. Against this it was objected that expositors of laws ought to have no hand in making them and arguments in favor of this had been drawn from England. What weight was due to them might be easily determined by an attention to facts. The truth was that the judges in England had a great share in the legislation. They are consulted in difficult and doubtful cases. They may be, and some of them are, members of the legislature. They are, or may be, members of the privy council and can there advise the executive, as they will do with us if the motion succeeds. The influence the English judges may have in the latter capacity, in strengthening the executive check, cannot be ascertained, as the King by his influence in a manner dictates the laws. There is one difference in the two cases, however, which disconcerts all reasoning from the British to our proposed Constitution. The British executive has so great an interest in his prerogatives and such power for means of defending them that he will never yield any part of them. The interest of our executive is so inconsiderable and so transitory and his means of defending it so feeble that there is the justest ground to fear his want of firmness in resisting encroachments. He was extremely apprehensive that the auxiliary firmness and weight of the judiciary would not supply the deficiency. He concurred in thinking the public liberty in greater danger from legislative usurpations than from any other source. It had been said that the legislature ought to be relied on as the proper guardians of liberty. The answer was short and conclusive. Either bad laws will be pursued or not. On the latter supposition, no check will be wanted; on the former, a strong check will be necessary. And this is the proper supposition. Emissions of paper money, largesses to the people, a remission of debts, and similar measures will at some times be popular and will be pushed for that reason. At other times, such measures will coincide with the interests of the legislature themselves, and that will be a reason not less cogent for pushing them. It may be thought that the people will not be deluded and misled in the latter case, but experience teaches another lesson. The press is indeed a great means of diminishing the evil, yet it is found to be unable to prevent it altogether.

Mr. L. Martin considered the association of the judges with the executive as a dangerous innovation, as well as one that could not produce the particular advantage expected from it. A knowledge of mankind and of legislative affairs cannot be presumed to belong in a higher degree to the judges than to the legislature. And as to the constitutionality of laws, that point will come before the judges in their official character. In this character they have a negative on the laws. Join them with the executive in the revision and they will have a double negative. It is necessary that the supreme judiciary should have the confidence of the people. This will soon be lost if they are employed in the task of remonstrating against popular measures of the legislature. Besides, in what mode and proportion are they to vote in the council of revision?

Mr. Madison could not discover in the proposed association of the judges with the executive, in the revisionary check on the legislature, any violation of the maxim which requires the great departments of power to be kept separate and distinct. On the contrary, he thought it an auxiliary precaution in favor of the maxim. If a constitutional discrimination of the departments on paper were a sufficient security to each against encroachments of the others, all further provisions would indeed be superfluous. But experience had taught us a distrust of that security and that it is necessary to introduce such a balance of powers and interests as will guaranty the provisions on paper. Instead, therefore, of contenting ourselves with laying down the theory in the Constitution that each department ought to be separate and distinct, it was proposed to add a defensive power to each, which should maintain the theory in practice. In so doing, we did not blend the departments together. We erected effectual barriers for keeping them separate. The most regular example of this theory was in the British constitution. Yet it was not only the practice there to admit the judges to a seat in the legislature and in the executive councils, and submit to their previous examination all laws of a certain description, but it was a part of their constitution that the executive might negative any law whatever; a part of *their* constitution, which had been universally regarded as calculated for the preservation of the whole. The objection against a union of the judiciary and executive branches in the revision of the laws had either no foundation or was not carried far enough. If such a union was an improper mixture of powers or such a judiciary check on the laws was inconsistent with the theory of a free constitution, it was equally so to admit the executive to any participation in the making of laws and the revisionary plan ought to be discarded altogether.

Mr. Mason observed that the defense of the executive was not the sole object of the revisionary power. He expected even greater advantages from it. Notwithstanding the precautions taken in the constitution of the legislature, it would still so much resemble that of the individual states that it must be expected frequently to pass unjust and pernicious laws. This restraining power was therefore essentially necessary. It would have the effect not only of hindering the final passage of such laws, but would discourage demagogues from attempting to get them passed. It has been said (by Mr. L. Martin) that if the judges were joined in this check on the laws, they would have a double negative, since in their expository capacity of judges they would have one negative. He would reply that in this capacity they could impede in one case only the operation of laws. They could declare an unconstitutional law void. But with regard to every law, however unjust, oppressive, or pernicious, that did not come plainly under this description, they would be under the necessity as judges to give it a free course. He wished the further use to be made of the judges of giving aid in preventing every improper law. Their aid will be the more valuable as they are in the habit and practice of considering laws in their true principles and in all their consequences.

Mr. Wilson: The separation of the departments does not require that they should have separate objects, but that they should act separately, though on the same objects. It is necessary that the two branches of the legislature should be separate and distinct, yet they are both to act precisely on the same object.

Mr. Gerry had rather give the executive an absolute negative for its own defense than thus to blend together the judiciary and executive departments. It will bind them together in an offensive and defensive alliance against the legislature and render the latter unwilling to enter into a contest with them.

Mr. Gouverneur Morris was surprised that any defensive provision for securing the effectual separation of the departments should be considered as an improper mixture of them. Suppose that the three powers were to be vested in three persons by compact among themselves; that one was to have the power of making, another of executing, and a third of judging, the laws. Would it not be very natural for the two latter, after having settled the partition on paper, to observe, and would not candor oblige the former to admit, that as a security against legislative acts of the former, which might easily be so framed as to undermine the powers of the two others, the two others ought to be armed with a veto for their own defense, or at least to have an opportunity of stating their objections against acts of encroachment? And would anyone pretend that such a right tended to blend and confound powers that ought to be separately exercised? As well might it be said that if three neighbors had three distinct farms, a right in each to defend his farm against his neighbors tended to blend the farms together.

Mr. Gorham: All agree that a check on the legislature is necessary. But there are two objections against admitting the judges to share in it which no observations on the other side seem to obviate. The first is that the judges ought to carry into the exposition of the laws no prepossessions with regard to them; the second, that as the judges will outnumber the executive, the revisionary check would be thrown entirely out of the executive hands and, instead of enabling him to defend himself, would enable the judges to sacrifice him.

Mr. Wilson: The proposition is certainly not liable to all the objections which have been urged against it. According to Mr. Gerry, it will unite the executive and judiciary in an offensive and defensive alliance against the legislature. According to Mr. Gorham, it will lead to a subversion of the executive by the judiciary influence. To the first gentleman the answer was obvious—that the joint weight of the two departments was necessary to balance the single weight of the legislature. To the first objection stated by the other gentleman, it might be answered that supposing the prepossession to mix itself with the exposition, the evil would be overbalanced by the advantages promised by the expedient; to the second objection, that such a rule of voting might be provided in the detail as would guard against it.

Mr. Rutledge thought the judges of all men the most unfit to be concerned in the revisionary council. The judges ought never to give their opinion on a law till it comes before them. He thought it equally unnecessary. The executive could advise with the officers of state, as of war, finance, and so forth, and avail himself of their information and opinions.

The question on Mr. Wilson's motion for joining the judiciary in the revision of laws passed in the negative.

Attempt to join judiciary to executive in veto power over legislature defeated, 4 to 3.

• Article III, Section 2: . . . The Trial of all Crimes, except in Cases of Impeachment, shall be by Jury; and such Trial shall be held in the State where the said Crimes shall have been committed; but when not committed within any State, the Trial shall be at such Place or Places as the Congress may by Law have directed.   THE CONSTITUTION OF THE UNITED STATES

Editor's note: Randolph's original resolutions had no provision for trials by jury in criminal cases, but the Committee of Detail included it in its judiciary article. It came to the floor of the convention on August 28, was amended slightly, and accepted without debate or dissent. Jury trials in civil cases were eventually guaranteed by Article VII of the Bill of Rights.

Amendment

CHAPTER SIX

• Article V: The Congress, whenever two thirds of both Houses shall deem it necessary, shall propose Amendments to this Constitution, or, on the Application of the Legislatures of two thirds of the several States, shall call a Convention for proposing Amendments, which, in either Case, shall be valid to all Intents and Purposes, as Part of this Constitution, when ratified by the Legislatures of three fourths of the several States, or by Conventions in three fourths thereof, as the one or the other Mode of Ratification may be proposed by the Congress; Provided that no Amendment which may be made prior to the Year One thousand eight hundred and eight shall in any Manner affect the first and fourth Clauses in the Ninth Section of the first Article; and that no State, without its Consent, shall be deprived of its equal Suffrage in the Senate.

THE CONSTITUTION OF THE UNITED STATES

AMENDMENT PROCEDURE DEBATED / *September 10*

Mr. Gerry moved to reconsider Article 19, "On the application of the legislatures of two-thirds of the states in the Union, for an amendment of this Constitution, the legislature of the United States shall call a convention for that purpose."

This Constitution, he said, is to be paramount to the state constitutions. It follows, hence, from this article, that two-thirds of the states may obtain a convention, a majority of which can bind the Union to innovations that may subvert the state constitutions altogether. He asked whether this was a situation proper to be run into.

Mr. Hamilton seconded the motion, but, he said, with a different view from Mr. Gerry. He did not object to the consequences stated by Mr. Gerry. There was no greater evil in subjecting the people of the United States to the major voice than the people of a particular state. It had been wished by many and was much to have been desired that an easier mode of introducing amendments had been provided by the Articles of the Confederation. It was equally desirable now that an easy mode should be established for supplying defects which will probably appear in the new system. The mode proposed was not adequate. The state legislatures will not apply for alterations, but with a view to increase their own powers. The national legislature will be the first to perceive, and will be most sensible to the necessity of, amendments and ought also to be empowered, whenever two-thirds of each branch should concur, to call a convention. There could be no danger in giving this power, as the people would finally decide in the case.

Mr. Madison remarked on the vagueness of the terms, "call a convention for the purpose," as sufficient reason for reconsidering the article. How was a convention to be formed? By what rule decide? What the force of its acts?

Mr. Gerry's motion passed, 9 to 1.

Mr. Sherman moved to add to the article:

". . . or the legislature may propose amendments to the several states for their approbation, but no amendments shall be binding until consented to by the several states."

Mr. Gerry seconded the motion.

Mr. Wilson moved to insert "two-thirds of" before the words "several states," as an amendment to the motion of Mr. Sherman.

Motion defeated, 6 to 5.

Mr. Wilson then moved to insert "three-fourths of" before "the several states," which was agreed to.

Mr. Madison moved to postpone the consideration of the amended proposition in order to take up the following:

"The legislature of the United States, whenever two-thirds of both houses shall deem necessary, or on the application of two-thirds of the legislatures of the several states, shall propose amendments to this Constitution, which shall be valid, to all intents and purposes, as part thereof, when the same shall have been ratified by three-fourths, at least, of the legislatures of the several states, or by conventions in three-fourths thereof, as one or the other mode of ratification may be proposed by the legislature of the United States."

Mr. Hamilton seconded the motion.

Mr. Rutledge said he never could agree to give a power by which the articles relating to slaves might be altered by the states not interested in that property and prejudiced against it. In order to obviate this objection, these words were added to the proposition: "provided that no amendments, which may be made prior to the year 1808, shall in any manner affect the Fourth and Fifth Sections of the Seventh Article."

The postponement being agreed to, the proposition of Mr. Madison and Mr. Hamilton, as amended, passed, 9 to 1.

AMENDMENT ON APPLICATION OF TWO-THIRDS OF STATES APPROVED / September 15

Article 4, Section 4. After the word "executive" were inserted the words "when the legislature cannot be convened."

Article 5: "The Congress, whenever two-thirds of both Houses shall deem necessary, or on the application of two-thirds of the legislatures of the several states, shall propose, amendments to this Constitution, which shall be valid to all intents and purposes as part thereof, when the same shall have been ratified by three-fourths at least of the legislatures of the several states, or by conventions in three-fourths thereof, as the one or the other mode of ratification may be proposed by the Congress: provided, that no amendment which may be made prior to the year 1808 shall in any manner affect the first and fourth clauses in the ninth section of article 1."

Mr. Sherman expressed his fears that three-fourths of the states might be brought to do things fatal to particular states, as abolishing them altogether or depriving them of their equality in the Senate. He thought it reasonable that the proviso in favor of the states importing slaves should be extended so as to provide that no state should be affected in its internal police or deprived of its equality in the Senate.

Mr. Mason thought the plan of amending the Constitution exceptionable and dangerous. As the proposing of amendments is in both the modes to depend, in the first immediately, and in the second ultimately, on Congress, no amendments of the proper kind would ever be obtained by the people if the government should become oppressive, as he verily believed would be the case.

Mr. Gouverneur Morris and Mr. Gerry moved to amend the article so as to require a convention on application of two-thirds of the states.

Mr. Madison did not see why Congress would not be as much bound to propose amendments applied for by two-thirds of the states as to call a convention on the like application. He saw no objection, however, against providing for a convention for the purpose of amendments, except only that difficulties might arise as to the form, the quorum, and so forth, which in constitutional regulations ought to be as much as possible avoided.

The motion of Gouverneur Morris and Mr. Gerry was agreed to.

Mr. Sherman moved to strike out of Article 5, after "legislatures," the words "of three-fourths," and so after the word "conventions," leaving future conventions to act in this matter, like the present convention, according to circumstances.

Motion defeated, 7 to 3.

Mr. Gerry moved to strike out the words "or by conventions in three-fourths thereof."

Motion defeated, 10 to 1.

Ratification

CHAPTER SEVEN

• Article VII: The Ratification of the Conventions of nine States, shall be sufficient for the Establishment of this Constitution between the States so ratifying the Same. THE CONSTITUTION OF THE UNITED STATES

THE RATIFICATION PROBLEM INTRODUCED / *June 5*

The fifteenth resolution, for "recommending conventions under appointment of the people to ratify the new Constitution," and so forth, being taken up, Mr. Sherman thought such a popular ratification unnecessary, the Articles of Confederation providing for changes and alterations with the assent of Congress and ratification of state legislatures.

Mr. Madison thought this provision essential. The Articles of Confederation themselves were defective in this respect, resting in many of the states on the legislative sanction only. Hence, in conflicts between acts of the states and of Congress, especially where the former are of posterior date and the decision is to be made by state tribunals, an uncertainty must necessarily prevail, or rather, perhaps, a certain decision in favor of the state authority. He suggested also that as far as the Articles of Union were to be considered as a treaty only of a particular sort among the governments of independent states, the doctrine might be set up that a breach of any one article by any of the parties absolved the other parties from the whole obligation. For these reasons, as well as others, he thought it indispensable that the new Constitution should be ratified in the most unexceptionable form and by the supreme authority of the people themselves.

Mr. Gerry observed that in the eastern states the Confederation had been sanctioned by the people themselves. He seemed afraid of referring the new system to them. The people in that quarter have at this time the wildest ideas of government in the world. They were for abolishing the Senate in Massachusetts, and giving all the other powers of government to the other branch of the legislature.

Mr. King supposed that the last article of the Confederation rendered the legislature competent to the ratification. The people of the southern states, where the Federal Articles had been ratified by the legislatures only, had since, impliedly, given their sanction to it. He thought, notwithstanding, that there might be policy in varying the mode. A convention being a single house, the adoption may more easily be carried through it than through the legislatures, where there are several branches. The legislatures, also, being (liable) to lose power, will be most likely to raise objections. The people having already parted with the necessary powers, it is immaterial to them by which government they are possessed, provided they be well employed.

Mr. Wilson took this occasion to lead the committee by a train of observations to the idea of not suffering a disposition, in the plurality of states, to confederate anew on better principles, to be defeated by the inconsiderate or selfish opposition of a few states. He hoped the provision for ratifying would be put on such a footing as to admit of such a partial union with a door open for the accession of the rest.

Mr. Pinckney hoped that in case the experiment should not unanimously take place, nine states might be authorized to unite under the same government.

The fifteenth resolution was postponed by unanimous vote.

In committee of the whole. The question was taken on the fifteenth resolution, to wit, referring the new system to the people of the United States for ratification.

It passed in the affirmative.

MODE OF RATIFICATION DEBATED / July 23

The nineteenth resolution, referring the new Constitution to assemblies to be chosen by the people for the express purpose of ratifying it, was next taken into consideration.

Mr. Ellsworth moved that it be referred to the legislatures of the states for ratification. Mr. Paterson seconded the motion.

Mr. Mason considered a reference of the plan to the authority of the people as one of the most important and essential of the resolutions. The legislatures have no power to ratify it. They are the mere creatures of the state constitutions and cannot be greater than their creators. And he knew of no power in any of the constitutions—he knew there was no power in some of them—that could be competent to this object. Whither, then, must we resort? To the people, with whom all power remains that has not been given up in the constitutions derived from them. It was of great moment, he observed, that this doctrine should be cherished as the basis of free government. Another strong reason was that, admitting the legislatures to have a competent authority, it would be wrong to refer the plan to them, because succeeding legislatures, having equal authority, could undo the acts of their predecessors and the national Government would stand in each state on the weak and tottering foundation of an act of assembly. There was a remaining consideration of some weight. In some of the states the governments were not derived from the clear and undisputed authority of the people. This was the case in Virginia. Some of the best and wisest citizens considered the constitution as established by an assumed authority. A national Constitution derived from such a source would be exposed to the severest criticism.

Mr. Randolph: One idea has pervaded all our proceedings, to wit, that opposition as well from the states as from individuals will be made to the system to be proposed. Will it not then be highly imprudent to furnish any unnecessary pretext by the mode of ratifying it? Added to other objections against a ratification by the legislative authority only, it may be remarked that there have been instances in which the authority of the common law has been set up in particular states against that of the Confederation, which has had no higher sanction than legislative ratification. Whose opposition will be most likely to be excited against the system? That of the local demagogues, who will be degraded by it from the importance they now hold. These will spare no efforts to impede that progress in the popular mind which will be necessary to the adoption of the plan and which every member will find to have taken place in his own, if he will compare his present opinions with those he brought with him into the convention. It is of great importance, therefore, that the consideration of this subject should be transferred from the legislatures, where this class of men have their full influence, to a field in which their efforts can be less mischievous. It is, moreover, worthy of consideration that some of the states are averse to any change in their constitutions and will not take the requisite steps, unless expressly called upon, to refer the question to the people.

Mr. Gerry: The arguments of Col. Mason and Mr. Randolph prove too much. They prove an unconstitutionality in the present federal system and even in some of the state governments. Inferences drawn from such a source must be inadmissible. Both the state and the Federal Government have been too long acquiesced in to be now shaken. He considered the Confederation to be paramount to any state constitution. The last article of it, authorizing alterations, must, consequently, be so well as the others, and everything done in pursuance of the article must have the same high authority with the article. Great confusion, he was confident, would result from a recurrence to the people. They would never agree on anything. He could not see any ground to suppose that the people will do what their rulers will not. The rulers will either conform to or influence the sense of the people.

Mr. Gorham was against referring the plan to the legislatures. 1. Men chosen by the people for the particular purpose will discuss the subject more candidly than members of the legislature, who are to lose the power which is to be given up to the General Government. 2. Some of the legislatures are composed of several branches. It will consequently be more difficult in these cases to get the plan through the legislatures than through a convention. 3. In the states many of the ablest men are excluded from the legislatures, but may be elected into a convention. Among these may be ranked many of the clergy, who are generally friends to good government. Their services were found to be valuable in the formation and establishment of the Constitution of Massachusetts. 4. The legislatures will be interrupted with a variety of little business, by artfully pressing which, designing men will find means to delay from year to year, if not to frustrate altogether, the national system. 5. If the last Article of the Confederation is to be pursued, the unanimous concurrence of the states will be necessary. But will anyone say that all the states are to suffer themselves to be ruined if Rhode Island should persist in her opposition to general measures? Some other states might also tread in her steps. The present advantage, which New York seems to be so much attached to, of taxing her neighbors by the regulation of her trade, makes it very probable that she will be of the number. It would, therefore, deserve serious consideration whether provision ought not to be made for giving effect to the system without waiting for the unanimous concurrence of the states.

Mr. Ellsworth: If there be any legislatures who should find themselves incompetent to the ratification, he should be content to let them advise with their constituents and pursue such a mode as would be competent. He thought more was to be expected from the legislatures than from the people. The prevailing wish of the people in the eastern states is to get rid of the public debt and the idea of strengthening the national Government carries with it that of strengthening the public debt. It was said by Col. Mason, in the first place, that the legislatures have no authority in this case, and in the second, that their successors, having equal authority, could rescind their acts. As to the second point, he could not admit it to be well-founded. An act to which the states by their legislatures make themselves parties becomes a compact from which no one of the parties can recede of itself. As to the first point, he observed that a new set of ideas seemed to have crept in since the Articles of Confederation were established. Conventions of the people or with power derived expressly from the people were not then thought of. The legislatures were considered as competent. Their ratification has been acquiesced in without complaint. To whom have Congress applied on subsequent occasions for further powers? To the legislatures, not to the people. The fact is that we exist at present, and we need not inquire how, as a Federal society united by a character, one article of which is that alterations therein may be made by the legislative authority of the states. It has been said that if the Confederation is to be observed, the states must unanimously concur in the proposed innovations. He would answer that if such were the urgency and necessity of our situation as to warrant a new compact among a part of the states founded on the consent of the people, the same pleas would be equally valid in favor of a partial compact founded on the consent of the legislatures.

Mr. Williamson thought the resolution (the nineteenth) so expressed as that it might be submitted either to the legislatures or to conventions recommended by the legislatures. He observed that some legislatures were evidently unauthorized to ratify the system. He thought, too, that conventions were to be preferred as more likely to be composed of the ablest men in the states.

Mr. Gouverneur Morris considered the inference of Mr. Ellsworth from the plea of necessity, as applied to the establishment of a new system on the consent of the people of a part of the states, in favor of a like establishment on the consent of a part of the legislatures, as a non sequitur. If the Confederation is to be pursued, no alteration can be made without the unanimous consent of the legislatures. Legislative alterations not conformable to the Federal compact would clearly not be valid. The judges would consider them as null and void. Whereas in case of an appeal to the people of the United States, the supreme authority, the Federal compact may be altered by a majority of them in like manner as the constitution of a particular state may be altered by a majority of the people of the state. The amendment moved by Mr. Ellsworth erroneously supposes that we are proceeding on the basis of the Confederation. This convention is unknown to the Confederation.

Mr. King thought with Mr. Ellsworth that the legislatures had a competent authority, the acquiescence of the people of America in the Confederation being equivalent to a formal ratification by the people. He thought with Mr. Ellsworth, also, that the plea of necessity was as valid in the one case as the other. At the same time, he preferred a reference to the authority of the people expressly delegated to conventions as the most certain means of obviating all disputes and doubts concerning the legitimacy of the new Constitution as well as the most likely means of drawing forth the best men in the states to decide on it. He remarked that among other objections made in the state of New York to granting powers to Congress, one had been that such power as would operate within the states could not be reconciled to the Constitution and, therefore, were not grantable by the legislative authority. He considered it as of some consequence also to get rid of the scruples which some members of the state legislature might derive from their oaths to support and maintain the existing constitutions.

Mr. Madison thought it clear that the legislatures were incompetent to the proposed changes. These changes would make essential inroads on the state constitutions and it would be a novel and dangerous doctrine that a legislature could change the constitution under which it held its existence. There might indeed be some constitutions within the Union which had given a power to the legislature to concur in alterations of the Federal compact. But there were certainly some which had not, and in the case of these a ratification must of necessity be obtained from the people. He considered the difference between a system founded on the legislatures only, and one founded on the people, to be the true difference between a league or treaty and a constitution. The former, in point of moral obligation, might be as inviolable as the latter. In point of political operation, there were two important distinctions in favor of the latter. First, a law violating a treaty ratified by a pre-existing law might be respected by the judges as a law, though an unwise or perfidious one. A law violating a constitution established by the people themselves would be considered by the judges as null and void. Secondly, the doctrine laid down by the law of nations in the case of treaties is that a breach of any one article by any of the parties frees the other parties from their engagements. In the case of a union of people under one constitution, the nature of the pact has always been understood to exclude such an interpretation. Comparing the two modes in point of expediency, he thought all the considerations which recommended this convention in preference to Congress for proposing the reform were in favor of state conventions in preference to the legislatures for examining and adopting it.

Question on Mr. Ellsworth's motion to refer the plan to the legislatures of the states defeated, 7 to 3.

Mr. Gouverneur Morris moved that the reference of the plan be made to one general convention, chosen and authorized by the people, to consider, amend, and establish the same. The motion was not seconded.

Ratification by "assemblies chosen by the people" passed, 9 to 1.

Article 21 being then taken up, "The ratifications of the conventions of _____ states shall be sufficient for organizing this Constitution," Mr. Wilson proposed to fill the blank with "seven," that being a majority of the whole number and sufficient for the commencement of the plan.

Mr. Carroll moved to postpone the article in order to take up the report of the committee of eleven, and the question was defeated, 8 to 3.

Mr. Gouverneur Morris thought the blank ought to be filled in a twofold way so as to provide for the event of the ratifying states being contiguous, which would render a smaller number sufficient, and the event of their being dispersed, which would require a greater number for the introduction of the government.

Mr. Sherman observed that the states being now confederated by articles which require unanimity in changes, he thought the ratification in this case of ten states, at least, ought to be made necessary.

Mr. Randolph was for filling the blank with "nine," that being a respectable majority of the whole and being a number made familiar by the constitution of the existing Congress.

Mr. Wilson mentioned "eight" as preferable.

Mr. Dickinson asked whether the concurrence of Congress is to be essential to the establishment of the system—whether the refusing states in the Confederacy could be deserted—and whether Congress could concur in contravening the system under which they acted.

Mr. Madison remarked that if the blank should be filled with "seven," "eight," or "nine" the Constitution, as it stands, might be put in force over the whole body of the people, though less than a majority of them should ratify it.

Mr. Wilson: As the Constitution stands, the states only which ratify can be bound. We must, he said, in this case go to the original powers of society. The house on fire must be extinguished without a scrupulous regard to ordinary rights.

Mr. Butler was in favor of "nine." He revolted at the idea that one or two states should restrain the rest from consulting their safety.

Mr. Carroll moved to fill the blank with "the thirteen," unanimity being necessary to dissolve the existing Confederacy which had been unanimously established.

Mr. King thought this amendment necessary; otherwise, as the Constitution now stands, it will operate on the whole though ratified by a part only.

Adjourned.

In convention. Mr. King moved to add to the end of Article 21 the words "between the said states," so as to confine the operation of the government to the states ratifying it.

The question passed, 9 to 1. Maryland voted no; Delaware was absent.

Mr. Madison proposed to fill the blank in the article with—"any seven or more states entitled to thirty-three members at least in the House of Representatives according to the allotment made in the Third Section of Article 4." This, he said, would require the concurrence of a majority of both the states and the people.

Mr. Sherman doubted the propriety of authorizing less than all the states to execute the Constitution, considering the nature of the existing Confederation. Perhaps all the states may concur, and on that supposition it is needless to hold out a breach of faith.

Mr. Clymer and Mr. Carroll moved to postpone the consideration of Article 21 in order to take up the reports of committees not yet acted on.

On this question the states were equally divided.

Mr. Gouverneur Morris moved to strike out "conventions of the," after "ratifications," leaving the states to pursue their own modes of ratification.

Mr. Carroll mentioned the mode of altering the Constitution of Maryland, pointed out therein, and that no other mode could be pursued in that state.

Mr. King thought that striking out "conventions" as the requisite mode was equivalent to giving up the business altogether. Conventions alone, which will avoid all the obstacles from the complicated formation of the legislatures, will succeed, and if not positively required by the plan, its enemies will oppose that mode.

Mr. Gouverneur Morris said he meant to facilitate the adoption of the plan by leaving the modes approved by the several state constitutions to be followed.

Mr. Madison considered it best to require conventions; among other reasons for this, that the powers given to the General Government being taken from the state governments, the legislatures would be more disinclined than conventions composed in part, at least, of other men, and if disinclined, they could devise modes apparently promoting, but really thwarting, the ratification. The difficulty in Maryland was no greater than in other states where no mode of change was pointed out by the constitution and all officers were under oath to support it. The people were, in fact, the fountain of all power and by resorting to them all difficulties were got over. They could alter constitutions as they pleased. It was a principle in the bills of rights that first principles might be resorted to.

Mr. McHenry said that the officers of government in Maryland were under oath to support the mode of alteration prescribed by the constitution.

Mr. Gorham urged the expediency of "conventions"; also Mr. Pinckney, for reasons formerly urged on a discussion of the question.

Mr. L. Martin insisted on a reference to the state legislatures. He urged the danger of commotions from a resort to the people and to first principles in which the government might be on one side and the people on the other. He was apprehensive of no such consequences, however, in Maryland, whether the legislature or the people should be appealed to. Both of them would be generally against the Constitution. He repeated also the peculiarity in the Maryland Constitution.

Mr. King observed that the Constitution of Massachusetts was made unalterable till the year 1790; yet this was no difficulty with him. The state must have contemplated a recurrence to first principles before they sent deputies to this convention.

Mr. Sherman moved to postpone Article 21 and to take up Article 22, which question was defeated, 6 to 5.

Mr. Gouverneur Morris' motion to strike out "conventions of the" was negatived, 6 to 4.

On the question for filling the blank in Article 21 with "thirteen," moved by Mr. Carroll and Mr. L. Martin, all states voted no, except Maryland.

Mr. Sherman and Mr. Dayton moved to fill the blank with "ten."

Mr. Wilson supported the motion of Mr. Madison requiring a majority both of the people and of states.

Mr. Clymer was also in favor of it.

Mr. Mason was for preserving ideas familiar to the people. Nine states had been required in all great cases under the Confederation and that number was on that account preferable.

The question for "ten" was defeated, 7 to 4.

The question for "nine" was passed, 8 to 3.

Article 21, as amended, was then agreed to by all the states, Maryland excepted, and Mr. Jenifer being aye.

Article 22 was then taken up, to wit—"This Constitution shall be laid before the United States, in Congress assembled, for their approbation; and it is the opinion of this convention that it should be afterwards submitted to a convention chosen in each state under the recommendation of its legislature in order to receive the ratification of such convention."

Mr. Gouverneur Morris and Mr. Pinckney moved to strike out the words "for their approbation."

The question passed, 8 to 3.

Mr. Gouverneur Morris and Mr. Pinckney then moved to amend the article so as to read:

"This Constitution shall be laid before the United States, in Congress assembled; and it is the opinion of this convention, that it should afterwards be submitted to a convention chosen in each state in order to receive the ratification of such convention; to which end the several legislatures ought to provide for the calling conventions within their respective states as speedily as circumstances will permit."

Mr. Gouverneur Morris said his object was to impress in stronger terms the necessity of calling conventions in order to prevent enemies to the plan from giving it the go-by. When it first appears with the sanction of this convention, the people will be favorable to it. By degrees the state officers and those interested in the state governments will intrigue and turn the popular current against it.

Mr. L. Martin believed Mr. Morris to be right, that after a while the people would be against it, but for a different reason from that alleged. He believed they would not ratify it unless hurried into it by surprise.

Mr. Gerry enlarged on the idea of Mr. L. Martin, in which he concurred; represented the system as full of vices, and dwelt on the impropriety of destroying the existing Confederation without the unanimous consent of the parties to it.

Ratification by nine states approved, 8 to 3.

Mr. Mason seconded the motion, declaring that he would sooner chop off his right hand than put it to the Constitution as it now stands. He wished to see some points not yet decided brought to a decision before being compelled to give a final opinion on this article. Should these points be improperly settled, his wish would then be to bring the whole subject before another general convention.

Mr. Gouverneur Morris was ready for a postponement. He had long wished for another convention that will have the firmness to provide a vigorous government, which we are afraid to do.

Mr. Randolph stated his idea to be, in case the final form of the Constitution should not permit him to accede to it, that the state conventions should be at liberty to propose amendments to be sub-

mitted to another general convention which may reject or incorporate them as may be judged proper. *439*
Postponement question defeated, 8 to 3.

APPROBATION OF CONGRESS REJECTED / *September 10*

Mr. Gerry moved to reconsider Articles 21 and 22, from the latter of which "for the approbation of Congress" had been struck out. He objected to proceeding to change the government without the approbation of Congress as being improper and giving just umbrage to that body. He repeated his objections also to an annulment of the Confederation with so little scruple or formality.

Mr. Hamilton concurred with Mr. Gerry as to the indecorum of not requiring the approbation of Congress. He considered this as a necessary ingredient in the transaction. He thought it wrong, also, to allow nine states, as provided by Article 21, to institute a new government on the ruins of the existing one. He would propose as a better modification of the two articles (21 and 22) that the plan should be sent to Congress in order that the same, if approved by them, may be communicated to the state legislatures to the end that they may refer it to state conventions; each legislature declaring that if the convention of the state should think the plan ought to take effect among nine ratifying states, the same should take effect accordingly.

Mr. Gorham: Some states will say that nine states shall be sufficient to establish the plan; others will require unanimity for the purpose, and the different and conditional ratifications will defeat the plan altogether.

Mr. Hamilton: No convention convinced of the necessity of the plan will refuse to give it effect on the adoption by nine states. He thought this mode less exceptionable than the one proposed in the article, while it would attain the same end.

Mr. Fitzsimmons remarked that the words "for their approbation" had been struck out in order to save Congress from the necessity of an act inconsistent with the Articles of Confederation under which they held their authority.

Mr. Randolph declared if no change should be made in this part of the plan, he should be obliged to dissent from the whole of it. He had from the beginning, he said, been convinced that radical changes in the system of the Union were necessary. Under this conviction, he had brought forward a set of republican propositions as the basis and outline of a reform. These republican propositions had, however, much to his regret, been widely and, in his opinion, irreconcilably departed from. In this state of things, it was his idea, and he accordingly meant to propose, that the state conventions should be at liberty to offer amendments to the plan and that these should be submitted to a second general convention with full power to settle the Constitution finally. He did not expect to succeed in this proposition, but the discharge of his duty in making the attempt would give quiet to his own mind.

Mr. Wilson was against a reconsideration for any of the purposes which had been mentioned.

Mr. King thought it would be more respectful to Congress to submit the plan generally to them than in such a form as expressly and necessarily to require their approbation or disapprobation. The assent of nine states he considered as sufficient and that it was more proper to make this a part of the Constitution itself than to provide for it by a supplemental or distinct recommendation.

Mr. Gerry urged the indecency and pernicious tendency of dissolving in so slight a manner the solemn obligations of the Articles of Confederation. If nine out of thirteen can dissolve the compact, six out of nine will be just as able to dissolve the new one hereafter.

Mr. Sherman was in favor of Mr. King's idea of submitting the plan generally to Congress. He thought nine states ought to be made sufficient, but that it would be better to make it a separate act, and in some such form as that intimated by Col. Hamilton, than to make it a particular article of the Constitution.

Mr. Hamilton then moved to postpone Article 21, in order to take up the following (resolution):

"Resolved, that the foregoing plan of a Constitution be transmitted to the United States in Congress assembled, in order that . . . it may be communicated to the legislatures of the several states to the end that they may provide for its final ratification . . . ; and that it be recommended to the said legislatures . . . to declare that if the said convention shall approve of the said Constitution, such approbation shall be binding and conclusive upon the state; and further that if the said convention that'll be of opinion that the same, upon the assent of any nine states thereto, ought to take effect between the states so assenting, such opinion shall thereupon be also binding upon such a state, and the said Constitution shall take effect between the states assenting thereto."

Mr. Gerry seconded the motion.

Mr. Wilson: This motion being seconded, it is necessary now to speak freely. He expressed in strong terms his disapprobation of the expedient proposed, particularly the suspending the plan of the convention on the approbation of Congress. He declared it to be worse than folly to rely on the concurrence of the Rhode Island members of Congress in the plan. Maryland had voted on this floor for requiring the unanimous assent of the thirteen states to the proposed change in the federal system. New York has not been represented for a long time past in the convention. Many individual deputies from other states have spoken much against the plan. Under these circumstances can it be safe to make the assent of Congress necessary? After spending four or five months in the laborious and arduous task of forming a government for our country, we are ourselves throwing insuperable obstacles in the way of its success.

Mr. Clymer thought that the mode proposed by Mr. Hamilton would fetter and embarrass Congress as much as the original one, since it equally involved a breach of the Articles of Confederation.

Mr. King concurred with Mr. Clymer. If Congress can accede to one mode, they can to the other. If the approbation of Congress be made necessary and they should not approve, the state legislatures will not propose the plan to conventions, or if the states themselves are to provide that nine states shall suffice to establish the system, that provision will be omitted, everything will go into confusion, and all our labor be lost.

Mr. Rutledge viewed the matter in the same light with Mr. King.

The question to postpone in order to take up Mr. Hamilton's motion was defeated, 10 to 1.

A question being then taken on the Article 21, it was agreed to unanimously.

Mr. Hamilton withdrew the remainder of the motion to postpone Article 22, observing that his purpose was defeated by the vote just given.

Mr. Williamson and Mr. Gerry moved to reinstate the words "for the approbation of Congress" in Article 22, which was disagreed to unanimously.

The Document

THE DRAFTING COMMITTEE / July 23

Mr. Gerry moved that the proceedings of the convention for the establishment of a national Government (except the part relating to the executive) be referred to a committee to prepare and report a constitution conformable thereto.

The appointment of a committee as moved by Mr. Gerry was agreed to.

The question, "Shall the committee consist of ten members, one from each state present?" was defeated, 10 to 1.

The vote on the question, "Shall it consist of seven members?" split, 5 to 5.

The latter question being lost by an equal division of votes, it was agreed unanimously that the committee should consist of five members to be appointed tomorrow.

Adjourned.

/ August 6

Mr. Rutledge delivered in the report of the Committee of Detail, as follows, a printed copy being at the same time furnished to each member.

COMPLETION OF THE DOCUMENT / *September 11*

In convention. The report of the Committee of Style and Arrangement not being made and being waited for, the house adjourned.

/ September 12

In convention. Dr. Johnson from the Committee of Style, and so forth, reported a digest of the plan of which printed copies were ordered to be furnished to the members. He also reported a letter to accompany the plan to Congress.

REPORT /

[Editor's note: Here follows a copy of the Constitution.]

LETTER /

"We have now the honor to submit to the consideration of the United States in Congress assembled that Constitution which has appeared to us the most advisable.

"The friends of our country have long seen and desired that the power of making war, peace, and treaties, that of levying money and regulating commerce and the correspondent executive and judicial authorities should be fully and effectually vested in the General Gov-

ernment of the Union. But the impropriety of delegating such exten- 443
sive trust to one body of men is evident. Thence results the necessity
of a different organization. It is obviously impracticable in the Federal Government of these states to secure all rights of independent
sovereignty to each and yet provide for the interest and safety of all.
Individuals entering into society must give up a share of liberty to preserve the rest. The magnitude of the sacrifice must depend as well on
situation and circumstances as on the object to be obtained. It is at all
times difficult to draw with precision the line between those rights
which must be surrendered and those which may be reserved. And
on the present occasion this difficulty was increased by a difference
among the several states as to their situation, extent, habits, and particular interests.

"In all our deliberations on this subject, we kept steadily in our
view that which appeared to us the greatest interest of every true
American, the consolidation of our Union, in which is involved our
prosperity, felicity, safety, perhaps our national existence. This important consideration, seriously and deeply impressed on our minds, led
each state in the convention to be less rigid in points of inferior magnitude than might have been otherwise expected. And thus the Constitution which we now present is the result of a spirit of amity and
of that mutual deference and concession which the peculiarity of our
political situation rendered indispensable.

"That it will meet the full and entire approbation of every state is
not, perhaps, to be expected. But each will doubtless consider that had
her interest alone been consulted, the consequences might have been
particularly disagreeable and injurious to others. That it is liable to
as few exceptions as could reasonably have been expected, we hope
and believe; that it may promote the lasting welfare of that country
so dear to us all and secure her freedom and happiness, is our most
ardent wish."

REPORT OF THE COMMITTEE ON STYLE / *September 13*

Dr. Johnson made a further report from the Committee of Style, and
so forth, of the following resolutions to be substituted for Articles 22
and 23:

"Resolved, that the preceding Constitution be laid before the
United States in Congress assembled; and that it is the opinion of this
convention that it should afterwards be submitted to a convention of
delegates chosen in each state by the people thereof, under the recommendation of its legislature, for their assent and ratification, and that

each convention assenting to and ratifying the same should give notice thereof to the United States in Congress assembled.

"Resolved, that it is the opinion of this convention that as soon as the conventions of nine states shall have ratified this Constitution, the United States in Congress assembled should fix a day on which electors should be appointed by the states which shall have ratified the same, and a day on which the electors should assemble to vote for the President, and the time and place for commencing proceedings under this Constitution: that after such publication, the electors should be appointed, and the senators and representatives elected; that the electors should meet on the day fixed for the election of the President and should transmit their votes, certified, signed, sealed, and directed, as the Constitution requires, to the Secretary of the United States in Congress assembled; that the senators and representatives should convene at the time and place assigned; that the senators should appoint a president for the sole purpose of receiving, opening, and counting the votes for President, and that after he shall be chosen, the Congress together with the President, should without delay proceed to execute this Constitution."

Adjourned.

Final Questions

PROPOSAL FOR PUBLIC
ADDRESS DEFEATED / *September 15*

Mr. Carroll reminded the house that no address to the people had yet been prepared. He considered it of great importance that such a one should accompany the Constitution. The people had been accustomed to such on great occasions and would expect it on this. He moved that a committee be appointed for the special purpose of preparing an address.

Mr. Rutledge objected on account of the delay it would produce and the impropriety of addressing the people before it was known whether Congress would approve and support the plan. Congress, if an address be thought proper, can prepare as good a one.

The members of the convention can also explain the reasons of what has been done to their respective constituents.

Mr. Sherman concurred in the opinion that an address was both unnecessary and improper.

Mr. Carroll's motion defeated, 6 to 4.

RANDOLPH REQUESTS
ANOTHER CONVENTION / September 10

Mr. Randolph took this opportunity to state his objections to the system. They turned on the Senate's being made the court of impeachment for trying the executive; on the necessity of three-fourths instead of two-thirds of each house to overrule the negative of the President; on the smallness of the number of the representative branch; on the want of limitation to a standing army; on the general clause concerning necessary and proper laws; on the want of some particular restraint on navigation acts; on the power to lay duties on exports; on the authority of the general legislature to interpose on the application of the executives of the states; on the want of a more definite boundary between the general and state legislatures and between the general and state judiciaries; on the unqualified power of the President to pardon treasons; on the want of some limit to the power of the legislature in regulating their own compensations. With these difficulties in his mind, what course, he asked, was he to pursue? Was he to promote the establishment of a plan which he verily believed would end in tyranny? He was unwilling, he said, to impede the wishes and judgment of the convention, but he must keep himself free, in case he should be honored with a seat in the convention of his state, to act according to the dictates of his judgment. The only mode in which his embarrassment could be removed was that of submitting the plan to Congress, to go from them to the state legislatures and from these to state conventions, having power to adopt, reject, or amend; the process to close with another general convention with full power to adopt or reject the alterations proposed by the state conventions and to establish finally the government. He accordingly proposed a resolution to this effect.

Dr. Franklin seconded the motion.

Mr. Mason urged and obtained that the motion should lie on the table for a day or two to see what steps might be taken with regard to the parts of the system objected to by Mr. Randolph.

MOTION UNANIMOUSLY DEFEATED / September 15

Mr. Randolph, animadverting on the indefinite and dangerous power given by the Constitution to Congress, expressing the pain he felt at differing from the body of the convention on the close of the great and awful subject of their labors, and anxiously wishing for some accommodating expedient which would relieve him from his embarrassments, made a motion importing "that amendments to the plan might be offered by the state conventions, which should be submitted to, and finally decided on by another general convention."

Should this proposition be disregarded, it would, he said, be impossible for him to put his name to the instrument. Whether he should oppose it afterwards, he would not then decide, but he would not deprive himself of the freedom to do so in his own state if that course should be prescribed by his final judgment.

Mr. Mason seconded and followed Mr. Randolph in animadversions on the dangerous power and structure of the government, concluding that it would end either in monarchy or a tyrannical aristocracy—which he was in doubt—but one or other he was sure. This Constitution had been formed without the knowledge or idea of the people. A second convention will know more of the sense of the people and be able to provide a system more consonant to it. It was improper to say to the people, take this or nothing. As the Constitution now stands, he could neither give it his support or vote in Virginia, and he could not sign here what he could not support there. With the expedient of another convention, as proposed, he could sign.

Mr. Pinckney: These declarations from members so respectable at the close of this important scene give a peculiar solemnity to the present moment. He descanted on the consequences of calling forth the deliberations and amendments of the different states on the subject of government at large. Nothing but confusion and contrariety will spring from the experiment. The states will never agree in their plans and the deputies to a second convention, coming together under the discordant impressions of their constituents, will never agree. Conventions are serious things and ought not to be repeated. He was not without objections, as well as others, to the plan. He objected to the power of a majority only of Congress over commerce. But apprehending the danger of a general confusion and an ultimate decision by the sword, he should give the plan his support.

Mr. Gerry stated the objections which determined him to withhold his name from the Constitution: one, the duration and re-eligibility of the Senate; two, the power of the House of Representatives to conceal their journals; three, the power of Congress over the places of election; four, the unlimited power of Congress over their own compensation; five, that Massachusetts has not a due share of representatives allotted to her; six, that three-fifths of the blacks are to be represented as if they were freemen; seven, that under the power over commerce, monopolies may be established; eight, the Vice President being made head of the Senate. He could, however, he said, get over all these if the rights of the citizens were not rendered insecure—first, by the general power of the legislature to make what laws they may please to call "necessary and proper"; secondly, to raise armies and money without limit; thirdly, to establish a tribunal without juries, which will be a star chamber as to civil cases. Under such a view of the Constitution, the best that could be done, he conceived, was to provide for a second general convention.

On the question on the proposition of Mr. Randolph, all the states answered no.

On the question to agree to the Constitution as amended, all the states voted aye.

The Constitution was then ordered to be engrossed, and the house adjourned.

THE JOURNAL OF THE PROCEEDINGS / *September 17*

Mr. King suggested that the journals of the convention should be either destroyed or deposited in the custody of the president. He thought, if suffered to be made public, a bad use would be made of them by those who would wish to prevent the adoption of the Constitution.

Mr. Wilson preferred the second expedient. He had at one time liked the first best, but as false suggestions may be propagated, it should not be made impossible to contradict them.

A question was then put on depositing the journals and other papers of the convention in the hands of the president.

The president, having asked what the convention meant should be done with the journals, and so forth, whether copies were to be allowed to the members if applied for, it was resolved "that he retain the journal and other papers, subject to the order of Congress, if ever formed under the Constitution."

Journal of Convention deposited with president, subject to the orders of the Congress when formed, was approved, 10 to 1.

The Signing

WASHINGTON APPEALS TO THE DELEGATES [1] / *September 17*

When the president rose for the purpose of putting the question, he said that although his situation had hitherto restrained him from of-

---

[1] This was Washington's only speech at the convention.

fering his sentiments on questions depending in the house and, it might be thought, ought now to impose silence on him, yet he could not forbear expressing his wish that the alteration proposed might take place. It was much to be desired that the objections to the plan recommended might be made as few as possible. The smallness of the proportion of representatives had been considered by many members of the convention an insufficient security for the rights and interests of the people. He acknowledged that it had always appeared to himself among the exceptionable parts of the plan, and late as the present moment was for admitting amendments, he thought this of so much consequence that it would give him much satisfaction to see it adopted.

FRANKLIN PRAISES THE CONSTITUTION / September 17

Dr. Franklin rose with a speech in his hand, which Mr. Wilson read:

"Mr. President: I confess that there are several parts of the Constitution which I do not at present approve, but I am not sure I shall never approve them. For having lived long, I have experienced many instances of being obliged by better information or fuller consideration to change opinions, even on important subjects, which I once thought right, but found to be otherwise. It is, therefore, that the older I grow the more apt I am to doubt my own judgment and to pay more respect to the judgment of others. Most men, indeed, as well as most sects in religion, think themselves in possession of all truth and that wherever others differ from them it is so far error. Steele, a Protestant, in a dedication tells the Pope that the only difference between our churches in their opinions of the certainty of their doctrines is 'the Church of Rome is infallible and the Church of England is never in the wrong.' But though many private persons think almost as highly of their own infallibility as of that of their sect, few express it so naturally as a certain French lady who in a dispute with her sister said, 'I don't know how it happens, sister, but I meet with nobody but myself that is always in the right—il n'y a que moi qui a toujours raison.'

"In these sentiments, sir, agree to this Constitution with all its faults, if they are such, because I think a General Government necessary for us—and there is no form of government but what may be a blessing to the people if well-administered—and believe further that this is likely to be well-administered for a course of years and can only end in despotism as other forms have done before it when the people shall become so corrupted as to need despotic government, being incapable of any other. I doubt, too, whether any other convention we can obtain may be able to make a better Constitution. For when you assemble a number of men to have the advantage of their joint wisdom, you inevitably assemble with those men all their prejudices, their passions, their errors of opinion, their local interests, and their selfish views. From such an assembly can a perfect production be expected? It, therefore, astonishes me, sir, to find this system approaching so near to perfection as it does, and I think it will astonish our enemies who are waiting with confidence to hear that our councils are confounded like those of the builders of Babel, and that our states are on the point of separation only to meet hereafter for the purpose of cutting one another's throats. Thus I consent, sir, to this Constitution, because I expect no better and because I am not sure that it is not the best. The opinions I have had of its errors I sacrifice to the public good. I have never whispered a syllable of them abroad. Within these walls they were born and here they shall die. If every one of us in returning to our constituents were to report the objections he has had to it, and endeavor to gain partisans in support of them, we might prevent its being generally received and thereby lose all the salutary effects and great advantages resulting naturally in our favor among foreign nations, as well as among ourselves, from our real or apparent unanimity. Much of the strength and efficiency of any government in procuring and securing happiness to the people depends on opinion—on the general opinion of the goodness of the government as well as of the wisdom and integrity of its governors. I hope, therefore, that for our own sakes, as a part of the people, and for the sake of posterity, we shall act heartily and unanimously in recommending this Constitution (if approved by Congress and confirmed by the conventions) whereever our influence may extend, and turn our future thoughts and endeavors to the means of having it well-administered.

"On the whole, sir, I cannot help expressing a wish that every member of the convention, who may still have objections to it, would with me on this occasion doubt a little of his own infallibility, and to make manifest our unanimity put his name to this instrument." He then moved that the Constitution be signed by the members and offered the following as a convenient form, namely, "Done in Convention by the unanimous consent of the states present, the 17th of September, etc. . . . In witness whereof, we have hereunto subscribed our names."

This ambiguous form had been drawn up by Mr. Gouverneur Morris in order to gain the dissenting members and put into the hands of Dr. Franklin that it might have the better chance of success.

On the question to agree to the Constitution, enrolled in order to be signed, it was agreed to, all the states answering aye.

Mr. Randolph then rose and with an allusion to the observations of Dr. Franklin apologized for his refusing to sign the Constitution, notwithstanding the vast majority and venerable names that would give sanction to its wisdom and its worth. He said, however, that he did not mean by this refusal to decide that he should oppose the Constitution without doors. He meant only to keep himself free to be governed by his duty as it should be prescribed by his future judgment. He refused to sign because he thought the object of the convention would be frustrated by the alternative which it presented to the people. Nine states will fail to ratify the plan and confusion must ensue. With such a view of the subject, he ought not, he could not, by pledging himself to support the plan, restrain himself from taking such steps as might appear to him most consistent with the public good.

Mr. Gouverneur Morris said that he too had objections, but considering the present plan as the best that was to be attained, he should take it with all its faults. The majority had determined in its favor and by that determination he should abide. The moment this plan goes forth all other considerations will be laid aside and the great question will be, shall there be a national Government or not? And this must take place or a general anarchy will be the alternative. He remarked that the signing in the form proposed related only to the fact that the states present were unanimous.

Mr. Williamson suggested that the signing should be confined to the letter accompanying the Constitution to Congress, which might perhaps do nearly as well and would be found satisfactory to some members who disliked the Constitution. For himself, he did not think a better plan was to be expected and had no scruples against putting his name to it.

Mr. Hamilton expressed his anxiety that every member should sign. A few characters of consequence, by opposing or even refusing to sign the Constitution, might do infinite mischief by kindling the latent sparks that lurk under an enthusiasm in favor of the convention which may soon subside. No man's ideas were more remote from the plan than his own were known to be, but is it possible to deliberate between anarchy and convulsion on one side, and the chance of good to be expected from the plan on the other.

Mr. Blount said he had declared that he would not sign so as to pledge himself in support of the plan, but he was relieved by the form proposed and would, without committing himself, attest the fact that the plan was the unanimous act of the states in convention.

Dr. Franklin expressed his fears, from what Mr. Randolph had said, that he thought himself alluded to in the remarks offered this morning to the house. He declared that when drawing up that paper, he did not know that any particular member would refuse to sign his name to the instrument and hoped to be so understood. He possessed a high sense of obligation to Mr. Randolph for having brought forward the plan in the first instance and for the assistance he had given in its progress, and hoped that he would yet lay aside his objections and, by concurring with his brethren, prevent the great mischief which the refusal of his name might produce.

Mr. Randolph could not but regard the signing in the proposed form as the same with signing the Constitution. The change of form, therefore, could make no difference with him. He repeated that in refusing to sign the Constitution, he took a step which might be the most awful of his life, but it was dictated by his conscience, and it was not possible for him to hesitate—much less to change. He repeated also his persuasion that the holding out this plan, with a final alternative to the people of accepting or rejecting it in toto, would really produce the anarchy and civil convulsions which were apprehended from the refusal of individuals to sign it.

Mr. Gerry described the painful feelings of his situation and the embarrassments under which he rose to offer any further observations on the subject, which had been finally decided. Whilst the plan was depending, he had treated it with all the freedom he thought it deserved. He now felt himself bound, as he was disposed, to treat it with the respect due to the act of the convention. He hoped he should not violate that respect in declaring on this occasion his fears that a civil war may result from the present crisis of the United States. In Massachusetts, particularly, he saw the danger of this calamitous event. In that state there are two parties, one devoted to democracy—the worst, he thought, of all political evils—the other, as violent in the opposite extreme. From the collision of these in opposing and resisting the Constitution, confusion was greatly to be feared. He had thought it necessary for this and other reasons that the plan should have been proposed in a more mediating shape in order to abate the heat and opposition of parties. As it had been passed by the convention, he was persuaded it would have a contrary effect. He could not, therefore, by signing the Constitution, pledge himself to abide by it at all events. The proposed form made no difference with him. But if it were not otherwise apparent, the refusals to sign should never be known from him. Alluding to the remarks of Dr. Franklin, he could not, he said, but view them as leveled at himself and the other gentlemen who meant not to sign.

Gen. Pinckney: We are not likely to gain many converts by the ambiguity of the proposed form of signing. He thought it best to be candid and let the form speak the substance. If the meaning of the signers be left in doubt, his purpose would not be answered. He should sign the Constitution with a view to support it with all his influence and wished to pledge himself accordingly.

The members then proceeded to sign the Constitution as finally amended as follows:

We, the people of the United States, in order to form a more perfect union, establish justice, insure domestic tranquility, provide for the common defence, promote the general welfare, and secure the blessings of liberty to ourselves and our posterity, do ordain and establish this Constitution for the United States of America. . . .[1]

DR. FRANKLIN HAS THE LAST WORD / *September 17*

The Constitution being signed by all the members, except Mr. Randolph, Mr. Mason, and Mr. Gerry, who declined giving it the sanction of their names, the convention dissolved itself by an adjournment *sine die.*

Whilst the last members were signing, Dr. Franklin, looking toward the president's chair, at the back of which a rising sun happened to be painted, observed to a few members near him that painters had found it difficult to distinguish in their art a rising from a setting sun. "I have," said he, "often and often in the course of the session, and the vicissitudes of my hopes and fears as to its issue, looked at that behind the president without being able to tell whether it was rising or setting, but now, at length, I have the happiness to know that it is a rising, and not a setting, sun."

---

[1] Again, the language of the Committee of Style. As originally proposed by the Committee of Detail, it read: "We, the people of the States of New Hampshire, Massachusetts, Rhode Island," etc.

Index of the Constitution

piration of the second Year, of the second Class at the Expiration of the fourth Year, and of the third Class at the Expiration of the sixth Year, so that one-third may be chosen every second Year; and if Vacancies happen by Resignation, or otherwise, during the Recess of the Legislature of any State, the Executive thereof may make temporary Appointments [until the next Meeting of the Legislature, which shall then fill such Vacancies]. 312

No Person shall be a Senator who shall not have attained to the Age of thirty Years, and been nine Years a Citizen of the United States, and who shall not, when elected, be an Inhabitant of that State for which he shall be chosen. 312-316

The Vice President of the United States shall be President of the Senate, but shall have no Vote, unless they be equally divided. 254-257, 391-392

The Senate shall chuse their other Officers, and also a President pro tempore, in the Absence of the Vice President, or when he shall exercise the Office of President of the United States. 254-257

The Senate shall have the sole Power to try all Impeachments. When sitting for that Purpose, they shall be on Oath or Affirmation. When the President of the United States is tried, the Chief Justice shall preside: And no Person shall be convicted without the Concurrence of two thirds of the Members present. 389-391

Judgment in Cases of Impeachment shall not extend further than to removal from Office, and disqualification to hold and enjoy any Office of honor, Trust, or Profit under the United States: but the Party convicted shall nevertheless be liable and subject to Indictment, Trial, Judgment and Punishment, according to Law. 389-391

SECTION 4

The Times, Places and Manner of holding Elections for Senators and Representa-

tives, shall be prescribed in each State by the Legislature thereof; but the Congress may at any time by Law make or alter such Regulations, except as to the Places of chusing Senators. 255-257

The Congress shall assemble at least once in every Year, and such Meeting shall be on the first Monday in December, unless they shall by Law appoint a different Day. 255-257

SECTION 5

Each House shall be the Judge of the Elections, Returns and Qualifications of its own Members, and a Majority of each shall constitute a Quorum to do Business; but a smaller Number may adjourn from day to day, and may be authorized to compel the Attendance of absent Members, in such Manner, and under such Penalties as each House may provide. 255-257, 260-263

Each House may determine the Rules of its Proceedings, punish its Members for disorderly Behaviour, and, with the Concurrence of two thirds, expel a Member. 255-257

Each House shall keep a Journal of its Proceedings, and from time to time publish the same, excepting such Parts as may in their Judgment require Secrecy; and the Yeas and Nays of the Members of either House on any question shall, at the Desire of one fifth of those Present, be entered on the Journal. 263-264

Neither House, during the Session of Congress shall, without the Consent of the other, adjourn for more than three days, nor to any other Place than that in which the two Houses shall be sitting. 255-257

SECTION 6

The Senators and Representatives shall receive a Compensation for their Services, to be ascertained by Law, and paid out of the Treasury of the United States. They shall in all Cases, except Treason, Felony and Breach of the Peace, be privileged from Arrest during their Attendance at the Session of their respective Houses, and in going to and returning from the same; and for any Speech or Debate in either House, they shall not be questioned in any other Place. 257-260, 302-305, 316-317

No Senator or Representative shall, during the Time for which he was elected, be appointed to any civil Office under the Authority of the United States, which shall have been created, or the Emoluments whereof shall have been encreased during such time; and no Person holding any Office under the United States, shall be a Member of either House during his Continuance in Office. 249-254, 302-305

SECTION 7

All Bills for raising Revenue shall originate in the House of Representatives; but the Senate may propose or concur with Amendments as on other Bills. 189-202

Every Bill which shall have passed the House of Representatives and the Senate, shall, before it becomes a Law, be presented to the President of the United States; If he approve he shall sign it, but if not he shall return it, with his Objections to that House in which it shall have originated, who shall enter the Objections at large on their Journal, and proceed to reconsider it. If after such Reconsideration two thirds of that House shall agree to pass the Bill, it shall be sent, together with the Objections, to the other House, by which it shall likewise be reconsidered, and if approved by two thirds of that House, it shall become a Law. But in all such Cases the Votes of both Houses shall be determined by Yeas and Nays, and the Names of the Persons voting for and against the Bill shall be entered on the Journal of each House respectively. If any Bill shall not be returned by the President within ten Days (Sundays excepted) after it shall have been presented to him, the Same shall be a Law, in like Manner as if he had signed it, unless the Congress by their Adjournment prevent its Return, in which Case it shall not be a Law. 375-384

Every Order, Resolution, or Vote to which the Concurrence of the Senate and House of Representatives may be necessary (except on a question of adjournment) shall be presented to the President of the United States; and before the Same shall take Effect, shall be approved by him, or being disapproved by him, shall be repassed by two thirds of the Senate and House of Representatives, according to the Rules and Limitations prescribed in the Case of a Bill. 375-384

SECTION 8

The Congress shall have Power.—1. To lay and collect Taxes, Duties, Imposts and Excises, to pay the Debts and provide for the common Defence and general Welfare of the United States; but all Duties, Imposts and Excises shall be uniform throughout the United States; [202-204, 209-211]

2. To borrow Money on the credit of the United States; [189-202]

3. To regulate Commerce with foreign Nations, and among the several States, and with the Indian Tribes; [212-219]

4. To establish an uniform Rule of Naturalization, and uniform Laws on the subject of Bankruptcies throughout the United States; [237-239]

5. To coin Money, regulate the Value thereof, and of foreign Coin, and fix the Standard of Weights and Measures; [189-202]

6. To provide for the Punishment of counterfeiting the Securities and current Coin of the United States; [189-202]

7. To establish Post Offices and post Roads; [237-239]

8. To promote the Progress of Science and useful Arts, by securing for limited Times to Authors and Inventors the exclusive

SECTION 9

ever, from any King, Prince, or foreign State. 237-239

No State shall enter into any Treaty, Alliance, or Confederation; grant Letters of Marque and Reprisal; coin Money; emit Bills of Credit; make any Thing but gold and silver Coin a Tender in Payment of Debts; pass any Bill of Attainder, ex post facto Law, or Law impairing the Obligation of Contracts, or grant any Title of Nobility. 179-181, 223-224

No State shall, without the Consent of the Congress, lay any Imposts or Duties on Imports or Exports, except what may be absolutely necessary for executing its inspection Laws: and the net Produce of all Duties and Imposts, laid by any State on Imports or Exports, shall be for the Use of the Treasury of the United States; and all such Laws shall be subject to the Revision and Control of the Congress. 180-181

No State shall, without the Consent of Congress, lay any Duty of Tonnage, keep Troops, or Ships of War in time of Peace, enter into any Agreement or Compact with another State, or with a foreign Power, or engage in War, unless actually invaded, or in such imminent Danger as will not admit of delay. 180-181

ARTICLE II

SECTION 1

The executive Power shall be vested in a President of the United States of America. He shall hold his Office during the Term of four Years, and, together with the Vice President, chosen for the same Term, be elected, as follows [327-345]

Each State shall appoint, in such Manner as the Legislature thereof may direct, a Number of Electors, equal to the whole Number of Senators and Representatives to which the State may be entitled in the Congress: but no Senator or Representative, or Person holding an Office of Trust or Profit under the United States, shall be appointed an Elector. 345-359

[The Electors shall meet in their respective States, and vote by Ballot for two Persons, of whom one at least shall not be an Inhabitant of the same State with themselves. And they shall make a List of all the Persons voted for, and of the Number of Votes for each; which List they shall sign and certify, and transmit sealed to the Seat of the Government of the United States, directed to the President of the Senate. The President of the Senate shall, in the Presence of the Senate and House of Representatives, open all the Certificates, and the Votes shall then be counted. The Person having the greatest Number of Votes shall be the President, if such Number be a Majority of the whole Number of Electors appointed; and if there be more than one who have such Majority, and have an equal Number of Votes, then the House of Representatives shall immediately chuse by Ballot one of them for President; and if no person have a Majority, then from the five highest on the List the said House shall in like Manner chuse the President. But in chusing the President, the Votes shall be taken by States, the Representation from each State having one Vote; A quorum for this Purpose shall consist of a Member or Members from two thirds of the States, and a Majority of all the States shall be necessary to a Choice. In every Case, after the Choice of the President, the Person having the greatest Number of Votes of the Electors shall be the Vice President. But if there should remain two or more who have equal Votes, the Senate should chuse from them by Ballot the Vice President.] 345-368

The Congress may determine the Time of chusing the Electors, and the Day on which they shall give their Votes; which Day shall be the same throughout the United States. 345-359

No Person except a natural born Citizen, or a Citizen of the United States, at the time of the Adoption of this Constitution, shall be eligible to the Office of President; neither shall any Person be eligible to that Office who shall not have attained to the Age of thirty five Years, and been fourteen Years a Resident within the United States. 372

In Case of the Removal of the President from Office, or of his Death, Resignation, or Inability to discharge the Powers and Duties of the said Office, the same shall devolve on the Vice President, and the Congress may by Law provide for the Case of Removal, Death, Resignation or Inability, both of the President and Vice President, declaring what Officer shall then act as President, and such Officer shall act accordingly, until the Disability be removed, or a President shall be elected. 392-393

The President shall, at stated Times, receive for his Services, a Compensation, which shall neither be encreased nor diminished during the Period for which he shall have been elected, and he shall not receive within that Period any other Emolument from the United States, or any of them. 369-372

Before he enter on the Execution of his Office, he shall take the following Oath or Affirmation:—"I do solemnly swear (or affirm) that I will faithfully execute the Office of President of the United States, and will to the best of my Ability, preserve, protect and defend the Constitution of the United States." 372-373

SECTION 2

The President shall be Commander in Chief of the Army and Navy of the United States, and of the Militia of the several States, when called into the actual Service of the United States; he may require the Opinion, in writing, of the principal Officer in each of the executive Departments, upon any subject relating to the Duties of their respective Offices, and he shall have Power to grant Reprieves

and Pardons for Offences against the United States, except in Cases of Impeachment. 204-208, 374-375, 393-394

He shall have Power, by and with the Advice and Consent of the Senate, to make Treaties, provided two thirds of the Senators present concur; and he shall nominate, and by and with the Advice and Consent of the Senate, shall appoint Ambassadors, other public Ministers and Consuls, Judges of the supreme Court, and all other Officers of the United States, whose Appointments are not herein otherwise provided for, and which shall be established by Law: but the Congress may by Law vest the Appointment of such inferior Officers, as they think proper, in the President alone, in the Courts of Law, or in the Heads of Departments. 317-322, 373-374, 401-407

The President shall have Power to fill up all Vacancies that may happen during the Recess of the Senate, by granting Commissions which shall expire at the End of their next Session. 394

SECTION 3

He shall from time to time give to the Congress Information of the State of the Union, and recommend to their Consideration such Measures as he shall judge necessary and expedient; he may, on extraordinary Occasions, convene both Houses, or either of them, and in Case of Disagreement between them, with Respect to the Time of Adjournment, he may adjourn them to such Time as he shall think proper; he shall receive Ambassadors and other public Ministers; he shall take Care that the Laws be faithfully executed, and shall Commission all the Officers of the United States. 394

SECTION 4

The President, Vice President and all civil Officers of the United States, shall be removed from Office on Impeachment for, and Conviction of, Treason, Bribery, or other high Crimes and Misdemeanors. 384-389

ARTICLE III

SECTION 1

The judicial Power of the United States, shall be vested in one supreme Court, and in such inferior Courts as the Congress may from time to time ordain and establish. The Judges, both of the supreme and inferior Courts, shall hold their Offices during good Behaviour, and shall, at stated Times, receive for their Services, a Compensation, which shall not be diminished during their Continuance in Office. 399-401, 407-409

SECTION 2

The judicial Power shall extend to all Cases, in Law and Equity, arising under this Constitution, the Laws of the United States, and Treaties made, or which shall be made, under their Authority;—to all Cases affecting Ambassadors, other public Ministers and Consuls;—to all Cases of Admiralty and maritime Jurisdiction; —to Controversies to which the United States shall be a Party;—to Controversies between two or more States;—between a State and Citizens of another State;— between Citizens of different States,— between Citizens of the same State claiming Lands under Grants of different States, and between a State, or the Citizens thereof, and foreign States, Citizens or Subjects. 409-418

In all Cases affecting Ambassadors, other public Ministers and Consuls, and those in which a State shall be Party, the supreme Court shall have original Jurisdiction. In all the other Cases before mentioned, the supreme Court shall have appellate Jurisdiction, both as to Law and Fact, with such Exceptions, and under such Regulations as the Congress shall make. 410-418

The Trial of all Crimes, except in Cases of Impeachment, shall be by Jury; and such Trial shall be held in the State where the said Crimes shall have been committed; but when not committed within any State, the Trial shall be at such Place or Places as the Congress may by Law have directed. 418-419

SECTION 3

Treason against the United States, shall consist only in levying War against them, or, in adhering to their Enemies, giving them Aid and Comfort. No Person shall be convicted of Treason unless on the Testimony of two Witnesses to the same overt Act, or on Confession in open Court. 219-222

The Congress shall have power to declare the Punishment of Treason, but no Attainder of Treason shall work Corruption of Blood, or Forfeiture except during the Life of the Person attainted. 219-222

ARTICLE IV

SECTION 1

Full Faith and Credit shall be given in each State to the public Acts, Records, and judicial Proceedings of every other State. And the Congress may by general Laws prescribe the Manner in which such Acts, Records and Proceedings shall be proved, and the Effect thereof. 181

SECTION 2

The Citizens of each State shall be entitled to all Privileges and Immunities of Citizens in the several States. 182-184

A Person charged in any State with Treason, Felony, or other Crime, who shall flee from Justice, and be found in another State, shall on Demand of the executive Authority of the State from which he fled, be delivered up, to be removed to the State having Jurisdiction of the Crime. 219-222

No Person held to Service or Labour in one State, under the Laws thereof, escaping into another, shall, in Consequence of any Law or Regulation therein, be discharged from such Service or Labour, but shall be delivered up on Claim of the Party to whom such Service or Labour may be due. 223

SECTION 3

New States may be admitted by the Congress into this Union; but no new State shall be formed or erected within the Jurisdiction of any other State; nor any State be formed by the Junction of two or more States, or Parts of States, without the Consent of the Legislatures of the States concerned as well as of the Congress. 182-184

The Congress shall have Power to dispose of and make all needful Rules and Regulations respecting the Territory or other Property belonging to the United States; and nothing in this Constitution shall be so construed as to Prejudice any Claims of the United States, or of any particular State. 182-184

SECTION 4

The United States shall guarantee to every State in this Union a Republican Form of Government, and shall protect each of them against Invasion; and on Application of the Legislature, or of the Executive (when the Legislature cannot be convened) against domestic Violence. 67,183-184

ARTICLE V

The Congress, whenever two thirds of both Houses shall deem it necessary, shall propose Amendments to this Constitution, or, on the Application of the Legislatures of two thirds of the several States, shall call a Convention for proposing Amendments, which, in either Case, shall be valid to all Intents and Purposes, as Part of this Constitution, when ratified by the Legislatures of three fourths of the several States, or by Conventions in three fourths thereof, as the one or the other Mode of Ratification may be proposed by the Congress; Provided that no Amendment which may be made prior to the Year One thousand eight hundred and eight shall in any Manner affect the first and fourth Clauses in the Ninth Section of the first Article; and that no State, without its Consent, shall be deprived of its equal Suffrage in the Senate. 423-425

461

ARTICLE VI

All Debts contracted and Engagements entered into, before the Adoption of this Constitution, shall be as valid against the United States under this Constitution, as under the Confederation. 211

This Constitution, and the Laws of the United States which shall be made in Pursuance thereof; and all Treaties made, or which shall be made, under the Authority of the United States, shall be the supreme Law of the Land; and the Judges in every State shall be bound thereby, any Thing in the Constitution or Laws of any State to the Contrary notwithstanding. 179-181

The Senators and Representatives before mentioned, and the Members of the several State Legislatures, and all executive and judicial Officers, both of the United States and of the several States, shall be bound by Oath or Affirmation, to support this Constitution; but no religious Test shall ever be required as a Qualification to any Office or public Trust under the United States. 80-82

ARTICLE VII

The Ratification of the Conventions of nine States shall be sufficient for the Establishment of this Constitution between the States so ratifying the Same. 429-437

Index of Delegates

438, 439, 440, 441, 446, 451, 452; description, 20, 22

GILMAN, NICHOLAS:
17

GORHAM, NATHANIEL:
17, 30, 34, 81, 120, 121, 136-137, 157, 163, 166, 168, 183, 184, 201, 203, 218, 230, 242, 243, 246, 255, 258, 260, 265, 274, 283, 291, 293, 303, 307, 317, 319, 322, 360, 367, 374, 381, 401, 402, 403, 404, 413, 418, 432, 437, 439; description, 20

HAMILTON, ALEXANDER:
17, 19, 23, 24, 27, 31, 32, 35, 37, 47, 56, 80, 92-100, 107, 108, 119, 135, 139-141, 273, 274, 281, 304, 305, 310, 367, 376, 383, 423, 439, 440, 441, 450; description, 20, 21

HOUSTON, WILLIAM:
16, 183, 287, 351, 353

HOUSTON, WILLIAM CHURCHILL:
16; description, 20

INGERSOLL, JARED:
16

JENIFER, DANIEL OF ST. THOMAS:
17, 33, 271, 277

JOHNSON, WILLIAM SAMUEL:
17, 31, 116, 122, 136, 141, 220, 221, 224, 297, 319, 442, 443

KING, RUFUS:
17, 19, 21, 31, 32, 34, 48, 56, 60, 76, 107, 149, 151, 164, 165, 167, 175-176, 184, 190, 211, 221, 222, 228, 230, 244, 256, 261, 262, 265, 274, 275, 285, 293, 299, 304, 321, 335, 341, 343, 365, 368, 373, 375, 386, 387, 410, 412, 429, 433, 435, 436, 437, 440, 441, 447; description, 19, 20, 22

LANGDON, JOHN:
17, 202, 204, 205, 207, 212, 213, 228, 230, 237, 246, 258, 264

LANSING, JOHN:
17, 26, 85-86, 110, 130, 156

LIVINGSTON, WILLIAM:
16; description, 20, 21

McCLURG, JAMES:
16, 332, 334; description, 19, 21

McHENRY, JAMES:
17, 19, 200, 214, 223, 437; description, 19, 20

MADISON, JAMES: *463*
16, 18, 19, 21, 23, 24, 26, 27, 31, 32, 34, 35, 38, 39, 56, 57, 59, 61, 62, 64, 66, 67, 69-71, 100-106, 117-119, 122, 131-134, 138-139, 145-147, 149, 156, 157-159, 162, 168, 171, 173, 175, 176-178, 183, 184, 189, 197-198, 200, 202, 205, 207, 208, 209, 213, 217, 219, 220, 222, 229, 230, 231, 234, 235, 236, 237, 241, 243, 244, 247, 248, 255, 256, 257, 258, 262, 263, 265, 266, 271, 273, 275, 276-277, 280, 281, 283, 287, 294-296, 304, 305, 306, 307-309, 313, 317, 318, 319, 320, 322, 328, 329, 333, 334, 342, 352, 356-358, 359, 360, 364, 367, 368, 373, 375, 377, 382, 384, 385, 388, 389, 394, 400, 402, 403, 404, 405, 406, 409, 411-412, 413, 416, 424, 425, 429, 434, 435, 436; description, 22

MARTIN, ALEXANDER:
16, 287

MARTIN, LUTHER:
17, 33, 81, 108, 113, 128-130, 141, 149, 153, 156, 157, 181, 183, 184, 192, 193, 204, 207, 222, 224, 235, 246, 260, 335, 338, 343, 351, 352, 401, 404, 415, 437, 438; description, 21

MASON, GEORGE:
16, 21, 22, 29, 32, 48, 55, 58, 66, 69, 111-113, 119, 122, 156, 163, 174, 183, 184, 191, 194-195, 201, 203, 204, 205, 206, 209, 214, 217, 219, 221, 222, 225, 229, 230, 231, 236, 239, 240, 243, 247, 248, 249, 256, 259, 261, 264, 265, 273, 274, 275, 277, 278, 283, 288, 289, 291, 293, 296, 303, 313, 317, 318, 331, 334, 336-337, 344, 346, 350, 361, 363, 364, 368, 373, 375, 378, 383, 385, 388, 390, 392, 393, 401, 404, 407, 412, 414, 416, 425, 430, 437, 438, 445, 446, 452; description, 19, 22

MERCER, JOHN FRANCIS:
17, 201, 210, 242, 248, 250, 253, 261, 262, 263, 282, 318

MIFFLIN, THOMAS:
16

MORRIS, GOUVERNEUR:
15, 16, 21, 22, 27, 28, 29, 31, 32, 34, 54, 55, 56, 153-155, 159-160, 162, 163, 166, 168-169, 171-172, 173, 180, 181, 182, 184, 190, 191, 196, 200, 209, 210, 212, 216, 219, 220, 221, 222, 223, 228, 229, 230, 235, 236, 237, 239, 240, 243, 246, 248, 251, 254, 255, 256, 258, 261, 262, 264, 265, 280, 282, 283, 286, 289, 292, 294, 296, 297, 300, 312, 314, 318, 319, 321, 322, 332, 334, 335, 337, 338-340, 344, 348, 349, 351, 354-356, 358, 361, 362,

Subject Index